GREEN PLANET BLUES

A project of the Harrison Program on
The Future Global Agenda, University of Maryland

GREEN PLANET BLUES

ENVIRONMENTAL POLITICS FROM STOCKHOLM
TO JOHANNESBURG

THIRD EDITION

KEN CONCA AND
GEOFFREY D. DABELKO, EDITORS

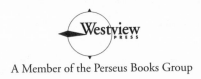

A Member of the Perseus Books Group

Copyright © 2004 by Westview Press, A Member of the Perseus Books Group

Published in the United States of America by Westview Press, A Member of the Perseus Books Group,
5500 Central Avenue, Boulder, Colorado 80301-2877, and in the United Kingdom by Westview Press,
12 Hid's Copse Road, Cumnor Hill, Oxford OX2 9JJ.

Find us on the world wide web at www.westviewpress.com

Westview Press books are available at special discounts for bulk purchases in the United States by corporations, institutions, and other organizations. For more information, please contact the Special
Markets Department at the Perseus Books Group, 11 Cambridge Center, Cambridge, MA 02142, or
call (617) 252–5298 or (800) 255–1514, or e-mail special.markets@perseusbooks.com.

Library of Congress Cataloging-in-Publication Data
   Green planet blues : environmental politics from Stockholm to Johannesburg /edited by Ken Conca
and Geoffrey D. Dabelko. — 3rd ed.
      p.   cm.
   A project of the Harrison Program on the Future Global Agenda.
   Includes bibliographical references.
   ISBN 0-8133-4201-5 (hardcover: alk. Paper)
   ISBN 0-8133-4200-7 (paperback: alk. Paper)
   1. environmental policy—Political aspects.   2. Sustainable development.   3. Green movement.
I. Conca, Ken.   II. Dabelko, Geoffrey D.   III. Harrison Program on the Future Global Agenda.
HC79.E5G6916   2004
363.7—dc21
                                                                                      2004-19814

The paper used in this publication meets the requirements of the American National Standard for Per-
manence of Paper for Printed Library Materials Z39.48–1984.

Text design by Reginald Thompson
Typeface used in this text: Minion

10   9   8   7   6   5   4   3   2   1

CONTENTS

PART SIX
FROM ECOLOGICAL CONFLICT
TO ENVIRONMENTAL SECURITY? 283

PART SEVEN
ECOLOGICAL JUSTICE 331

PREFACE

This book originated as a project of the University of Maryland's Harrison Program on the Future Global Agenda. We are grateful to Horace Harrison for making the program possible, to then-director Dennis Pirages for supporting the idea, and to Michael Alberty for his help as coeditor on the first edition. We also appreciate the support of the Woodrow Wilson International Center for Scholars and its Environmental Change and Security Project. For their help, advice, and support as we prepared the third edition, we thank Jon Barnett, Michele Betsill, Steve Catalano, Elizabeth DeSombre, Shannon Green, Peter Jacques, Sara Kamins, Elisabeth Malzahn, John M. Meyer, Ronald Mitchell, Adil Najam, Kate O'Neill, Dennis Pirages, Kurt Rakouskas, Armin Rosencranz, Jennifer Swearingen, Marietta Urban, Stacy VanDeveer, and Greg White. We are also grateful to several anonymous respondents to the student and faculty surveys we distributed to collect feedback on the second edition.

For the third edition we have updated the text to take account of several new developments including the emergence of the idea of globalization as a way of understanding world politics and the changed political climate in the wake of the unraveled Kyoto climate accord and the Johannesburg summit. In doing so, we have tried to remain true to the book's original goals of discussing cross-cutting issues of power and authority, juxtaposing different environmental paradigms, and presenting a diversity of voices. At the end of the introduction to each part, we have included a list of questions that we have found useful in stimulating critical thought, discussion, and learning. For the third edition we have also added an open-access Web site (www.bsos.umd.edu/harrison) with background information, links to a wide array of useful sites, sources, and simulations, and suggestions for additional reading.

Because many of the selections presented in this volume are excerpts, a brief explanation of our editing philosophy is in order. In those cases where space limitations precluded reprinting an entire essay, our goal has been to edit in such a way as to emphasize the underlying ideas and concepts. In many cases, this has meant leaving out complex elaborations, trenchant asides, or supporting examples. We have preserved the original notes corresponding to the material reproduced here but left out notes corresponding to passages of text not included. For one essay (Lélé) containing a large number of in-line citations in the original, we have preserved the factual citations but removed several of the more general references to enhance readability and conserve space. Readers seeking further background, greater detail, or additional references should consult the original material.

INTRODUCTION:
THREE DECADES OF GLOBAL
ENVIRONMENTAL POLITICS

KEN CONCA AND
GEOFFREY D. DABELKO

Think globally, act locally. Spaceship Earth. The common heritage of humanity. Pollution does not respect national borders. The Earth is one, but the world is not. We have not inherited the Earth from our parents; we have borrowed it from our children. The global commons. Each of these well-known phrases invokes similar themes: the interconnectedness of the global environment; the close ties between environmental quality and human well-being; and the common fate that these realities impose upon all of the planet's occupants, present and future. We live, as we have for some time, in an era of global environmental politics.

Pollution, ecosystem destruction, and natural resource depletion are not new problems. Many regions and localities were grappling with these issues long before the industrial revolution or even the emergence of the modern system of nation-states. And just as environmental problems have a long-standing history, so do the political struggles that inevitably accompany those problems. Thus, severe wood shortages led to conservation efforts in Babylonia during the time of Hammurabi.[1] Measures to protect wetlands in recognition of their importance as sources of fish, game, and fuel have been traced to the sixth century A.D. in the Huang-Huai-Hai plain of northeastern China.[2] Air-quality crises in London during the early stages of the industrial revolution led to the formation of smoke-abatement societies advocating legislative action.[3] One can easily imagine the political controversies that must have engulfed each of these episodes, given that these measures protecting environmental quality or altering access to natural resources would have offended powerful interests.

Today, the dramas of environmental politics are increasingly played out on a global stage. It is generally agreed that human transformation of the environment is a global-scale problem.[4] In some cases this is because the system under stress is globally interconnected in a physical sense, as in the case of the Earth's climate, the oceans, or the atmosphere's protective ozone layer. In other cases, accumulated local events produce consequences of global significance, as in the depletion of the world's fisheries or the reduction of the planet's biological diversity.

People increasingly speak of global environmental problems. But what do we mean when we speak of *global environmental politics*? To answer this question, consider what people see when they look at a forest. Some see a stock of timber to be exploited for economic gain. Others see a complex ecological system that holds the soil in place, stabilizes the local water cycle, moderates the local climate, and fosters biological diversity. Still others see the forest as a home for people and other living things, or perhaps as an ancestral burial ground. Finally, some see the forest as a powerful cultural symbol on broader scales: The forest as a dynamic living system reflects the potential harmony between humanity and nature and provides a link between the past and the future.

We live in a world that is at once fragmented by the political division into sovereign states and reassembled by pervasive flows of people, goods, money, ideas, images, and technology across borders. In such a world, conflicting visions of the forest take on international significance. Some see in the forest an important source of international economic power, giving those who control it influence in international markets and a reliable source of foreign exchange. Others see it as a powerful symbol of global interdependence: The forest reflects the global consequences of local acts in that its destruction may alter the global climate or deplete the global stock of biological diversity. Still others see a very different sort of international symbol: The forest represents national sovereignty in that it confirms the right of a nation to do as it sees fit within its territory. Such rights may seem luxuries that a crowded planet cannot afford. But this is not often the view of people who feel their sovereign rights immediately threatened—particularly if those rights were won in a struggle for independence that forged their very nation.

Often these competing visions reflect different interests held by individuals, groups, and perhaps even entire nations. They are also a product, however, of the structures that govern world politics. The institution of national sovereignty, the division of labor in the capitalist world economy, the rise of transnational networks of environmentalists, the predominance of powerful beliefs about the links between consumption and "progress"—all of these underlying features of contemporary world politics shape what people see when they look at the forest.

Competing visions, values, and interests often lead to conflict. Actors disagree about the nature of the problem, the effectiveness or fairness of proposed solutions, and the appropriate location of responsibility. Thus, studying global environmental politics means understanding the conflicts of interest that surround environmental issues—but also asking how interests, values, and visions related to the environment are shaped.

The study of global environmental politics also involves the search for cooperative solutions to ecological dilemmas. The idea that global environmental problems require "international cooperation" is widely accepted, but the appropriate scope and content of such cooperation are hotly contested. Does international cooperation mean formal, treaty-based agreements among governments? Does it mean a broader "global bargain" between North and South, linking a number of issues in a single package? Or does it refer to a still broader process of global dialogue not limited to governments, in which different societies move toward a global convergence of values? Does an increasingly global network of environmental organizations represent an effective new form of international cooperation, or is it simply one more way in which the strong impose their will upon the weak? Is the goal of international cooperation to create an increasingly dense web of transnational linkages, one that binds nations to a common future and a common commitment to environmental protection? Or should we be agreeing instead to begin delinking an ever more tightly coupled, "globalizing" world system, so that various localities and regions have more flexibility to pursue responses appropriate to their unique circumstances?

Finally, an important dimension of the study of global environmental politics is connecting the patterns of international conflict and cooperation we see over the environment to some of the larger changes under way in world politics. If studying the structure of world politics gives us insight into the character of global environmental problems, the reverse is also true. It is no surprise that as the world has tumbled into the twenty-first century, environmental problems have emerged as a critical theme in the study of international relations and world politics. At a time when much conventional wisdom in international relations is under challenge, studying the politics of the global environment may also give us greater insight into the emerging patterns of world politics as a whole.

From Stockholm to
Johannesburg—and Beyond

Three global summit meetings—the 1972 U.N. Conference on the Human Environment, held in Stockholm, Sweden; the 1992 U.N. Conference on Environment and Development, held in Rio de Janeiro, Brazil
(known popularly as the "Earth Summit"); and the 2002 World Summit
on Sustainable Development, held in Johannesburg, South Africa—
provide useful benchmarks for the evolution of global environmental
politics.[5] The contrasts among these three events reflect many underlying changes in the world during the intervening three decades.

One important shift is that of international political context. The first
global environmental summit, in Stockholm, occurred in the shadow of
the Cold War. The governments of Eastern Europe and the Soviet
Union boycotted the conference after a dispute over the representation of divided Germany. Two decades later, the Rio summit took place
in the relatively optimistic afterglow of the end of the Cold War, amid
a general sense of new opportunities for global cooperation. A decade
later in Johannesburg, much of that optimism had faded in the light of
globalization controversies, increasingly muscular American unilateral-
ism, the gritty reality of enduring global political, economic, and cultural conflicts, and the shocking events of September 11, 2001.

A second clear change was the emergence of global public awareness and concern. The Stockholm conference took place in the wake of
the first Earth Day (1970) and at a time of rising popular concern in the
United States and Europe about environmental problems, particularly
air and water pollution. Many of the participants at Stockholm—particularly those from the North—framed environmental problems as the
by-products of an affluent, industrialized lifestyle. The implication was
that the poorer regions of the world do not suffer as much from environmental problems as do the wealthy, nor do they exhibit the same
level of concern about such problems. By the time of the Rio conference, however, the notion that there is both a "pollution of affluence"
and a "pollution of poverty" had gained much broader acceptance. As
the environmental causes of poverty became clearer, what many of
those suffering from poverty have presumably known all along became more generally understood: Environmental concerns were not
the exclusive property of affluent people or industrialized countries,
hence Rio's linkage between environment and development. By the
time of the Johannesburg summit, development issues had become
central to the discussion (so much so that some environmental advocates felt the environmental agenda was being largely ignored).

A third important trend over the past three decades has been the
tremendous growth in the scientific understanding of environmental

problems. Stockholm focused attention principally on relatively narrowly defined problems of air and water pollution, whereas Rio embraced a far broader and more complex agenda. This shift reflected in
part a changing scientific paradigm—one that views the Earth as a
single integrated system with complex linkages among the large-scale
ecological systems of land, oceans, atmosphere, and biosphere.[6] The
discussion at Rio, especially the ambitious goals embodied in
"Agenda 21," also reflected the greater capacity of scientists to measure, monitor, and model complex processes of environmental
change.[7] Yet the growth of scientific knowledge is not immune to political context; as delegates gathered in Johannesburg one year after
the destruction of the World Trade Center, the continued commitment of governments to open information flows and exchange of environmental data could not be taken for granted in the light of fears
about "environmental terrorism."

Governments and other actors gathering to discuss global environmental problems themselves have also undergone notable changes in
the decades since the Stockholm conference. Almost none of the governments gathered in Stockholm had any form of national environmental bureaucracy; virtually all did two decades later in Rio. In many
cases, these agencies enabled governments to take advantage of the
growth of environmental knowledge so as to analyze more effectively the causes and consequences of environmental problems. In
some cases these agencies had evolved into advocates for various environmental protection programs, producing more complex internal
debates within national delegations. By the time of the Johannesburg summit ten years later, environmental considerations had also
been mainstreamed in the rhetoric and policy guidelines—if not always the practice—of development organizations such as the World
Bank and were increasingly prominent in the debates surrounding
trade and financial organizations such as the International Monetary
Fund and World Trade Organization (see Part Four of this volume).

Nongovernmental organizations have also undergone substantial
change. During the Stockholm conference, 134 NGOs, virtually all
from the industrialized world, were officially accredited participants.
Two decades later, there were more than 1,400 NGOs participating officially in the Rio summit, with about one-third of these groups from
the global South—and countless more unofficial participants.[8] Over
time, international networking and coalition building among environmental groups have become much more common.[9]

A final measure of the changes from Stockholm to Johannesburg is
the growth in the number of international environmental treaties,
agreements, and cooperative accords. By some estimates there are now
more than one thousand international environmental agreements in

place. Many of these are relatively narrow in scope: agreements between two neighboring countries on specific environmental problems
or regional agreements involving small numbers of countries and narrow agendas. But the list also includes several major international accords adopted since the Stockholm conference, including agreements
on ocean pollution, acid rain, preservation of the ozone layer, the international trade in endangered species, and environmental protection
in Antarctica. The designers of international accords at Rio had a much
broader set of examples upon which to draw than did their predeces-
sors at Stockholm; as a result, they also had at least a crude understanding of what makes various approaches to international environmental cooperation effective.[10] Between Rio and Johannesburg, some
important new international agreements were reached, such as the
Cartagena Protocol on Biosafety and the Stockholm Convention on
Persistent Organic Pollutants. By the time of the Johannesburg summit,
however, the tenuous compromise of the 1997 Kyoto Protocol to the
Framework Convention on Climate Change had come unraveled with
the U.S. decision to withdraw from the agreement, casting a pall over
the prospects for ambitious multilateral environmental diplomacy.

It is equally important to stress what did *not* change in the thirty
years between Stockholm and Johannesburg. Many of the stumbling
blocks to effective global response seen at Stockholm were also in full
evidence at the subsequent gatherings. These include the tremendous mistrust and suspicion governing relations between North and
South in world politics; the tenacious embrace of traditional conceptions of national sovereignty by governments, even as they acknowledge the need for coordinated global responses to problems that do
not respect borders; and the tensions between the long-term vision
necessary for ecologically sane planning and the short-term concern
for economic growth and political stability that preoccupies most
governments.

Perhaps the most important continuity in the more than three
decades since Stockholm is that global environmental change has
continued at an alarming rate. Between 1970 and 2000, global commercial energy consumption, a major source of environmental impacts, roughly doubled; other global indicators of human impact on
the environment, including food production, water use, overall economic activity, and population, increased in roughly similar proportions. To be sure, these very crude indicators of human stress on environmental systems can mask as much as they reveal. They say nothing
about how underlying activities actually affect the environment,
about who or what may be responsible, or who suffers the consequences most directly and immediately. But they do indicate the scale
of the problem and the enormity of the challenge of reorienting fun-

damental practices that drive growth, production, consumption, and environmental transformation in the current world system.

This mixed picture of continuity and change raises an obvious question: Compared to where things stood at the Stockholm conference, where do we stand in the wake of the Johannesburg summit and as we look to the future? Many environmental advocates were dismayed with the Johannesburg summit, turning the official notion of "Rio plus 10" into the dismissive label "Rio minus 10." Whereas Rio had produced multilateral treaties on climate and biodiversity and Agenda 21, an ambitious eight-hundred-page blueprint for sustainable development in the twenty-first century, Johannesburg focused instead on the lag in implementation of these commitments; although many welcomed the focus on implementation, the meeting produced little in the way of tangible products or specific targets and timetables for action (see the essay by Speth in Part Three).

Do the past three decades tell an optimistic story of global society moving to meet the challenges of ecological interdependence, or do they chronicle unwillingness or inability to grapple with the root causes of the problem? Perhaps both are true. Growing knowledge and awareness, organizational adjustments, and occasional substantive breakthroughs over the past thirty years may reveal important possibilities for change, learning, and effective global cooperation. At the same time, enduring divisions and the far less optimistic tenor of Johannesburg when compared to Rio serve to underscore the depth of the political challenge posed by global environmental problems.

Conflicting Views of the Environmental Problematique

Growing scientific understanding and shared levels of public concern do not automatically translate into a shared understanding of the social causes of environmental problems. One of the first challenges facing students of global environmental politics is to sort out a potentially bewildering debate on the causes of pollution and environmental degradation. Some of this uncertainty lies in the realm of science. The physical, chemical, and biological mechanisms involved in processes such as climate change, desertification, and deforestation are sometimes quite poorly understood by leading experts, to say nothing of citizens, policymakers, or interest groups. For example, the global interaction of oceans, atmosphere, land, and biosphere has only recently become a central concern of disciplines like oceanography, atmospheric science, and terrestrial ecology (causing a growing number of scholars to rethink traditional disciplinary boundaries in these fields). Although knowledge is expanding rapidly on many fronts, scientific uncertainty remains substantial in the face of the complexity of processes of environmental change.

These aspects of technical complexity are matched by similar controversies, debates, and uncertainties surrounding the social dimensions of environmental change. In explaining why human populations have had such a substantial impact on planetary ecosystems, different analysts invoke factors as diverse as values, technology, culture, ideology, public policy, demographic change, and the social structures of class, race, or gender. Some observers elevate one or a few of these factors to the role of central cause, treating the others as mere symptoms. Others have sought to develop more complex models that stress the interaction of these various forces and processes.

Many see the problem as essentially one of values—in particular, the value that modern societies attach to consumption. Alan Durning asserts that

> [t]he soaring consumption lines that track the rise of the consumer society are, from another perspective, surging indicators of environmental harm. The consumer society's exploitation of resources threatens to exhaust, poison, or unalterably disfigure forests, soils, water, and air. We, its members, are responsible for a disproportionate share of all the global environmental challenges facing humanity.[11]

Our consumer culture translates wants into needs, stresses material-intensive forms of social gratification, and overwhelms older, more ecologically sustainable traditions that stand in its way. As consumerism spreads through increasingly sophisticated advertising, pop culture, and the global media, more and more regions of the planet adopt the aspirations of the consumer society.[12]

Technology is another commonly cited culprit. Barry Commoner, a key figure in raising public awareness about environmental problems in the United States through books such as *The Closing Circle,* used the simple example of the production of beer bottles in the United States to illustrate the technological dimension.[13] Writing in the mid-1970s, Commoner investigated the impact of three factors commonly cited as causes of environmental problems—population growth, rising levels of consumption per capita, and technological change. He found that the number of beer bottles produced in America increased by a dramatic 593 percent from 1950 to 1967, even though the population grew by only 30 percent and beer consumption by only 5 percent per capita. Clearly, a technological change—the replacement of reusable beer kegs and returnable bottles with single-use, throwaway ones—led to the bulk of the increase, and hence, to the bulk of the environmental impact in terms of energy use, trash, and so on. Commoner argued that similar technological changes at work across most of the key sectors of modern society are at the heart of the environmental crisis. The surge in popularity of sport-utility vehicles in the United States provides a contemporary example.

Some observers argue that prevailing technologies and values are expressions of underlying power dynamics in society. For example, Murray Bookchin—though not necessarily disagreeing with Durning's assessment of the consumer society or Commoner's cautions about technology—stresses the importance of social inequality. He warns against attributing environmental problems to such vague and impersonal formulations as "values," "technology," and "humanity." Such reasoning "serves to deflect our attention from the role society plays in producing ecological breakdown."[14] According to Bookchin,

[a] mythic "Humanity" is created—irrespective of whether we are talking about oppressed ethnic minorities, women, Third World people, or people in the First World—in which everyone is brought into complicity with powerful corporate elites in producing environmental dislocations. In this way, the social roots of ecological problems are shrewdly obscured. A new kind of biological "original sin" is created in which a vague group of animals called "Humanity" is turned into a destructive force that threatens the survival of the living world.[15]

According to Bookchin, the key to understanding lies instead in seeing how social inequality feeds environmental degradation and resource overexploitation. Societies constructed upon hierarchies of race, class, and gender are, in this view, fundamentally based on exploitation and thus have an inherent tendency to seek domination over nature rather than a means of living in harmony with it, just as they promote the domination of some people by others.[16]

Vandana Shiva, who has written extensively about forestry issues in postcolonial India, provides a model aimed at linking diverse causal forces such as technology, values, and social structure.[17] For Shiva, history is key: Technological and demographic change, hierarchical patterns of social structure, and consumption-oriented values are coevolutionary products of Indian society's dominant historical experience—the political, economic, and social transformations brought about by more than a century of British colonial rule. Thus, in her view, "causes" of environmental degradation in India as diverse as the industrial revolution, the capitalist world economy, and the destructive power of modern science and technology are "the philosophical, technological, and economic components of the same process."[18]

Sorting out this diverse array of claims about social causes of environmental change requires carefully detailed, historical study of the ways in which economic, social, and political institutions in society coevolve over time.[19] Many of the selections in this volume present models of the causes of environmental problems, at varying levels of detail and complexity. It will become apparent to the reader that these various causal claims are based on very different understandings of the sources of power, interest, authority, and legitimacy in society. Sorting out such diverse claims does not guarantee that effective policies and institutions will be designed. Actors may agree on the causes of a problem but still disagree on the appropriate responses; they may see their interests affected differently or hold different views about the fairness or effectiveness of a particular response. But grappling with the complex array of causes does seem to be a necessary preliminary step if appropriate responses are to be crafted. Perhaps just as importantly, examining the diversity of claims also helps us to understand the equally diverse beliefs about history, justice, and responsibility that various actors bring to the debate.

Global Environmental Politics:
Power, Ideas, and Voices

The material in this book has been selected with three goals in mind. One goal has been to pay particular attention to underlying questions of power, interest, authority, and legitimacy that shape global environmental debates. The challenge of the global environment is often framed as a largely technical and administrative task of promoting policy coordination among governments. Clearly, rational policies and effective intergovernmental cooperation will be a crucial part of any meaningful response to the challenge. But a narrow focus on governments, treaties, and public policies can blur our understanding of some of the deeper components of the problematique. The environmental problems facing the global community also raise deeper questions of governmental authority, of the relationship between the state and society, and of processes of economic and cultural globalization that challenge state sovereignty.

Second, we have tried to emphasize the *ideas* that have most powerfully shaped the evolving debate over the global environment. By assembling under one cover some of the most influential voices in the debate, we hope to provide a firsthand sense of how ideas have shaped action, while at the same time stressing the obstacles to changing the world through new ideas. Thus we examine some of the most powerful paradigms that prevailed at the time of the Stockholm conference and the controversies engendered by those views. We also explore the powerful and controversial new paradigms that have emerged, in the three decades since the Stockholm conference, around themes of sustainability, environmental security, and ecological justice. Comparing these sets of ideas over time reveals how people's thinking has changed at the same time as it highlights enduring themes.

Our third goal has been to present a broad range of voices in what is and must be a *global* debate. This goal might appear to conflict with our previously stated intention of presenting the most powerful and influential ideas: One might be tempted by a sense of urgency to try to narrow the debate to what the most powerful voices consider feasible or desirable (much as some governments have tried to woo an increasingly reluctant United States to participate in the global climate regime). In our view, any such narrowing of the debate on the grounds of political expediency would be deeply troubling on moral grounds, given the stakes involved for people, their livelihoods, their health, and all forms of life on the planet. It also strikes us as potentially disastrous—not expedient at all—given the current lack of global consensus on so many fundamental issues. The poor and powerless might lack the ability to shape the ecological future they desire, but they might well have the power to veto proposed "solutions" that ignore their needs and interests. Although universal agreement is a utopia difficult to imagine, durable responses to global environmental problems can be achieved only through a broad social consensus. Thus we have chosen essays for this book with the intent of including perspectives from South as well as North, with voices that are rural as well as urban, female as well as male, and critical of existing institutions as well as broadly comfortable working within them.

The book's organization is meant to serve these goals. We begin in Part One with a discussion of the dominant paradigms and controversies that shaped debate at the time of the Stockholm conference and during the conference itself. The views and debates that prevailed in that era provide a useful reference point for measuring what has changed since then. Part One focuses in particular on three provocative and influential ideas of that era: first, the notion that there are inherent "limits to growth" on a planet of finite natural resources and limited ecological resilience; second, the claim that where nature is concerned, self-interested individual behavior often adds up to a collective "tragedy of the commons"; and third, the idea that environmental threats increasingly demand controlling, perhaps even authoritarian, responses.

In Part Two we examine how the structure of the international system shapes the types of problems we face and the types of solutions we can imagine. The discussion focuses on the roles of national sovereignty and transnational capitalism in shaping political and economic institutions, patterns of environmental harm, and the possibilities for political responses. Part Two also examines environmentalism as a global social movement, investigating whether we might be seeing the emergence of new and different forms of political authority that challenge these dominant aspects of system structure.

Parts Three and Four examine the challenges of international cooperation and institutional reform. Part Three focuses on international cooperation, presenting a range of views on the prospects for cooperation and the appropriate form and substance of such cooperation. Part Four examines the possibilities for reforming some deeply embedded international practices in ways that foster environmental protection. The section focuses in particular on international trade and international development assistance or "foreign aid," two institutionalized practices that have been at the center of the ongoing debate about the relationship between the world economy and the global environment.

The volume concludes with three powerful and controversial paradigms that have crystallized and given form to the debates in the period since the Stockholm conference: sustainability (Part Five), environmental security (Part Six), and ecological justice (Part Seven). For some observers, these three paradigms are complementary and potentially harmonious facets of a single vision for the planet and its people. Others see tensions and contradictions inherent in the simultaneous pursuit of development, security, and justice in world affairs. Convergent or not, they are likely to remain the conceptual building blocks for environmental initiatives of the future.

In compiling this material, we have deliberately avoided organizing the book around a conventional list of environmental "issue areas" (climate change, deforestation, toxics, acid rain, and so on) or generic "classes" of environmental problems, such as transboundary pollution flows versus problems of the global commons. To be sure, these are useful ways to organize one's thinking about complex, multidimensional problems. However, by focusing on crosscutting themes of power, authority, and responsibility, we hope this book will provide a useful complement to these other approaches, which are already well represented in the literature.

Notes

1. John Perlin, *A Forest Journey: The Role of Wood in the Development of Civilization* (Cambridge, MA: Harvard University Press, 1991), p. 46.

2. Zoo Daqing and Zhang Peiyuan, "The Huang-Huai-Hai Plain," in B. L. Turner II, William C. Clark, Robert W. Kates, John F. Richards, Jessica T. Mathews, and William B. Meyer, eds., *The Earth as Transformed by Human Action* (New York: Cambridge University Press, 1990).

3. Peter Brimblecombe, *The Big Smoke: A History of Air Pollution in London since Medieval Times* (London: Methuen, 1987).

4. Turner et al., *The Earth as Transformed by Human Action.*

5. For an overview of the Stockholm conference, see Lynton Caldwell, *International Environmental Policy,* 3rd ed. (Durham, NC: Duke University Press, 1996). On Rio, see Peter M. Haas, Marc A. Levy, and Edward A. Parson, "Appraising the Earth Summit: How Should We Judge UNCED's Success?" *Environment* 34, no. 8 (1992); Michael Grubb, Matthias Koch, Abby Munson, Francis Sullivan, and Koy Thomson, *The Earth Summit Agreements: A Guide and Assessment* (London: Earthscan Publications, 1993); Pratap Chatterjee and Matthias Finger, *The Earth Brokers: Power, Politics and World Development* (London: Routledge, 1994). On Johannesburg, see the contribution of Speth to this volume.

6. See National Academy of Sciences, *One Earth, One Future: Our Changing Global Environment* (Washington, DC: National Academy Press, 1990), especially pp. 15–19.

7. On the growth of scientific knowledge about the environment from Stockholm to Rio, see Mostafa K. Tolba, Osama A. El-Kholy, E. El-Hinnawi, M. W. Holdgate, D. F. McMichael, and R. E. Munn, *The World Environment, 1972–1992: Two Decades of Challenge* (London: Chapman & Hall, 1992), chapter 20.

8. Haas, Levy, and Parson, "Appraising the Earth Summit."

9. One example of such a coalition in action can be seen in the campaign to change World Bank lending practices; see Part Four. On international coalitions and networking, see the contributions of Wapner and Barker and Soyez in Part Two; see also Margaret Keck and Katherine Sikkink, *Activists Beyond Borders: Advocacy Networks and International Politics* (New York: Cornell University Press, 1998).

10. On the effectiveness of international environmental regimes, see Peter M. Haas, Robert O. Keohane, and Mark A. Levy, eds., *Institutions for the Earth: Sources of Effective International Environmental Protection* (Cambridge, MA: MIT Press, 1993).

11. Alan Durning, *How Much Is Enough? The Consumer Society and the Future of the Earth* (New York: W. W. Norton, 1992), p. 23.

12. See Thomas Princen, Michael Maniates, and Ken Conca, *Confronting Consumption* (Cambridge, MA: MIT Press, 2002).

13. Barry Commoner, *Making Peace with the Planet,* 5th ed. (New York: New Press, 1992), pp. 148–150.

14. Murray Bookchin, *Remaking Society: Pathways to a Green Future* (Boston: South End Press, 1990), p. 9.

15. Bookchin, *Remaking Society,* pp. 9–10.

16. This theme is central to much of the literature on ecological justice; see Part Seven of this book.

17. Vandana Shiva, "People's Ecology: The Chipko Movement," in Saul Mendlovitz and R.B.J. Walker, eds., *Towards a Just World Peace* (London: Butterworths, 1987). See also Vandana Shiva, *Ecology and the Politics of Survival: Conflicts over Natural Resources in India* (Newbury Park, CA: Sage, 1991); Ramachandra Guha, *The Unquiet Woods: Ecological Change and Peasant Resistance in the Himalayas* (Berkeley: University of California Press, 1989).

18. Shiva, "People's Ecology," p. 262.

19. On the concept of coevolution see Richard B. Norgaard, "Sociosystem and Ecosystem Coevolution in the Amazon," *Journal of Environmental Economics and Management* 8 (1981):238–254.

PART ONE

THE DEBATE AT STOCKHOLM

As discussed in the introductory chapter, the 1972 U.N. Conference on the Human Environment, held in Stockholm, was a seminal event in the history of global environmental politics. Many important international agreements had already been concluded by the time of the Stockholm conference, including a treaty governing Antarctica (1959), a partial nuclear-test-ban treaty (1963), a treaty governing the exploration and use of outer space (1967), and several international agreements on ocean-related matters such as whaling, the use of marine resources, and pollution. But the Stockholm conference was the first broadly international effort to evaluate and discuss the environment in systematic, comprehensive terms, and it helped establish the trajectory of future efforts—the complex array of diplomatic initiatives and debates, attempts at transnational institution building, and global movements for social change that unfolded during the decades that followed.

Although the Stockholm conference took place more than three decades ago, many of its central debates are still current. These include several key questions revisited later in this book: Is global pollution mainly a problem of poverty or a problem of affluence? What is the balance of responsibility between North and South in global environmental degradation? Does the institution of national sovereignty help or hinder the effort to construct international responses to environmental problems? An understanding of the dominant ideas and controversies at the Stockholm conference provides an important historical perspective on the debates and disputes that dominate contemporary global environmental politics.[1]

In this section we introduce some of the ideas that shaped debate during the Stockholm era. We pay particular attention to three powerful and controversial claims from that era: the idea that there are inherent "limits to growth" facing the international economy, the world's population, and global consumption; the idea that self-interested individual behavior toward the environment adds up to a collective "tragedy of the commons"; and the claim that the environmental crisis demands a firm, authoritarian state to deal with the problems facing a "scarcity society."

Although thinking about the environment has evolved considerably in the years since the Stockholm conference, these themes are not just of historical interest. They have strongly influenced the nature of scientific and social-scientific inquiry since the conference, with many analysts and activists working to either prove or disprove the existence of limits to growth, a tragedy of the commons, or a political basis for ecological authoritarianism. These ideas also have shaped the political strategies pursued by governments, corporations, environmentalists, and other actors seeking to promote or hinder various forms of international environmental cooperation.

For the industrialized countries of the North, the Stockholm conference was a response to mounting public anxiety over the environmental consequences of industrial society. By the early 1970s, concerns over problems as diverse as air and water pollution, wilderness preservation, toxic chemicals, urban congestion, nuclear radiation, and rising prices for natural-resource commodities began to fuse into the notion that the world was rapidly approaching natural limits to growth in human activity. The best-selling book *The Limits to Growth* did much to galvanize public fears. Using a technique known as systems modeling, the authors tried to predict the consequences of unlimited growth in human numbers and consumption. As the passage presented here indicates, they concluded that the convergence of several trends—accelerating industrialization, rapid population growth, widespread malnutrition, depletion of nonrenewable resources, and a deteriorating environment—was moving the world rapidly toward overall limits on global growth. In order to avoid a potentially catastrophic collapse of the world's economic and social systems, it would be necessary to implement planned restraints on growth in population and in resource consumption.

Critics of *The Limits to Growth* argued that the book overstated the urgency of the problem, overlooked the possibility of substituting less-scarce inputs, and underestimated the possibility for technological solutions.[2] (These arguments foreshadowed the emergence in the 1980s of the concept of "sustainable development," which argues that some forms of economic growth can be compatible with natural limits; see Part Five.) The book's central claims were highly controversial, and most Northern governments were reluctant to fully endorse or embrace its findings. But the fears articulated in *The Limits to Growth* found widespread popular support in industrial societies, where they converged with the arguments of the growing coalition of environmental organizations.

Not surprisingly, the idea of limits to growth, and the controversy surrounding it, was received quite differently in the South. Among the less-industrialized countries, the idea of limits to growth evoked not only intellectual skepticism but also political suspicions. These suspicions were expressed eloquently in a 1972 essay by João Augusto de Araujo Castro, at that time Brazilian ambassador to the United States and an influential voice in North-South diplomacy. The South has never been monolithic in its views on problems of development and the environment. But as Castro made clear, many in the South linked the North's environmental concerns to the broader pattern of North-South relations. Thus, there was widespread agreement among Third World governments at the Stockholm conference that the North was responsible for the global environmental crisis; that the North, having reaped the fruits of industrialization, now sought to close the door on the South; that the environmental problems of poverty differed fundamentally from those of affluence; and that solutions crafted with the North's problems in mind would be ineffective, or worse, if imposed on the South.

The South's unity at the Stockholm conference made it clear that a *global* response to environmental problems would require linking the environmental debate to the development concerns of the South and to a broader dialogue about the political and economic "rules of the game" in the international system. The message was clear: If such connections were not drawn, the South would not participate.

Just as the idea of limits to growth dominated the debate over the *consequences* of environmental problems, the debate over *causes* crystallized around the powerful and controversial idea of the "tragedy of the commons." This view was popularized by biologist Garrett Hardin in a now-famous essay that appeared in the influential scholarly journal *Science* in 1968. According to Hardin, the "tragedy" occurred when self-interested actors enjoyed open access to, or unlimited use of, natural resources or environmental systems. Because consumers could benefit fully from additional exploitation while bearing only a small part of the "costs" of that exploitation (for example, environmental degradation)—costs shared with all other users—the overwhelming tendency would be toward greater exploitation of the resource. Each actor would pursue this logical individual behavior until the result for the system as a whole was the destruction or degradation of the resource in question. Individual logic would produce collective disaster—hence the notion of tragedy. Using the example of overgrazing on the town commons of medieval England (hence the "tragedy of the commons"), Hardin suggested that the same combination of self-interest and open access that had caused this earlier catastrophe was at the root of current problems of pollution and overpopulation. The solutions offered by Hardin were either to replace open access with enforceable private property rights, so that individual users would reap the full costs as well as the full benefits of their actions, or to impose governmental restrictions on access.

Hardin's model has been enormously influential in shaping thinking about global environmental problems, particularly for the so-called global commons such as the oceans and atmosphere, which fall under the domain of no single government. One reason for its influence is the model's simple elegance: The tragedy of the commons combines a recognizable human motive (self-interest) with a recognizable set of social rules (those allowing open access to natural resources and the environment) to produce a result that most would recognize as undesirable (rapid depletion or destruction of the resource in question).

Yet Hardin's model is, at heart, just a metaphor: The English commons is invoked as a simplified representation of the complex social rules, customs, goals, and behavioral incentives that shape how people interact with the environment individually and collectively. Whether such a "tragedy" actually lies at the center of global environmental problems depends on whether this abstraction is in fact an accurate representation of human behavior and social institutions. Even if the tragedy seems plausible conceptually, how widely does it apply as a description of the real world?

Susan J. Buck argues that despite its widespread acceptance, Hardin's tragedy does not even describe accurately the situation of the commons in medieval England on which the metaphor is based. According to Buck, access to the town commons was never unrestrained but rather was governed by a complex set of community rules that ensured sustainable use. The commons system was destroyed not by population growth and self-interested individual behavior, as Hardin asserted, but by changing political and economic conditions in Britain, which gave powerful actors the incentive and ability to privatize the commons and to overwhelm community-based systems of property rights. Thus, rather than representing a tragedy, the endurance of the commons system, in some cases for several hundred years, shows that there may be possibilities other than the stark choice Hardin poses between purely private property and purely open access.

In the decades since Hardin's essay was published, scholars have produced a large body of empirical evidence addressing the question of whether Hardin's tragedy actually exists.[3] Research has focused on a wide range of natural-resource and environmental systems—often referred to as "common-pool resources"—that are potentially subject to the "tragedy," including fisheries, wildlife populations, surface water, groundwater, rangelands, and forests. Much of this work has found that Hardin's formulation, though sometimes applicable, is by no means universal. Whether a "tragedy" of overconsumption ensues depends on the type of social rules governing these natural resources or environmental systems. The enforceable private property rights advocated by Hardin are just one such set of rules, and not necessarily the most appropriate for all situations. Elinor Ostrom's influential book *Governing the Commons*, published in 1990, provided both theory and evidence that self-organizing, sustainable management of shared resources is possible under certain conditions.[4] Ostrom and her colleagues argue that common-pool resources are more likely to be governed sustainably if governing rules and institutions follow certain design principles:

Given the large variation in common-pool resources, their patterns of use, and their users, researchers agree that no single institutional design can be devised that will work in all of the many different common-pool resource situations. Researchers also agree, however, that we can discuss a set of general principles that increase performance of an institutional design:

1. Rules are devised and managed by resource users.
2. Compliance with rules is easy to monitor.
3. Rules are enforceable.
4. Sanctions are graduated.
5. Adjudication is available at low cost.
6. Monitors and other officials are accountable to users.
7. Institutions to regulate a given common-pool resource may need to be devised at multiple levels.
8. Procedures exist for revising rules.[5]

The work of Buck, Ostrom, and others is of critical importance in the effort to craft international responses to environmental problems. If Hardin's tragedy does apply to the global commons, it will be exceedingly difficult to craft effective international responses to global environmental problems. This is so because both of Hardin's preferred solutions, privatizing the commons or subjecting it to the control of a powerful central authority, are infeasible in the current international system. If these are the only choices, the tragedy seems likely to proceed apace. However, if systems of collective management can be shown to have been effective on the local or regional level, it may also be possible to design such systems to operate on the international level.[6] Under these circumstances there could still be a tragedy of the commons, but it would result from our lack of skill and effectiveness in designing fair and efficient international responses rather than from some ironclad logic of nature.

What would be the political consequences of the limits to growth and the tragedy of the commons? A provocative answer to this question was provided by William Ophuls in his 1977 book *Ecology and the Politics of Scarcity* (on which the later essay excerpted here was based). According to Ophuls, a new era of scarcity would be marked by an authoritarian political response, just as scarcity in the past had been the trigger for various forms of violence, oppression, and war. The "scarcity society" that Ophuls described would perceive "the necessity for political control" in order to avoid "ecological self-destruction." The result Ophuls foresaw was a political future "much less libertarian and much more authoritarian, much less individualistic and much more communalistic than our present." Ophuls did see an alternative to this grim scenario, which he labeled a "democracy of restraint." In this scenario, it would be possible to forge an ecologically rational future without coercive authority, provided that human gratification could be decoupled from material consumption. But a democracy of restraint would demand a prompt response to environmental problems and a broad social consensus on the importance of taking action—circumstances that Ophuls deemed unlikely.

Ophuls's notions about the likelihood of authoritarian responses to environmental problems remain controversial. Nor is it clear that authoritarian responses would be effective. In Part Seven, on the question of ecological justice, we present very different interpretations of the links between freedom, democracy, justice, and the environment. But the questions Ophuls raised about the ability of today's governments to respond effectively and in a timely fashion, and the attention he drew to the close link between control of nature and control of people, remain critical themes in environmental politics.

Despite their critics, and despite changes in our understanding in the decades since the Stockholm conference, the concepts of "limits to growth," "the tragedy of the commons," and "the scarcity society" remain powerfully influential in global environmental politics. Not only did they help shape the pathway from Stockholm; they are also readily seen in contemporary controversies. The dispute about growth limits has reemerged in current debates over the environmental consequences of international trade (see Part Four) and the prospects for sustainability (see Part Five). Similarly, those skeptical about the prospects for effective international cooperation invoke both the logic of self-interested behavior and the commons-like features of global environmental systems (see Part Three)—just as Hardin did thirty years ago. And the increasingly widespread fear that environmental degradation threatens national and international security raises for some the specter of authoritarian solutions, as posited by Ophuls (see Part Six). The evolution of global environmental politics cannot be understood without examining the history of these ideas; weighing their claims carefully and critically is as important today as it was in the Stockholm era.

Thinking Critically

1. How well have the essays by Meadows, Castro, Hardin, and Ophuls, which were all written between 1968 and 1977, withstood the test of time? Do they still provide an adequate framework for understanding and addressing global environmental problems? What aspects of their essays seem anachronistic? What aspects ring true today? Imagine what a dialogue among these thinkers would be like if they were to meet today and discuss the durability of each other's claims.

2. Contrast Castro's claims about the environment and development with the essays on sustainability in Part Five. Do either the advocates or the critics of the sustainability paradigm frame the problem in the same way as Castro?

3. Does the criticism of Hardin presented in Buck's essay invalidate his central claim about the tragedy of the commons? In other words, can Hardin still be right about the larger problem even if he misread the history of the English commons, and even if exceptions to his pessimistic scenario can be found? What do you think Hardin would say to his critics?

4. If Buck, Ostrom, and others are correct to argue that sustainable governance of the commons is feasible on a local scale, can we imagine similar forms of governance on a larger scale? What are the limits of scale for these forms of governance, and at what scale are these limits likely to be encountered?

5. Consider Ostrom's list, above, of design principles for sustainable management of common-pool resources. Would it be difficult politically or administratively to incorporate these principles into international environmental agreements on a regional or global commons? Which would likely be the sticking points in international negotiations, and why?

6. Contrast Ophuls's arguments about the need for strong command-and-control governance with the essays on environmental justice in Part Seven. Is the concentration of power in the hands of the state part of the problem or part of the solution? In an era in which many governments face profound skepticism and frequent crises of authority, are people likely to look to the state for solutions to the problems of the "scarcity society"?

Notes

1. Lynton Caldwell, *International Environmental Policy,* 3rd ed. (Durham, NC: Duke University Press, 1996).

2. Several of these criticisms are summarized in W. D. Nordhaus, "World Dynamics: Measurement without Data," *Economic Journal* 83, no. 332 (December 1973):1156–1183. See also Julian Simon and Herman Kahn, *The Resourceful Earth* (Oxford: Basil Blackwell, 1984).

3. Much of this research is summarized in Nives Dolšak and Elinor Ostrom, *The Commons in the New Millennium: Challenges and Adaptation* (Cambridge, MA: MIT Press, 2003). See also David Feeny, Fikret Berkes, Bonnie J. McCay, and James M. Acheson, "The Tragedy of the Commons: Twenty-Two Years Later," *Human Ecology* 18, no. 1 (1990):1–19.

4. See Elinor Ostrom, *Governing the Commons: The Evolution of Institutions for Collective Action* (London: Cambridge University Press, 1990).

5. Nives Dolšak and Elinor Ostrom, "The Challenges of the Commons," in Dolåak and Ostrom, *The Commons in the New Millennium,* p. 22.

6. See Robert O. Keohane and Elinor Ostrom, eds., *Local Commons and Global Interdependence* (London: Sage, 1995).

I

THE LIMITS TO GROWTH

Donella H. Meadows, Dennis L. Meadows, Jørgen Randers, and William W. Behrens III

Problems and Models

Every person approaches his problems . . . with the help of models. A model is simply an ordered set of assumptions about a complex system. It is an attempt to understand some aspect of the infinitely varied world by selecting from perceptions and past experience a set of general observations applicable to the problem at hand. . . .

Decisionmakers at every level unconsciously use mental models to choose among policies that will shape our future world. These mental models are, of necessity, very simple when compared with the reality from which they are abstracted. The human brain, remarkable as it is, can only keep track of a limited number of the complicated, simultaneous interactions that determine the nature of the real world.

We, too, have used a model. Ours is a formal, written model of the world.* It constitutes a preliminary attempt to improve our mental models of long-term, global problems by combining the large amount of information that is already in human minds and in written records with the new information-

Excerpted from Donella H. Meadows, Dennis L. Meadows, Jørgen Randers, and William W. Behrens III, *The Limits to Growth* (Washington, D.C.: Potomac Associates, 1972). Reprinted with permission.

*The prototype model on which we have based our work was designed by Professor Jay W. Forrester of the Massachusetts Institute of Technology. A description of that model has been published in his book *World Dynamics* (Cambridge, Mass.: Wright-Allen Press, 1971).

processing tools that mankind's increasing knowledge has produced—the scientific method, systems analysis, and the modern computer.

Our world model was built specifically to investigate five major trends of global concern—accelerating industrialization, rapid population growth, widespread malnutrition, depletion of nonrenewable resources, and a deteriorating environment. These trends are all interconnected in many ways, and their development is measured in decades or centuries, rather than in months or years. With the model we are seeking to understand the causes of these trends, their interrelationships, and their implications as much as one hundred years in the future.

The model we have constructed is, like every other model, imperfect, oversimplified, and unfinished. We are well aware of its shortcomings, but we believe that it is the most useful model now available for dealing with problems far out on the space-time graph. To our knowledge it is the only formal model in existence that is truly global in scope, that has a time horizon longer than thirty years, and that includes important variables such as population, food production, and pollution, not as independent entities, but as dynamically interacting elements, as they are in the real world. . . .

In spite of the preliminary state of our work, we believe it is important to publish the model and our findings now. Decisions are being made every day, in every part of the world, that will affect the physical, economic, and social conditions of the world system for decades to come. These decisions cannot wait for perfect models and total understanding. They will be made on the basis of some model, mental or written, in any case. . . .

Our conclusions are:

1. If the present growth trends in world population, industrialization, pollution, food production, and resource depletion continue unchanged, the limits to growth on this planet will be reached sometime within the next one hundred years. The most probable result will be a rather sudden and uncontrollable decline in both population and industrial capacity.
2. It is possible to alter these growth trends and to establish a condition of ecological and economic stability that is sustainable far into the future. The state of global equilibrium could be designed so that the basic material needs of each person on earth are satisfied and each person has an equal opportunity to realize his individual human potential.
3. If the world's people decide to strive for this second outcome rather than the first, the sooner they begin working to attain it, the greater will be their chances of success.

These conclusions are so far-reaching and raise so many questions for further study that we are quite frankly overwhelmed by the enormity of the job that must be done. We hope that this book will serve to interest other people

. . . to raise the space and time horizons of their concerns and to join us in understanding and preparing for a period of great transition—the transition from growth to global equilibrium. . . .

A Finite World

We have mentioned many difficult trade-offs . . . in the production of food, in the consumption of resources, and in the generation and clean-up of pollution. By now it should be clear that all of these trade-offs arise from one simple fact—the earth is finite. The closer any human activity comes to the limit of the earth's ability to support that activity, the more apparent and unresolvable the trade-offs become. When there is plenty of unused arable land, there can be more people and also more food per person. When all the land is already used, the trade-off between more people or more food per person becomes a choice between absolutes.

In general, modern society has not learned to recognize and deal with these trade-offs. The apparent goal of the present world system is to produce more people with more (food, material goods, clean air, and water) for each person. . . . We have noted that if society continues to strive for that goal, it will eventually reach one of many earthly limitations. . . . It is not possible to foretell exactly which limitation will occur first or what the consequences will be, because there are many conceivable, unpredictable human responses to such a situation. It is possible, however, to investigate what conditions and what changes in the world system might lead society to collision with or accommodation to the limits to growth in a finite world. . . .

Technology and the Limits to Growth

Although the history of human effort contains numerous incidents of mankind's failure to live within physical limits, it is success in overcoming limits that forms the cultural tradition of many dominant people in today's world. Over the past three hundred years, mankind has compiled an impressive record of pushing back the apparent limits to population and economic growth by a series of spectacular technological advances. Since the recent history of a large part of human society has been so continuously successful, it is quite natural that many people expect technological breakthroughs to go on raising physical ceilings indefinitely. These people speak about the future with resounding technological optimism. . . .

The hopes of the technological optimists center on the ability of technology to remove or extend the limits to growth of population and capital. We have shown that in the world model the application of technology to apparent problems of resource depletion or pollution or food shortage has no impact on the essential problem, which is exponential growth in a finite and complex system. Our attempts to use even the most optimistic estimates of the benefits of technology in the model did not prevent the ultimate decline of population and industry, and in fact did not in any case postpone the collapse beyond the year 2200. . . .

Applying technology to the natural pressures that the environment exerts against any growth process has been so successful in the past that a whole culture has evolved around the principle of fighting against limits rather than learning to live with them. . . . But the relationship between the earth's limits and man's activities is changing. The exponential growth curves are adding millions of people and billions of tons of pollutants to the ecosystem each year. Even the ocean, which once appeared virtually inexhaustible, is losing species after species of its commercially useful animals. . . .

There may be much disagreement with the statement that population and capital growth must stop soon. But virtually no one will argue that material growth on this planet can go on forever. . . . Man can still choose his limits and stop when he pleases by weakening some of the strong pressures that cause capital and population growth, or by instituting counterpressures, or both. Such counterpressures will probably not be entirely pleasant. They will certainly involve profound changes in the social and economic structures that have been deeply impressed into human culture by centuries of growth. The alternative is to wait until the price of technology becomes more than society can pay, or until the side-effects of technology suppress growth themselves, or until problems arise that have no technical solutions. At any of those points the choice of limits will be gone. Growth will be stopped by pressures that are not of human choosing, and that, as the world model suggests, may be very much worse than those which society might choose for itself.

. . . Technological optimism is the most common and the most dangerous reaction to our findings from the world model. Technology can relieve the symptoms of a problem without affecting the underlying causes. Faith in technology as the ultimate solution to all problems can thus divert our attention from the most fundamental problem—the problem of growth in a finite system—and prevent us from taking effective action to solve it. . . .

The Transition from Growth to Global Equilibrium

We can say very little at this point about the practical, day-by-day steps that might be taken to reach a desirable, sustainable state of global equilibrium. Neither the world model nor our own thoughts have been developed in sufficient detail to understand all the implications of the transition from growth to equilibrium. Before any part of the world's society embarks deliberately on such a transition, there must be much more discussion, more extensive analysis, and many new ideas contributed by many different people. . . .

Although we underline the need for more study and discussion of these difficult questions, we end on a note of urgency. We hope that intensive study and debate will proceed simultaneously with an ongoing program of action. The details are not yet specified, but the general direction for action is obvious. Enough is known already to analyze many proposed policies in terms of their tendencies to promote or to regulate growth.[1] . . . Efforts are weak at the moment, but they could be strengthened very quickly if the goal of equilibrium were recognized as desirable and important by any sizable part of human society. . . .

Taking no action to solve these problems is equivalent to taking strong action. Every day of continued exponential growth brings the world system closer to the ultimate limits to that growth. A decision to do nothing is a decision to increase the risk of collapse. We cannot say with certainty how much longer mankind can postpone initiating deliberate control of his growth before he will have lost the chance for control. We suspect on the basis of present knowledge of the physical constraints of the planet that the growth phase cannot continue for another one hundred years. Again, because of the delays in the system, if the global society waits until those constraints are unmistakably apparent, it will have waited too long.

If there is cause for deep concern, there is also cause for hope. Deliberately limiting growth would be difficult, but not impossible. The way to proceed is clear, and the necessary steps, although they are new ones for human society, are well within human capabilities. Man possesses, for a small moment in his history, the most powerful combination of knowledge, tools, and resources the world has ever known. He has all that is physically necessary to create a totally new form of human society—one that would be built to last for generations. The two missing ingredients are a realistic, long-term goal that can guide mankind to the equilibrium society and the human will to achieve that goal. Without such a goal and a commitment to it, short-term concerns will generate the exponential growth that drives the world system toward the limits of the earth and ultimate collapse. With that goal and that commitment mankind would be ready now to begin a controlled, orderly transition from growth to global equilibrium.

Notes

1. See, for example, "Fellow Americans Keep Out!" *Forbes,* June 15, 1971, p. 22, and *The Ecologist,* January 1972.

2

ENVIRONMENT AND DEVELOPMENT: THE CASE OF THE DEVELOPING COUNTRIES

João Augusto de Araujo Castro

Introduction

Interest in the field of ecology, which is centered in the developed countries, has recently increased due to the sudden discovery of a possible imbalance between man and earth. Resulting from the population explosion and the misuse of existing and newly developed technologies, this potential imbalance could bring about an environmental crisis menacing the future of mankind. In several countries the emergence of an interest in ecological problems has not been confined to the realm of the scientific community. It has aroused public concern which has expressed itself, although sometimes vaguely, in such initiatives as Earth Week, celebrated in the United States in April 1970, and the mushrooming of a specialized literature.

As would be expected, the methods envisaged to resolve on a world basis the so-called environmental crisis were inspired by the realities of a fraction of that very same world: the family of the developed countries. Furthermore, the bulk of the solutions in hand, mainly of a technical nature, seek primarily to make healthier the consequences of the Industrial Revolution without necessarily providing a tool for a further distribution of its benefits among states.

Excerpted from "Environment and Development: The Case of the Developing Countries," in David A. Kay and Eugene B. Skolnikoff, eds., *World Eco-crisis: International Organizations in Response.* © 1972. Reprinted by permission of the University of Wisconsin Press.

This study seeks to introduce some neglected aspects of the interests of developing countries into discussions about a world ecological policy. The working hypothesis is that the implementation of any worldwide environmental policy based on the realities of the developed countries tends to perpetuate the existing gap in socioeconomic development between developed and developing countries and so promote the freezing of the present international order. . . .

Developed Countries

Although there does not yet exist a systematic body of doctrine, the new ecological policy of the developed countries contains several elements that have already stimulated important developments in academic thought, as indicated by the growing literature on the matter, and attitudes of governments and private sectors in these countries, mainly in their relations with the developing countries.

A short historical digression may help in analyzing the rationale of this ecological policy. As a localized phenomenon in the countries of the Northern Hemisphere, the Industrial Revolution of the eighteenth century was not brought about by one single factor. It was not, for instance, the result of inventions or the coming into operation of new machines. As in the case of other major movements in history, it was the result of the interplay of many factors, some obscure in themselves, whose combined effort laid down the foundations of a new industrial system. Growing organically, cell by cell, new patterns of industrial organization were soon translated into the establishment of a new international order. Around the group of countries enjoying the benefits of the Industrial Revolution there existed an increasing family of countries, trying, mostly unsuccessfully, to modernize their own means of production.

This new international order and the relatively uneven distribution of political power among states, based on the use and monopoly of advanced technologies, may be considered one of the most enduring effects of the Industrial Revolution. And since then, as a normal corollary of the new order, the technologically advanced countries have been endeavoring to maintain their political and economic position in the world while the technologically less endowed countries have been seeking to alter, through development, this global status quo.

This permanent struggle between the two groups of countries persists in the present days and it is unlikely that it will cease in the near future. For this to happen one would have to assume a perfectly homogeneous world community whose conflicts would have been eliminated through a perfect satisfaction, on a homogeneous basis, of all human needs. This condition is most likely to be found only in the realms of utopia. . . .

According to a helpful image taken from academic and governmental sources in the developed countries our planet could be visualized as a "spaceship earth," where life could only be sustained, nay simply possible, through maintenance of a delicate equilibrium between the needs of the passengers and the ability of the craft to respond to those needs. Undisturbed until recently, this equilibrium would now be menaced by an excess of population and the consequences of the use of both previously existing and newly developed technologies. Elaborating the same image, "spaceship earth" would be divided into two classes of passengers, the first coincident with the technologically advanced countries and the second representative of the technologically less endowed countries, which would necessarily have to trade off positions with a view to maintaining the equilibrium of the vessel. . . .

In order to maintain the equilibrium of the vessel the problems created by population explosion and the use of both previously existing and new technologies should, in the view of developed countries, now be dealt with globally, irrespective of the unequal distribution, on a world scale, of the benefits and related destructive effects on the environment engendered by the Industrial Revolution. Germane to such a global ecological policy is the need for world planning for development which, to be successful, might purposely aim at freezing the present relative positions of the two classes inside the vessel.

Provided that the first class already enjoys low average rates of population growth and is unlikely to opt for a slower rate of industrial growth for the sole purpose of guaranteeing a purer atmosphere or cleaner water, the new ecology-saving policy would be more successful if applied in the areas where the environmental crisis has not yet appeared, even in its least acute forms. Actually, these areas would mainly comprise the territory of the second class. Thus: the second class should be taught to employ the most effective and expeditious birth control methods and to follow an orderly pollution-reducing process of industrialization. In the case of industrialization, the mainstream of socioeconomic development, the lesson must be even harsher: The second class must organize production in accordance with environment-saving techniques already tested by the first class or be doomed to socioeconomic stagnation. . . .

Nowadays some ecologists do not hesitate to say that the developing countries can never hope to achieve the consumption patterns of the developed countries. Some seemingly appalling calculations are offered as proof of this. To raise the living standards of the world's existing population to American levels the annual production of iron would have to increase 75 times, that of copper 100 times, that of lead 200 times, and that of tin 250 times. Were a country such as India to make use of fertilizers at the per capita level of the Netherlands, it would consume one-half of the world's total output of fertilizers. Clearly, the parity of the developing countries with the developed ones is no longer compatible with the existing stocks of natural resources. Again, according to those wise men, the increasing expectations in developing countries, which are sometimes associated with something approaching a revolution, are nothing more than expectations of elites and therefore must be curbed. Most of the population of these countries, it is claimed, do not have an ambition to reach Western standards and do not even know that "such a thing as development is on the agenda."

Now, the alleged exhaustion of natural resources is accompanied, in general, by forecasts of the fateful coming of formidable ecological hecatombs.

The continuing progress of developed countries would require an economic lebensraum in the Southern Hemisphere. In the name of the survival of mankind developing countries should continue in a state of underdevelopment because if the evils of industrialization were to reach them, life on the planet would be placed in jeopardy. . . .

Very few reasonable people underwrite these fanciful ideas. Yet, it cannot be denied that the environment in developed countries is threatened and that it should be preserved. The difficulty in dealing with environmental problems nowadays is that they have become a myth. . . . From an uttermost neglect of ecological problems public opinion in the United States has swung to an outright "geolatry." The environment has been rediscovered and Mother Earth now has a week dedicated to her in the calendar. School children crusade to clean up the streets; college students organize huge demonstrations; uncivilized industries that dump their wastes in the air, in the water, or on the ground are denounced as public enemies.

. . . The simplistic concepts that ecology is disturbed because there are "too many people" or because they "consume too much" must be discarded as nothing more than fallacies. There is abundant evidence that the earth is capable of supporting a considerably greater population at much higher levels of consumption. The simple fact that in half a century mankind found it possible to wage four major wars, with a terrible waste of wealth, is a clear indication that we are not after all so short of resources although we may be short of common sense. . . .

Environmental problems not only pose a new and compelling argument for disarmament and peace but also call attention to the question of efficiency in the organization of production. It is widely known, but seldom remembered when the availability of natural resources is discussed, that in developed countries billions of dollars are spent every year to purchase so-called farm surpluses. Millions of tons of agricultural products have been regularly stored or destroyed to keep prices up in the world markets. . . . These figures and these facts evidently do not agree with the superficial statements which have been made about the irreparable strain being put on natural resources.

Pollution of the air and water and related damages to the environment are loosely attributed, in general, to faulty technologies, but few have bothered to assess objectively the exact proportions of the problem. According to experts at the Organization for Economic Cooperation and Development (OECD) safeguarding the environment in the United States would require annual expenditures of . . . less than 2 percent of the American GNP [Editors' note: gross national product]. Clearly, there is no real cause for most of the fuzzy agitation about the environment. Put in their proper perspective, environmental problems are little more than a question of the reexamination of national priorities. . . .

When discussing the environment some ecologists and other wise men, as often happens in many other instances, try haphazardly to superimpose peculiar situations prevailing in developed countries onto the realities of the developing countries. . . . If the peculiarities of developing countries are taken into account, it will not be difficult to recognize that, in broad terms, they are still at a prepollution stage or, in other words, have not yet been given the chance to become polluted. . . . The 24 countries of Latin America, the least under-developed region in the developing world, have less than one-tenth of the total number of motor vehicles in the United States. Only a few ecologists and other wise men would say that Latin Americans should rather have fewer cars and cleaner air.

There is a pollution of affluence and a pollution of poverty. It is imperative to distinguish between the two lest some pollution be prevented at the cost of much economic development. Were it not for the dangers arising from the confusion between the two kinds of pollution, there would be no need for calling attention to the precarious housing conditions, poor health, and low sanitary standards not to mention starvation in developing countries. The linear transposition of ecological problems of the developed countries to the context of the developing ones disregards the existence of such distressing social conditions. Wherever these conditions prevail, the assertion that income means less pollution is nonsense. It is obvious, or should be, that the so-called pollution of poverty can only be corrected through higher incomes, or more precisely, through economic development.

The most sensible ecologists are of the opinion that the pollution levels can be attributed not so much to population or affluence as to modern technologies. In the United States the economy would have grown enough, in the absence of technological change, to give the increased population about the same per capita amounts of goods and services today as in 1946. The ecological crisis has resulted mainly from the sweeping progress in technologies. Modern technologies have multiplied the impact of growth on the environment and, consequently, generated most of the existing pollution. Those who haphazardly transpose developed countries' situations to the milieu of an underdeveloped country repeatedly warn the latter against the dangers of modern technologies and rapid industrialization. "Don't let happen to your cities what happened to New York; keep your beautiful landscapes." It is ironic that developed countries, which create and sell modern technologies, should caution developing countries against utilizing them. Is this done to justify the second-hand technologies that sometimes accompany foreign direct investments?

Developing Countries

A somewhat apathetic attitude on the part of the developing countries regarding the environmental issue does not imply negation of the relevance of the matter and the need for true international cooperation to solve the problem it poses for the survival of mankind. This apathetic attitude, however, clearly is derived from the developing countries' socioeconomic experience which differs, to a large extent, from that of the developed countries. Consequently, one has to bear in mind that, not having enjoyed the opportunity to experience their own

Industrial Revolution, the developing countries have not been stimulated to think about the environmental crisis as posed in the present days. The phenomenon of urbanization in the Southern Hemisphere, even in the countries experiencing a considerable degree of progress, may raise questions about poor living standards in some areas but has not thus far led to industrial congestion.

As indicated in the elements of the ecological policy of the developed countries, the equilibrium of "spaceship earth" would depend on the enforcement of measures bearing on population and on the use of the previously existing and new technologies chiefly in the second class of the vessel or, in other words, in the territory of the developing countries. Even if applied to their full extent, those measures would not result at some foreseeable date in a single-class carrying vessel, preferably closer to the first steerage. This ecological policy, which aims primarily at the equilibrium of the vessel, could better succeed if the relative positions of the classes were maintained, for the emergence of one single class would presuppose a considerable change in the living standards of the first class, something that may not be attained in the light of present global socioeconomic realities. . . .

On the question of the preservation of the environment the passenger's survival would call for the enforcement of a drastic decision, globally applied, to maintain a "green area reserve" which would have to coincide mainly with the territories of the developing countries. This step would safeguard, against complete exhaustion, the natural elements (soil, atmosphere, and water) still available on the planet just to provide some sort of counteraction to the spoilage of the same natural elements used up in the countries where the benefits of the Industrial Revolution were massively concentrated.

Besides the ethical question raised by this policy, as expressed in the ostensive imbalance between responsibility for the damage and obligation for repair, the developing countries, in abiding by its prescriptions, would make a commitment to conservatism rather than to conservation. Furthermore, the possibility of a widespread application of developed countries' ecological policy, theoretically conceived to secure the equilibrium of "spaceship earth," may risk transforming the Southern Hemisphere countries into the last healthy weekend areas for the inhabitants of a planet already saturated with the environment created by the Industrial Revolution. As a token of compensation the Southern Hemisphere countries could claim to have resurrected, and adequately preserved, the environmental milieu for the living and the survival of Rousseau's "happy savage." In expressing their concern over the environmental crisis the developing countries cannot accept, without further refinement, the ecological policy devised by the developed countries whose socioeconomic structure was deeply influenced by the unique phenomenon of the Industrial Revolution.

The first step toward the refinement of that policy may be the rejection of the principle that the ecology issue, taken on a global basis, can be dealt with exclusively through a technical approach, as suggested by the developed countries. Given the implications for the international order, including the freezing of the status quo, any environment-saving policy must necessarily be imbued with a solid and well-informed political approach. This would provide an opportunity for the developing countries, by preserving their national identities, to join safely in the effort of the international community to preserve the equilibrium of "spaceship earth."

As a normal corollary of the political approach, ecological policy should not depart from the broader framework of socioeconomic development. In this regard a second step of refinement would require a corresponding universal commitment to development if the task of preserving the environment is to be shared by the world community. . . .

Evidently, no country wants any pollution at all. But each country must evolve its own development plans, exploit its own resources as it thinks suitable, and define its own environmental standards. The idea of having such priorities and standards imposed on individual countries or groups of countries, on either a multilateral or a bilateral basis, is very hard to accept.

That is why it is disturbing to see the International Bank for Reconstruction and Development (IBRD) set up its own ecological policy. Repercussions on the environment, defined according to IBRD ecologists, have become an important factor in determining whether financial assistance by that institution should be granted for an industrial project in developing countries. It seems reasonable that the preservation of the environment should not exclude the preservation of national sovereignty. Ecological policies should rather be inserted into the framework of national development.

It is perhaps time for the developing countries to present their own views on the framing of an environmental policy in spite of the fact that the developed countries have not yet ended their own controversial debate or furnished definite and convincing data on the issue. In adopting a position the developing countries recognize the existence of environmental problems in the world and the possibility of finding solutions through both national efforts and international cooperation.

The first point to be touched on concerns the question of national sovereignty. In this regard any ecological policy, globally applied, must not be an instrument to suppress wholly or in part the legitimate right of any country to decide about its own affairs. In reality this point would simply seek to guarantee on an operational level the full exercise of the principle of juridical equality of states as expressed, for instance, in the Charter of the United Nations. . . . Sovereignty, in this context, should not be taken as an excuse for isolationism and consequently for escapism in relation to international efforts geared to solving environmental problems. For the developing countries it is crucial to consider, in the light of their own interests, nationally defined, the whole range of alternative solutions devised or implemented in the developed countries. Naturally, it is assumed that all countries can act responsibly and that none is going to deliberately favor policies that may endanger the equilibrium of "spaceship earth."

Closely linked to the problem of sovereignty, the question of national priorities calls for an understanding of the distinction between the developmental characteristics of developed and developing countries. As has been previously pointed out in this article, while the ecological issue came to the forefront of public concern as a by-product of postindustrial stages of development, it is not yet strikingly apparent in the majority of the developing countries. And different realities, of course, should be differently treated or, at least, given the fittest solutions.

In the developing countries the major concern is an urgent need to accelerate socioeconomic development, and a meaningful ecological policy must not hamper the attainment of that goal in the most expeditious way. . . . In this context the developing countries, while rejecting the implementation of any ecological policy which bears in itself elements of socioeconomic stagnation, could only share a common responsibility for the preservation of the environment if it was accompanied and paralleled by a corresponding common responsibility for development. . . .

Conclusion

This study has probed very briefly some aspects of an ecological policy in the light of the interests of the developing countries. . . . Emphasis has been laid on the undesirability of transposing, uncritically, into the realities of the developing countries the solutions already envisaged by the developed countries to eliminate or reduce the so-called environmental crisis to the extent that those solutions may embody elements of socioeconomic stagnation. . . . Finally, a preliminary and broad picture of a position of the developing countries has stressed the relation between preservation of environment and the urgent need to speed up socioeconomic development and the desirability of a common world effort to tackle both these aspects simultaneously. This common effort, however, should not preclude or trespass on national interest as a departing point for the setting up of concepts and operational guidelines of an ecological policy for the developing countries.

In conclusion, a discussion of any meaningful ecological policy for both developed and developing countries . . . would better reflect a broad socioeconomic concern, as tentatively suggested in this article, rather than confine itself to a strictly scientific approach. Man's conceptual environment, and nothing else, will certainly prevail in shaping the future of mankind, for the preservation of the environment presupposes a human being to live in it and a human mind to conceive a better life for man on this planet. From the point of view of man—and we have no other standpoint—Man, Pascal's "roseau pensant," is still more relevant than Nature.

3

THE TRAGEDY
OF THE COMMONS

GARRETT HARDIN

Tragedy of Freedom in a Commons

. . . The tragedy of the commons develops in this way. Picture a pasture open to all. It is to be expected that each herdsman will try to keep as many cattle as possible on the commons. Such an arrangement may work reasonably satisfactorily for centuries because tribal wars, poaching, and disease keep the numbers of both man and beast well below the carrying capacity of the land. Finally, however, comes the day of reckoning, that is, the day when the long-desired goal of social stability becomes a reality. At this point, the inherent logic of the commons remorselessly generates tragedy.

As a rational being, each herdsman seeks to maximize his gain. Explicitly or implicitly, more or less consciously, he asks, "What is the utility to *me* of adding one more animal to my herd?" This utility has one negative and one positive component.

1. The positive component is a function of the increment of one animal. Since the herdsman receives all the proceeds from the sale of the additional animal, the positive utility is nearly +1.
2. The negative component is a function of the additional overgrazing created by one more animal. Since, however, the effects of overgrazing

are shared by all the herdsmen, the negative utility for any particular
decisionmaking herdsman is only a fraction of −1.

Adding together the component partial utilities, the rational herdsman concludes that the only sensible course for him to pursue is to add another animal
to his herd. And another; and another. . . . But this is the conclusion reached by
each and every rational herdsman sharing a commons. Therein is the tragedy.
Each man is locked into a system that compels him to increase his herd without limit—in a world that is limited. Ruin is the destination toward which all
men rush, each pursuing his own best interest in a society that believes in the
freedom of the commons. Freedom in a commons brings ruin to all.

Some would say that this is a platitude. Would that it were! In a sense, it was
learned thousands of years ago, but natural selection favors the forces of psychological denial.[1] The individual benefits as an individual from his ability to
deny the truth even though society as a whole, of which he is a part, suffers.
Education can counteract the natural tendency to do the wrong thing, but the
inexorable succession of generations requires that the basis for this knowledge
be constantly refreshed. . . .

In an approximate way, the logic of the commons has been understood for
a long time, perhaps since the discovery of agriculture or the invention of private property in real estate. But it is understood mostly only in special cases
which are not sufficiently generalized. Even at this late date, cattlemen leasing
national land on the western ranges demonstrate no more than an ambivalent
understanding, in constantly pressuring federal authorities to increase the
head count to the point where overgrazing produces erosion and weed dominance. Likewise, the oceans of the world continue to suffer from the survival
of the philosophy of the commons. Maritime nations still respond automatically to the shibboleth of the "freedom of the seas." Professing to believe in the
"inexhaustible resources of the oceans," they bring species after species of fish
and whales closer to extinction.[2]

The National Parks present another instance of the working out of the
tragedy of the commons. At present, they are open to all, without limit. The
parks themselves are limited in extent—there is only one Yosemite Valley—
whereas the population seems to grow without limit. The values that visitors
seek in the parks are steadily eroded. Plainly, we must soon cease to treat the
parks as commons or they will be of no value to anyone.

What shall we do? We have several options. We might sell them off as private property. We might keep them as public property, but allocate the right
to enter them. The allocation might be on the basis of wealth, by the use of an
auction system. It might be on the basis of merit, as defined by some agreed-
upon standards. It might be by lottery. Or it might be on a first-come, first-
served basis, administered to long queues. These, I think, are all the reasonable possibilities. They are all objectionable. But we must choose—or
acquiesce in the destruction of the commons that we call our National Parks.

Pollution

In a reverse way, the tragedy of the commons reappears in problems of pollution. Here it is not a question of taking something out of the commons, but of putting something in—sewage, or chemical, radioactive, and heat wastes into water; noxious and dangerous fumes into the air; and distracting and unpleasant advertising signs into the line of sight. The calculations of utility are much the same as before. The rational man finds that his share of the cost of the wastes he discharges into the commons is less than the cost of purifying his wastes before releasing them. Since this is true for everyone, we are locked into a system of "fouling our own nest," so long as we behave only as independent, rational, free-enterprisers.

The tragedy of the commons as a food basket is averted by private property, or something formally like it. But the air and waters surrounding us cannot readily be fenced, and so the tragedy of the commons as a cesspool must be prevented by different means, by coercive laws or taxing devices that make it cheaper for the polluter to treat his pollutants than to discharge them untreated. We have not progressed as far with the solution of this problem as we have with the first. Indeed, our particular concept of private property, which deters us from exhausting the positive resources of the earth, favors pollution. The owner of a factory on the bank of a stream—whose property extends to the middle of the stream—often has difficulty seeing why it is not his natural right to muddy the waters flowing past his door. The law, always behind the times, requires elaborate stitching and fitting to adapt it to this newly perceived aspect of the commons.

The pollution problem is a consequence of population. It did not much matter how a lonely American frontiersman disposed of his waste. "Flowing water purifies itself every 10 miles," my grandfather used to say, and the myth was near enough to the truth when he was a boy, for there were not too many people. But as population became denser, the natural chemical and biological recycling processes became overloaded, calling for a redefinition of property rights.

How to Legislate Temperance?

Analysis of the pollution problem as a function of population density uncovers a not generally recognized principle of morality, namely: *the morality of an act is a function of the state of the system at the time it is performed.*[3] Using the commons as a cesspool does not harm the general public under frontier conditions, because there is no public; the same behavior in a metropolis is unbearable. A hundred and fifty years ago a plainsman could kill an American bison, cut out only the tongue for his dinner, and discard the rest of the animal. He was not in any important sense being wasteful. Today, with only a few thousand bison left, we would be appalled at such behavior. . . .

That morality is system-sensitive escaped the attention of most codifiers of ethics in the past. "Thou shalt not . . ." is the form of traditional ethical directives which make no allowance for particular circumstances. The laws of our society follow the pattern of ancient ethics, and therefore are poorly suited to governing a complex, crowded, changeable world. Our epicyclic solution is to augment statutory law with administrative law. Since it is practically impossible to spell out all the conditions under which it is safe to burn trash in the back yard or to run an automobile without smog-control, by law we delegate the details to bureaus. The result is administrative law, which is rightly feared for an ancient reason—*Quis custodiet ipsos custodes?*—"Who shall watch the watchers themselves?" John Adams said that we must have "a government of laws and not men." Bureau administrators, trying to evaluate the morality of acts in the total system, are singularly liable to corruption, producing a government by men, not laws.

Prohibition is easy to legislate (though not necessarily to enforce); but how do we legislate temperance? Experience indicates that it can be accomplished best through the mediation of administrative law. We limit possibilities unnecessarily if we suppose that the sentiment of *Quis custodiet* denies us the use of administrative law. We should rather retain the phrase as a perpetual reminder of fearful dangers we cannot avoid. The great challenge facing us now is to invent the corrective feedbacks that are needed to keep custodians honest. We must find ways to legitimate the needed authority of both the custodians and the corrective feedbacks.

Freedom to Breed Is Intolerable

The tragedy of the commons is involved in population problems in another way. In a world governed solely by the principle of "dog eat dog"—if indeed there ever was such a world—how many children a family had would not be a matter of public concern. Parents who bred too exuberantly would leave fewer descendants, not more, because they would be unable to care adequately for their children. David Lack and others have found that such a negative feedback demonstrably controls the fecundity of birds.[4] But men are not birds, and have not acted like them for millenniums, at least.

If each human family were dependent only on its own resources; *if* the children of improvident parents starved to death; *if*, thus, overbreeding brought its own "punishment" to the germ line—*then* there would be no public interest in controlling the breeding of families. But our society is deeply committed to the welfare state,[5] and hence is confronted with another aspect of the tragedy of the commons.

In a welfare state, how shall we deal with the family, the religion, the race, or the class (or indeed any distinguishable and cohesive group) that adopts overbreeding as a policy to secure its own aggrandizement?[6] To couple the concept of freedom to breed with the belief that everyone born has an equal right to the commons is to lock the world into a tragic course of action. . . .

Conscience Is Self-Eliminating

It is a mistake to think that we can control the breeding of mankind in the long run by an appeal to conscience. . . .

People vary. Confronted with appeals to limit breeding, some people will undoubtedly respond to the plea more than others. Those who have more children will produce a larger fraction of the next generation than those with more susceptible consciences. The difference will be accentuated, generation by generation. . . . The argument has here been stated in the context of the population problem, but it applies equally well to any instance in which society appeals to an individual exploiting a commons to restrain himself for the general good—by means of his conscience. To make such an appeal is to set up a selective system that works toward the elimination of conscience from the race.

Pathogenic Effects of Conscience

. . . To conjure up a conscience in others is tempting to anyone who wishes to extend his control beyond the legal limits. Leaders at the highest level succumb to this temptation. Has any President during the past generation failed to call on labor unions to moderate voluntarily their demands for higher wages, or to steel companies to honor voluntary guidelines on prices? I can recall none. The rhetoric used on such occasions is designed to produce feelings of guilt in noncooperators.

For centuries it was assumed without proof that guilt was a valuable, perhaps even an indispensable, ingredient of the civilized life. Now, in this post-Freudian world, we doubt it.

Paul Goodman speaks from the modern point of view when he says: "No good has ever come from feeling guilty, neither intelligence, policy, nor compassion. The guilty do not pay attention to the object but only to themselves, and not even to their own interests, which might make sense, but to their anxieties."[7]

One does not have to be a professional psychiatrist to see the consequences of anxiety. We in the Western world are just emerging from a dreadful two-centuries-long Dark Ages of Eros that was sustained partly by prohibition laws, but perhaps more effectively by the anxiety-generating mechanisms of education. . . .

Since proof is difficult, we may even concede that the results of anxiety may sometimes, from certain points of view, be desirable. The larger question we should ask is whether, as a matter of policy, we should ever encourage the use of a technique the tendency (if not the intention) of which is psychologically pathogenic. We hear much talk these days of responsible parenthood; the coupled words are incorporated into the titles of some organizations devoted to birth control. Some people have proposed massive propaganda campaigns to instill responsibility into the nation's (or the world's) breeders. But what is the meaning of the word responsibility in this context? Is it not merely a synonym for the word conscience? When we use the word responsibility in the absence of substantial sanctions are we not trying to browbeat a free man in a commons into acting against his own interest? Responsibility is a verbal counterfeit for a substantial quid pro quo. It is an attempt to get something for nothing.

If the word responsibility is to be used at all, I suggest that it be in the sense Charles Frankel uses it.[8] "Responsibility," says this philosopher, "is the product of definite social arrangements." Notice that Frankel calls for social arrangements—not propaganda.

Mutual Coercion
Mutually Agreed Upon

The social arrangements that produce responsibility are arrangements that create coercion, of some sort. Consider bank-robbing. The man who takes money from a bank acts as if the bank were a commons. How do we prevent such action? Certainly not by trying to control his behavior solely by a verbal appeal to his sense of responsibility. Rather than rely on propaganda we follow Frankel's lead and insist that a bank is not a commons; we seek the definite social arrangements that will keep it from becoming a commons. That we thereby infringe on the freedom of would-be robbers we neither deny nor regret.

The morality of bank-robbing is particularly easy to understand because we accept complete prohibition of this activity. We are willing to say "Thou shalt not rob banks," without providing for exceptions. But temperance also can be created by coercion. Taxing is a good coercive device. To keep downtown shoppers temperate in their use of parking space we introduce parking meters for short periods, and traffic fines for longer ones. We need not actually forbid a citizen to park as long as he wants to; we need merely make it increasingly expensive for him to do so. Not prohibition, but carefully biased options are what we offer him. A Madison Avenue man might call this persuasion; I prefer the greater candor of the word coercion.

Coercion is a dirty word to most liberals now, but it need not forever be so. As with the four-letter words, its dirtiness can be cleansed away by exposure to the light, by saying it over and over without apology or embarrassment. To many, the word coercion implies arbitrary decisions of distant and irresponsible bureaucrats; but this is not a necessary part of its meaning. The only kind of coercion I recommend is mutual coercion, mutually agreed upon by the majority of the people affected.

To say that we mutually agree to coercion is not to say that we are required to enjoy it, or even to pretend we enjoy it. Who enjoys taxes? We all grumble about them. But we accept compulsory taxes because we recognize that voluntary taxes would favor the conscienceless. We institute and (grumblingly) support taxes and other coercive devices to escape the horror of the commons.

An alternative to the commons need not be perfectly just to be preferable. . . . The alternative of the commons is too horrifying to contemplate. Injustice is preferable to total ruin.

It is one of the peculiarities of the warfare between reform and the status quo that it is thoughtlessly governed by a double standard. Whenever a reform measure is proposed it is often defeated when its opponents triumphantly discover a flaw in it. As Kingsley Davis has pointed out,[9] worshippers of the status quo sometimes imply that no reform is possible without unanimous agreement, an implication contrary to historical fact. As nearly as I can make out, automatic rejection of proposed reforms is based on one of two unconscious assumptions: (i) that the status quo is perfect; or (ii) that the choice we face is between reform and no action; if the proposed reform is imperfect, we presumably should take no action at all, while we wait for a perfect proposal.

But we can never do nothing. That which we have done for thousands of years is also action. It also produces evils. Once we are aware that the status quo is action, we can then compare its discoverable advantages and disadvantages with the predicted advantages and disadvantages of the proposed reform, discounting as best we can for our lack of experience. On the basis of such a comparison, we can make a rational decision which will not involve the unworkable assumption that only perfect systems are tolerable.

Recognition of Necessity

Perhaps the simplest summary of this analysis of man's population problems is this: the commons, if justifiable at all, is justifiable only under conditions of low-population density. As the human population has increased, the commons has had to be abandoned in one aspect after another.

First we abandoned the commons in food gathering, enclosing farm land and restricting pastures and hunting and fishing areas. These restrictions are still not complete throughout the world.

Somewhat later we saw that the commons as a place for waste disposal would also have to be abandoned. Restrictions on the disposal of domestic sewage are widely accepted in the Western world; we are still struggling to close the commons to pollution by automobiles, factories, insecticide sprayers, fertilizing operations, and atomic energy installations.

In a still more embryonic state is our recognition of the evils of the commons in matters of pleasure. There is almost no restriction on the propagation of sound waves in the public medium. The shopping public is assaulted with mindless music, without its consent. Our government is paying out billions of dollars to create supersonic transport which will disturb 50,000 people for every one person who is whisked from coast to coast 3 hours faster. Advertisers muddy the airwaves of radio and television and pollute the view of travelers. We are a long way from outlawing the commons in matters of pleasure. Is this because our Puritan inheritance makes us view pleasure as something of a sin, and pain (that is, the pollution of advertising) as the sign of virtue?

Every new enclosure of the commons involves the infringement of somebody's personal liberty. Infringements made in the distant past are accepted because no contemporary complains of a loss. It is the newly proposed infringements that we vigorously oppose; cries of "rights" and "freedom" fill the air. But what does "freedom" mean? When men mutually agreed to pass laws against robbing, mankind became more free, not less so. Individuals locked into the logic of the commons are free only to bring on universal ruin; once they see the necessity of mutual coercion, they become free to pursue other goals. I believe it was Hegel who said, "Freedom is the recognition of necessity."

The most important aspect of necessity that we must now recognize is the necessity of abandoning the commons in breeding. No technical solution can rescue us from the misery of overpopulation. Freedom to breed will bring ruin to all. At the moment, to avoid hard decisions many of us are tempted to propagandize for conscience and responsible parenthood. The temptation must be resisted, because an appeal to independently acting consciences selects for life disappearance of all conscience in the long run, and an increase in anxiety in the short.

The only way we can preserve and nurture other and more precious freedoms is by relinquishing the freedom to breed, and that very soon. "Freedom is the recognition of necessity"—and it is the role of education to reveal to all the necessity of abandoning the freedom to breed. Only so, can we put an end to this aspect of the tragedy of the commons.

Notes

1. G. Hardin, ed., *Population, Evolution, and Birth Control* (Freeman, San Francisco, 1964), p. 56.

2. S. McVay, *Sci. Amer.* 216 (No. 8), 13 (1966).

3. J. Fletcher, *Situation Ethics* (Westminster, Philadelphia, 1966).

4. D. Lack, *The Natural Regulation of Animal Numbers* (Clarendon Press, Oxford, 1954).

5. H. Girvetz, *From Wealth to Welfare* (Stanford Univ. Press, Stanford, Calif., 1950).

6. G. Hardin, *Perspec. Biol. Med.* 6, 366 (1963).

7. P. Goodman, *New York Rev. Books* 10(8), 22 (23 May 1968).

8. C. Frankel, *The Case for Modern Man* (Harper, New York, 1955), p. 203.

9. J. D. Roslansky, *Genetics and the Future of Man* (Appleton-Century-Crofts, New York, 1966), p. 177.

4

NO TRAGEDY
ON THE COMMONS

SUSAN J. BUCK

Introduction

In 1951, Josephine Tey published her classic detective story *Daughter of Time*. In this defense of Richard III, she coined the term *Tonypandy*, which is the regrettable situation which occurs when a historical event is reported and memorialized inaccurately but consistently until the resulting fiction is believed to be the truth.[1] History is not the only field in which Tonypandy occurs. A prime example of Tonypandy in the field of economics is the "tragedy of the commons."

Academics are often too facile in labeling an article as "seminal," but Garrett Hardin's 1968 article, "The Tragedy of the Commons," deserves the accolade.[2] The article has been reprinted over fifty times,[3] and entire books have been devoted to exploring the meaning and implications of Hardin's memorable title.[4] The phrase "tragedy of the commons" has slipped into common parlance at colleges and universities and is rapidly becoming public property.[5] Discussion of the inevitability of such a tragedy is the lawful prey of economists, sociologists, philosophers, and theologians. Certainly we cannot deny that the phenomenon exists: the ruination of a limited resource when confronted with unlimited access by an expanding population. Where, then, lies Tonypandy in the tragedy of the commons?

Originally published as Susan Jane Buck Cox, "No Tragedy on the Commons," in *Environmental Ethics* 7 (Spring 1985):49–61. Reprinted with permission.

Although the tragedy of the commons may occur, that it regularly occurred on the common lands of medieval and post-medieval England is
not true; the historical antecedents of the tragedy of the commons as developed by Hardin and others following the 1968 article, and as commonly
understood by students and professors, are inaccurate.[6] . . . Decline was
not the result of unlimited access, but rather was the result of the historical
forces of the industrial revolution, agrarian reform, and improved agricultural practices.

"The Tragedy of
the Commons" Defined

. . . [Hardin's original] language is relatively free of cultural phenomena. . . .
Later references to Hardin's tragedy of the commons, however, reflect a more
explicit historical perspective. In 1977 Hardin used allusions to the Enclosure
Acts of the late eighteenth and early nineteenth centuries to explain how the
tragedy might be cured.[7] In 1969, Beryl Crowe wrote:

> The commons is a fundamental social institution that has a history going back
> through our own colonial experience to a body of English common law which ante-
> dates the Roman conquest. That law recognized that in societies there are some envi-
> ronmental objects which have never been, and should never be, exclusively appropri-
> ated to any individual or group of individuals. In England the classic example of the
> commons is the pasturage set aside for public use, and the "tragedy of the commons"
> to which Hardin refers was a tragedy of overgrazing and lack of care and fertilization
> which resulted in erosion and underproduction so destructive that there developed
> in the late 19th century an enclosure movement.[8]

. . . Perhaps the most extensive anglicization of the commons is found in
This Endangered Planet by Richard Falk. He writes that Hardin "has evolved
an effective metaphor of [the paradox of aggregation] from a historical experience, the destruction of the common pastures of English country towns in
the 1700s and 1800s through overgrazing herds."[9]
    Further examples can be found, almost ad infinitum and certainly ad nau-
seam. Moreover, questioning of graduate students in economics or planning
or public administration elicits the same historical background on the tragedy
of the commons as described by Falk. Such evidence suggests that there is a
general impression among most people today that the tragedy was a regular
occurrence on the common lands of the villages in medieval and post-
medieval England—a belief which, despite its wide acceptance as fact, is historically false.

The Commons Defined

In order to dispel the myth of the tragedy of the commons, we must first discover the definition of *commons* as it was understood in medieval England. The legal right of common is "a right which one or more persons have to take or use some portion of that which another's soil produces . . . and is a right to part of the profits of the soil, and to part only, the right of the soil lying with another and not with the person who claims common."[10] This right is an ancient one: "Recent archaeological and historical work indicates that in many places nucleated villages did not come into being until the ninth, tenth, or even the eleventh centuries. . . . But whatever their origins, the classic common field system probably developed with them. . . ."[11] These rights "were not something specifically granted by a generous landlord, but were the residue of rights that were much more extensive, rights that are in all probability older than the modern conception of private property. They probably antedate the idea of private property in land, and are therefore of vast antiquity."[12] The right of common was a right granted to specific persons because these persons had some prior claim to the land or because the actual owner of the land granted them that right in return for their services.

Our modern-day notions of *common* as a public right does not accurately describe the medieval commons. Gonner wrote in 1912:

> [Common] now is taken as denoting the claims, somewhat vague and precarious, of the public as against those holding the land and engaged in its cultivation. But this finds no sanction in a time when over very many, if not most, cultivated districts common was a result of claim to land, and formed a necessary condition of its proper management. . . . The early rights of common were anything but vague, and were invariably vested in those employed in cultivation of their representatives; they were anything rather than a general claim on the part of the public. . . . [Common rights] were a necessary element in the agricultural system, they were involved in the ownership and cultivation of the land, and they were largely the source of the profits obtained from the land and the means of rendering its cultivation effective.[13]

Clearly our use of common to describe public access to national parks or to deep-sea fishing is at variance with the original use of the term. . . .

We thus have a picture of the legal status of a common. Either by common-law right as freehold tenant or through usage and grants, a villager was entitled to pasture limited numbers of specific animals on the lord's waste. It is important to note that even from the beginning, the use of the common was not unrestricted: "Common pasture of stubble and fallow was a feature of open-field husbandry from the start . . . and with it went communal control."[14] The English common was not available to the general public but was only available to certain individuals who owned or were granted the right to use it. Use of the common even by these people was not unregulated. The types and in some cases the numbers of animals each tenant could pasture were limited, based at least partly on a recognition of the limited carrying capacity of the land.

The Management of the Commons

The earliest records for communal farming regulations are the manor court rolls of the mid-thirteenth century.[15] The earliest record for a village meeting is the fourteenth century. Joan Thirsk writes:

> From these dates the evidence points unequivocally to the autonomy of village communities in determining the form of, and the rules governing their field system. . . . In villages which possessed no more than one manor, matters were agreed in the manorial court, and the decisions sometimes, but not always, recorded on the court roll. Decisions affecting villages which shared the use of commons were taken at the court of the chief lord, at which all the villages were represented. In villages where more than one manor existed, agreement might be reached at a village meeting at which all tenants and lords were present or represented.[16]

. . . Such agreements among the neighbors are recorded in the village bylaws. These bylaws "emphasize the degree to which . . . agricultural practice was directed and controlled by an assembly of cultivators, the manorial court, who coordinated and regulated the season-by-season activities of the whole community. Arable and meadowland were normally thrown open for common pasturing by the stock of all the commoners after harvest and in fallow times, and this necessitated some rules about cropping, fencing, and grazing beasts. Similarly, all the cultivators of the intermixed strips enjoyed common pasturage in the waste, and in addition, the rights to gather timber, peat and other commodities were essential concomitants of the possession of arable and meadow shares."[17] There was, however, an extraordinary diversity of bylaws among the various regions of England. In one Lincolnshire fenland village, for example, "strangers coming into the town but having no land could enjoy free common for their cattle for one year. After that they had to abide by the rules governing all other inhabitants. These were generous provisions that reflected the abundance of grazing."[18] In contrast, in 1440, the village of Launton decreed that "any tenant who has a parcel of meadow in East Brokemede shall not mow there now or ever until his neighbors are agreed under pain of 3s.4d.,"[19] a clear reflection of the need to conserve and to regulate. What is important to note here is the detail with which the open fields were regulated. Ault notes that bylaws covered such points as where field workers were paid (at the granary rather than in the field, where payment in kind might lead to accusations of theft), and at what age boys could begin to pasture sheep on the common (sixteen). The commons were carefully and painstakingly regulated, and those instances in which the common deteriorated were most often due to lawbreaking and to oppression of the poorer tenant rather than to egoistic abuse of a common resource.

Abuses of the Commons

The commons were subject to several forms of abuse. Often the regulations governing the commons were broken, as when greedy farmers took in unauthorized animals, or when wealthy landowners or squatters took grazing to which they were not entitled because of lack of agreement among the tenants. The common thread in these abuses is their illegality.

One of the methods of controlling grazing was "stinting," allocating the number and type of beasts that could be grazed on the waste. Stinting developed more from lack of winter feed when stock was pastured on the arable land than from a desire to protect the summer grazing. This summer grazing "was as carefully controlled as the manorial courts could make it."[20] . . . In Westmorland in 1695, "Occasionally, these stinting rules were broken, resulting in the 'Townfield . . . being sore abused and misorderly eaten.' The remedy was to employ a pounder who had to make sure the stints were carefully maintained."[21] Hence, we have one abuse of the common: simple lawbreaking which was remedied by resort to the law.

A similar problem with a less happy solution occurred when the wealthier landholders took advantage of the poorer tenants. In the early sixteenth century, Fitzherbert noted that the rich man benefitted from overcharging the common.[22] According to Gonner, it was "pointed out alike in the sixteenth, seventeenth and eighteenth centuries that the poor owning rights may be largely kept out of their rights by the action of large farmers who exceed their rights and thus surcharge the common to the detriment of all, or by the lack of winter feed in the absence of which summer grazing could be of little worth. . . . The unfortunate poor tenant was denied his remedy at law for the illegal abuses of the more powerful landowners. The ultimate conclusion was the enclosure of the common land, most effective in the parliamentary enclosure acts from 1720 to 1880."[23] Such change was perhaps inevitable, but it is social change and the perennial exploitation of the poor by the less poor rather than Hardin's tragedy.[24]

A third problem arose on unstinted land. In the sixteenth century the "unstinted common was almost invariably overburdened. . . . This state of things was largely to the advantage of rich commoners or the lord of the manor, who got together large flocks and herds and pastured them in the common lands to the detriment of the poorer commoners, who, unlike them, could do little in the way of providing winter feed, and now found themselves ousted even from their slender privileges in the commons."[25] . . . By 1800 in the East Riding, "there was a good deal of overstocking. Some of the commons were stinted but others were not, and it was here that overstocking occurred. Many of the commons were frequently waterlogged when a small expenditure would have drained them, but what was everyone's business was nobody's business."[26] Of course, by 1800 parliamentary enclosure was well under way and this report from East Riding was made by an employee of the newly formed board of agriculture, established in response to a "widespread campaign for the more effective use of the land-resources of the country, with particular reference to the large areas of remaining open fields and to the vast areas of common lands and wastes."[27] Sponsored by wealthy landowners, the land reform was frequently no more than a sophisticated land-grab, justified in part by the admittedly striking increase in productivity of enclosed common land.

The Inevitable
Decline of the Commons

The increased productivity was often touted by land reformers—wealthy or otherwise—as proof of the evils of the commons system. However, the change was the result of many factors, and not just of enclosure. Some of the increase would probably have occurred without enclosure, but enclosure hastened the process. The common land was not the best land. The lord's waste was often reclaimed land, cultivated from forest and marsh. . . . Enclosure took the better land and subjected it to the new and improved methods of agriculture which had been all but impossible under the common system, for the management of the common could not be changed unless all commoners agreed and, just as important, remained agreed.[28] Improved roads and transportation facilities made marketing easier, and of course, the land had fewer people to support. Economies of scale made it profitable to use improved stock. In 1760, Robert Bakewell, the founder of modern methods of livestock improvement, began selective breeding of farm animals.[29] Previously forbidden by ecclesiastical authorities as incest, inbreeding of animals with desirable qualities soon led to dramatic improvements in stock.[30] Planting the enclosure with nitrogen-fixing crops such as clover improved the soil; drainage improved livestock health. Animals were disturbed less by driving to and from land pasture. All of these factors combined to improve the productivity of the formerly common land.

That enclosure improved productivity is neither a surprise nor a shame to the commons. The commons system "was falling into disuse, a new system was taking its place, and with the change the actual use made of the common or common rights declined. It might indeed have been retorted [to advocates of inclosure] that what was wanted was a stricter enforcement of the whole common right system."[31] A related view was expressed in 1974 by Van Rensselaer Potter:

> When I first read Hardin's article [on the tragedy of the commons], I wondered if the users of the early English commons weren't prevented from committing the fatal error of overgrazing by a kind of 'bioethics' enforced by the moral pressure of their neighbors. Indeed, the commons system operated successfully in England for several hundred years. Now we read that, before the colonial era in the Sahel, 'overpasturage was avoided' by rules worked out by tribal chiefs. When deep wells were drilled to obtain water 'the boreholes threw into chaos the traditional system of pasture use based on agreements among tribal chieftains.' Thus, we see the tragedy of the commons not as a defect in the concept of a 'commons' but as a result of the disastrous transition period between the loss of an effective bioethic and its replacement by a new bioethic that could once again bring biological realities and human values into a viable balance.[32]

Conclusion

Hardin writes that the "view that whatever is owned by many people should be free for the taking by anyone who feels a need for it . . . is precisely the idea of the commons."[33] Why should it matter if this "idea of the commons" is historically inaccurate?

Any academic should feel an aversion to Tonypandy, but the issue is more important than a possible pedantic dislike of inaccuracy. It is beyond dispute that issues such as depletion of limited resources, environmental quality, fisheries economics, and national land management are of great and increasing concern. How those issues are dealt with depends in large part on our perceptions of the disposition of similar issues in the past. If we misunderstand the true nature of the commons, we also misunderstand the implications of the demise of the traditional commons system. Perhaps what existed in fact was not a "tragedy of the commons" but rather a triumph: that for hundreds of years—and perhaps thousands, although written records do not exist to prove the longer era—land was managed successfully by communities. That the system failed to survive the industrial revolution, agrarian reform, and transfigured farming practices is hardly to be wondered at.

Our reexamination of the commons requires a dual focus. The first is to search for the ideas and practices which led to successful commoning for centuries and to try to find lessons and applications for our own times. The second focus is epistemological: are our perceptions of the nature of humankind awry? Since it seems quite likely if "economic man" had been managing the commons that tragedy really would have occurred, perhaps someone else was running the common.

In 1968, Hardin wrote that "'ruin' is the destruction toward which all men rush, each pursuing his own best interest in a society that believes in the freedom of the commons. Freedom in a common brings ruin to all."[34] But the common is not free and never was free. Perhaps in the changed perception of the common lies a remedy for ruin.

Notes

1. Tonypandy was a Welsh mining town where, in 1910, Winston Churchill sent unarmed London policemen to quell rioting strikers. The version popularly believed in Wales is that government troops shot Welsh miners who were striking for their workers' rights. In precise Tey-usage, *Tonypandy* exists when such a fiction is allowed to persist even by those people who know better. An example of Tonypandy in American history is the Boston Massacre. Josephine Tey, *Daughter of Time* (New York: Macmillan, 1951).

2. Garrett Hardin, "The Tragedy of the Commons," *Science* 162 (1968):1243–48.

3. Gordon Foxall, "A Note on the Management of 'Commons,'" *Journal of Agricultural Economics* 30 (1979):55.

4. For example, Garrett Hardin and John Baden, eds., *Managing the Commons* (San Francisco: Freeman, 1977).

5. Who could mistake the content—or inspiration—of articles such as "The Use of the Commons Dilemma in Examining the Allocation of Common Resources" (R. Kenneth Godwin and W. Brace Shepard, Resources for the Future Reprint 179), or "Legislating Commons: The Navajo Tribal Council and the Navajo Range" (Gary D. Libecap and Ronald N. Johnson, *Economic Inquiry* 18 [1980]:69–86), or Hardin and Baden, *Managing the Commons.* See also basic American government texts such as Robert Lineberry, *Government in America,* 2nd ed. (Boston: Little, Brown, 1983), in which he identifies the tragedy of the commons as "a parable about sheep overgrazing a common meadow" (pp. 579–80).

6. This is not to imply that the tragedy of the commons *never* occurred in those centuries; records are incomplete and to assert positively that something never occurred is to court contradiction and exposure.

7. Garrett Hardin, "Denial and Disguise," in Hardin and Baden, *Managing the Commons,* pp. 45–52. Hardin acknowledges the injustice of the Enclosure Acts but applauds the increase in agricultural productivity that they entailed.

8. Beryl Crowe, "The Tragedy of the Commons Revisited," in Hardin and Baden, *Managing the Commons,* 54–55.

9. Richard A. Falk, *This Endangered Planet* (New York: Random, 1971), p. 48.

10. E. C. K. Gonner, *Common Land and Inclosure,* 2nd ed. (London: Cass, 1966). The first portion of this quote is quoted by Gonner without attribution. This is not, however, an outmoded or esoteric definition: basic American college dictionaries provide the same definition.

11. C. C. Taylor, "Archaeology and the Origins of Open-Field Agriculture," in Trevor Rowley, ed., *The Origins of Open-Field Agriculture* (London: Groom Helm, 1981), p. 21. See also Della Hooke, "Open-field Agriculture—The Evidence from the Pre-Conquest Charters of the West Midlands," ibid., p. 58: "Land held in common by a community is clearly in evidence by the tenth century."

12. W. G. Hoskins and L. Dudley Stamp, *The Common Lands of England and Wales* (London: Collins, 1965), p. 6.

13. Gonner, *Common Land,* pp. 3–4.

14. W. O. Ault, *Open-Field Farming in Medieval England* (London: Allen and Unwin, 1972), p. 17.

15. Ibid., p. 18. Ault gives 1246 as the earliest manor court rolls; the earliest manorial reeve's accounts are for 1208–9.

16. Joan Thirsk, "Field Systems of the East Midlands," in Alan R. H. Baker and Robin A. Butlin, eds., *Studies of Field Systems in the British Isles* (Cambridge, England: Cambridge University Press, 1973), p. 232.

17. B. K. Roberts, "Field Systems of the West Midlands," in Baker and Butlin, *Studies,* p. 199.

18. Thirsk, "Field Systems," p. 251.

19. Westminster Muniments, 1550; quoted in Ault, *Open-Field Farming,* p. 26.

20. G. Elliot, "Field Systems of Northwest England," in Baker and Butlin, *Studies,* p. 67. As an example, in Denwick in 1567 the stint of "each husbandland was 6 old beasts above two years old, 37 sheep above one year old besides lambs and other young cattle, four pigs above one year old, two geese and one horse or mare" (R. A. Butlin, "Field Systems of Northumberland and Durham," in Baker and Butlin, *Studies,* p. 138).

21. Elliot, "Field Systems," p. 83. The internal quote is from the Westmorland Record office, Musgrave D. P., Court Rolls 1695.

22. Edward Scrutton, *Commons and Common Fields* (1887; reprint ed., New York: Lenox Hill, 1970), p. 122.

23. Roberts, "Field Systems," p. 190.

24. A classic example of exploitation is the Statute of Merton (1236), which allowed "chief tenants to assart land for their own or their villeins' exclusive use, provided that 'sufficient' common land was left for the needs of the village community." June A. Sheppard, "Field Systems of Yorkshire," in Baker and Bullin, *Studies,* pp. 176–77.

25. Gonner, *Common Land,* p. 103.

26. Hoskins and Stamp, *Common Lands,* p. 55.

27. Ibid., p. 54.

28. Scrutton, *Commons,* pp. 120–21. For example, all the farmers might agree to let one field lie fallow against custom for two years. If, in the second year, one tenant decided to return to the customary management and to graze his cattle in the field, the rest were powerless to stop him, and of course, the result would be the use of the field by all the tenants.

29. Victor Rice, Frederick Andrews, Everett Warwick, and James Legates, *Breeding and Improvement of Farm Animals* (New York: McGraw-Hill, 1957), p. 16.

30. For example, between 1710 and 1790, the weight at Smithfield of cattle changed from 370 pounds to 800 pounds, of calves from 50 to 148, of sheep from 28 to 80, and of lambs from 18 to 50. This weight change is of course due to a multitude of causes. Scrutton, *Commons,* p. 121.

31. Gonner, *Common Land,* pp. 306–7.

32. Van Rensselaer Potter, *Science* 185 (1974):813.

33. Garrett Hardin, "Denial and Disguise," in Hardin and Baden, *Managing the Commons,* p. 47.

34. Hardin, "Tragedy of the Commons," in Hardin and Baden, *Managing the Commons,* p. 20.

5

THE SCARCITY SOCIETY

WILLIAM OPHULS

For the past three centuries, we have been living in an age of abnormal abundance. The bonanza of the New World and other founts of virgin resources, the dazzling achievements of science and technology, the availability of "free" ecological resources such as air and water to absorb the waste products of industrial activities and other lesser factors allowed our ancestors to dream of endless material growth. Infinite abundance, men reasoned, would result in the elevation of the common man to economic nobility. And with poverty abolished, inequality, injustice, and fear—all those flowers of evil alleged to have their roots in scarcity—would wither away. Apart from William Blake and a few other disgruntled romantics, or the occasional pessimist like Thomas Malthus, the Enlightenment ideology of progress was shared by all in the West.* The works of John Locke and Adam Smith, the two men who gave bourgeois political economy its fundamental direction, are shot through with the assumption that there is always going to be more—more land in the colonies, more wealth to be dug from the ground, and so on. Virtually all the philosophies, values, and institutions typical of modern capitalist society—the legitimacy of self-interest, the primacy of the individual and his inalienable rights, economic laissez-faire, and democracy as we know it—are the luxuriant fruit of an era of apparently endless abundance. They cannot continue to exist in their current form once we return to the more normal condition of scarcity.

Worse, the historic responses to scarcity have been conflict—wars fought to control resources, and oppression—great inequality of wealth and the political measures needed to maintain it. The link between scarcity and oppression

*Marxists tend to be more extreme optimists than non-Marxists, differing only on how the drive to Utopia was to be organized.

is well understood by spokesmen for underprivileged groups and nations, who react violently to any suggested restraint in growth of output.

Our awakening from the pleasant dream of infinite progress and the abolition of scarcity will be extremely painful. Institutionally, scarcity demands that we sooner or later achieve a full-fledged "steady-state" or "spaceman" economy. Thereafter, we shall have to live off the annual income the earth receives from the sun, and this means a forced end to our kind of abnormal affluence and an abrupt return to frugality. This will require the strictest sort of economic and technological husbandry, as well as the strictest sort of political control.

The necessity for political control should be obvious from the use of the spaceship metaphor: political ships embarked on dangerous voyages need philosopher-king captains. However, another metaphor—the tragedy of the commons—comes even closer to depicting the essence of the ecopolitical dilemma. The tragedy of the commons has to do with the uncontrolled self-seeking in a limited environment that eventually results in competitive over-exploitation of a common resource, whether it is a commonly owned field on which any villager may graze his sheep, or the earth's atmosphere into which producers dump their effluents.

Francis Carney's powerful analysis of the Los Angeles smog problem indicates how deeply all our daily acts enmesh us in the tragic logic of the commons:

> Every person who lives in this basin knows that for twenty-five years he has been living through a disaster. We have all watched it happen, have participated in it with full knowledge. . . . The smog is the result of ten million individual pursuits of private gratification. But there is absolutely nothing that any individual can do to stop its spread. . . . An individual act of renunciation is now nearly impossible, and, in any case, would be meaningless unless everyone else did the same thing. But he has no way of getting everyone else to do it.

If this inexorable process is not controlled by prudent and, above all, timely political restraints on the behavior that causes it, then we must resign ourselves to ecological self-destruction. And the new political strictures that seem required to cope with the tragedy of the commons (as well as the imperatives of technology) are going to violate our most cherished ideals, for they will be neither democratic nor libertarian. At worst, the new era could be an anti-Utopia in which we are conditioned to behave according to the exigencies of ecological scarcity.

Ecological scarcity is a new concept, embracing more than the shortage of any particular resource. It has to do primarily with pollution limits, complex trade-offs between present and future needs, and a variety of other physical constraints, rather than with a simple Malthusian overpopulation. The case for the coming of ecological scarcity was most forcefully argued in the Club of Rome study *The Limits to Growth*. That study says, in essence, that man lives on a finite planet containing limited resources and that we appear to be approaching some of these major limits with great speed. To use ecological jargon, we are about to overtax the "carrying capacity" of the planet.

Critical reaction to this Jeremiad was predictably reassuring. Those wise in the ways of computers were largely content to assert that the Club of Rome people had fed the machines false or slanted information. "Garbage in, garbage out," they soothed. Other critics sought solace in less empirical directions, but everyone who recoiled from the book's apocalyptic vision took his stand on grounds of social or technological optimism. Justified or not, the optimism is worth examining to see where it leads us politically.

The social optimists, to put their case briefly, believe that various "negative feedback mechanisms" allegedly built into society will (if left alone) automatically check the trends toward ever more population, consumption, and pollution, and that this feedback will function smoothly and gradually so as to bring us up against the limits to growth, if any, with scarcely a bump. The market-price system is the feedback mechanism usually relied upon. Shortages of one resource—oil, for example—simply make it economical to substitute another in more abundant supply (coal or shale oil). A few of these critics of the limits-to-growth thesis believe that this process can go on indefinitely.

Technological optimism is founded on the belief that it makes little difference whether exponential growth is pushing us up against limits, for technology is simultaneously expanding the limits. To use the metaphor popularized during the debate, ecologists see us as fish in a pond where all life is rapidly being suffocated by a water lily that doubles in size every day (covering the whole pond in thirty days). The technological optimists do not deny that the lily grows very quickly, but they believe that the pond itself can be made to grow even faster. Technology made a liar out of Malthus, say the optimists, and the same fate awaits the neo-Malthusians. In sum, the optimists assert that we can never run out of resources, for economics and technology, like modern genii, will always keep finding new ones for us to exploit or will enable us to use the present supply with ever-greater efficiency.

The point most overlooked in this debate, however, is that politically it matters little who is right: the neo-Malthusians *or* either type of optimist. If the "doomsdayers" are right, then of course we crash into the ceiling of physical limits and relapse into a Hobbesian universe of the war of all against all, followed, as anarchy always has been, by dictatorship of one form or another. If, on the other hand, the optimists are right in supposing that we can adjust to ecological scarcity with economics and technology, this effort will have, as we say, "side effects." For the collision with physical limits can be forestalled only by moving toward some kind of steady-state economy—characterized by the most scrupulous husbanding of resources, by extreme vigilance against the ever-present possibility of disaster should breakdown occur, and, therefore, by tight controls on human behavior. However we get there, "Spaceship Earth" will be an all-powerful Leviathan—perhaps benign, perhaps not.

A Bird in the Bush

The scarcity problem thus poses a classic dilemma. It may be possible to avoid crashing into the physical limits, but only by adopting radical and unpalatable measures that, paradoxically, are little different in their ultimate political and social implications from the future predicted by the doomsdayers.

Why this is so becomes clear enough when one realizes that the optimistic critics of the doomsdayers, whom I have artificially grouped into "social" and "technological" tendencies, finally have to rest their different cases on a theory of politics, that is, on assumptions about the adaptability of leaders, their constituencies, and the institutions that hold them together. Looked at closely, these assumptions also appear unrealistic.

Even on a technical level, for example, the market-price mechanism does not coexist easily with environmental imperatives. In a market system a bird in the hand is always worth two in the bush. This means that resources critically needed in the future will be discounted—that is, assessed at a fraction of their future value—by today's economic decision-makers. Thus decisions that are economically "rational," like mine-the-soil farming and forestry, may be ecologically catastrophic. Moreover, charging industries—and, therefore, consumers—for pollution and other environmental harms that are caused by mining and manufacturing (the technical solution favored by most economists to bring market prices into line with ecological realities) is not politically palatable. It clearly requires political decisions that do not accord with current values or the present distribution of political power; and the same goes for other obvious and necessary measures, like energy conservation. No consumer wants to pay more for the same product simply because it is produced in a cleaner way; no developer wants to be confronted with an environmental impact statement that lets the world know his gain is the community's loss; no trucker is likely to agree with any energy-conservation program that cuts his income.

We all have a vested interest in continuing to abuse the environment as we have in the past. And even if we should find the political will to take these kinds of steps before we collide with the physical limits, then we will have adopted the essential features of a spaceman economy on a piecemeal basis—and will have simply exchanged one horn of the dilemma for the other.

Technological solutions are more roundabout, but the outcome—greater social control in a planned society—is equally certain. Even assuming that necessity always proves to be the mother of invention, the management burden thrown on our leaders and institutions by continued technological expansion of that famous fishpond will be enormous. Prevailing rates of growth require us to double our capital stock, our capacity to control pollution, our agricultural productivity, and so forth every fifteen to thirty years. Since we already start from a very high absolute level, the increment of required new construction and new invention will be staggering. For example, to accommodate world population growth, we must, in roughly the next thirty years, build houses, hospitals, ports, factories, bridges, and every other kind of facility in numbers that almost equal all the construction work done by the human race up to now.

The task in every area of our lives is essentially similar, so that the management problem extends across the board, item by item. Moreover, the complexity of the overall problem grows faster than any of the sectors that comprise it, requiring the work of innovation, construction, and environmental management to be orchestrated into a reasonably integrated, harmonious whole. Since delays, planning failures, and general incapacity to deal effectively with even our current level of problems are all too obvious today, the technological response further assumes that our ability to cope with large-scale complexity will improve substantially in the next few decades. Technology, in short, cannot be implemented in a political and social vacuum. The factor in least supply governs, and technological solutions cannot run ahead of our ability to plan, construct, fund, and man them.

Planning will be especially difficult. For one thing, time may be our scarcest resource. Problems now develop so rapidly that they must be foreseen well in advance. Otherwise, our "solutions" will be too little and too late. The automobile is a critical example. By the time we recognized the dangers, it was too late for anything but a mishmash of stopgap measures that may have provoked worse symptoms than they alleviated and that will not even enable us to meet health standards without painful additional measures like rationing. But at this point we are almost helpless to do better, for we have ignored the problem until it is too big to handle by any means that are politically, economically, and technically feasible. . . .

Another planning difficulty: the growing vulnerability of a highly technological society to accident and error. The main cause for concern is, of course, some of the especially dangerous technologies we have begun to employ. One accident involving a breeder reactor would be one too many: the most minuscule dose of plutonium is deadly, and any we release now will be around to poison us for a quarter of a million years. Thus, while we know that counting on perfection in any human enterprise is folly, we seem headed for a society in which nothing less than perfect planning and control will do.

At the very least, it should be clear that ecological scarcity makes "muddling through" in a basically laissez-faire socioeconomic system no longer tolerable or even possible. In a crowded world where only the most exquisite care will prevent the collapse of the technological society on which we all depend, the grip of planning and social control will of necessity become more and more complete. Accidents, much less the random behavior of individuals, cannot be permitted; the expert pilots will run the ship in accordance with technological imperatives. Industrial man's Faustian bargain with technology therefore appears to lead inexorably to total domination by technique in a setting of clockwork institutions. C. S. Lewis once said that "what we call Man's power over Nature turns out to be a power exercised by some men over other men with Nature as its instrument," and it appears that the greater our technological power over nature, the more absolute the political power that must be yielded up to some men by others.

These developments will be especially painful for Americans because, from the beginning, we adopted the doctrines of Locke and Smith in their most libertarian form. Given the cornucopia of the frontier, an unpolluted environment, and a rapidly developing technology, American politics could afford to be a more or less amicable squabble over the division of the spoils, with the government stepping in only when the free-for-all pursuit of wealth got out of hand. In the new era of scarcity, laissez-faire and the inalienable right of the individual to get as much as he can are prescriptions for disaster. It follows that the political system inherited from our forefathers is moribund. We have come to the final act of the tragedy of the commons.

The answer to the tragedy is political. Historically, the use of the commons was closely regulated to prevent overgrazing, and we need similar controls . . . to prevent the individual acts that are destroying the commons today. Ecological scarcity imposes certain political measures on us if we wish to survive. Whatever these measures may turn out to be—if we act soon, we may have a significant range of responses—it is evident that our political future will inevitably be much less libertarian and much more authoritarian, much less individualistic and much more communalistic than our present. The likely result of the reemergence of scarcity appears to be the resurrection in modern form of the preindustrial polity, in which the few govern the many and in which government is no longer of or by the people. Such forms of government may or may not be benevolent. At worst, they will be totalitarian, in every evil sense of that word we know now, and some ways undreamed of. At best, government seems likely to rest on engineered consent, as we are manipulated by Platonic guardians in one or another version of Brave New World. The alternative will be the destruction, perhaps consciously, of "Spaceship Earth."

A Democracy of Restraint

There is, however, a way out of this depressing scenario. To use the language of ancient philosophers, it is the restoration of the civic virtue of a corrupt people. By their standards, by the standards of many of the men who founded our nation (and whose moral capital we have just about squandered), we are indeed a corrupt people. We understand liberty as a license for self-indulgence, so that we exploit our rights to the full while scanting our duties. We understand democracy as a political means of gratifying our desires rather than as a system of government that gives us the precious freedom to impose laws on ourselves—instead of having some remote sovereign impose them on us without our participation or consent. Moreover, the desires we express through our political system are primarily for material gain; the pursuit of happiness has been degraded into a mass quest for what wise men have always said would injure our souls. We have yet to learn the truth of Burke's political syllogism, which expresses the essential wisdom of political philosophy: man is a passionate being, and there must therefore be checks on will and appetite; if these checks are not self-imposed, they must be applied externally as fetters by a sovereign power. The way out of our difficulties, then, is through the abandonment of our political corruption.

The crisis of ecological scarcity poses basic value questions about man's place in nature and the meaning of human life. It is possible that we may learn from this challenge what Lao-tzu taught two-and-a-half millennia ago:

> Nature sustains itself through three precious
> principles, which one does well to embrace and follow.
> These are gentleness, frugality, and humility.

A very good life—in fact, an affluent life by historic standards—can be lived without the profligate use of resources that characterizes our civilization. A sophisticated and ecologically sound technology, using solar power and other renewable resources, could bring us a life of simple sufficiency that would yet allow the full expression of the human potential. Having chosen such a life, rather than having had it forced on us, we might find it had its own richness.

Such a choice may be impossible, however. The root of our problem lies deep. The real shortage with which we are afflicted is that of moral resources. Assuming that we wish to survive in dignity and not as ciphers in some ant-heap society, we are obliged to reassume our full moral responsibility. The earth is not just a banquet at which we are free to gorge. The ideal in Buddhism of compassion for all sentient beings, the concern for the harmony of man and nature so evident among American Indians, and the almost forgotten ideal of stewardship in Christianity point us in the direction of a true ethics of human survival—and it is toward such an ideal that the best among the young are groping. We must realize that there is no real scarcity in nature. It is our numbers and, above all, our wants that have outrun nature's bounty. We become rich precisely in proportion to the degree in which we eliminate violence, greed, and pride from our lives. As several thousands of years of history show, this is not something easily learned by humanity, and we seem no readier to choose the simple, virtuous life now than we have been in the past. Nevertheless, if we wish to avoid either a crash into the ecological ceiling or a tyrannical Leviathan, we must choose it. There is no other way to defeat the gathering forces of scarcity.

PART TWO

ECOLOGY AND THE STRUCTURE OF THE INTERNATIONAL SYSTEM

As discussed in the introductory chapter to this volume, environmental problems are the result of a complex array of social forces, including technology, political and economic institutions, social structures, and human values. In this part we are particularly interested in the subset of causes that can be attributed to the structure of the international system. The term *structure* is sometimes used by scholars in international relations to refer to the international distribution of power among states. Thus, during the Cold War, the structure of the system was often said to be bipolar in that the two superpowers wielded by far the most power in international affairs. Here we use the term more generally to refer to the relatively stable, unchanging characteristics of world politics, such as the political division of the world into sovereign states, or the capitalist global economy, which shapes transactions among societies.[1] These relatively permanent features of the world system give shape and definition to the interactions among governments, international organizations, multinational corporations, nongovernmental organizations, and other agents of world politics.

A few aspects of system structure seem particularly important in shaping the array of global environmental problems we face and the possibilities for responding to those problems. The first is state sovereignty, which many scholars take to be the central feature of world politics. As the World Commission on Environment and Development put it, "The Earth is one, but the world is not."[2] One of the main reasons for this absence of unity is the sovereignty of individual states, which gives them, at least in principle, decisionmaking autonomy over matters falling within their territorial jurisdiction.

The tensions between ecology and sovereignty are due in part to the fact that the boundaries of states and the boundaries of ecosystems do not perfectly coincide, meaning that individual states cannot effectively manage many of their most serious environmental problems. Most large-scale environmental problems cross national borders; many are tied to global systems, such as the atmosphere and oceans, which are beyond the control of individual states.

Yet governments have clung tenaciously to the notion that they retain exclusive authority over the activities within their territory that affect the global environment. The primacy of state sovereignty was one of the few points on which governments could agree during the contentious Stockholm conference:

> States have . . . the sovereign right to exploit their own resources pursuant to their own environmental policies, and the responsibility to ensure that activities within their jurisdiction or control do not cause damage to the environment of other states or of areas beyond the limits of their national jurisdiction.[3]

Although this principle refers not only to the sovereign *rights* of states but also to their *responsibilities,* it has generally been seen as a reinforcement of state sovereignty. In most instances, states have guarded this right emphatically when pressured by the global community—whether the state in question is a tropical rain-forest country, such as Brazil, or a leading emitter of greenhouse gases, such as the United States.

Some observers see global environmental challenges as eroding sovereignty, as states are forced to accept restrictions on domestic actions. Others argue that international environmental cooperation is boosting the problem-solving abilities of many states, thereby reaffirming their sovereign authority. But as Ken Conca points out, sovereignty is more complex than simply the right of nations to do as they please or the authority of governments to act. Conca argues that sovereignty is indeed being changed by global ecological interdependence, but in many ways at once. Using the example of the Brazilian Amazon, Conca sees Brazilian sovereignty as simultaneously being bounded by new international norms, broadened as the state is made the foundation for forest protection strategies, and rendered more brittle as the enormity of the task and likelihood of failure put state legitimacy at risk. Seen in this light, sovereignty is not an unchanging structural feature of the world system but rather a historical social institution that may or may not successfully adapt to global ecological interdependence.

A second crucial feature of system structure is the existence of an increasingly interconnected capitalist world economy. If nature refuses to sit still for governance within national borders, so too does commerce. It has long been apparent that the world's major centers of industrial production and consumption, including the United States, Europe, and Japan, are not "ecologically self-contained."[4] These regions rely upon imports of a wide range of commodities, both as raw materials for production and as food for consumption. As a result, the core industrial regions of the world economy draw upon the "ecological capital" of the places that supply those inputs. The production that takes place in the industrialized world thus casts an ecological shadow far beyond the borders of individual industrialized countries.

To be sure, we have had a world-scale economic system since at least the colonial era. Nevertheless, economic interconnectedness is being deepened and broadened dramatically by the increasing mobility of goods, services, money, people, technology, ideas, and symbols—the phenomenon often referred to as "globalization." What are the ramifications of globalization for the environment? One is the greater dispersion of both positive and negative repercussions: negative in the sense of invasive species and cross-border pollutant flows; positive in the sense of cross-border environmental cooperation of the sort discussed in later sections.

Also, globalization seems to both lengthen and shorten sociogeographic distances. On the one hand, globalization means the growth of genuinely global-scale production chains that snake in and out of nominally sovereign territories. People at any one node along that chain—be they citizens, consumers, workers, activists, government regulators—are further "distanced" from the other nodes.[5] Most modern consumers, for example, have almost no knowledge of the environmental impact attached to the production of that which they consume, be it an auto or an apple. On the other hand, the communications revolution forges important new linkages that shorten virtual distances, making some forms of knowledge exchange, cooperation, and coalition building possible on a far broader scale.

One of the most contentious debates about globalization is its effect on environmental regulation. As the essay presented here by Lyuba Zarsky points out, "Globalization heightens the influence of market forces—most importantly, the influence of competition—on the making and enforcement of environmental policy. . . . The most significant impact of globalization is that it limits the unilateral policymaking capability of nation-states." Many have expressed fears that the result of these hypercompetitive economic pressures is the gutting of environmental regulations and standards, as governments and businesses seek to lower producer costs, attract foreign investment, and render economies more competitive in international trade. Zarsky suggests that a better metaphor is that of being "stuck in the mud," in the sense that needed strengthening of and innovation in environmental policy will not take place.

The transnational character of modern capitalism also raises important questions of responsibility. Who is responsible for the destruction of tropical rain forests, when the "causes" of that destruction range from the chain saws in the hands of local timber cutters to the global economic system that creates a demand for tropical timber products? Do we blame local people, the transnational banks and corporations that carry economic practices across borders, distant people who may benefit from these activities, or the structure of the world capitalist economy as a whole?

Just as state sovereignty imposes a pattern of political authority that does not correspond exactly to the underlying ecological reality, so transnational capitalism imposes patterns of economic activity that do not wholly correspond to the prevailing pattern of political authority. Both features of system structure give environmental problems an inherently transnational dimension, and both greatly complicate the prospects for global cooperation. Yet it is important to keep in mind that these "structural" properties of the international system are not natural or automatic features of world politics—they are the results of human choice and behavior. This leads us to the question of how ideas, beliefs, and worldviews give structure to the behavior of the various actors in world politics. Obviously, sovereignty and capitalism are two ideas that have had a powerful structuring influence. Some observers have argued that these two ideas are embedded in the more fundamental ethos of "modernity"—a complex set of beliefs that came to dominate European culture in the modern era and subsequently spread to the Americas, Africa, and Asia via colonialism and other manifestations of European power.[6] Some of the principal ideas that make up the modern worldview involve beliefs about the autonomy of the individual, the power of science and technology, the desirability of increased consumption, and the inevitability of progress. Thus, the ideological bedrock of modernity is as important a feature of world politics as the political structure of state sovereignty and the economic structure of global capitalism.[7]

But not all actors embrace the dominant social paradigm. Indeed, many environmentalists argue that environmentalism is a social movement that rejects core features of the dominant paradigm. Is this the case? Does environmentalism transcend the limits of state sovereignty, oppose the unfettered operation of global capitalism, and reject many central tenets of the modern worldview? Is it possible that the idea of environmentalism is itself building a new global structure: a network of individuals and groups with an "antisystemic" orientation in the sense that they reject many values and preferences of the dominant social paradigm?[8] Or is environmentalism better understood as a set of ideas that fits comfortably within the confines of a statist, capitalist, modernist world? These questions are hotly debated by environmentalists and their critics, and there may be no single answer: The environmental movement consists of a patchwork of groups with widely differing goals and views, working at levels ranging from local to global. As Parts Five, Six, and Seven make clear, the diversity of ideas driving various forms of environmental advocacy can make collaboration among environmentalists as difficult as collaboration among sovereign states.

Nevertheless, the environmental movement has emerged as a force to be reckoned with in international affairs. We conclude this part with three essays that present three important ways in which environmental NGOs and movement groups are changing world politics:

through domestic political struggles, transnational networking, and the promotion of large-scale sociocultural change.

The autobiography of Brazilian activist Chico Mendes reminds us that environmentalism around the world has historically drawn most of its energy from the grass roots. Despite the growing internationalization of environmental politics, domestic political struggles remain the most important pathway to change. Mendes was a labor activist and environmentalist working in the western Amazon state of Acre. He led a movement for the preservation of the Amazon forest and the livelihood of its occupants. Mendes advocated a brand of environmentalism that struggled as much against the oppression of people as the destruction of nature. Mendes was killed in 1988, assassinated by powerful local landowning interests that were threatened by his efforts to organize rural workers in the region. The powerful vision he expressed, which made him an important political leader of the forest peoples' movement in Brazil, also made him in death a martyr and an international symbol. The global outcry following his murder greatly enhanced the pressures on the Brazilian government to reverse policies that promote deforestation in the Amazon region.[9]

We also include a short interview with Kenyan environmental activist Wangari Maathai, another local activist who has become famous around the world for her efforts to protect forests and their people. Kenyan and Brazilian forest politics differ dramatically, and Mendes and Maathai come from very different personal backgrounds. Yet some of the similar themes in their experiences—including the emphasis on people's livelihoods, the centrality of struggle, and the challenges of organizing and mobilizing a sustained movement—should be apparent. Maathai also points to the significant role of gender dynamics, a theme taken up in more detail in Part Seven.

Mary Barker and Dietrich Soyez illustrate the increasingly transnational character of such local struggles. Drawing their examples from environmental disputes in Canada, the authors point out that urban industrial societies cast an ecological shadow over their domestic "hinterlands." Canadians resisting the effects of this shadow have increasingly reached across borders to network with allies, to lobby governments and corporations that have dealings with Canada, and to bring external pressures to bear on the Canadian government. Their activities reverse one of the traditional axioms of environmentalism: These communities are thinking locally but acting globally.

If a sustained global movement of environmentalism is to exert political power, it will be because movement groups as diverse as those seen in these Brazilian, Kenyan, and Canadian examples can find ways to establish effective and durable international networks to coordinate efforts, exchange information, and pool resources. The barriers to such cooperation are formidable: a lack of resources compared to the activities they oppose; the frequent opposition of governments, corporations, and other powerful actors; conflicting viewpoints on goals and means; and unequal power between relatively well-heeled and influential groups from the North and some of the less institutionalized, grassroots groups of both North and South. Nor can we assume that international environmentalism automatically produces environmental or social benefits; Part Seven presents troubling cases in which transnational environmental groups have sometimes sought to preserve Latin American rain forests or African wildlife in ways that fail to involve local communities, perhaps even contributing to their continued oppression.

Despite these obstacles and potential pitfalls, there have been examples of effective international networking among environmentalists, as in the case of the internationally coordinated campaigns to change the environmental practices of the World Bank or confront unfettered trade liberalization (see Part Four). Moreover, as Paul Wapner reminds us in the final essay of this part, the activities of transnational environmental networks need not be limited to lobbying efforts by well-heeled organizations with access to power. Wapner argues that too much attention has been paid to the lobbying activities of environmental NGOs and movement groups, and not enough to the ways in which they cross borders to alter directly the practices of large numbers of people. Groups such as Greenpeace, the World Wildlife Fund, and Friends of the Earth use available political resources—including symbolic gestures, boycotts, economic pressures, and local networking—to promote the environmental agenda in ways that often bypass governments entirely. Wapner sees this as a form of "world civic politics" rooted in a thin but expanding global civil society.

As Ronnie Lipschutz suggests,

> The notion of "civil society" is one with a long history, but it generally refers to those forms of association among individuals that are explicitly not part of the public, state apparatus, the private, household realm or the atomistic market. Civil society is important in global politics in that it is a sector of the state-society complex where social change often begins. This does not mean that global civil society is a unity; it is riven by many divisions, more than one finds in even the international state system. Nonetheless, there are segments of this global civil society that are oriented in ways that specifically promote social and political change.[10]

Whether it makes sense to extend to the global realm the idea of "civil society," which originated with the study of domestic politics in industrial democracies, remains the subject of much debate. But even for skeptics, the idea serves as an important reminder that the state is not the sole or even the primary source of political, social, and cultural change.

Thinking Critically

1. Are the problems confronting the Brazilian state in the Amazon generalizable? Is the pattern of transformation of Brazilian sovereignty hypothesized in Conca's essay likely to be found on a broader scale? What makes sovereignty endure in the face of such pressures?

2. Does globalization promote or inhibit international environmental cooperation? Which seems to be growing more quickly—the pressures on countries to solve problems collectively or the loss of control in an increasingly transnationalized world economy?

3. Are Mendes and Maathai describing similar struggles? What are the constants and what are the variables? In other words, what aspects of these movements, their obstacles, and the context in which they operate are likely to be inherent to such struggles? What aspects are likely to be place-specific?

4. Contrast the activities of the environmental organizations and movement groups discussed in the essays by Mendes, Maathai, Wapner, and Barker and Soyez. Are the forces that push people to mobilize politically the same in each case? Are the political resources available to these groups the same in each case? What gives these groups power? What limits their power?

5. Do the cases from Canada, Kenya, and Brazil provide evidence for Wapner's claim that we are seeing the emergence of a global civil society? Or do they describe locally grounded political struggles that have little in common beyond occasional, expedient cooperation?

Notes

1. The term "structure" is used in this sense in Ken Conca, "Environmental Change and the Deep Structure of World Politics," in Ronnie D. Lipschutz and Ken Conca, *The State and Social Power in Global Environmental Politics* (New York: Columbia University Press, 1993).

2. World Commission on Environment and Development, *Our Common Future* (New York: Oxford University Press, 1987).

3. Mostafa K. Tolba, Osama A. El-Kholy, E. El-Hinnawi, M. W. Holdgate, D. F. McMichael, and R. E. Munn, *The World Environment, 1972–1992: Two Decades of Challenge* (London: Chapman & Hall, 1992), p. 808. This principle was reiterated twenty years later at the Earth Summit; see "Rio Declaration on Environment and Development," United Nations Conference on Environment and Development, U.N. Doc. A/CONF.151/5/Rev. 1(1992).

4. Jim MacNeill, Pieter Winsemius, and Taizo Yakushiji, *Beyond Interdependence* (New York: Oxford University Press, 1991).

5. See Ken Conca, "Consumption and Environment in a Global Economy," *Global Environmental Politics* 1, no. 3 (Summer 2001):53–71.

6. On the role of colonialism in promoting the spread of European values, see Edward Said, *Culture and Imperialism* (New York: Random House, 1993).

7. This theme is developed in Conca, "Environmental Change and the Deep Structure of World Politics."

8. The term "antisystemic movement" is taken from G. Arrighi, T. K. Hopkins, and I. Wallerstein, *Antisystemic Movements* (London: Verso, 1989).

9. On the international pressures surrounding deforestation in the Amazon, see Susanna Hecht and Alexander Cockburn, *The Fate of the Forest: Developers, Destroyers, and Defenders of the Amazon* (New York: HarperCollins, 1990).

10. Ronnie D. Lipschutz with Judith Mayer, *Global Civil Society and Global Environmental Governance: The Politics of Nature from Place to Planet* (Albany, NY: SUNY Press, 1996), p. 2.

6

RETHINKING THE ECOLOGY-SOVEREIGNTY DEBATE

KEN CONCA

How do mounting international pressures for environmental protection affect state sovereignty? Does it even make sense to speak of sovereignty in a world marked by tight ecological interdependence, massive transboundary pollutant flows and severe threats to key global environmental services? How will the evolving roles, rules and understandings that have institutionalised sovereignty adapt to these new ecological realities?

These questions are of particular concern in the South, where the full range of rights and opportunities promised by sovereignty have rarely been realised to the extent enjoyed in the industrialised world. When Third World governments have voiced resistance to the institutionalisation of new standards of environmental behaviour, they have often done so on the grounds that such rules violate their sovereignty.[1]

In this paper I present a critique of prevailing perspectives on the sovereignty-ecology link. Though the focus is not exclusively on the Third World, the critique illustrates the limited utility of prevailing formulations in a Third World context. I also point the way toward some elements of an alternative conceptualisation, and illustrate these propositions with a brief discussion of the case of the Brazilian Amazon.

Two Perspectives on
Ecology and Sovereignty

My reading of the ecology-sovereignty literature is that two perspectives dominate the debate. The first argues that we are in fact seeing an erosion or weakening of sovereignty. Environmental concerns are said to be erecting new and effectively global standards for state behaviour. These new global standards are said to manifest themselves in several ways: in formal dealings among states (such as the creation of international environmental regimes), in rules of environmental conditionality, attached to the actions of international organisations such as the World Bank;[2] in the evolving norms of a growing body of international environmental law;[3] and in the political pressures brought to bear on governments by increasingly transnational environmental movements, citizens' networks, and non-governmental organisations.[4] Such pressures and constraints are unevenly applied and imperfectly enforced, to be sure; but they are beginning, it is claimed, to constrain the autonomy of state action by imposing limits on the menu of policy choices available to states.

This perspective is sometimes, though not inevitably, tied to the view that sovereignty and ecology are inherently at odds. Because ecosystems and environmental processes do not respect state borders, sovereignty itself becomes a key institution of global-scale environmental destruction. It creates a scale for decision-making, adjudication, and authority that does not coincide with fundamental ecological realities, and thus frustrates ecologically responsible management.[5]

These claims about eroding sovereignty can be contrasted with a second identifiable point of view in the literature. Here the claim is that international processes and, in particular, the emergence of multilateral institutions for environmental protection, do not inevitably erode state sovereignty and may even strengthen it. By placing states at the centre of institutional responses and strengthening their capacity to act collectively, it is argued, the menu of choices available to states is being expanded, not restricted.

For example, Levy, Keohane and Haas have argued that, although environmental regimes may limit the scope of governments to act unilaterally, they also facilitate collective state-based problem solving.[6] The authors draw a distinction between 'operational' sovereignty, defined as the legal freedom of the state to act under international law, and 'formal' sovereignty, defined in terms of the state's legal supremacy and independence.[7] International environmental institutions constrain operational sovereignty, but formal sovereignty remains largely intact. Implicit in this reasoning is the argument that enhanced problem-solving capabilities more than offset the external limitations on the scope of state authority.

A Critique

These two perspectives inevitably embody normative stances toward the state. In one view, the state is a large part of the problem, whereas in the other it is the foundation for solutions—or, at the very least, a central feature of the terrain on which solutions will have to be built. We can also examine them, however, as claims of what is happening to sovereignty, for better or for worse. Here, although they do make different sets of claims, the two are not necessarily irreconcilable. It is perfectly plausible, for example, that the scope of state autonomy is being narrowed (as the first claim would suggest) at the same time that the problem-solving capacity of states is increasing (as the second claim would argue).

However, before concluding that this represents the full range of consequences for sovereignty in an ecologically interdependent world, several observations are in order. The picture sketched above is in fact seriously incomplete, particularly when applied to contemporary international politics in the Third World. I hypothesise that for many Third World states, sovereignty is in fact being transformed as a result of global ecological interdependence, but not in the manner sketched by either of the above claims, or even by the net effect of the two taken together.

I base this hypothesis on two sets of observations. First, both arguments fail to disaggregate what is in fact a complex and highly unevenly distributed set of international pressures on states to solve environmental problems. Second, both are based on an incomplete characterisation of sovereignty itself. They only partially capture what has made sovereignty endure over time, and therefore misrepresent what sovereignty has actually meant for most states.

Let me stress here that the point is not to set up two straw arguments for easy dismissal. There are important insights in both of these perspectives. But they also appear to miss some potentially important effects on sovereignty, in part because their conceptual approaches to sovereignty limit the range of hypotheses they entertain.

Characterisation of
Environmental Pressures on the State

One problem is an overly general representation of the types of environmental pressure states feel. Clearly, governments do feel mounting pressure to respond to international environmental problems. Cross-national comparisons of public opinion data show consistently high levels of public awareness and concern.[8] While not all peoples, classes, regions and cultures define the problem in exactly the same terms, widespread concerns about environmental quality cut across simplistic distinctions between rich and poor, North and South, overdeveloped and underdeveloped.[9] The growth of pressures on states can also be seen in the contrast between the 1992 UNCED Conference in Rio de Janeiro and the UN Conference on the Human Environment, held two decades earlier in Stockholm. Stockholm was a gathering of 114 nations but was attended by only 2 heads of state; Rio represented an assemblage of more than 150 nations, including over 100 heads of state. The 134 non-governmental organisations at Stockholm were dwarfed by the 1400 non-governmental organisations and more than 8000 journalists from 111 countries who attended the Rio Conference.[10]

If it is clear that pressures are mounting, it is also clear that there have been consequences for the range of choices available to states. It has become much more difficult (though by no means impossible) to construct large dams, indiscriminately export toxic wastes, clear-cut forests, traffic in endangered species, or emit unlimited quantities of chemicals that destroy the ozone layer. That governments of both the North and the South so often see these limits (at least when applied to them) as interference in their sovereign right to use natural resources as they see fit, indicates a strong perception that the consequences are real.

However, while we may very well be seeing the birth of a generalisable, universal norm of environmental responsibility, the specific pressures on states have thus far followed a much more selective pattern. First, to the extent that a new norm is emerging, it is manifest in a highly segmented set of activities, including the lobbying of scientists, the pressure of public opinion, the calculations of governments, and the targeted political pressures of eco-activists. There is no reason to suppose that these all carry the same implications for sovereignty, or even push in the same general direction.

Second, regardless of their origin, the pressures states are feeling typically flow through multiple channels, including intergovernmental relations, dealings with international organisations, transnational linkages among environmental groups, and the workings of the media. Can pressures to join state-based international regimes be assumed to affect sovereignty in the same manner as pressures to accept the World Bank's environmental conditions on lending?

Third, current pressures clearly do not touch all states equally. Instead, what we have seen is something akin to assigning ecological pariah status to specific states on specific issues, whether it be Brazil and Indonesia in the case of tropical deforestation, China and India on dam construction, Japan on the trade in endangered species, or the former Soviet Union on reactor safety. Whatever the implications for sovereignty, they are unevenly distributed.

Fourth, and perhaps most important, responding to international environmental pressures can create resources and purchase legitimacy at the same time that it may constrain the menu of policy choices. This is in fact generally acknowledged when the gains for states are directly linked to efforts at environmental management. But these are not the only plausible effects; some of the resources gained or legitimacy purchased may speak to more general questions of the state's legitimacy and capacity to govern.[11]

Conceptions of Sovereignty

A second set of problems involves the specific conceptualisation of sovereignty itself that underlies these perspectives. One problem is that both sovereignty and the challenge to it are viewed in essentially functionalist terms. By this reasoning, states exist because they perform key functions better than alternative forms of social organisation, and pressures on the state exist because one increasingly important function—environmental protection—is being performed inadequately. The problems with functionalist arguments are well known, and stem from their *post hoc* character: causes are imputed from observed effects.[12] Problems emerge when the function is incorrectly specified—that is, when causal significance is given to an observed effect that is in reality an unintended consequence or less-than-central function. A straightforward example: the notion that international environmental regimes exist because states want to solve environmental problems may in fact be wrong. Regimes may be thrust on states by increasingly powerful non-state actors, or they may serve other fundamental purposes of state, e.g., those having to do with state legitimacy and perceptions of effectiveness. Functionalist interpretations based on each of these widely differing "functions" would lead us to dramatically different conclusions about the implications for sovereignty.

The conceptualisation of sovereignty is also excessively general. Sovereignty in historical practice has carried with it the presumption of a complex *bundle* of rights: equality among states, non-intervention, exclusive territorial jurisdiction, the presumption of state competence, restrictions on binding adjudication without consent, exclusive rights to wield violence, and the embeddedness of international law in the free will of states.[13]

There is no reason to expect that a particular set of international pressures affects these various component norms of sovereignty equally or in parallel fashion. Indeed, to the extent that ecological interdependence highlights *tensions* among such norms, one would expect just the opposite—that some normative pillars of sovereignty can be strengthened as others are undermined or eroded. Consider transboundary pollutant flows: institutional mechanisms to control them could erode the sovereign right to exclusive territorial jurisdiction, but at the same time *strengthen* aspects of the principle of non-intervention, if the flows themselves are viewed as unjustified interventions.

Third, the view of sovereignty is largely ahistorical. What rules, practices or beliefs reproduce sovereignty as an institution? Has this process of reproduction been broadly similar in all entities we regard as states, or is there more than one way to reproduce oneself as a sovereign entity? Are there differences in what sovereignty has meant for states whose organised existence is largely a product of colonialism? Does the territorial basis of the state differ fundamentally in frontier societies or in multi-ethnic ones? Clearly, the answers are unlikely to be uniform across time and for all states. This suggests that we cannot describe in universal terms either the processes rendering states sovereign or the way in which they may be changing as a result of ecological interdependence. Sovereignty as a global institution changes because of what happens to different states over time, at different rates and in different ways.

These weaknesses—functionalist logic, excessive generality, and ahistorical character—are symptoms of more fundamental conceptual problems. One of these is the unresolved tension over whether sovereignty represents, as Robert Jackson has put it, "a norm or a fact." In other words, is sovereignty based on the "fact" of material capabilities that enable organised entities to claim standing as states? Or is it based on the selective extension of recognition as a legitimate state? As Jackson and others have argued, we need to understand sovereignty as at once *both* "fact" *and* "norm."[14]

The perspectives examined here tend instead to fall on one or the other side of this divide. The ecology-erodes-sovereignty view typically frames sovereignty as a formal legal right, de-emphasising the foundations of the state that make it able to claim domestic authority and international standing. Alternately, the claim of enduring sovereignty in the face of environmental pressures stresses states as problem-solvers (albeit with varying degrees of capability). It thus emphasises sovereignty as the maintenance of a certain set of capabilities with which to act.

Finally, and perhaps most importantly, sovereignty in both perspectives is essentially conceived as freedom from external constraints on state action and choice. This one-dimensional view overlooks the fact that sovereignty looks inward as well as outward. It finds its basis not only in autonomy relative to external actors, but also in the state's jurisdictional power over civil society. According to Ruth Lapidoth:

> Usually, a distinction is made between the internal and external aspect of sovereignty. The former [internal] means the highest, original—as opposed to derivative—power within a territorial jurisdiction; this power is not subject to the executive, legislative, or judicial jurisdiction of a foreign state or any foreign law other than public international law. The external aspect of sovereignty underlines the independence and equality of states and the fact that they are direct and immediate subjects of international law.[15]

John Ruggie's definition of sovereignty as "the institutionalisation of public authority within mutually exclusive jurisdictional domains" also captures this internal dimension.[16]

Historically, the ability to control rules of access to the environment and natural resources—to define who may alter, and to what extent, which specific natural materials, systems, and processes—has been a central component of state authority and legitimacy.[17] Thus the full effects of international environmental pressures on state sovereignty as a collective institution cannot be understood without examining this inward-looking dimension. This is particularly so for much of the South, given the legacy of colonialism and the orientation of so many Third World political economies toward commodity exports.

Like the outward-looking dimension, the state-society dimension of sovereignty represents both fact and norm. It demands not only some minimal level of social recognition of the state's legitimacy, but also a complex bundle of state capabilities. Joel Migdal, for example, disaggregates the notion of state capacity into such varied components as the penetration of civil society, the regulation of social relations, the extraction of resources from civil society, and the use of those resources for defined state purposes.[18] International pressures, whether manifest in state-state, state-IO, or state-NGO interactions, are unlikely to affect these varied capabilities equally. Moreover, state capacity and social legitimacy may be at odds, as appears to be the case when coercive means are used to "protect" ecosystems from local use and encroachment.[19]

Toward an Alternative View of the Sovereignty-Ecology Link

What would an alternative conceptualisation look like? Clearly, it will require a multi-dimensional, less readily operational definition of sovereignty. Sovereignty must be conceived as having both external and internal dimensions; it must be seen as having a basis in both norms of recognition and material capabilities; and both its normative and material bases must be seen as consisting of multi-faceted bundles of norms and capabilities, respectively. These complexities should make us humble about drawing general conclusions outside the context of specific cases. A corollary is that there is little to be gained in speaking in general unified terms about sovereignty being 'strengthened,' 'eroded,' or 'maintained,' either with regard to specific states or the institution of state sovereignty as a whole.

The multiple dimensions of sovereignty should not, however, automatically lead us down the path of static 2x3 matrices and reductionist thinking. The focus should be on whether and how *specific* state actions and *specific* aspects of state-society relations create the conditions of authority, legitimacy, and capability necessary for states to make effectively sovereign claims. When the Brazilian government builds a road through the jungle, this must be seen as an act that speaks to *each* of the dimensions of sovereignty alluded to above: legitimacy as well as capability, international as well as domestic. If the idea of a two-level game is an apt metaphor (and it may not be, for this reason), it is a game in which most of the moves resonate on both boards at once.

An Example: The Brazilian Amazon

Consider the example of the Brazilian Amazon, perhaps the single most widely noted and contentious case to date in the ecology-sovereignty debate.[20] Before the ink had dried on the major agreements signed at the 1992

UNCED Conference in Rio de Janeiro, Brazilian diplomat Marcos Azambuja offered the following analysis:

> Brazilian interests are reinforced in the majority of the documents. At no time did we face opposition to our basic interests. . . . (W)e came out of the negotiations without the slightest scratch to our sovereignty.[21]

As evidence, the ambassador could have pointed to the conference declaration of principles on environment and development. Here the sovereign right of states to 'exploit their own resources' is reaffirmed using exactly the same language enshrined in the well-known Principle 21 of the Stockholm Conference 20 years earlier.[22] Or, the ambassador could turn to the specific agreements on climate and biodiversity, which did little to contradict this principle.

The absence of 'scratches' on the wall of Brazilian sovereignty was particularly noteworthy with respect to the issue of predominant concern to the Brazilians at the conference: the fate of tropical rainforests, and of the Amazon in particular. Efforts to scratch that wall, by constructing a regime for the preservation (or at least controlled depletion) of the world's remaining rainforests, were soundly defeated. Key points of disagreement included whether to link the regime specifically to an agreement on climate change and whether to cover temperate as well as tropical forests.

But walls have two surfaces, and in the Brazilian case the inside surface has suffered more than a slight scratch. Consider the following testimony of one veteran field researcher in the Amazon:

> Wherever one looks in the Amazonian economy, the state is in retreat: unable to finance tax breaks or build highways without the aid of multilateral banks, unable to include more than one per cent of the rural population in official colonisation schemes, unable to control land titling or land conflicts, unable to register or tax the greater part of the Amazonian economy, unable to enforce federal law on more than a sporadic basis.[23]

The irony is that this assessment of the limits of state capabilities comes at a time when the Brazilian state has been placed squarely at the centre of most schemes for sustainable development in the region. Clearly, some state actions have been proscribed by international pressures. But, far from prohibiting state action, the net effect of international pressures has been to stimulate a more active, interventionist state role in the region, under the rubric of supporting sustainable development. Far from simply "eroding" sovereignty, these pressures strengthen the presence of the state in the region and in Brazilian society as a whole. They also create opportunities for state actors to pursue longstanding goals having little to do with ecology. In the specifically Brazilian case such goals include the control of remote territories or indigenous peoples, the demarcation and fortification of Brazil's borders, and the reorganisation of existing patterns of land tenure.[24]

These extensions of the state are not without cost, however; they can only be realised at substantial risk to state legitimacy, given the enormous complexity of the task of sustainable development and the limited effectiveness of many state actions as sketched in the above quote. Moreover, the risk to state legitimacy may extend beyond the relatively narrow realm of environmental management. Consider the following commentary in the leading Brazilian newsweekly, *Veja*, discussing the highly publicised murder of a group of indigenous people at the Haximu settlement. "The Haximu massacre shows that, in reality, these minorities [indigenous peoples] are protected with the same courage and efficiency that guard the public hospital network and the pensions of the retired."[25] The state's inability to protect the lives and land of indigenous peoples is being linked directly to its other widely perceived inadequacies.

Under such circumstances, it means little to say that Brazilian sovereignty over the Amazon is eroding, strengthening, or maintaining the *status quo*. Rather, it seems that we are seeing a more complex, dynamic process in which sovereignty is simultaneously being narrowed in scope (by international prohibitions), deepened (by strengthening state capacities and state penetration of civil society), and rendered more brittle (by eroding state legitimacy).

Conclusion

. . . A strong case can be made for both of the perspectives sketched at the outset of this paper. Clearly, the freedom of states to undertake, promote or tolerate processes of environmental degradation is being limited, and many of the limits emanate from sources external to the state itself. At the same time, there is little doubt that new international institutions have made some governments more effective problem solvers (although we should always be careful about assumptions that the problem to be solved is, from the point of view of state actors, environmental and not political). That both effects could be happening at once is testimony to the multi-faceted character of sovereignty.

Whether these represent the full set of effects is another matter. Consider an analogy to the origins of the modern welfare state. States were faced with a new set of challenges (macroeconomic stabilisation, creating a social safety net, and so on). In response, states evolved new institutions, some national and some international, and in the process thrust themselves into a whole new set of state-society relationships. The consequences were hardly a lessening of the state's penetration of civil society or a decline in the size and reach of state institutions. At the same time, however, by assuming these new tasks, state legitimacy (both domestic and international) was put substantially at risk. The entire process was of course intensely politicised and political, with both state and non-state actors seeking to turn the new agenda to maximum advantage.

Much the same process may be at work with the challenge of environmental protection. New tasks, for which states are poorly suited and to which they are often opposed, have been thrust upon them by rising social demands. This challenge renders some choices more remote, but it also creates new opportunities, in the form of international resources for state responses and new mandates for state management and regulation. However, because most of the solutions being promulgated have a strongly statist cast, state legitimacy is put at substantial risk. A growing body of evidence suggests that participation, democracy, and legitimate authority are the keys to solving environmental problems. If so, the implications for state legitimacy may ultimately be the greatest consequence, both for sovereignty and for ecology.

Notes

1. See for example the comments of the Malaysian Prime Minister, Mahathir Mohamad, at the 1992 U.N. Conference on Environment and Development (UNCED), in *Environmental Policy and Law* 22, no. 4 (1992), p. 232, and Somaya Saad, "For Whose Benefit? Redefining Security," *Ecodecisions* (September 1991), pp. 59–60. See also the "Beijing Declaration of 41 Developing Countries," 18–19 June 1991, reprinted in *China Daily* (20 June 1991), p. 4, cited in the introduction to Andrew Hurrell and Benedict Kingsbury, eds., *The International Politics of the Environment* (Oxford, UK: Clarendon Press, 1992), p. 39, note 60.

2. On environmental conditionality, see Andrew Hurrell, "Green Conditionality," Overseas Development Council Policy Paper, March 1993 (Washington, DC: Overseas Development Council, 1993).

3. See Patricia Birnie, "International Environmental Law: Its Adequacy for Present and Future Needs," in Hurrell and Kingsbury, eds., *The International Politics of the Environment,* p. 84 (note 1). Birnie refers to what has been described as an emerging, bounded concept of "reasonable sovereignty."

4. On emergent global environmental values carried by transnational networks of activists and advocates see Margaret Keck and Kathryn Sikkink, "International Issue Networks in the Environment and Human Rights," a paper presented at the 17th Congress of the Latin American Studies Association, Los Angeles, California, 24–27 September 1992. See also Kathryn Sikkink, "Human Rights, Principled Issue-networks, and Sovereignty in Latin America," *International Organization* 47, no. 3 (Summer 1993), pp. 411–441, and Ronnie D. Lipschutz, "Reconstructing World Politics: The Emergence of Global Civil Society," *Millennium: Journal of International Studies* 21, no. 3 (Winter 1992), pp. 389–420.

5. For a discussion of this view, see Hurrell and Kingsbury, "Introduction," in Hurrell and Kingsbury, eds., *International Politics of the Environment,* pp. 6–8. The authors cite the work of Richard Falk and John Dryzek as representative examples.

6. Mark A. Levy, Robert O. Keohane, and Peter M. Haas, "Improving the Effectiveness of International Environmental Institutions," in Haas, Keohane, and Levy, eds., *Institutions for the Earth: Sources of Effective International Environmental Protection* (Cambridge, MA: MIT Press, 1993), especially pp. 415–417.

7. Ibid., p. 416.

8. See Riley E. Dunlap et al., "Of Global Concern: Results of the Health of the Planet Survey," *Environment* 35, no. 9 (November 1993), pp. 6–15 and 33–39.

9. One interesting result of the study by Dunlap and colleagues was the strikingly similar pattern of environmental concerns found in polling data across twenty-four countries of widely differing income levels (see Dunlap et al., "Of Global Concern").

10. These figures are from Peter M. Haas, Marc A. Levy, and Edward A. Parson, "Appraising the Earth Summit: How Should We Judge UNCED's Success?" *Environment* 34, no. 6 (October 1992), pp. 7–11 and 26–33.

11. This observation points to the basically functionalist logic of much of the ecology-sovereignty debate, a theme to which I return below.

12. For a discussion of the limits of functionalist theories, see Robert O. Keohane, *After Hegemony: Cooperation and Discord in the World Political Economy* (Princeton, NJ: Princeton University Press, 1984), pp. 80–83.

13. This list is from Ruth Lapidoth, "Sovereignty in Transition," *Journal of International Affairs* 45, no. 2 (Winter 1992), pp. 325–346.

14. Robert Jackson, *Quasi-States: Sovereignty, International Relations, and the Third World* (Cambridge, UK: Cambridge University Press, 1990), chapter 3.

15. Ibid., p. 327.

16. John G. Ruggie, "Continuity and Transformation in the World Polity: Toward a Neorealist Synthesis," in Robert O. Keohane, ed., *Neorealism and Its Critics* (New York: Columbia University Press, 1986), p. 143, as cited in J. Samuel Barkin and Bruce Cronin, "The State and the Nation: Changing Norms and the Rules of Sovereignty in International Relations," *International Organization* 48, no. 1 (Winter 1994), pp. 107–130.

17. See Ronnie D. Lipschutz and Judith Mayer, "Not Seeing the Forest for the Trees: Rights, Rules, and the Renegotiation of Resource Management Regimes," in Ronnie D. Lipschutz and Ken Conca, eds., *The State and Social Power in Global Environmental Politics* (New York: Columbia University Press, 1993), pp. 246–273.

18. Joel Migdal, *Strong Societies and Weak States* (Princeton, NJ: Princeton University Press, 1988).

19. For a discussion of this effect in the specific context of wildlife in Kenya and forests in Indonesia, see Nancy Peluso, "Coercing Conservation," in Lipschutz and Conca, eds., *The State and Social Power,* pp. 46–70.

20. I discuss this case in greater detail in Ken Conca, "Environmental Protection, International Norms, and National Sovereignty: The Case of the Brazilian Amazon," in Gene Lyons and Michael Mastanduno, eds., *Beyond Westphalia? National Sovereignty and International Intervention* (Baltimore, MD: Johns Hopkins University Press, 1995).

21. "Summit Documents Safeguard Brazilian Interests," *Daily Report: Latin America,* FBIS-LAT–92–114-S, June 12, 1992, p. 27 (supplement); original source *O Globo,* 11 June 1992, Rio '92 section, p. 1.

22. Principle 2: "States have, in accordance with the Charter of the United Nations and the principles of international law, the sovereign right to exploit their own resources, pursuant to their own environmental and developmental policies, and the responsibility to ensure that activities within their jurisdiction or control do not cause damage to the environment of other States or of areas beyond the limits of national jurisdiction." See "Rio Declaration on Environment and Development," United Nations Conference on Environment and Development, U.N. Document A/CONF.151/5/Rev.1 (1992).

23. David Cleary, "After the Frontier: Problems with Political Economy in the Modern Brazilian Amazon," *Journal of Latin American Studies* 25, part 2 (May 1993), pp. 331–349.

24. These themes are discussed in detail in Conca, "Environmental Protection, International Norms, and National Sovereignty."

25. "Um Grito do Fundo da Selva," *Veja* (August 25, 1993), p. 27. The translation is mine.

7

STUCK IN THE MUD? NATION-STATES, GLOBALIZATION, AND ENVIRONMENT

Lyuba Zarsky

Introduction

Environmental and resource management is largely the preserve of nation-states. Economic globalization, however, constrains the unilateral management capacities of nation-states and creates new imperatives on states to co-operate internationally—not only to manage global resources, but also to coordinate domestic environmental policies.

This chapter presents the hypothesis that, in the absence of effective multilateralism, economic globalization inhibits innovation in national environmental policy, and thus also inhibits the rate of improvement in environmental performance. Rather than a "race to the bottom," heightened competition for global markets causes environmental policy to be "stuck in the mud." Nation-states are pulled toward environmental policy convergence by market-driven and political pressures, primarily to maintain or gain competitiveness. In the balance and over time, the effect of convergence pressures on the average level of national environmental performance may be positive. Without effective international policy cooperation, how-

Excerpted from Lyuba Zarsky, "Stuck in the Mud? Nation-States, Globalization, and Environment," in *Globalization and Environment: Preliminary Perspectives*, OECD 1997. Reprinted with permission.

ever, the terms of convergence will be "too low" and "too slow" to point development towards sustainability.

The central challenge of globalization is therefore to raise the terms of policy convergence through effective supranational governance (both global and regional), by states and within the private sector. Good environmental management in the age of globalization also requires new approaches to national policy—approaches in tune with a highly open economy. Far from making nation-states irrelevant, globalization makes new and difficult demands on them. . . .

Environmental Management in the Age of Globalization

Economic globalization is fundamentally changing the nature of environmental management. On the one hand, globalization heightens the influence of market forces—most importantly, the influence of competition—on the making and enforcement of environmental policy. On the other hand, it subjects national environment policy to the discipline (or chaos) of international economic institutions.

On both counts, the most significant impact of globalization is that it limits the unilateral policymaking capability of nation-states. Overcoming these constraints will require strengthening subnational capacities for environmental management on the one hand, and international collective action on the other (to build supranational governance capacities). In the age of globalization, nation-states face new imperatives to coordinate domestic environmental and resource management policy, as well as to develop new unilateral approaches to the government-market interface. The existing institutional framework for environmental multilateralism, however, is rudimentary at best, and its integration with international economic governance is nearly nonexistent.

The case for international environmental cooperation is usually made in terms of the need to manage global or regional commons and transboundary resources.[1] These types of collective action problems stem from ecological, rather than from economic, interdependence: autarkic, as well as open, economies would still have to cooperate to establish sustainable utilization regimes for global commons. However, globalization constrains and conditions cooperation by changing the matrix of incentives within and among nations.

The central and specific effects of globalization on environmental management are the new limits on unilateral policymaking in the areas of ecosystem and natural resource management. With increasing global economic integration, domestic economic and social policies affect global prices, market shares, and investor expectations—and vice versa. For the large and rich countries of the Organization for Economic Cooperation and Development (OECD), the reverberations from domestic policy to global markets are greater than they are for small or poor countries. Even the largest market economies, however, are subject to cost, price, and exchange rate pressures imposed by global markets. OECD countries are particularly sensitive to impacts on markets from policies adopted in *other OECD countries.*

The impact of globalization on environmental management capacities cuts two ways: it constrains governments, and it enhances the influence of markets on social and economic outcomes. Markets, in turn, influence environmental performance through technology transfer, changes in the level of demand for environmentally intensive goods, substitution effects, "green" consumerism, and other channels. Indeed, in the context of globalization, markets become important vehicles and arenas for the generation and transmission of social norms and behaviors. The nub of the relationship between globalization and environmental management is that globalization changes the character of the government-market interface.

Given this change, the two key questions are: (i) what, in the aggregate, is the likely impact of global market integration on environmental performance, in the current global institutional regime? and (ii) what institutional innovations, supranational or national, could significantly raise the level of environmental performance in the context of globalization? . . .

Convergence in a Global Economy

Market-driven economic globalization creates pressures for countries to become more alike. Convergence trends encompass economic performance, economic policy, and social—including environmental—policy.[2]

Convergence trends in economic performance have been extensively studied, from both a theoretical and an empirical perspective. With increasing integration of markets, capital will flow toward those economic activities which promise the highest returns. In theory, if all markets—capital, labor, ideas, and goods and services—were fully integrated, there would be absolute convergence over time in the performance of key economic indicators, such as productivity (output per worker), real wages, rates of return on capital, and living standards.[3]

In practice, markets are not perfect; nor are they perfectly open. Market imperfections and obstacles generate economic gaps, even among fairly homogenous countries, like members of the OECD. Moreover, large and seemingly entrenched gaps between rich/developed and poor/developing countries continue to plague the world economy. Nonetheless, empirical studies suggest that globalization drives a discernible, if less-than-absolute, process of economic convergence, both within and between broad categories of "rich" and "poor" countries.[4] These studies are based largely on the "prior wave" of globalization, which took place in the late nineteenth century.

The hypothesis of this chapter is that market integration also drives *policy* convergence. The deeper and broader the level of market integration among countries, the greater the tendency towards economic and social policy convergence. Moreover, the larger a nation's market share in global trade and capital, the greater the forces of convergence toward the policies of that nation. At a global level, the rich countries of the OECD are simultaneously the "large-market" countries, and the most highly integrated. Policy convergence is therefore likely both within the OECD group, as well as (over time) from the developing countries toward the OECD.

Market integration impels governments to undertake similar economic policies, especially macroeconomic policies. Obviously, broad international agreement on open market policies is the *sine qua non* of globalization. Moreover, given technological and communication capabilities, governments would not be able to restrict capital outflows, even if they so desired.

But governments also have to keep key aspects of their domestic macroeconomic policies, including interest rates, within bands that are similar to each other. An interest rate too far below average international rates would spark capital outflows and exchange rate depreciation, triggering or exacerbating domestic inflation. The highly speculative character of unregulated international financial markets aggravates the problem enormously: small changes, or expectations thereof, in interest or exchange rates can ignite huge waves of capital movement.

The market forces of convergence also affect social policy. While theoretical and empirical studies are scarce, historical accounts suggest that the broadest parameter of social policy—the social contract among government, capital, labor, and communities—is pulled by global market forces towards "sameness." In the period after World War II, for example, the social contract within Western nations was based on full employment and the welfare state. The unraveling of this social contract in Britain and the United States generated market pressures on other OECD countries to follow suit.[5] It is unlikely that radically different social contract terms among countries, especially among OECD countries, would be sustainable in the global economy.

Environmental Policy Convergence

Environmental policy can be seen as part of the social contract. Like other aspects of social governance, environmental policy is subject to international market forces, primarily the forces of competition. Indeed, environmental and resource management policies are especially sensitive to international market forces because these policies are so deeply bound up with costs of production. The deeper the exposure to international competition, the more the particular resource or environmental management policy will be subject to convergence pressures.

There are few empirical studies of how globalization affects national environmental policy formation. An analytical framework suggests that environmental degradation and good environmental management will both impose economic costs. Unless specific policy measures are taken, these costs will not be reflected in market prices, but will be borne socially (either today or in the future). An individual country or company which takes measures to internalize its own local or global environmental costs could be priced out of export markets, or lose attractiveness as a production site for domestic or foreign investors.

Even if the change in relative costs is negligible, the fear or threat of such an effect can create "policy paralysis." Policymakers are subject to a wide variety of domestic political economy pressures, in the form of advocacy, lobbying, and campaign contributions by international business, as well as by labor and community groups. Political pressures to promote competitiveness will intensify as the share of income (including both wages and profits) derived from international trade and investment increases.

There are thus strong incentives for the costs to producers imposed by environmental management standards to converge towards those of primary competitors. More subtly, global markets provide incentives for the total costs to business of meeting environmental requirements to converge. "Total costs" include compliance costs, as well as information, regulatory, and other transaction costs. More efficient regulatory regimes may generate a higher level of environmental performance for the same cost.

Among the possible competitors subject to convergence pressures will be nations competing for export markets and for overseas investment projects, including countries seeking to become "production platforms." This category also includes multinational corporations competing for export markets, for government procurement contracts, or for investment projects more generally. Even wholly domestic firms are subject to convergence pressures, if their product markets or inputs are sourced internationally. Moreover, to facilitate trade and investment, policymakers have an additional incentive to harmonize environmental policy in order to reduce transaction costs—the extra costs to business of obtaining information about environmental requirements, and of meeting these requirements. Transnational firms can also reduce learning and management costs by maintaining global standards.

In addition to competitiveness, convergence in environmental product standards is driven by state regulation, especially by import requirements existing in large-market countries. For example, product standards in OECD and other countries often require importers to meet a host of consumer safety and health criteria. The larger the import market, the greater will be the impact of domestic product standards on international standards. Moreover, OECD policymakers expressly work to facilitate trade by seeking convergence. Cases where U.S. and E.U. product standards or procedures differ radically, such as eco-labeling, quickly induce policymaker efforts to find commonality.

Environmental standards for production and resource management are less subject to policy transmission effects than product standards are. The World Trade Organization prohibits states from unilaterally imposing process and production method (PPM) standards on imports. Eco-labeling standards are controversial, in part because they introduce the possibility of discrimination between products on the basis of production processes. Within some regional groupings, such as the European Union, policy convergence for both products and PPMs is driven by regional intergovernmental cooperation, as well as by market forces.

Like economic performance, the process of environmental policy convergence is not likely to be either absolute or uniform on a global scale. The process called "globalization" is far from truly global: the overwhelming portion of goods and services is still produced by local producers within individual countries for domestic markets.[6] Moreover, the processes of economic integration are largely *regional*. And while the North-South divide has been blurred by the emergence of the newly industrializing economies (NIEs), the gap between the OECD countries and all the rest is still glaring (as is the gap between the very poorest and all others).

Policy convergence is likely to be most pronounced among countries whose markets are the most highly integrated, as well as among those that are the most homogeneous in economic capacity. Among rich countries, environmental product and production standards are therefore likely to converge around an "OECD average," or around industry-wide averages, in the case of internationally exposed industries.

For developing countries, the primary export markets are OECD countries. Product standards, therefore, are pulled toward the OECD average, as export markets become more deeply and broadly integrated with the OECD. The primary competition to serve as production platforms, on the other hand, comes from other developing countries. Without regulation, environmental production standards in this case are likely to converge not towards the OECD but toward some kind of NIE or developing country benchmark (at least in the short term). Over time, as the sectoral composition of production becomes more like that existing in OECD countries, as the environmental management capacities of developing countries improve, or as market forces themselves bring new norms, developing country environmental production standards may increasingly be pulled toward the OECD average.

"Stuck in the Mud"?
The Constraints of Competitiveness

What will market-driven trends toward environmental policy convergence mean for environmental performance? Some analysts have argued that globalization will generate a "race to the bottom" in terms of environmental performance standards.[7] The operational dynamic in this framework is competition, especially between high- and low-standard countries, to serve as "production platforms." The idea is that the search for higher returns and lower costs will drive international investment toward the low-standard countries, while capital outflow and/or the threat of relocation will create pressures to lower standards in high standard countries.

Empirical studies, however, have generally failed to detect any effects of differential environmental management costs on investment location decisions. One exception is a study in progress suggesting that U.S. mining capital relocated its investment to Europe during the 1980s, in order to escape the high transaction costs of U.S.-style "adversarial legalism" in environmental regulation.[8] This study presumes, however, that European standards are no lower than U.S. standards and that investors were ultimately attracted by a more *efficient*, rather than a more lax, regulatory regime. Since the study provides no environmental performance indicators, it is inconclusive as to whether the cheaper regulatory regime in Europe generated the same, better, or worse environmental performance, relative to that achieved in the United States.

One reason often cited for the failure to detect "race to the bottom" effects is that environmental compliance costs in most industries are low, and form a small fraction of either investment or operating costs. Given environmental performance indicators (e.g., greenhouse gas emissions, generation of toxic waste, loss of biodiversity), low environmental compliance costs suggest that industry production costs (and hence, market prices) do not incorporate environmental costs and commitments. In other words, the reason that environmental regulations seem to matter little in investment decisions may be that they are universally low.

The central argument of this chapter is that, rather than triggering a downward spiral, the primary impact of globalization is to keep environmental policy initiatives "stuck in the mud." On the one hand, the constraints of competitiveness induced by globalization retard the capacity and willingness of *all* nation-states to take *any* unilateral measures which impose the costs of good environmental management on domestic producers. On the other hand, the pressures of policy convergence mean that those measures which *are* taken will only be those that are in step with primary competitors. The net results are: (i) that markets become the primary drivers of changes in environmental performance, and (ii) that environmental managers are pressured to maintain the status quo, or to change it only incrementally.

Relative market prices and patterns of competitive advantage, however, usually grow out of an institutional context in which environment is left out of the equation. The pressures of globalization to maintain the status quo mean that improvements in environmental performance will be slow. Given the large new demands on global ecosystems posed by rapid economic growth in developing countries, slow progress—even if steady—points toward a pessimistic assessment for the prospects of global sustainability.

Environmental performance in the context of globalization, in both OECD and developing countries, is nevertheless propelled upward by other forces, including consumer trends, industry self-regulation, and the advocacy efforts of citizen groups (both internal and external). Moreover, the drive for international competitiveness is itself a two-edged sword: the push to compete in markets can act to undermine inefficient, ecologically damaging national policies, such as resource subsidies. For businesses, it can also promote innovation in waste-saving and input efficient production processes.

In short, market-driven pressures to be competitive can *enhance,* as well as *retard,* improvements in environmental performance. In a global economy, cross-border flows of capital, commodities, and people will promote technological and managerial change. Indeed, over the long run, globalization may be positively correlated with improvements in environmental performance—even taking scale effects into account—as resources are better allocated, as environmentally cleaner technologies are disseminated, and as the environmental standards of the worst performers are pulled gradually upward.

The problem is that, since each nation or firm will be reluctant to take unilateral action which could undermine its competitiveness, the average level of environmental performance in the OECD is likely to be low, and most importantly, the rate of innovation in *improving* environmental performance will be slow in all countries. Nation-states and businesses will be willing to innovate only in incremental ways that increase costs slightly or which generate "win-win" outcomes that improve both competitiveness and environmental performance at the same time.

The pressures of competitiveness affect not only the management of *domestic* resources, but also unilateral and collective policy responses to *international* environmental problems, such as climate change. The greater the potential impact on domestic producers and export markets, the more difficult it is to build political support for policy change—even when the change is fully justifiable at a domestic level in economic and/or environmental terms.

A market-driven process of convergence is not just "low and slow," it is bound to be "blunt" as well. Good ecosystem and resource management requires sensitivity to local ecological and social conditions. *Diversity* of goals and approaches across and within nations will generally yield better environmental results than will *uniformity.*

Overcoming the problems of uniformity and inertia requires collective action by governments and/or by firms, to set broad, common, environmental and resource management frameworks which promote continuous improvement in environmental performance. In Europe, the "common standards" problem was tackled primarily by "side payments" from more- to less-powerful nations, in order to raise their standards.[9] In the global context, however, gaps between low- and high-standard countries are much greater, making the potential costs of a "side-payment" strategy politically problematic. Indeed, most OECD countries have either cut, or not increased, their foreign aid flows in the past decade. . . .

Creative Institutional Responses

Imagine a wondrous new machine, strong and supple, a machine that reaps as it destroys. It is huge and mobile . . . running over open terrain and ignoring familiar boundaries . . . [throwing] . . . off enormous mows of wealth and bounty while it leaves behind great furrows of wreckage.

Now imagine that there are skilful hands on board, but *no one is at the wheel.* In fact, this machine has no wheel nor any internal governor to control the speed and direction. It is sustained by its own forward motion, guided mainly by its own appetites. And it is accelerating.[10]

Market forces, especially at the global level, are wondrous things. Markets coordinate millions of consumption and production decisions every second. Market-based competition spurs innovation and learning, including rapid changes in technology, and promotes social transformation. Economic interdependence brings people from many cultures and nations into contact, often to undertake common projects. But global markets can also promote undesirable and even dangerous outcomes: social upheaval and inequality within and between countries, which sows seeds of civil and international conflict;[11] cultural homogenization; and degradation of the earth's life-support systems.

The key to reducing the social impacts of market forces is the institutional structure in which they are embedded. If market forces are like great torrential rains, institutions—with both big and small "I's"—are the channels and aqueducts which guide them over the land. Or, to use Greider's metaphor of global markets as Terminator-like machines, institutions are the software programs which put someone "at the wheel."

Institutional dynamism is the key to overcoming the inertia of global market competition which keeps rapid improvements in environmental and resource management "stuck in the mud." Institutional innovation is needed at two levels—supranational and national—in order to change the ways that states and markets interact in a global economy. At the *supranational* level, the primary goals of institutional innovation are to increase the average level of environmental performance within OECD countries, by enhancing policy coordination (especially for PPMs), and to close the gaps between the OECD and developing countries in both product and production standards, by promoting development and capacity-building. At the *national* level, the primary goal is to enhance the efficiency and reduce the cost of strategies to greatly enhance environmental performance. One of the key ways to do this is to strengthen subnational capacities for environmental management at both municipal and provincial levels. . . .

Conclusions

This chapter has argued that the central challenge of globalization for environmental management is the need for international coordination to manage, and raise, the terms of policy convergence. It has also offered some rudimentary suggestions for institutional innovations to take on this task.

The problems in moving down this path should not be underestimated. In particular, there are three main "stumbling blocks." The first has to do with *leadership.* Globalization creates a kind of leadership vacuum. On the one hand, globalization makes nation-states increasingly interdependent and homogeneous, both creating common problems and making it easier to identify common solutions. On the other hand, globalization heightens the sensitivity of the government of each nation-state, big and small, to competitiveness, and thereby reduces its willingness to suffer costs for the common good.

This problem is especially acute, given constraints on the United States. In much of the post-war period, the United States has been looked to for leadership in international economic, security, and environmental affairs. Still dominant in many markets, the United States is nonetheless subject to chronic trade and budget deficits, as well as to financial market pressures. Since the 1980s, American trade negotiators have often pushed agendas in international institutions which reflect U.S. sectoral trade rather than broad strategic ones.

The problem is a structural one: in a global economy without effective multilateral governance, each nation is pressed toward conceiving of economic diplomacy in terms of its own commercial interests. U.S. and E.U. negotiators often complain bitterly of the reluctance of the other side to take leadership initiatives. Progress towards effective supranational governance will require both greater vision and policy integration within countries (especially OECD countries) and an effective style of collective leadership.

The second problem in achieving effective environmental multilateralism concerns the large global gaps between rich and poor nations. "At a global level," argues one analyst, "the key stumbling block is the problem of inequity. True commitment to 'development' has to be part of the institutional framework of environmental and economic institutions."[12] Besides being a moral imperative, such a commitment by the rich countries is needed to move forward the project of multilateral governance.

The third, and perhaps most tractable, set of problems stems from the informational and analytical requirements of policy coordination. Work is needed to develop—and to standardize—indicators of environmental performance. Research is needed to develop common definitions and measures of financial subsidies, to analyze the relationship between subsidies and the environment, and to determine where "double dividends" are possible. Finally, research is needed on the institutional dynamics of globalization and the environment. This chapter has offered some thoughts about how this particular research effort might be better focused.

Notes

1. O. R. Young, *International Governance: Protecting the Environment in a Stateless Society* (Ithaca: Cornell University Press, 1994); P. M. Haas, R. O. Keohane, and M. A. Levy, eds., *Institutions for the Earth: Sources of Effective Environmental Protection* (Cambridge: MIT Press, 1993). For global or regional commons, like the atmosphere or regional seas, international cooperation is needed to overcome coordination (prisoner's dilemma and free-rider) problems. Because individual nation-states cannot be excluded from the benefits of investment in sustainable resource utilization, they have no incentive to pay for those improvements in the first place. Coordination would improve the welfare of all, but the costs of the improvements would have to be apportioned (and enforced). For cross-border resources like rivers, nation-states have incentives to capture the benefits of (and to "sluff-off" the costs) of environmental externalities from neighboring states.

2. Globalization also seems to drive countries to be more alike in key social dimensions, especially internal wage and income distribution, at least within the broad categories of "rich" and "poor" countries. See J. G. Williamson, *Globalization and Inequality Then and Now: The Late 19th and Late 20th Centuries Compared*. Working Paper 5491, National Bureau of Economic Research, Cambridge, Mass., March 1996.

3. M. Obstfeld and K. Rogoff, *Foundations of International Macro-economics* (Cambridge: MIT Press, 1996), Chapter 7.

4. Williamson, *Globalization and Inequality*; K. H. O'Rourke and J. G. Williamson, *Around the European Periphery 1870–1913: Globalization, Schooling, and Growth*. Working Paper 5392, National Bureau for Economic Research, Cambridge, Mass., December 1995.

5. B. Eichengreen and P. B. Kenen, "Managing the World Economy Under the Bretton Woods System: An Overview," in P. B. Kenen, ed., *Managing the World Economy, Fifty Years After Bretton Woods* (Washington, DC: Institute for International Economics, 1994); R. Boyer and D. Drache, eds., *States Against Markets: The Limits of Globalization* (London and New York: Routledge, 1996).

6. R. E. Lipsey, M. Blomstrom, and E. Ramstetter, *Internationalized Production in World Output*. Working Paper 5385, National Bureau of Economic Research, Cambridge, MA, December 1995.

7. R. L. Revesz, "Rehabilitating Inter-State Competition: Rethinking the 'Race to the Bottom,'" New *York University Law Review* 67 (1992).

8. L. Andersen and R. A. Kagan, "Adversarial Legalism, Transaction Costs, and the Industrial Flight Hypothesis." Draft paper for Trade and Environment Policy Project, a collaboration of the Berkeley Roundtable on the International Economy, Nautilus Institute for Security and Sustainable Development, and the National Wildlife Federation.

9. R. Steinberg, "Trade-Environment Rules and Practices: Globalization, Westernization or Regionalization?" Paper to Workshop on Innovative Approaches to Trade and Environment in Asia-Pacific, Nautilus Institute and Berkeley Roundtable on the International Economy.

10. W. Greider, *One World, Ready or Not: The Manic Logic of Global Capitalism* (New York: Simon and Schuster, 1997); emphasis added.

11. "It . . . appears that the inequality trends which globalization produced prior to World War I were at least partly responsible for the inter-war retreat from globalization. Will the world economy of the next century also retreat from its commitment to globalization, because of its inequality side effects?" Williamson, *Globalization and Inequality*.

12. T. Athanasiou, *Divided Planet: The Ecology of Rich and Poor* (New York: Little, Brown, 1996).

8

FIGHT FOR THE FOREST

Chico Mendes
(with Tony Gross)

Building Bridges

We realised that in order to guarantee the future of the Amazon we had to find a way to preserve the forest while at the same time developing the region's economy.

So what were our thoughts originally? We accepted that the Amazon could not be turned into some kind of sanctuary that nobody could touch. On the other hand, we knew it was important to stop the deforestation that is threatening the Amazon and all human life on the planet. We felt our alternative should involve preserving the forest, but it should also include a plan to develop the economy. So we came up with the idea of extractive reserves.

What do we mean by an extractive reserve? We mean the land is under public ownership but the rubber tappers and other workers that live on that land should have the right to live and work there. I say "other workers" because there are not only rubber tappers in the forest. In our area, rubber tappers also harvest brazil nuts, but in other parts of the Amazon there are people who earn a living solely from harvesting nuts, while there are others who harvest babaçu and jute. . . .

Where did we get the idea of setting up the CNS [Editors' note: National Council of Rubber Tappers]? We discovered there is something called the National Rubber Council which represents the interests of landowners and busi-

Originally published in Chico Mendes with Tony Gross, *Fight for the Forest: Chico Mendes in His Own Words* (London: Latin America Bureau, 1989). Reprinted with permission.

nessmen but not the interests of the rubber tappers, so we thought, why not create an organisation as a counterweight to all that bureaucracy and try to stop the government messing the rubber tappers about? The First National Congress set up the CNS and elected a provisional executive committee.

The CNS is not meant to be a kind of parallel trade union, replacing the Xapuri Rural Workers' Union, for example. [Editors' note: Xapuri is the town where Mendes lived and worked until his assassination in December of 1988. It is located in the western Amazonian state of Acre, near the Brazilian border with Bolivia.] It is just an organisation for rubber tappers. The growth of the trade unions was very important for us, but other agricultural workers including day labourers and so on are also members of the same union. Other kinds of agricultural workers have been seen as having particular needs and interests, but not rubber tappers; it's as though we were something that existed only in the past. So one of the reasons for creating the CNS was to recognise the rubber tappers as a particular group of workers fighting for a very important objective—the defence of the Amazon forest. The idea went down very well.

The Indians

We also wanted to seek out the leaders of the Indian peoples in Acre and discuss how to unite our resistance movements, especially since Indians and rubber tappers have been at odds with each other for centuries. In Acre the leaders of the rubber tappers and Indian peoples met and concluded that neither of us was to blame for this. The real culprits were the rubber estate owners, the bankers and all the other powerful interest groups that had exploited us both.

People understood this very quickly, and from the beginning of 1986 the alliance of the peoples of the forest got stronger and stronger. Our links with the Indians have grown even further this year. For example, a meeting of the Tarauacá rubber tappers was attended by 200 Indians and six of them were elected to the Tarauacá Rubber Tappers' Commission. Indians are now beginning to participate in the CNS organising commissions. In Cruzeiro do Sul about 200 Indians are active in the movement and this year they have even joined in our *empates* [Editors' note: The term *empate* means "tie" or "standoff" in Portuguese. It refers here to a common tactic of the movement in which local people physically occupy the area threatened by deforesters. The goals are to create a standoff that inhibits the destruction of the forest and to convince the workers involved in deforestation that their interests lie in forest preservation].

Our proposals are now not just ours alone, they are put forward together by Indians and rubber tappers. Our fight is the fight of all the peoples of the forest.

When the Minister of Agriculture met a joint commission of Indians and rubber tappers in his office, he was really taken aback. "What's going on?," he said, "Indians and rubber tappers have been fighting each other since the last century! Why is it that today you come here together?"

We told him things had changed and this meant the fight to defend the Amazon was stronger. People really took notice of that. . . .

The Landowners Strike Back

We know we face powerful opposition. As well as the landowners and businessmen who dominate the Amazon region, we are up against the power of those who voted against land reform in the Constituent Assembly. The voting power of these people in Congress has been a problem for us and has encouraged the growth of the right-wing landowners' movement, the Rural Democratic Union (UDR). The defeat of the land reform proposal was a big victory for the landowners and land speculators. Now, since the establishment of the UDR in Acre, we've got a real fight on our hands. However, we also believe our movement has never been stronger.

You can already see how strong the UDR is in Acre—it's just organised its first cattle auction to raise funds. We know, through people who have been to UDR meetings here, that their aim is to destroy the Xapuri union by striking at the grassroots organisations of the Xapuri rubber tappers. They think if they can defeat Xapuri they can impose their terms on the whole state and further afield in the Amazon region as well. The Governor of Acre himself told me this. Just to give you an idea, it was after the UDR's official launch here in Acre that the first drops of blood were spilt in Xapuri. . . .

The Government Takes Sides

There was a time when the state government seemed to be paying a lot of attention to environmental problems and to the rubber tappers. But we soon realised it was just putting on a show of defending the environment so the international banks and other international organisations would approve its development projects.

We can't see how the authorities can say they defend the ecological system while at the same time deploying police to protect those who are destroying the forest. That happened, for example, in the case of the Ecuador rubber estate where there were many nut and rubber trees. The Governor was warned several times about what was going on there. In fact, I personally warned him and suggested he go and look at what was happening for himself. I told him he was being very hasty in sending police there. Fifty acres of virgin forest were cut down, but thanks to the pressure, thanks to the hundreds of telegrams sent to the Governor by national and international organisations, we managed to get him to withdraw the police from the area and so saved about 300 hectares of forest.

In the area they destroyed there, the last harvest produced 1,400 cans of brazil nuts, a good crop. We challenged the owner of the land and the Governor himself to work out the annual income per hectare produced by forest products such as brazil nuts and rubber and then compare it with that produced by grazing cattle there. They refused because they knew we could prove the income from one hectare of forest is 20 times greater than when the forest is cleared and given over to cattle.

We quoted decree law 7.511 of 30 July 1986 and regulation 486 of 28 October 1986 which prohibit the cutting down and sale of brazil nut and rubber trees and the deforestation of hillsides. There were two hillsides in the area being cut down on the Ecuador rubber estate and the law was completely flouted. After the second empate, when the rubber tappers managed to stop work going ahead, the local IBDF [Editors' note: Brazilian Forestry Development Institute] representative appeared and without even inspecting what was going on, told the landowner he could go ahead and clear the forest. He gave the landowner a licence even though the landowner did not present, as he should have done, a written plan for managing the area.

Another law—I can't remember its number—says you can only clear up to 50 hectares of forest without presenting a forestry management plan. Further on it adds that it's forbidden to cut down any area of forest on hillsides or where there is a concentration of brazil nut and rubber trees. None of these laws were respected. The Governor himself didn't even consider them and the IBDF certainly didn't.

We do have a good relationship with the Acre Technology Foundation (FUNTAC) which is a state government agency. They really understand how difficult the lives of rubber tappers are and recognise that deforestation is a problem. But despite the good relationship we've got with FUNTAC, we have no confidence left in the state government. How can we believe a Governor who says he defends the forest, and visits Rio and Japan to talk about defending the forest, but who then orders the police to go and protect the people who are destroying it? He ought to be using the political power that his office gives him. If he used his power in favour of the workers he'd certainly get their support. . . .

The rubber tappers aren't saying that nobody should lay a finger on the Amazon. No. We've got our own proposals for organising production. The rubber tappers and the Indians have always grown their subsistence crops but they've never threatened the existence of the forest. It's the deforestation carried out by the big landowners to open up pasture for their cattle that is threatening the forest. Often, these people are just speculating with the land. What happens in Xapuri and other parts of the Amazon is that these people cut down 10,000 hectares, turn half of it into pasture for their cattle and let the other half grow wild. They are really just involved in land speculation.

The landowners use all the economic power at their disposal. They bribe the authorities; it's common knowledge that they've bought off the IBDF staff in the Amazon region. They also use the law. They request police protection for the workers hired to cut down the trees, saying it is their land so they can do whatever they like with it. They accuse the rubber tappers of trespassing when we try and stop the deforestation. They turn to the courts for support and protection, claiming the land is private property. But the rubber tappers have been here for centuries!

There has been less pressure from the police in the last two years because we are able to present reasoned arguments to them. When we organise an *empate,* the main argument we use is that the law is being flouted by the landowners and our *empate* is only trying to make sure the law is respected.

The other tactic the landowners use, and it's a very effective one, is to use hired guns to intimidate us. Our movement's leaders, not just myself but quite a few others as well, have been threatened a lot this year. We are all on the death list of the UDR's assassination squads. Here in Xapuri, these squads are led by Darlí and Alvarino Alves da Silva, owners of the Paraná and other ranches round here. They lead a gang of about 30 gunmen—I say 30 because we've counted them as they patrol the town. Things have changed recently because we managed to get an arrest warrant issued in Umuarama, in the state of Paraná, for the two of them. I don't know whether it was the federal police, but somebody tipped them off. Now they're both in hiding and have said they'll only give themselves up when I'm dead.

We are sure this will be the landowners' main tactic from now on. They are going to fight our movement with violence and intimidation. There's no doubt in our minds about that. The level of violence that has been common in the south of the state of Pará is already spreading to Xapuri, to Acre.

9

KENYA'S GREEN MILITANT: AN INTERVIEW WITH WANGARI MUTA MAATHAI

Interview by
Ethirajan Anbarasan of
the *UNESCO Courier*

In a country where women play a marginal role in political and social affairs, fifty-nine-year-old Wangari Muta Maathai's achievements stand out as an exception. A biologist, she was the first woman from East Africa to receive a doctorate, to become a professor and chair a department—all at the University of Nairobi.

Maathai began to be active in the National Council of Women of Kenya in 1976 and it was through the council that she launched a tree-planting project called "Save the Land Harambee" (a Swahili word meaning let's all pull together). The project was renamed the Green Belt Movement (GBM) in 1977.

The GBM initiated programs to promote and protect biodiversity, to protect the soil, to create jobs especially in rural areas, to give women a positive image in the community and to assert their leadership qualities.

The overall aim of the GBM has been to create public awareness of the need to protect the environment through tree planting and sustainable management. Nearly 80 percent of the 20 million trees planted by the GBM have survived. At present the GBM has over 3,000 nurseries, giving job opportunities to about 80,000 people, most of them rural women.

In 1986 the GBM established a Pan-African Green Belt Network and has organized workshops and training programs on environmental awareness for

Originally published in *UNESCO Courier*, December 1999. Reprinted from the new *Courier*.

scores of individuals from other African countries. This has led to the adoption of Green Belt methods in Tanzania, Uganda, Malawi, Lesotho, Ethiopia, and Zimbabwe. Maathai, who is a member of the UN Secretary General's Advisory Board on Disarmament, has won fourteen international awards, including the prestigious Right Livelihood Award. She won the award, presented by a Swedish foundation and often referred to as an Alternative Nobel Prize, in recognition of her "contributions to the well-being of humankind."

In a country where single-party rule prevailed for decades, Maathai has been teargassed and severely beaten by police during demonstrations to protect Kenya's forests. "The government thinks that by threatening me and bashing me they can silence me," says Maathai. "But I have an elephant's skin. And somebody must raise their voice."

Maathai, a mother of three children, is currently involved in a struggle to save the 2,500-acre Karura forests, northwest of Nairobi, where the government wants to build housing complexes.

You once said that the quality of the environment cannot be improved unless and until the living conditions of ordinary people are improved. Could you enlarge on this?

If you want to save the environment you should protect the people first, because human beings are part of biological diversity. And if we can't protect our own species, what's the point of protecting tree species?

It sometimes looks as if poor people are destroying the environment. But they are so preoccupied with their survival that they are not concerned about the long-term damage they are doing to the environment simply to meet their most basic needs.

So it is ironic that the poor people who depend on the environment are also partly responsible for its destruction. That's why I insist that the living conditions of the poor must be improved if we really want to save our environment. For example, in certain regions of Kenya, women walk for miles to get firewood from the forests, as there are no trees left nearby. When fuel is in short supply, women have to walk further and further to find it. Hot meals are served less frequently, nutrition suffers, and hunger increases. If these women had enough resources they would not be depleting valuable forest.

What is at stake in the forests of Kenya and East Africa today?

Since the beginning of this century, there has been a clear tendency to cut down indigenous forests and to replace them with exotic species for commercial exploitation. We've now become more aware of what this involves and have realized that it was wrong to cut down indigenous forests, thereby destroying our rich biological diversity. But much damage has already been done.

When the Green Belt Movement started its campaign in 1977 to plant trees, Kenya had about 2.9 percent of forest cover. Today the forested area has further dwindled to around 2 percent. We are losing more trees than we are planting.

The other important issue is that the East African environment is very vulnerable. We are very close to the Sahara Desert, and experts have been warning that the desert could expand southward like a flood if we keep on felling trees indiscriminately, since trees prevent soil erosion caused by rain and wind. By clearing remaining patches of forests we are in essence creating many micro-Sahara Deserts. We can already see evidence of this phenomenon.

We hold civic education seminars for rural people, especially farmers, as part of campaigns to raise public awareness about environmental issues. If you were to ask a hundred farmers how many of them remember a spring or a stream that has dried up in their lifetime, almost thirty of them would raise their hands.

What has your Green Belt Movement (GBM) achieved and in particular to what extent has it prevented environmental degradation in Kenya?

The most notable achievement of the GBM in my view has been in raising environmental awareness among ordinary citizens, especially rural people. Different groups of people now realize that the environment is a concern for everybody and not simply a concern for the government. It is partly because of this awareness that we are now able to reach out to decisionmakers in the government. Ordinary citizens are challenging them to protect the environment.

Secondly, the GBM introduced the idea of environmental conservation through trees because trees meet many basic needs of rural communities. We started out by planting seven trees in a small park in Nairobi in 1977. At that time we had no tree nursery, no staff and no funds, only a conviction that ordinary country people had a role to play in solving environmental problems. We went on from there and now we have planted over 20 million trees all over Kenya.

The act of planting trees conveys a simple message. It suggests that at the very least you can plant a tree and improve your habitat. It increases people's awareness that they can take control of their environment, which is the first step toward greater participation in society. Since the trees we have planted are visible, they are the greatest ambassadors for our movement.

Despite the Rio earth summit of 1992 and the Kyoto climate summit in 1997, there has been no significant progress in environmental protection programs and campaigns at a global level. Why?

Unfortunately, for many world leaders development still means extensive farming of cash crops, expensive hydroelectric dams, hotels, supermarkets, and luxury items, which plunder human and natural resources. This is shortsighted and does not meet people's basic needs— for adequate food, clean water, shelter, local clinics, information and freedom.

As a result of this craze for so-called development, environmental protection has taken a back seat. The problem is that the people who are responsible for much of the destruction of the environment are precisely those who should be providing leadership in environmental protection campaigns. But they are not doing so.

Also, political power now is wielded by those who have business interests and close links with multinational corporations (MNCs). The only aim of these MNCs is to make profit at the expense of the environment and people. We also know that many world political leaders are persuaded by MNCs not to pay attention to declarations made in international environmental conferences. I strongly believe that as citizens we should refuse to be at the mercy of these corporations. Corporations can be extremely merciless, as they have no human face.

You started your career as an academic. Later you became an environmentalist, and now you are called a pro-democracy activist. How would you describe your evolution in the last twenty-five years?

Few environmentalists today are worried about the welfare of bees, butterflies and trees alone. They know that it is not possible to keep the environment pure if you have a government that does not control polluting industries and deforestation.

In Kenya, for example, real estate developers have been allowed to go into the middle of indigenous forests and build expensive houses. As concerned individuals we should oppose that. When you start intervening at that level, you find yourself in direct confrontation with policymakers and you start to be called an activist.

I was teaching at the University of Nairobi in the 1970s, when I felt that the academic rights of women professors were not being respected because they were women. I became an activist at the university, insisting that I wanted my rights as an academic.

Meanwhile, I found myself confronted by other issues that were directly related to my work but were not clear to me at the outset, like human rights. This directly led me to another area, governance. As a result I was drafted into the pro-democracy campaign.

I realized in the 1970s that in a young democracy like ours it was very easy for leaders to become dictators. As this happened they started using national resources as though they were their personal property. I realized that the constitution had given them powers to misuse official machinery.

So I became involved in the pro-democracy movement and pressed for constitutional reforms and political space to ensure freedom of thought and expression. We cannot live with a political system that kills creativity and produces cowardly people.

With your academic qualifications you could have lived a comfortable life in the United States or elsewhere in the West. But you decided to come back and settle down in Kenya. In the last twenty-five years, you have been verbally abused, threatened, beaten, put behind bars and on many occasions forbidden to leave the country. Have you ever regretted returning to Kenya and becoming an activist?

I did not deliberately decide to become an activist, but I have never regretted the fact that I decided to stay here and to contribute to the development of this country and my region. I know that I have made a little difference. Many people come up to me and tell me that my work has inspired them. This gives me great satisfaction because in the earlier days, especially during the dictatorship, it was difficult to speak.

Until a few years ago, people used to come up to me in the street and whisper "I am with you and I am praying for you." They were so scared of being identified with me that they did not want to be heard. I know a lot of people were afraid of talking to me and being seen with me because they might be punished.

I have been a greater positive force by staying here and going through trials and tribulations than if I had gone to other countries. It would have been very different to live in the West and say my country should do this and that. By being here I encourage many more people.

Do you think you were subjected to virulent attacks and abuses because you questioned men's decisions?

Our men think African women should be dependent and submissive, definitely not better than their husbands. There is no doubt that at first many people opposed me because I am a woman and resented the idea that I had strong opinions.

I know that at times men in positions of influence, including President Daniel Arap Moi, ridiculed me. At one time Members of Parliament accused me and ridiculed me for being a divorced woman. I have felt that deep inside they were hoping that by calling into question my womanhood I would be subdued. Later they realized they were wrong. In 1989, for example, we had a big confrontation with the authorities when we were fighting to save Uhuru Park in Nairobi. I argued that it would be ridiculous to destroy this beautiful park in the center of the city and replace it with a multistoried complex.

Uhuru Park was the only place in Nairobi where people could spend time with their families outdoors. The park was a wonderful place for people to go because it was a place where no one bothered them.

When I launched the campaign opposing the construction of the "Park-monster," as the project later came to be known, I was ridiculed and accused of not understanding development. I didn't study development but I do know that you need space in a city. Fortunately other nongovernmental organizations and thousands of ordinary people joined our protests and finally the park was saved. The government, which wanted to destroy that park, has since declared it a national heritage. That's wonderful. They could have done that without fighting and without ridiculing me.

What made you stand in the presidential elections in 1997? Despite your popularity, why didn't you win a sizeable number of votes?

I decided to stand for election for several reasons. In 1992, when a multiparty system was legalized in Kenya for the first time, I tried very hard with other political groups to unite the opposition, but in vain. When there were many opposition candidates running for the presidency, I withdrew from the campaign.

As expected, the opposition lost those elections and everybody now accepts that the campaign we launched for them to unite was right. We wanted to form a government of national unity within the opposition in 1992. This is exactly what they are now clamoring for.

In the 1997 general elections, my idea was to persuade the opposition to unite and field a strong candidate from one ethnic community against the ruling Kenya African National Union (KANU). But I was called a tribalist by some opposition groups for proposing that idea. When all my efforts to unite the opposition failed, I decided to run for president.

But during the campaign I also came to realize that in this country it is very difficult to get elected without money. I didn't have money. I realized that it doesn't matter how good you are, how honest you are and how pro-democratic you are, if you don't have money to give to the voter you won't get elected. So I lost.

All this gave me a new experience. Now I can speak as an insider. I also realized that people here are not yet ready for democracy and we need a lot of civic education and political consciousness. People here are still controlled by ethnicity and vote along ethnic lines. The ethnic question became a very important issue during the last elections.

Despite having enormous natural resources Africa still lags behind other continents in terms of development and growth. Why is this?

Poor leadership, without any doubt. This generation of African leaders will go down in history as a very irresponsible one that has brought Africa to its knees. During the past three decades, Africa has suffered from a lack of visionary and altruistic leaders committed to the welfare of their people.

There are historical reasons for this. Just before independence was granted to many African countries, young Africans were promoted by colonial rulers to positions until then unoccupied by the local people and were trained to take over power from the colonial administration. The new black administrators and burgeoning elites enjoyed the same economic and social lifestyles and privileges that the imperial administrators enjoyed. The only difference between the two in terms of the objectives for the country was the color of their skin.

In the process, the African leaders abandoned their people, and in order to maintain their hold on power they did exactly what the colonial system was doing, namely to pit one community against another. This internal conflict continued for decades in many African countries, draining their scarce resources.

So what we need is to improve our leadership. If we don't there is no hope, because history teaches us that if you cannot protect what is your own, somebody will come and take it. If our people cannot protect themselves they will continue to be exploited. Their resources will continue to be exploited.

It is also true that Western powers, especially the former colonial masters of this region, have continued to exploit Africa and have continued to work very closely with these dictators and irresponsible leaders. That is why we are now deep in debt, which we cannot repay.

Africa also needs assistance from international governments to improve its economic standing. For example, most foreign aid to Africa comes in the form of curative social welfare programs such as famine relief, food aid, population control programs, refugee camps, peace-keeping forces and humanitarian missions.

At the same time, hardly any resources are available for sustainable human development programs such as functional education and training, development of infrastructure, food production, and promotion of entrepreneurship. There are no funds for the development of cultural and social programs which would empower people and release their creative energy.

I am hoping that in the new millennium a new leadership will emerge in Africa, and I hope this new leadership will show more concern for the people and utilize the continent's resources to help Africans get out of poverty.

1 0

THINK LOCALLY, ACT GLOBALLY? THE TRANSNATIONALIZATION OF CANADIAN RESOURCE-USE CONFLICTS

MARY L. BARKER
AND DIETRICH SOYEZ

Conflicts over resource use and development projects in northern Canada are being played out increasingly in the international arena. When transboundary impacts or water diversion and export are at issue, the interactions are primarily among people, organizations, and processes in Canada and its neighbor, the United States.[1] Foreign investment in resource projects can trigger even wider-ranging interactions, as in the case of Japanese involvement in large-scale clearcut logging and pulp mill construction in northern Alberta. Canadian aboriginal peoples and environmental groups, concerned about the impacts of logging in the northern boreal forest, have attempted to gain support in the "end-user" country (where the wood or wood products are used) by forging links with Japanese environmentalists and by developing an information campaign aimed at Japanese tourists visiting Canada.[2]

In the last three years, the German media have frequently covered clearcut logging in western Canada, and, in 1993, the German Greenpeace organization initiated a publicity campaign against logging the remaining old-growth

Environment vol. 36, no. 5, pp. 12–20 and 32–36, June 1994. Reprinted with permission of the Helen Dwight Reid Educational Foundation. Published by Heldref Publications, 1319 Eighteenth St. N.W., Washington, D.C. 20036-1802. © 1994.

temperate rain forest in coastal British Columbia. German activists participated in roadblock protests on the Canadian west coast and organized a domestic lobbying campaign against German publishing companies that use paper imported from Canada and Scandinavia.[3] Because of these activities, the
Canadian forest industry and government attempted to counteract the spread
of what they considered to be misinformation in the European end-user
countries about temperate rain forests, logging methods, and forest products.

The strategies of internationally based interest groups have been an effective political catalyst in the past. In the early 1980s, for example, controversies
surrounding the Newfoundland offshore seal hunt and the trapping of northern fur-bearing animals pitted the international animal rights movement and
Greenpeace International against the Canadian government, the fur industry,
and both aboriginal and nonaboriginal hunters. The European Common
Market became the main arena for the dispute, which led to a consumer fur
boycott, an import ban on seal products, and major repercussions for the subsistence economy of aboriginal peoples.[4] Increasingly, opponents as well as
proponents of particular resource-use regimes or large development projects
seek to influence the political outcome of the conflicts by forging and capital-
izing on international linkages.

The common denominator and triggering mechanism behind many such
conflicts are the "ecological shadows"[5] that urban-industrial societies cast
over their hinterlands. These shadows include the negative impacts of resource extraction as well as pollution from distant sources.[6] They are caused
by social and cultural conceptions and institutional failures that prevent an
adequate assessment and fair distribution of the risks and benefits of economic growth and consumption patterns. The concept of the ecological
shadow has been applied to the global debate between the "North" and
"South" over the inequitable relations between developed and developing
nations.[7] In Canada, this north-south dichotomy is reversed: The environmental and social costs often are borne by economically and socially marginalized groups in the sparsely populated north, whereas the large majority of
Canadians, who live in the south, reap most of the benefits.[8] Comparable
north-south patterns exist in Norway, Sweden, Japan, and Australia. The
costs are engendered not only by resource projects but by water- and air-
borne pollutants from distant sources; the perceptions, values, and economic
strategies of a distant but powerful urban society (such as the seal-hunt opponents in Europe) also may have major repercussions on northern environments, economies, and peoples.

Both the injection of large-scale technologies—with international financing and external end-users—and the imposition of outside ideologies meet
with opposition from indigenous peoples in the affected regions. Many no
longer expect their concerns to be addressed appropriately within their own
nation-state, and so, increasingly during the last few years, they have appealed
to the international public, the media, and international organizations. These

appeals have built on expressions of solidarity, information strategies, and links established in the 1970s among indigenous peoples around the world.[9] Indigenous peoples have also tried to forge alliances in end-user regions at home and abroad. Thus, the catch phrase of sustainable development— "think globally, act locally"—has been reversed, as populations seek outside support for their causes to "think locally, act globally." These interactions are transnational in nature not only because more than one nation is involved but also because the players often include multinational corporations, international banks, and indigenous peoples active in international forums, such as United Nations organizations.[10]

A Question of Rights

International resource transfers and the reactions of northern aboriginal peoples who bear the environmental and cultural impacts exported by the end-user states are a special example of a much broader problem: the adverse distributional effects of facilities siting and environmental degradation borne by any marginal group whose property rights are not recognized or adequately protected by the state.[11] Northern aboriginal peoples occupy a geographically, economically, and socially marginal position in today's world. But urban ethnic minorities and the nonaboriginal rural and elderly poor also lack the political empowerment and resources to resist externally imposed impacts.

Northern Canadian development conflicts involve several interwoven themes, including sustainable resource use, center-periphery relations, transboundary impacts, and minority-majority relations. Sustainable resource use has become a key theme in public debates over megaproject proposals in the north, where the dominant development-oriented interests impinge on aboriginal communities, many of which are showing severe symptoms of cultural dislocation but are seeking to return to or at least maintain remnants of a world view that values long-term stability.[12]

Environmental damage and land (or water) losses from resource extraction and construction projects, along with resource competition (such as hunting pressures) from incoming workers, can undermine or block aboriginal subsistence activities. Thus, the concept of sustainable resource use relates not only to resources but also to the ecological and cultural rights that enable people to choose future paths in keeping with their cultural aspirations.[13] When such rights are not recognized or guaranteed, populations often seek public (and media) support and forge alliances with other groups to exert pressure on political decisionmakers. If their efforts meet with little success in their own country, people begin to explore and develop transnational links.

In Canada, aboriginal aspirations and the complex issue of First Nation rights have gained increasing public attention over the last 20 years. Aboriginal leaders have long argued the need to redefine the relationship of the First Peoples with the Canadian state in order to fulfill their aspirations: self-government, settlement of outstanding land claims, and guaranteed rights that reflect their special historical status.[14] Section 35 of the Constitution Act of 1982 "recognized and confirmed" existing aboriginal and treaty rights, but there has been much disagreement and legal uncertainty about what this actually means. Decisions handed down by the Supreme Court of Canada in 1990 clarified some of the key issues, such as those concerning wildlife harvesting.

Aboriginal peoples assert a special relationship with the land—one that is inextricably linked with their cultural distinctiveness. The settlement of outstanding land claims is therefore crucial in areas where aboriginal title has never been extinguished by treaty. In 1973, the federal government adopted a policy of accepting for negotiation land claims based on traditional land use and occupancy. The first two comprehensive claims of aboriginal groups to be settled dealt with the James Bay Territory. Other Indian and Inuit organizations are now negotiating land claims with the Canadian government and, where applicable, provincial governments. These negotiations cover a wide range of issues, including ownership of certain land areas, guaranteed wildlife-harvesting rights, participation in resource-management decisions, resource revenue-sharing, and financial compensation. Although aboriginal leaders consider self-government to be an essential component, the federal government argues that this is a topic for later, separate negotiation.

The settlement of comprehensive land claims, even if successful, involves years of negotiation. The legal interpretation of broad, inherent aboriginal rights—for example, via Supreme Court decisions—is also a lengthy process. Until such rights are established and land claims settlements are negotiated to the satisfaction of the aboriginal peoples, some will seek to attain their goals by influencing political opinion within Canada and abroad.

Two Northern Conflicts

Two large projects in northern Canada, Phase 2 of the James Bay hydroelectric power scheme in Quebec and military low-altitude flight training over Labrador and eastern Quebec by member countries of the North Atlantic Treaty Organization (NATO), have generated conflicts featuring pervasive transnationalization. At first glance, the two cases have little in common: One concerns energy supply and demand, and the other, NATO defense policy. The James Bay project involves end-users in southern Quebec and the northeastern United States, but the aquatic environment, wetland habitats, wildlife, and aboriginal communities pursuing subsistence hunting and fishing are greatly affected. Although low-level flight training is not a permanent construction project like a storage reservoir or power station, its impacts are nonetheless serious. The key issues are rights over territory and airspace; noise impacts on people and wildlife; and the economic, social, and environmental effects of the project. The end-users are European NATO partners who export low-level flight training from their own densely populated countries because of increasing public opposition.

The James Bay Project

The government of Quebec and the provincial power utility, Hydro-Quebec, are committed to harnessing 28,000 megawatts of hydroelectric capacity from northern rivers whose total catchment area covers almost 400,000 square kilometers. Phase 1, which has harnessed La Grande River, is nearly completed, and Phase 2, which would place three dams on the Great Whale River is just now undergoing environment review.[15] A third phase of development is projected for the turn of the century. The end-users—consumers of electricity generated from the dams—live in southern Quebec, New York, and the New England states. Ultimately, Europeans and the Japanese may also be end-users if electricity-based hydrogen production and liquid hydrogen export (by tanker) prove to be feasible.

The project is greatly modifying the hydrological regime—including water volumes, discharge rates, temperature patterns, and ice formation—of the rivers flowing into James Bay and thus should result in substantial changes to the inland waters and coastal region. Although the scale of the project makes impact prediction and evaluation difficult, substantial habitat loss as well as changes in habitat and wildlife populations are already evident, especially in highly biologically productive wetland areas.[16] The accumulation of methyl mercury in the storage reservoirs and its concentration in food chains constitute a critical problem. Mercury contamination of fish has had a serious impact on the traditional subsistence economy of the aboriginal population in the region.[17]

Impacts seen by project proponents as controllable or capable of mitigation are viewed by opponents as irreversible and existence-threatening.[18] The affected peoples are mostly Cree Indians and Inuit living on the northern fringe of the project area and a small population (450) of Naskapi near Schefferville in northeastern Quebec. Some 4,700 aboriginal people live in two Cree and four Inuit communities located within the area of the Great Whale project alone. (More than 10,500 Cree and 8,500 Inuit live in Quebec.)[19]

In response to a Cree court challenge aimed at halting Phase 1, the Quebec government negotiated a treaty with the Cree and Inuit in 1975 that became known as the James Bay and Northern Quebec Agreement.[20] This agreement exchanged future provincial development rights for protection of aboriginal subsistence rights and monetary compensation. The Naskapi band, left out of this original treaty, signed a separate James Bay and Northeastern Quebec Agreement in 1978. Confronted with Phase 2 and possibly a third phase of development, the Cree are now challenging the provisions of the 1975 agreement. Key actors in the current dispute include the government of Quebec, local and international corporations, the Grand Council of the Cree, and environmental and human rights groups in Canada and the United States. The conflict has been played out before the courts, in state energy hearings in the northeastern United States, and in the heated constitutional dispute between French-speaking Québécois and the rest of Canada.

Military Flight Training

The Department of National Defence and Canada's NATO partners are engaging in low-level military flight training over a 100,000-square-kilometer area in Labrador and eastern Quebec. NATO training began in 1979, using the existing Canadian Forces Base at Goose Bay, Labrador, and expanded in 1986, when Canada signed 10-year agreements with its NATO partners Germany, Great Britain, and the Netherlands. These agreements allow up to 18,000 flights a year at elevations as low as 30 meters above ground level in two designated training areas connected by three flight corridors.[21] A proposal for a NATO tactical training center, which would have involved up to 40,000 flights a year, an offshore bombing range, and the use of live ammunition, was dropped in 1991 in response to profound shifts in the world strategic balance of power.

In 1992, approximately 7,400 low level flights were flown in the two designated areas during the April to October training season. The impact of noise (especially the "startle effect" of fast, low-flying jets) on human health and wildlife,[22] pollutant discharges on vegetation and water bodies, and the social impacts of the base on the local communities should be weighed against the benefits to the local economy, which is almost totally dependent on the military presence.

The aboriginal peoples affected by the overflights are mostly Montagnais and Innu Indians in Quebec and Labrador, respectively, as well as Inuit living on the Labrador coast and, more distantly, the small Naskapi band near Schefferville.[23] There are approximately 9,500 Montagnais living in Quebec and some 1,100 Innu and 4,500 Inuit and Settlers (people of mixed Inuit and European ancestry) living in Labrador. In the fall, about 1,200 Innu, Montagnais, and Naskapi engage in wildlife harvesting in the two flight training areas in Quebec and Labrador.[24] The Labrador Inuit are less immediately affected, but caribou hunters from the northernmost coastal community, Nain, have been overflown when they travel inland in April and May. Nonaboriginal hunters and commercial outfitters also use the two flight-training areas.

The flight-training proponents argue that there is no permanent population living within the two designated training areas and that potential effects—on the estimated 600,000 caribou of the George River herd and on local resource users, for example—can be mitigated by an impact-avoidance program, which was recently put in place. The aboriginal peoples who use the flight area for seasonal subsistence hunting express grave concerns about the environmental and health effects, question the justification for low-level flight training, and doubt the effectiveness of the avoidance program.[25] The Innu and Montagnais also object to the militarization of their homeland.

The Montagnais, Innu, and Labrador Inuit have never signed treaties with Canada or the former British colonial authorities. All three groups have engaged in lengthy land-claim negotiations with the federal and respective provincial governments to define their "homeland" rights.[26] Each group has taken a different position and adopted a particular political strategy with respect to the low-level flight training and land-claim negotiations. Since 1986, the ongoing military project has been the subject of a federal environmental assessment, which will not be concluded before mid-1994 at the earliest. Key actors in the conflict include the federal Department of National Defence and the three NATO partners, the provincial governments of Quebec and New-foundland-Labrador, regional business interests, the Montagnais and Naskapi in Quebec, the Innu and Inuit in Labrador, and peace, church, and aboriginal support groups in Canada and Europe.

A Match of Scale

These two cases can be viewed at three different scales: global, supraregional, and regional/local. At the global level, the concepts of sustainable resource use and equitable development have been mentioned already. At the supraregional scale, where the two basic issues are energy and defense, the broad global concepts manifest themselves as specific elements, many of which are common to both conflicts even though they take place in different physical settings and political arenas with, to a large extent, different actors. The James Bay dispute must be seen in the context of Quebec's sovereignty aspirations as well as the energy debate in potential end-user states. Two themes are unique to the military flying dispute: the NATO defense debate in Europe (and the role it played in justifying low-level flight training in the past) and the regional development policy of Newfoundland-Labrador, which has encouraged any development that held the promise of income and employment in remote Labrador. All the other elements at this supraregional level are common to both conflicts. These include the question of First Nation rights, the environmental behavior of corporations (the public utility, Hydro-Quebec) and of state institutions (the Canadian Department of National Defence), and the intercultural communication barriers, which go well beyond language differences and involve contrasting perceptions, values, and knowledge systems.[27]

At the regional/local scale of analysis, other elements appear that are embedded in and interact with the larger themes already mentioned. At this

microscale, it is important to recognize not only that there are differences between aboriginal and nonaboriginal peoples but also that subgroupings of
both peoples vary in their perceptions, values, aspirations, degree of empowerment, and political strategies. For example, in both conflicts, the Inuit and
Indian leaderships have pursued different strategies. The Inuit traditionally
have sought negotiated solutions through existing institutional channels, such
as the land-claim negotiations. In specific resource-use or management conflicts, their aim has been to convince people by presenting factual documentation. The Montagnais and Innu have sponsored research and published reports documenting their traditional land use, culture, and the perceived
impacts of military flying.[28] But they have also followed a different course,
which has included nonparticipation in formal proceedings in which they
have little or no faith. The Labrador Innu have refused to recognize Canadian
jurisdictional authority in some cases and have pursued strategies of civil disobedience, publicity-seeking, and alliances with other groups.[29]

Returning once more to the global and supraregional scales, both projects
are located in peripheral, or "frontier," regions in the boreal and sub-Arctic
north, which is, to a high degree, economically, politically, and socially dependent on southern, urban core regions. The indigenous peoples occupy a
"Fourth World"[30] within an urban-industrial state, and there is a collision of
the constitutional rights and claims of Canada, the provinces of Quebec and
Newfoundland-Labrador, and the First Nations. In both conflicts, there are
transnationalization processes at work in the environmental, political, economic, and cultural spheres. For example,

   confidential power contracts, concluded by the Quebec government with
      several multinational aluminum consortia, were first made public in
      Norway and Australia, not in Canada;
   Hydro-Quebec, the publicly owned power utility, has set up an office in
      Brussels, headed by a vice president, to lobby both parliaments and the
      media in Europe;
   Cree Indians are putting pressure on the Canadian government and its
      diplomats by lobbying international organizations, including various
      United Nations bodies;
   the Department of National Defence and Labrador supporters lobbied
      NATO partners at the Brussels headquarters to gain support for the
      construction of a tactical training center;
   the Inuit Circumpolar Conference, a nongovernmental organization
      representing the Inuit of Alaska, Canada, and Greenland, has pro-
      posed a transnational Inuit Regional Conservation Strategy for the
      Arctic[31] and has lobbied internationally for the demilitarization of
      the north; and
   representatives of the Labrador Innu, the Naskapi, and the Montagnais
      from Quebec have toured Europe on a number of occasions to lobby
      against military flight training over their homelands. In October 1992,

representatives of the Innu Nation were arrested after blocking a military base in the Netherlands in an act of civil disobedience to protest low-level flying by the Dutch in Canada.

These and other events show that the conflict arenas have extended well beyond the affected regions in Quebec and Labrador and even beyond the decision centers in southern Canada.

The Protagonists in Action

Transnationalization affects many domains, including the economic, cultural, and legal spheres. Although the focus here is on the international arena, these processes and events are often mirrored on the domestic front. A three-stage sequence can be identified as proponents and opponents act and react, as the conflict unfolds. First, international linkages are developed as proponents promote the project abroad. In the cases discussed here, Hydro-Quebec sought to secure electric power contracts in New York and the New England states and signed confidential power contracts with multinational aluminum consortia. And the Department of National Defence lobbied NATO headquarters in Brussels to win a competition against Turkey for the siting of the proposed tactical training center. The project was promoted as a means for Canada to fulfill its NATO obligations, and Canada's competitive advantages over Turkey (such as the availability of empty space) were emphasized.

Second, indigenous peoples make direct attempts to stop the intrusion of large-scale technologies into their territories. In these cases, aboriginal people have

called for independent assessment by international bodies (for example, a delegation from the International Human Rights Federation visited Quebec and Labrador at the request of the Quebec Montagnais and submitted its report criticizing low-altitude flying in 1986);

prepared factual documentation of the perceived impacts, including self-assessments, and commissioned consultant studies;[32]

performed acts of civil disobedience in Canada and abroad (Innu protesters repeatedly occupied the Goose Bay airbase runway and, in 1992, penetrated a military airbase in Holland);

organized lobbying activities overseas (in the case of James Bay, representatives of the Grand Council of the Cree and supporters lobbied the state legislatures of New York, Massachusetts, and Vermont; in the case of the military flying dispute, the Innu and Cree lobbied the European Parliament, the Innu Nations lobbied Dutch, German, and British parliamentarians, and the Innu, Cree, and Montagnais have lobbied in United Nations forums);

run information campaigns abroad by linking their causes to highly symbolic events, such as the 500th anniversary of Columbus's landing, the
1992 Olympic Games, and the Amsterdam International Water Tribunal,
by networking (for example, the Crees established contacts with several
U.S. public-interest groups, such international organizations as Greenpeace, Friends of the Earth, and the Sierra Club, and prestigious national
organizations abroad, such as the Audubon Society, and the Innu made
contact with international human rights organizations and aboriginal
support groups in Europe),[33] and by setting up protest marches and news
conferences abroad, as well as meetings, such as those of the Innu-Mon-
tagnais delegations to Europe and their audience with the Pope;
participated in foreign legal and administrative procedures, as when representatives of the Grand Council of the Crees attended hearings of
the New York State Standing Committee on Energy; and
formed alliances with supporter groups abroad (for example, the Cree allied themselves with environmental grassroots activists and organizations in the United States and Innu supporters allied themselves with
U.S. groups opposed to military training in the southwestern states).

Third, project proponents respond directly to the initiatives of the opponents. For the James Bay project, Hydro-Quebec attempted to influence the media's discussion in Europe and the United States, and its lobbyists were active at
state assemblies in New York and New England and at the European Parliament.
For the flight training, Canada's Department of National Defence circulated a
position paper called "Facts and Fallacies" in Canada and Europe to refute the
opponents' arguments about low-altitude flight training. It has also organized
tours to Goose Bay and selected Labrador communities for European journalists and parliamentarians. Another set of proponents, the Goose Bay–Happy
Valley Town Council, has consulted with public relations experts to devise a
campaign to promote the base and refute its critics. In addition, Canadian
diplomats have attempted to abort, modify, or veto certain human rights and
land-claims resolutions by international bodies, such as the International Human Rights Federation and the Centre for Transnational Corporations.

Two conclusions can be drawn from these examples: First, many of these
events and activities must be seen as indicators of international networks,
built up by the protagonists, and second, the protagonists' main interest lies in
influencing the flow of information and its impact at the international level.

Thinking Locally, Acting Globally

Clearly, the interplay among marginalized groups in the north, southern domestic proponents (with substantial political empowerment), and foreign

end-users has turned the conflicts over the James Bay hydroelectric power projects and low-level military flight training in Labrador and eastern Quebec into transnational, rather than purely Canadian, issues. When marginal groups lack power, believe that existing institutions and decisionmaking processes—such as the environmental assessment procedures and land-claim negotiations—are not sufficiently responsive, and feel that their rights are not recognized or protected, some try to gain bargaining power by seeking support in the international arena. The strategy is to "think locally" but "act globally."

It would be premature to draw definite conclusions about the effects of transnationalization on the outcomes of the two conflicts before the final decisions are made. However, it is clear that the protagonists are interested in influencing opinion abroad that might lend support to their own causes and weaken those of their opponents. Of course, the outcomes may be concrete and substantial, such as cancellation, modification, or postponement of the project, or more indirect and contextual, such as changes in the general or specific context of policies, activities, and so forth. Once networks are built up by the protagonists, pressure can be increased by information or disinformation campaigns aimed at forcing the opponent to react, preferably in the desired direction. The most striking example of such a reaction in the James Bay controversy was the cancellation of an important contract by the New York Power Authority in early 1992. However, this action resulted not only because of pressure from the Cree and their allies but also because of slumping energy demand caused by conscious demand-side management, energy conservation strategies, and the recession.

The decision to cancel Component 2 of the Goose Bay project, the NATO tactical training center, was a direct consequence of radically changed strategic relations in the world and not the result of opponents' lobbying abroad. But pressures from the Innu and Inuit, although very different in nature, did place the Department of National Defence and its performance of the environmental assessment under much public scrutiny. This scrutiny may well have contributed to the decision to design impact avoidance criteria for the selection of flight paths (however controversial these may be).

The visits of Innu delegations to the Netherlands and Germany did not result in the two NATO partners pulling out of low-level flight training in Canada: It is considered to be strategically necessary and cannot be carried out domestically because of opposition from their own residents. At best, sensitivity to the concerns of the Innu and acceptance of the need for impact avoidance measures, such as flight restrictions, may have grown. (If the outcome of the environmental assessment is increased flying restrictions, the three NATO partners may well decide to withdraw.) This is just one example of an opponent generating indirect, contextual impacts: The use of information campaigns at home and abroad can make the proponents more willing to listen and compromise because of real or perceived pressure. These two Canadian examples are by no means unique, as the transnationalization of disputes over tropical deforestation, whaling, and the ivory trade shows. All of these issues compete for public attention in a world flooded with information from diverse and opposing sources. The extent to which the protagonists are successful in influencing the outcome of each conflict depends on a constellation of factors and varies from case to case. One trend is clear, however: Interest groups that do not necessarily share the same agenda—for example, aboriginal peoples and environmentalists—will continue to seek more effective strategies and wider, albeit often temporary, coalitions in an effort to level what they consider to be very uneven political playing fields.

Notes

1. J. C. Day and F. Quinn, *Water Diversion and Export: Learning from Canadian Experience*, Pub. Series, no. 36 (Waterloo, Ont.: University of Waterloo, Department of Geography, 1992).

2. C. Bryson, "Forest Industry in Alberta: An International Issue?" *Environment News* 13 (Summer 1991):20–23. See, also, J. Goddard, *Last Stand of the Lubicon Cree* (Vancouver, B.C.: Douglas & McIntyre, 1991).

3. A number of press reports about the Greenpeace campaign appeared in late 1993. For example, the *Süddeutsche Zeitung* printed two articles on November 1993: "Protestaktion gegen Abholzung: Greenpeace Mitarbeiter in Kanada festgenommen" and "Kettensägenmassaker vor dem Burda-Verlag: Umweltschutzer protestieren gegen Papier, dessen Produktion die Natur zerstört." Canada reacted to the campaign with visits to Europe by forest industry and political representatives. For an exchange between Paul Heinbecker, Canadian ambassador to Germany, and Christoph Thies, a representative of German Greenpeace, see "Kahlschlag für den Kiosk? Der Streit Zwischen Greenpeace und Kanada über die Waldnutzung," *Der Spiegel Dokument*, no. 1 (February 1994).

4. See G. Wenzel, *Animal Rights, Human Rights: Ecology, Economy and Ideology in the Canadian Arctic* (Toronto: University of Toronto Press, 1991); and R. F. Keith and A. Saunders, eds., *A Question of Rights: Northern Wildlife Management and the Anti-Harvest Movement* (Ottawa: Canadian Arctic Resources Committee, 1989).

5. J. MacNeill, J. P. Winsemius, and T. Yakushiji, *Beyond Interdependence: The Meshing of the World's Economy and the Earth's Ecology* (New York: Oxford University Press, 1991).

6. The widespread diffusion of pollutants and the presence of contaminants in boreal, sub-Arctic, and Arctic environments are reasonably well documented. Examples range from the damage caused by acid rain to northern lakes and forests to the accumulation of pesticides, heavy metals, and PCBs in the far north. See, for example, Canada, Department of Environment, *The State of Canada's Environment* (Ottawa, 1992).

7. See, for example, R. R. White, *North, South, and the Environmental Crisis* (Toronto: University of Toronto Press, 1993).

8. For various perspectives on center-periphery relations in Canada and the historical role of northern resource developments, see L. D. McCann, ed., *Heartland and Hinterland: A Geography of Canada*, 2nd ed. (Scarborough, Ont.: Prentice-Hall Canada, 1987); L.-E. Hamelin, *La nordicité canadienne* (Ville LaSalle, Que.: Hurtubise HMH, 1978); R. Page, *Northern Development: The Canadian Dilemma* (Toronto: McClelland and Stewart, 1986);

and K. Coates and W. Morrison, *The Forgotten North: A History of Canada's Provincial Norths* (Toronto: James Lorimer, 1992).

9. J. R. Ponting, "Internationalization: Perspectives on an Emerging Direction in Aboriginal Affairs," *Canadian Ethnic Studies* 12, no. 3 (1990):85–109.

10. Other researchers refer to the same process as internationalization or globalization. See, for example, M. Featherstone, ed., *Global Culture: Nationalism, Globalization and Modernity* (London: Sage Press, 1990).

11. Aboriginal rights are a special case because, in both historical and recent treaties, they usually refer to limited property rights and to collective, not private, property. (The concept of individually owned property is foreign to aboriginal cultures in Canada.) For an introduction to this complex field, see M. Asch, *Home and Native Land: Aboriginal Rights and the Canadian Constitution* (Toronto: Methuen, 1984); B. Slattery, "Understanding Aboriginal Rights," *Canadian Bar Review* 66 (1987):727–783; "Collective Rights and Powers," *Inuit Studies* 16, no. 1–2 (1992); and S. Weaver, "A New Paradigm in Canadian Indian Policy for the 1990s," *Canadian Ethnic Studies* 12, no. 3 (1990):8–18.

12. A. Tanner, "Northern Indigenous Cultures in the Face of Development," in J. O. Saunders, ed., *The Legal Challenge of Sustainable Development* (Calgary, Alb.: Canadian Institute of Resource Law, 1990), 252–268.

13. For a discussion of sustainable resource use, see R. Chambers, *Sustainable Livelihoods: An Opportunity for the World Commission on Environment and Development* (Brighton, England: University of Sussex, Institute of Development Studies, 1986); and T. O'Riordan, "The Politics of Sustainability," in R. K. Turner, ed., *Sustainable Environmental Management: Principles and Practice* (Boulder, Colo.: Westview Press, 1988), 29–50.

14. See note 11 above; and A. Fleras and T. L. Elliott, *The Nations Within: Aboriginal-State Relations in Canada, the United States and New Zealand* (Toronto: Oxford University Press, 1992).

15. Hydro-Québec, *Document Synthèse: Proposition de Plan et développement Hydro-Québec 1990–1992 Horizon 1999* (Montreal, 1990); and Hydro-Québec, "Grand Baleine Complex," *Bulletin* 5 (Montreal, 1991).

16. F. Berkes, "The Intrinsic Difficulty of Predicting Impacts: Lessons from the James Bay Hydro Project," *Environmental Impact Assessment Review* 8, no. 1 (1988):201–220.

17. Comité de la Baie James sur le Mercure, *Rapport D'activités* (Montreal, 1991).

18. Grand Council of the Crees (of Quebec)/Cree Regional Authority, *Environmental, Economic, & Social Issues Related to the James Bay Phase II Project* (Ottawa, 1991).

19. Hydro-Québec, Communications et Relations Publiques, "Grand Baleine Complex," *Highlights*, no. 19 (1993); and Gouvernement du Québec, Secrétariat aux Affaires Autochtones, en collaboration avec les Publications du Québec, *Les Amerindians et les Inuits du Québec d'Aujourd'hui* (Quebec City, 1992).

20. T. Morantz, "Aboriginal Land Claims in Quebec," in K. Coates, ed., *Aboriginal Land Claims in Canada: A Regional Perspective* (Toronto: Copp Clark Pitman, 1992), 101–130; and H. Feit, "Negotiating Recognition of Aboriginal Right: History, Strategies, and Reactions to the James Bay and Northern Quebec Agreement," *Canadian Journal of Anthropology* 1, no. 2 (1980):159–172.

21. Canada, Department of National Defence, *Goose Bay EIS: An Environmental Impact Statement on Military Flying in Labrador and Quebec* (Ottawa, 1989), 3 volumes.

22. F. H. Harrington and A. M. Veitch, "Short-Term Impacts of Low-Level Jet Fighter Training on Caribou in Labrador," *Arctic* 44, no. 4 (1991):318–327; and Canadian Public

Health Association, *CPHA Task Force on the Health Effects of Increased Flying Activity in the Labrador Area: Final Report* (Ottawa, 1987).

23. The Montagnais, Naskapi, and Inno are, in fact, members of a single aboriginal people whose total population is approximately 10,000, living in small communities in Labrador and eastern Quebec. The names Montagnais and Naskapi were used by early European settlers to describe what were then thought to be distinct aboriginal groups.

24. P. Armitage and J. C. Kennedy, "Redbaiting and Racism on Our Frontier: Military Expansion in Labrador and Quebec," *Canadian Revue of Sociology & Anthropology* 26, no. 5 (1989):801.

25. See, for example, P. Armitage, *Homeland or Wasteland?: Contemporary Land Use and Occupancy Among the Innu of Utshimassit and Sheshatshit and the Impact of Military Expansion* (Sheshatshit, Nf.: Naskapi Montagnais Innu Association, 1989); idem, "Indigenous Homelands and the Security Requirements of Western Nation-States: Irmo Opposition to Military Flight Training in Eastern Quebec and Labrador," in A. Kirby, ed., *The Pentagon and the Cities* (London: Sage, 1992), 126–153; and M. Weiler, *Caribou Hunters vs. Fighter Jets*, Mundus Reihe Ethnologie Band 49 (Bonn: Holos, 1992).

26. For an overview, see A. Tanner and S. Henderson, "Aboriginal Land Claims in the Atlantic Provinces," in Coates, ed., *Aboriginal Land Claims in Canada,* pages 131–166; and Canada, Department of Indian and Northern Affairs, *Federal Policy for the Settlement of Native Claims* (Ottawa, 1993).

27. Attention is now being paid to significant differences between the scientific and traditional aboriginal knowledge systems and to their relevance for environmental management. See, for example, M. Freeman and L. N. Carbyn, eds., *Traditional Knowledge and Renewable Resource Management* (Edmonton, Alb.: Boreal Institute, 1988) and P. Usher, "Indigenous Management Systems and Conservation of Wildlife in the Canadian North," *Alternatives* 14, no. 1 (1987):3–9.

28. The Labrador Inuit Association (LIA) chose to cooperate with the consultants hired by the Department of National Defence to prepare an environmental impact statement. Extensive records of land use and ecological data were provided by LIA (J. Rowell, environmental advisor to the LIA, Nain, Nf., personal communication with the authors, 18 October 1992). Both the Labrador Innu and the Conseil des Atikamekw et des Montagnais withdrew from the formal federal environmental assessment process shortly after it was initiated in 1986, citing lack of faith in the proceedings. Both groups participated indirectly by submitting substantive critiques of the environmental impact statement after its release in 1989 (see, for example, note 21 above).

29. A. Tanner, "History and Culture in the Generation of Ethnic Nationalism," in M. D. Levin, ed., *Ethnicity and Aboriginality* (Toronto: University of Toronto Press, in press).

30. N. Dyck, "Aboriginal Peoples and Nation-States: An Introduction to the Analytical Issues," in N. Dyck, ed., *Indigenous Peoples and the Nation-State: "Fourth World" Politics in Canada, Australia and Norway,* Social and Economic Papers, no. 14 (St. John's, Nf.: Memorial University of Newfoundland, Institute of Social and Economic Research, 1985), 1–26.

31. Inuit Circumpolar Conference, *Principles and Elements for a Comprehensive Policy* (Montreal: McGill University, Center for Northern Studies and Research, 1992).

32. See, for example, Comité de la Baie James sur le Mercure, note 17 above; and Armitage, note 25 above.

33. Networking among the various groups, including environmental and aboriginal nongovernmental organizations can take many pathways, including e-mail and Greenet. It

is important to distinguish between networking as an ineffective game and communication strategies that do produce results. Cree contacts with environmentalists in the Northeastern United States did lead to a fundamental change in the nature of the electricity demand debate in New York and the New England states, which put pressure on Hydro-Quebec to justify its policies. Of course, there is always the risk that one partner in such an alliance will capture the agenda of the other partner, who then loses control over the situation.

POLITICS BEYOND THE STATE: ENVIRONMENTAL ACTIVISM AND WORLD CIVIC POLITICS

PAUL WAPNER

Interest in transnational activist groups such as Greenpeace, European Nuclear Disarmament (END), and Amnesty International has been surging. . . . This work is important, especially insofar as it establishes the increasing influence of transnational nongovernmental organizations (NGOs) on states. Nonetheless, for all its insight, it misses a different but related dimension of activist work—the attempt by activists to shape public affairs by working within and across societies themselves.

Recent studies neglect the societal dimension of activists' efforts in part because they subscribe to a narrow understanding of politics. They see politics as a practice associated solely with government and thus understand activist efforts exclusively in terms of their influence upon government. Seen from this perspective, transnational activists are solely global pressure groups seeking to change states' policies or create conditions in the international system that enhance or diminish interstate cooperation. Other efforts directed toward societies at large are ignored or devalued because they are not considered to be genuinely political in character. . . .

This article focuses on activist society-oriented activities and demonstrates that activist organizations are not simply transnational pressure groups, but

Wapner, Paul. "Politics Beyond the State: Environmental Activism and World Civic Politics," *World Politics* 47:3 1995: 311–340. © 1995 The Johns Hopkins University Press. Reprinted with permission of The Johns Hopkins University Press.

rather are political actors in their own right. The main argument is that the best way to think about transnational activist societal efforts is through the concept of "world civic politics." When activists work to change conditions without directly pressuring states, their activities take place in the civil dimension of world collective life or what is sometimes called global civil society.[1] Civil society is that arena of social engagement which exists above the individual yet below the state.[2] It is a complex network of economic, social, and cultural practices based on friendship, family, the market, and voluntary affiliation.[3] Although the concept arose in the analysis of domestic societies, it is beginning to make sense on a global level. The interpenetration of markets, the intermeshing of symbolic meaning systems, and the proliferation of transnational collective endeavors signal the formation of a thin, but nevertheless present, public sphere where private individuals and groups interact for common purposes. Global civil society as such is that slice of associational life which exists above the individual and below the state, but also across national boundaries. When transnational activists direct their efforts beyond the state, they are politicizing global civil society.

. . . In the following I analyze the character of world civic politics by focusing on one relatively new sector of this activity, transnational environmental activist groups (TEAGs). . . . This article demonstrates that, while TEAGs direct much effort toward state policies, their political activity does not stop there but extends into global civil society. In the following, I describe and analyze this type of activity and, in doing so, make explicit the dynamics and significance of world civic politics. . . .

Disseminating an Ecological Sensibility

Few images capture the environmental age as well as the sight of Greenpeace activists positioning themselves between harpoons and whales in an effort to stop the slaughter of endangered sea mammals. Since 1972, with the formal organization of Greenpeace into a transnational environmental activist group, Greenpeace has emblazoned a host of such images onto the minds of people around the world. Greenpeace activists have climbed aboard whaling ships, parachuted from the top of smokestacks, plugged up industrial discharge pipes, and floated a hot air balloon into a nuclear test site. These direct actions are media stunts, exciting images orchestrated to convey a critical perspective toward environmental issues. Numerous other organizations, including the Sea Shepherds Conservation Society, EarthFirst! and Rainforest Action Network, engage in similar efforts. The dramatic aspect attracts journalists and television crews to specific actions and makes it possible for the groups themselves to distribute their own media presentations. Greenpeace, for example, has its own media facilities; within hours it can provide photographs to newspapers and circulate scripted video news spots to television stations in eighty-eight countries.[4] The overall intent is to use international mass communications to expose antiecological practices and thereby inspire audiences to change their views and behavior vis-à-vis the environment.[5]

Direct action is based on two strategies. The first is simply to bring what are often hidden instances of environmental abuse to the attention of a wide audience: harpooners kill whales on the high seas; researchers abuse Antarctica; significant species extinction takes place in the heart of the rain forest; and nuclear weapons are tested in the most deserted areas of the planet. Through television, radio, newspapers, and magazines transnational activist groups bring these hidden spots of the globe into people's everyday lives, thus enabling vast numbers of people to "bear witness" to environmental abuse.[6] Second, TEAGs engage in dangerous and dramatic actions that underline how serious they consider certain environmental threats to be. That activists take personal risks to draw attention to environmental issues highlights their indignation and the degree of their commitment to protecting the planet. Taken together, these two strategies aim to change the way vast numbers of people see the world—by dislodging traditional understandings of environmental degradation and substituting new interpretive frames. This was put particularly well by Robert Hunter, a founding member of Greenpeace, who participated in the group's early antiwhaling expeditions. For Hunter, the purpose of the effort was to overturn fundamental images about whaling: where the predominant view was of brave men battling vicious and numerous monsters of the deep, Greenpeace documented something different. As Hunter put it:

> Soon, images would be going out into hundreds of millions of minds around the world, a completely new set of basic images about whaling. Instead of small boats and giant whales, giant boats and small whales; instead of courage killing whales, courage saving whales; David had become Goliath, Goliath was now David; if the mythology of Moby Dick and Captain Ahab had dominated human consciousness about Leviathan for over a century, a whole new age was in the making.[7]

Raising awareness through media stunts is not primarily about changing governmental policies, although this may of course happen as state officials bear witness or are pressured by constituents to codify into law shifts in public opinion or widespread sentiment. But this is only one dimension of TEAG direct action efforts. The new age envisioned by Hunter is more than passing environmental legislation or adopting new environmental policies. Additionally, it involves convincing all actors—from governments to corporations, private organizations, and ordinary citizens—to make decisions and act in deference to environmental awareness. Smitten with such ideas, governments will, activists hope, take measures to protect the environment. When the ideas have more resonance outside government, they will shift the standards of good conduct and persuade people to act differently even though governments are not requiring them to do so. In short, TEAGs work to disseminate an ecological sensibility to shift the governing ideas that animate societies, whether institutionalized within government or not, and count on this to reverberate throughout various institutions and collectivities.

The challenge for students of international relations is to apprehend the effects of these efforts and their political significance. As already mentioned, scholars have traditionally focused on state policy and used this as the criterion for endowing NGOs with political significance. Such a focus, however, misses the broader changes initiated by NGOs beyond state behavior. To get at this dimension of change requires a more sociological orientation toward world affairs.[8] One such orientation is a so-called fluid approach.

The fluid approach has been used in the study of domestic social movements but can be adopted to analyze TEAGs.[9] It gauges the significance of activist groups by attending to cultural expressions that signal cognitive, affective, and evaluative shifts in societies. Observers are attuned to the quickening of actions and to changes in meaning and perceive that something new is happening in a wide variety of places. When analyzing the peace movement, for instance, a fluid approach recognizes that activists aim not only to convince governments to cease making war but also to create more peaceful societies. This entails propagating expressions of nonviolence, processes of conflict resolution, and, according to some, practices that are more cooperative than competitive. A fluid approach looks throughout society and interprets shifts in such expressions as a measure of the success of the peace movement.[10] Similarly, a fluid approach acknowledges that feminist groups aim at more than simply enacting legislation to protect women against gender discrimination. Additionally, they work to change patriarchal practices and degrading representations of women throughout society. Thus, as Joseph Gusfield notes, the successes of the feminist movement can be seen "where the housewife finds a new label for discontents, secretaries decide not to serve coffee and husbands are warier about using past habits of dominance."[11] A fluid approach, in other words, interprets activist efforts by noticing and analyzing, in the words of Herbert Blumer, a "cultural drift," "societal mood," or "public orientation" felt and expressed by people in diverse ways.[12] It focuses on changes in lifestyle, art, consumer habits, fashion, and so forth and sees these, as well as shifts in laws and policies, as consequences of activist efforts.

Applied to the international arena, a fluid approach enables one to appreciate, however imperfectly, changes initiated by transnational activists that occur independently of state policies. With regard to TEAGs, it allows one to observe how an environmental sensibility infiltrates deliberations at the individual, organizational, corporate, governmental, and interstate levels to shape world collective life.

Consider the following. In 1970 one in ten Canadians said the environment was worthy of being on the national agenda; twenty years later one in three felt not only that it should be on the agenda but that it was the most pressing issue facing Canada.[13] In 1981, 45 percent of those polled in a U.S. survey said that protecting the environment was so important that "requirements and standards cannot be too high and continuing environmental improvements must be made regardless of cost"; in 1990, 74 percent supported the statement.[14] This general trend is supported around the world. In a recent Gallup poll majorities in twenty countries gave priority to safeguarding the environment even at the cost of slowing economic growth; additionally, 71 percent of the people in sixteen countries, including India, Mexico, South Korea, and Brazil, said they were willing to pay higher prices for products if it would help to protect the environment.[15]

These figures suggest a significant shift in awareness and concern about the environment over the past two decades. It is also worth noting that people have translated this sentiment into changes in behavior. In the 1960s the U.S. Navy and Air Force used whales for target practice. Twenty-five years later an international effort costing $5 million was mounted to save three whales trapped in the ice in Alaska.[16] Two decades ago corporations produced products with little regard for their environmental impact. Today it is incumbent upon corporations to reduce negative environmental impact at the production, packaging, and distribution phases of industry.[17] When multilateral development banks and other aid institutions were established after the Second World War, environmental impact assessments were unheard of; today they are commonplace.[18] Finally, twenty years ago recycling as a concept barely existed. Today recycling is mandatory in many municipalities around the world, and in some areas voluntary recycling is a profit-making industry. (Between 1960 and 1990 the amount of municipal solid waste recovered by recycling in the United States more than quintupled.)[19] In each of these instances people are voluntarily modifying their behavior in part because of the messages publicized by activists. If one looked solely at state behavior to account for this change, one would miss a tremendous amount of significant world political action.

A final, if controversial, example of the dissemination of an ecological sensibility is the now greatly reduced practice of killing harp seal pups in northern Canada. Throughout the 1960s the annual Canadian seal hunt took place without attracting much public attention or concern. In the late 1960s and throughout the 1970s and 1980s the International Fund for Animals, Greenpeace, the Sea Shepherds Conservation Society, and a host of smaller preservation groups saw this—in hindsight inaccurately, according to many—as a threat to the continued existence of harp seals in Canada. They brought the practice to the attention of the world, using, among other means, direct action. As a result, people around the globe, but especially in Europe, changed their buying habits and stopped purchasing products made out of the pelts. As a consequence, the market for such merchandise all but dried up with the price per skin plummeting.[20] Then, in 1983, the European Economic Community (EEC) actually banned the importation of seal pelts.[21] It is significant that the EEC did so only after consumer demand had already dropped dramatically.[22] Governmental policy, that is, may have simply been an afterthought and ultimately unnecessary. People acted in response to the messages propagated by activist groups.[23]

When Greenpeace and other TEAGs undertake direct action or follow other strategies to promote an ecological sensibility, these are the types of changes they are seeking. At times, governments respond with policy measures and changed behavior with respect to environmental issues. The failure of governments to respond, however, does not necessarily mean that the efforts of activists have been in vain. Rather, they influence understandings of good conduct throughout societies at large. They help set the boundaries of what is considered acceptable behavior.[24]

When people change their buying habits, voluntarily recycle garbage, boycott certain products, and work to preserve species, it is not necessarily because governments are breathing down their necks. Rather, they are acting out of a belief that the environmental problems involved are severe, and they wish to contribute to alleviating them. They are being "stung," as it were, by an ecological sensibility. This sting is a type of governance. It represents a mechanism of authority that can shape widespread human behavior.

Multinational Corporate Politics

In 1991 the multinational McDonald's Corporation decided to stop producing its traditional clamshell hamburger box and switch to paper packaging in an attempt to cut back on the use of disposable foam and plastic. In 1990 Uniroyal Chemical Company, the sole manufacturer of the apple-ripening agent Alar, ceased to produce and market the chemical both in the United States and abroad. Alar, the trade name for daminozide, was used on most kinds of red apples and, according to some, found to cause cancer in laboratory animals. Finally, in 1990 Starkist and Chicken of the Sea, the two largest tuna companies, announced that they would cease purchasing tuna caught by setting nets on dolphins or by any use of drift nets; a year later Bumble Bee Tuna followed suit. Such action has contributed to protecting dolphin populations around the world.

In each of these instances environmental activist groups—both domestic and transnational—played an important role in convincing corporations to alter their practices. To be sure, each case raises controversial issues concerning the ecological wisdom of activist pressures, but it also nevertheless demonstrates the effects of TEAG efforts. In the case of McDonald's, the corporation decided to abandon its foam and plastic containers in response to prodding by a host of environmental groups. These organizations, which included the Citizens Clearinghouse for Hazardous Waste, Earth Action Network, and Kids against Pollution, organized a "send-back" campaign in which people mailed McDonald's packaging to the national headquarters. Additionally, Earth Action Network actually broke windows and scattered supplies at a McDonald's restaurant in San Francisco to protest the company's environmental policies. The Environmental Defense Fund (EDF) played a mediating role by organizing a six-month, joint task force to study ways to reduce solid waste in McDonald's eleven thousand restaurants worldwide. The task force provided McDonald's with feasible responses to activist demands.[25] What is clear from most reports on the change is that officials at McDonald's did not believe it necessarily made ecological or economic sense to stop using clamshell packaging but that they bent to activist pressure.[26]

Uniroyal Chemical Company ceased producing Alar after groups such as Ralph Nader's Public Interest Research Group (PIRG) and the Natural Resources Defense Council (NRDC) organized a massive public outcry about the use of the product on apples in the U.S. and abroad. In 1989 NRDC produced a study that found that Alar created cancer risks 240 times greater than those declared safe by the U.S. Environmental Protection Agency (EPA).[27] This was publicized on CBS's *60 Minutes* and led to critical stories in numerous newspapers and magazines. Moreover, activists pressured supermarket chains to stop selling apples grown with Alar and pressured schools to stop serving Alar-sprayed apples. The effects were dramatic. The demand for apples in general shrank significantly because of the scare, lowering prices well below the break-even level.[28] This led to a loss of $135 million for Washington State apple growers alone.[29] Effects such as these and pressure by activist groups convinced Uniroyal to cease production of the substance not only in the U.S. but overseas as well. Like McDonald's, Uniroyal changed its practices not for economic reasons nor to increase business nor because it genuinely felt Alar was harmful. Rather, it capitulated to activist pressure. In fact, there is evidence from nonindustry sources suggesting that Alar did not pose the level of threat publicized by activists.[30]

Finally, in the case of dolphin-free tuna, Earth Island Institute (EII) and other organizations launched an international campaign in 1985 to stop all drift-net and purse seine fishing by tuna fleets. For unknown reasons, tuna in the Eastern Tropical Pacific Ocean swim under schools of dolphins. For years tuna fleets have set their nets on dolphins or entangled dolphins in drift nets as a way to catch tuna. While some fleets still use these strategies, the three largest tuna companies have ceased doing so. TEAGs were at the heart of this change. Activists waged a boycott against all canned tuna, demonstrated at stockholders' meetings, and rallied on the docks of the Tuna Boat Association in San Diego. Furthermore, EII assisted in the production of the film *Where Have All the Dolphins Gone?* which was shown throughout the United States and abroad; it promoted the idea of "dolphin-safe" tuna labels to market environmentally sensitive brands; and it enlisted Heinz, the parent company of Starkist, to take an active role in stopping the slaughter of dolphins by all tuna companies. Its efforts, along with those of Greenpeace, Friends of the Earth, and others, were crucial to promoting dolphin-safe tuna fishing.[31] One result of these efforts is that dolphin kills associated with tuna fishing in 1993 numbered fewer than 5,000. This represents one-third the mortality rate of 1992, when 15,470 dolphins died in nets, and less than one-twentieth of the number in 1989, when over 100,000 dolphins died at the hands of tuna fleets.[32] These numbers represent the effects of activist efforts. Although governments did eventually adopt domestic dolphin conservation policies and negotiated partial international standards to reduce dolphin kills, the first such actions came into force only in late 1992 with the United Nations moratorium on drift nets. Moreover, the first significant actions against purse seine fishing, which more directly affects dolphins, came in June 1994 with the United States International Dolphin Conservation Act.[33] As with the Canadian seal pup hunt, government action in the case of tuna fisheries largely codified changes that were already taking place.

In each instance, activist groups did not direct their efforts at governments. They did not target politicians; nor did they organize constituent pressuring. Rather, they focused on corporations themselves. Through protest, research, exposés, orchestrating public outcry, and organizing joint consultations, activists won corporate promises to bring their practices in line with environmental concerns. The levers of power in these instances were found in the economic realm of collective life rather than in the strictly governmental realm. Activists understand that the economic realm, while not the center of traditional notions of politics, nevertheless furnishes channels for effecting widespread changes in behavior; they recognize that the economic realm is a form of governance and can be manipulated to alter collective practices.

Perhaps the best example of how activist groups, especially transnational ones, enlist the economic dimensions of governance into their enterprises is the effort to establish environmental oversight of corporations. In September 1989 a coalition of environmental, investor, and church interests, known as the Coalition for Environmentally Responsible Economies (CERES), met in New York City to introduce a ten-point environmental code of conduct for corporations. One month later CERES, along with the Green Alliance, launched a similar effort in the United Kingdom. The aim was to establish criteria for auditing the environmental performance of large domestic and multinational industries. The code called on companies to, among other things, minimize the release of pollutants, conserve nonrenewable resources through efficient use and planning, utilize environmentally safe and sustainable energy sources, and consider demonstrated environmental commitment as a factor in appointing members to the board of directors. Fourteen environmental organizations, including TEAGs such as Friends of the Earth and the International Alliance for Sustainable Agriculture, publicize the CERES Principles (formerly known as the Valdez Principles, inspired by the Exxon *Valdez* oil spill) and enlist corporations to pledge compliance. What is significant from an international perspective is that signatories include at least one

Fortune 500 company and a number of multinational corporations. Sun Company, General Motors, Polaroid, and a host of other MNCs have pledged compliance or are at least seriously considering doing so. Because these companies operate in numerous countries their actions have transnational effects.

The CERES Principles are valuable for a number of reasons. In the case of pension funds, the code is being used to build shareholder pressure on companies to improve their environmental performance. Investors can use it as a guide to determine which companies practice socially responsible investment. Environmentalists use the code as a measuring device to praise or criticize corporate behavior. Finally, the Principles are used to alert college graduates on the job market about corporate compliance with the code and thus attempt to make environmental issues a factor in one's choice of a career. Taken together, these measures force some degree of corporate accountability by establishing mechanisms of governance to shape corporate behavior. To be sure, they have not turned businesses into champions of environmentalism, nor are they as effectual as mechanisms available to governments. At work, however, is activist discovery and manipulation of economic means of power.[34]

Via the CERES Principles and other forms of pressure, activists thus influence corporate behavior.[35] McDonald's, Uniroyal, and others have not been changing their behavior because governments are breathing down their necks. Rather, they are voluntarily adopting different ways of producing and distributing products. This is not to say that their actions are more environmentally sound than before they responded to activists or that their attempt to minimize environmental dangers is sincerely motivated. As mentioned, environmental activist groups do not have a monopoly on ecological wisdom, nor is corporate "greening" necessarily well intentioned.[36] Nonetheless, the multinational corporate politics of transnational groups are having an effect on the way industries do business. And to the degree that these enterprises are involved in issues of widespread public concern that cross state boundaries, activist pressure must be understood as a form of world politics.

Empowering Local Communities

For decades TEAGs have worked to conserve wildlife in the developing world. Typically, this has involved people in the First World working in the Third World to restore and guard the environment. First World TEAGs—ones headquartered in the North—believed that Third World people could not appreciate the value of wildlife or were simply too strapped by economic pressures to conserve nature. Consequently, environmental organizations developed, financed, and operated programs in the field with little local participation or input.

While such efforts saved a number of species from extinction and set in motion greater concern for Third World environmental protection, on the whole they were unsuccessful at actually preserving species and their habitats from degradation and destruction.[37] A key reason for this was that they attended more to the needs of plants and especially animals than to those of the nearby human communities. Many of the earth's most diverse and biologically rich areas are found in parts of the world where the poorest peoples draw their livelihood from the land. As demographic and economic constraints grow tighter, these people exploit otherwise renewable resources in an attempt merely to survive.[38] Ecological sustainability in these regions, then, must involve improving the quality of life of the rural poor through projects that integrate the management of natural resources with grassroots economic development.

Often after having supported numerous failed projects, a number of TEAGs have come to subscribe to this understanding and undertake appropriate actions. World Wildlife Fund (WWF) or World Wide Fund for Nature, as it is known outside English-speaking countries, is an example of such an organization. WWF is a conservation group dedicated to protecting endangered wildlife and wildlands worldwide. It originated in 1961 as a small organization in Switzerland, making grants to finance conservation efforts in various countries. Over the past thirty years it has grown into a full-scale global environmental organization with offices in over twenty countries. Within the past decade, WWF has established a wildlands and human needs program, a method of conservation to be applied to all WWF projects linking human economic well-being with environmental protection. It structures a game management system in Zambia, for example, which involves local residents in antipoaching and conservation efforts, and the channeling of revenues from tourism and safaris back into the neighboring communities that surround the preserves.[39] It informs a WWF-initiated Kilum Mountain project in the Cameroon that is developing nurseries for reforestation, reintroducing indigenous crops, and disseminating information about the long-term effects of environmentally harmful practices.[40] Finally, it is operative in a project in St. Lucia, where WWF has lent technical assistance to set up sanitary communal waste disposal sites, improved marketing of fish to reduce overfishing, and protected mangroves from being used for fuel by planting fast-growing fuel-wood trees.[41] WWF is not alone in these efforts. The New Forests Project, the Association for Research and Environmental Aid (AREA), the Ladakh Project, and others undertake similar actions.

In these kinds of efforts, TEAGs are not trying to galvanize public pressure aimed at changing governmental policy or directly lobbying state officials; indeed, their activity takes place far from the halls of congresses, parliaments, and executive offices. Rather, TEAGs work with ordinary people in diverse regions of the world to try to enhance local capability to carry out sustainable development projects. The guiding logic is that local people must be enlisted in protecting their own environments and that their efforts will then reverberate through wider circles of social interaction to affect broader aspects of world environmental affairs.[42]

Independent of the content of specific projects, the efforts of TEAGs almost always bring local people together.[43] They organize people into new forms of social interaction, and this makes for a more tightly woven web of associational life. To the degree that this is attentive to ecological issues, it partially fashions communities into ecologically sensitive social agents. This enables them more effectively to resist outside forces that press them to exploit their environments, and it helps them assume a more powerful role in determining affairs when interacting with outside institutions and processes. To paraphrase Michael Bratton, hands-on eco-development projects stimulate and release popular energies in support of community goals.[44] This strengthens a community's ability to determine its own affairs and influence events outside its immediate domain.

The dynamics of environmental destruction often do not originate at the local or state level. Poor people who wreck their environments are generally driven to do so by multiple external pressures. Embedded within regional, national, and ultimately global markets, living under political regimes riven by rivalries and controlled by leadership that is not popularly based, penetrated by MNCs, and often at the mercy of multilateral development banks, local people respond to the consumptive practices and development strategies of those living in distant cities or countries.[45] Once empowered, however, communities can respond to these pressures more successfully. For example, since 1985 tens of thousands of peasants, landless laborers, and tribal people have demonstrated against a series of dams in the Narmada Valley that critics believe will cause severe environmental and social damage. The Sardar Sarovar projects are intended to produce hydroelectric energy for the states of Gujarat, Madhya Pradesh, and Maharashtra and have been supported by the governments of these states, the Indian government, and until recently the World Bank. Resistance started locally, but since 1985 it has spread with the formation by local and transnational groups of an activist network that operates both inside India and abroad to thwart the project. While the final outcome has yet to be determined, local communities have already redefined the debate about the environmental efficacy of large dam projects, as well as those having to do with displacement and rehabitation. As a result, the Indian government, the World Bank, and other aid agencies now find themselves profoundly hesitant about future dam projects; indeed, in 1993 the Indian government withdrew its request for World Bank funding to support the Sardar Sarovar project.[46] Finally, local communities have served notice, through their insistence that they will drown before they let themselves be displaced, that they are better organized to resist other large-scale, external environmental and developmental designs.[47]

Local empowerment affects wider arenas of social life in a positive, less reactive fashion when communities reach out to actors in other regions, countries, and continents. Indeed, the solidification of connections between TEAGs and local communities itself elicits responses from regional, national, and international institutions and actors. This connection is initially facilitated when TEAGs that have offices in the developed world transfer money and resources to Third World communities. In 1989, for example, northern NGOs distributed $6.4 billion to developing countries, which is roughly 12 percent of all public and private development aid.[48] Much of this aid went to local NGOs and helped to empower local communities.[49]

This pattern is part of a broader shift in funding from First World governments. As local NGOs become better able to chart the economic and environmental destinies of local communities, First World donors look to them for expertise and capability. For instance, in 1975 donor governments channeled $100 million through local NGOs; in 1985 the figure had risen to $1.1 billion.[50] This represents a shift on the part of Official Development Assistance (ODA) countries. In 1975 they donated only 0.7 percent of their funding through Third World NGOs; in 1985 the figure rose to 3.6 percent.[51] This pattern is further accentuated when First World governments turn to transnational NGOs in the North for similar expertise. According to a 1989 OECD report, by the early 1980s virtually all First World countries adopted a system of co-financing projects implemented by their national NGOs. "Official contributions to NGOs' activities over the decades have been on an upward trend, amounting to $2.2 billion in 1987 and representing 5 percent of total ODA," according to the report.[52] While much of this was funneled through voluntary relief organizations such as Catholic Relief Services, overall there has been an upgrading in the status of NGOs concerned with development and environmental issues.[53]

Increased aid to local NGOs has obvious effects on local capability. It enhances the ability of communities to take a more active and effectual role in their economic and environmental destinies. The effects are not limited, however, to a more robust civil society. Many of the activities and certainly the funding directly challenge or at least intersect with state policies; thus, governments are concerned about who controls any foreign resources that come into the country. When funds go to NGOs, state activity can be frustrated. This is most clear in places like Kenya and Malaysia, where environmental NGOs are part of broader opposition groups. In these instances outside aid to local groups may be perceived as foreign intervention trying to diminish state power. At a lesser degree of challenge, outside support may simply minimize the control government exercises over its territory. Empowering local communities diminishes state authority by reinforcing local loyalties at the expense of national identity. At a minimum, this threatens government attempts at nation building. Put most broadly, TEAGs pose a challenge to state sovereignty and more generally redefine the realm of the state itself. Thus, while TEAGs may see themselves working outside the domain of the state and focusing on civil society per se, their actions in fact have a broader impact and interfere with state politics.

Nevertheless, it would be misleading to think about TEAGs as traditional interest groups. Rather, with their hands-on development/environmental efforts TEAGs attempt to work independent of governmental activity at the level of communities themselves. That their activities end up involving them in the political universe of the state is indicative of the porous boundary between local communities and the state or, more broadly, between the state and civil society. It does not mean that activist efforts in civil society gain political relevance only when they intersect state activities.[54]

The grassroots efforts of transnational environmental activists aim to engage people at the level at which they feel the most immediate effects—their own local environmental and economic conditions. At this level, TEAGs try to use activism itself, rooted in the actual experience of ordinary people, as a form of governance. It can alter the way people interact with each other and their environment, literally to change the way they live their lives. To the degree that such efforts have ramifications for wider arenas of social interaction—including states and other actors—they have world political significance.

World Civic Politics

The predominant way to think about NGOs in world affairs is as transnational interest groups. They are politically relevant insofar as they affect state policies and interstate behavior. In this article I have argued that TEAGs, a particular type of NGO, have political relevance beyond this. They work to shape the way vast numbers of people throughout the world act toward the environment using modes of governance that are part of global civil society.

Greenpeace, Sea Shepherds Conservation Society, and EarthFirst! for example, work to disseminate an ecological sensibility. It is a sensibility not restricted to governments nor exclusively within their domain of control. Rather, it circulates throughout all areas of collective life. To the degree this sensibility sways people, it acts as a form of governance. It defines the boundaries of good conduct and thus animates how a host of actors—from governments to voluntary associations and ordinary citizens—think about and act in reference to the environment.

A similar dynamic is at work when TEAGs pressure multinational corporations. These business enterprises interact with states, to be sure, and state governments can restrict their activities to a significant degree. They are not monopolized by states, however, and thus their realm of operation is considerably beyond state control. Due to the reach of multinational corporations into environmental processes, encouraging them to become "green" is another instance of using the governing capacities outside formal government to shape widespread activities.

Finally, when TEAGs empower local communities, they are likewise not focused primarily on states. Rather, by working to improve people's day-to-day economic lives in ecologically sustainable ways, they bypass state apparatuses and activate governance that operates at the community level. As numerous communities procure sustainable development practices, the efforts of TEAGs take effect. Moreover, as changed practices at this level translate up through processes and mechanisms that are regional, national, and global in scope, the efforts by TEAGs influence the activities of larger collectivities, which in turn shape the character of public life.

I suggested that the best way to think about these activities is through the category of "world civic politics." When TEAGs work through transnational networks associated with cultural, social, and economic life, they are enlisting forms of governance that are civil as opposed to official or state constituted in character. Civil, in this regard, refers to the quality of interaction that takes place above the individual and below the state yet across national boundaries. The concept of world civic politics clarifies how the forms of governance in global civil society are distinct from the instrumentalities of state rule. . . .

Notes

1. On the concept of "global civil society," see Richard Falk, *Explorations at the Edge of Time* (Philadelphia: Temple University Press, 1992); and Ronnie Lipschutz, "Restructuring World Politics: The Emergence of Global Civil Society," *Millennium* 21 (Winter 1992).

2. There is no single, static definition of civil society. The term has a long and continually evolving, if not contestable, conceptual history. For an appreciation of the historical roots of the term and its usage in various contexts, see Jean Cohen and Andrew Arato, *Civil Society and Political Theory* (Cambridge: MIT Press, 1992); John Keane, "Despotism and Democracy: The Origins and Development of the Distinction between Civil Society and the State, 1750–1850," in Keane, ed., *Civil Society and the State: New European Perspectives* (London: Verso, 1988).

3. I follow a Hegelian understanding of civil society, which includes the economy within its domain. Later formulations, most notably those offered by Gramsci and Parsons, introduce a three-part model that differentiates civil society from both the state and the economy. See Talcott Parsons, *The System of Modern Societies* (Englewood Cliffs, NJ: Prentice-Hall, 1971); Antonio Gramsci, *Prison Notebooks* (New York: International Publishers, 1971). For an extensive argument to exclude the economy from civil society, see Cohen and Arato (fn. 5).

4. Michael Harwood, "Daredevils for the Environment," *New York Times Magazine,* October 2, 1988, p. 7. Also confirmed in private interviews at the time. See also Clive Davidson, "How Greenpeace Squeezed onto Satellite Link," *New Scientist* 135 (July 1992), 20.

5. For discussions on the media-directed dimension of ecological political action, see Rik Scarce, *Eco-Warriors: Understanding the Radical Environmental Movement* (Chicago: Noble Press, 1990); David Day, *The Environmental Wars* (New York: Ballantine Books, 1989); Robert Hunter, *Warriors of the Rainbow: A Chronicle of the Greenpeace Movement* (New York: Holt, Rinehart and Winston, 1979); Walter Truett Anderson, *Reality Isn't What It Used to Be* (San Francisco: Harper and Row, 1990), chap. 7.

6. Bearing witness is a type of political action that originated with the Quakers. It requires that one who has observed a morally objectionable act (in this case an ecologically destructive one) must either take action to prevent further injustice or stand by and attest to its occurrence; one may not turn away in ignorance. For bearing witness as used by Greenpeace, see Hunter (fn. 33); Michael Brown and John May, *The Greenpeace Story*

(Ontario: Prentice-Hall Canada, 1989); Greenpeace, "Fifteen Years at the Front Lines," *Greenpeace Examiner* 11 (October–December 1986).

7. Hunter (fn. 33), 229.

8. Sociological perspectives on world politics have proliferated over the past few years. See, for example, Leslie Sklair, *Sociology of the Global System* (Baltimore: Johns Hopkins University Press, 1991); and David Jacobson, "The States System in the Age of Rights" (Ph.D. diss., Princeton University, 1991).

9. Joseph Gusfield, "Social Movements and Social Change: Perspectives on Linearity and Fluidity," in Louis Kriesberg, ed., *Research in Social Movements: Conflicts and Change* (Greenwich, Conn.: JAI Press, 1981) 4:326.

10. Paul Joseph, *Peace Politics* (Philadelphia: Temple University Press, 1993), 147–151; Johan Galtung, "The Peace Movement: An Exercise in Micro-Macro Linkages," *International Social Science Journal* 40 (August 1989), 377–382.

11. Gusfield (fn. 37), 326.

12. Blumer, "Social Movements," in Barry McLaughlin, ed., *Studies in Social Movements: A Social Psychological Perspective* (New York: Free Press, 1969).

13. Linda Starke, *Signs of Hope: Working toward Our Common Future* (New York: Oxford University Press, 1990), 2, 105.

14. Mathew Wald, "Guarding the Environment: A World of Challenges," *New York Times,* April 22, 1990, p. A1.

15. George Gallup International Institute, "The Health of the Planet Survey," quoted in "Bush Out of Step, Poll Finds," *Terra Viva: The Independent Daily of the Earth Summit* (Rio de Janeiro), June 3, 1992, p. 5. See, generally, Riley Dunlap, George Gallup, Jr., and Alec Gallup, "Of Global Concern: Results of the Health of the Planet Survey," *Environment* 53 (November 1993).

16. David Day, *The Whale War* (San Francisco: Sierra Club Books, 1987), 157. For a critical view of Operation Breakout, see Tom Rose, *Freeing the Whales: How the Media Created the World's Greatest Non-Event* (New York: Birch Lane Press, 1989).

17. See Council on Economic Priorities, *Shopping for a Better World* (New York: Council on Economic Priorities, 1988); Cynthia Pollock Shea, "Doing Well by Doing Good," *World Watch* 2 (November–December 1989). According to a 1991 Gallup poll, 28 percent of the U.S. public claimed to have "boycotted a company's products because of its record on the environment," and according to Cambridge Reports, in 1990, 50 percent of respondents said that they were "avoiding the purchase of products by a company that pollutes the environment"—an increase of 18 percent since 1987. Quoted in Riley Dunlap, "Public Opinion in the 1980s: Clear Consensus, Ambiguous Commitment," *Environment* 33 (October 1991), 36. See, more generally, Bruce Smart, *Beyond Compliance: A New Industry View of the Environment* (Washington, D.C.: World Resources Institute, 1992).

18. Jeremy Warford and Zeinab Partow, "Evolution of the World Bank's Environmental Policy," *Finance and Development,* no. 26 (December 1989).

19. U.S. Bureau of the Census, Statistical abstract of the United States, 1993 (Washington, D.C.: Bureau of the Census, 1993), 227, table 372.

20. The average price per seal pup skin dropped from $23.09 in 1979 to $10.15 in 1983. See George Wenzel, *Animal Rights, Human Rights* (Toronto: University of Toronto Press, 1991), 124, table 6.12.

21. This led to a further drop in price. By 1985 the price per skin had dropped to $6.99. See fn. 48.

22. Wenzel (fn. 48), 52–53; idem, "Baby Harp Seals Spared," *Oceans* 21 (March–April 1988); see, generally, Day (fn. 33), 60–64.

23. This example also demonstrates that environmental activists are not always accurate in assessing environmental threats and guaranteeing the ecological soundness of the sensibility they wish to impart. There is no evidence that harp seals were ever an endangered species. This is particularly troubling because the activities of Greenpeace, IFAW, and others produced severe social dislocation and hardship for communities as far away as Greenland, Iceland, and the Faroe Islands, as well as in the coastal communities of Newfoundland and Baffin Island. See Oran Young, *Arctic Politics: Conflict and Cooperation in the Circumpolar North* (Hanover, N.H.: University Press of New England, 1992), 128; J. Allen, "Anti-Sealing as an Industry," *Journal of Political Economy* 87 (April 1979); Leslie Spence et al., "The Not So Peaceful World of Greenpeace," *Forbes*, November 11, 1991; Wenzel (fn. 46).

24. On the issue of good conduct, see Gary Orren, "Beyond Self-Interest," in Robert Reich, ed., *The Power of Public Ideas* (Cambridge: Harvard University Press, 1988).

25. Bramble and Porter (fn. 2), 238; Porter and Brown (fn. 2), 61; Michael Parrish, "McDonald's to Do Away with Foam Packages," *Los Angeles Times*, November 2, 1990, p. A1.

26. "McDonalds Admits to Bowing to Ill-Informed Opinion on Polystyrene," *British Plastics and Rubber* (January 1991), 35; Phyllis Berman, "McDonald's Caves In," *Forbes*, February 4, 1991; Brian Quinton, "The Greening of McDonalds," *Restaurants and Institutions* 100 (December 1990), 28; John Holusha, "Packaging and Public Image: McDonald's Fills a Big Order," *New York Times*, November 2, 1990.

27. Natural Resources Defense Council, "Intolerable Risk: Pesticides in Our Children's Food: Summary," *A Report by the Natural Resources Defense Council* (New York, February 27, 1989).

28. Timothy Egan, "Apple Growers Bruised and Bitter after Alar Scare," *New York Times*, July 9, 1991, p. A1.

29. Michael Fumento, *Science under Siege: Balancing Technology and the Environment* (New York: William Morrow, 1993), 20.

30. "Revenge of the Apples," *Wall Street Journal*, December 17, 1990, p. A8. See generally Allan Gold, "Company Ends Use of Apple Chemical," *New York Times*, October 17, 1990; Adrian de Wind, "Alar's Gone, Little Thanks to the Government," *New York Times*, July 30, 1991; Lesli Roberts, "Alar: The Numbers Game," *Science* (March 24, 1989), 1430. For criticisms of the Alar campaign, see Fumento (fn. 57), 19–44; Bruce Ames, "Too Much Fuss about Pesticides," *Consumer's Research Magazine* (April 1990); and more generally idem, "Misconceptions about Pollution and Cancer," *National Review* 42 (December 1990).

31. Dave Phillips, "Breakthrough for Dolphins: How We Did It," *Earth Island Journal* 5 (Summer 1990); idem, "Taking Off the Gloves with Bumble Bee," *Earth Island Journal* 6 (Winter 1991); "Three Companies to Stop Selling Tuna Netted with Dolphins," *New York Times*, April 13, 1990, pp. A1, A14.

32. "Dolphin Dilemmas," *Environment* 35 (November 1993), 21.

33. "U.S. Law Bans Sale of Dolphin-Unsafe Tuna," *Earth Island Journal* 9 (Summer 1994), 7.

34. See CERES Coalition, *The 1990 Ceres Guide to the Valdez Principles* (Boston: CERES, 1990); Valerie Ann-Zondorak, "A New Face in Corporate Environmental Responsibility: The Valdez Principles," *Boston College Environmental Affairs Law Review* 18 (Spring 1991); Jack Doyle, "Valdez Principles: Corporate Code of Conduct," *Social Policy* 20 (Winter

1990); Joan Bavaria, "Dispatches from the Front Lines of Corporate Social Responsibility," *Business and Society Review*, no. 81 (Spring 1992).

35. For an extended discussion of NGO corporate politics that provides additional examples, see Starke (fn. 41), 89ff.

36. See, for example, Jack Doyle, "Hold the Applause: A Case Study of Corporate Environmentalism," *Ecologist* 22 (May–June 1992); David Beers and Catherine Capellaro, "Greenwash!" *Mother Jones* (March–April 1991). For sympathetic views, see Stephan Schmidheiny, *Changing Course: A Global Business Perspective on Development and the Environment* (Cambridge: MIT Press, 1992); Smart (fn. 45).

37. See, for example, Philip Hurst, *Rainforest Politics: Ecological Destruction in South East Asia* (Atlantic Highlands, N.J.: Zed Books, 1990); H. Jeffrey Leonard, ed., *Environment and the Poor: Development Strategies for a Common Agenda* (New Brunswick, N.J.: Transaction Books, 1989).

38. The relationship between the world's poor and environmental destruction is a complicated one. See, for example, Robin Broad, "The Poor and the Environment: Friends or Foes?" *World Development* 22 (June 1994); and Robert W. Kates and Viola Haarmann, "Where the Poor Live: Are the Assumptions Correct?" *Environment* 34 (May 1992).

39. See World Wildlife Fund, *The African Madagascar Program* (pamphlet) (April 1994); Nyamaluma Conservation Camp Lupande Development Project, *Zambian Wildlands and Human Needs Newsletter* (Mfuwe) (March 1990); Gabrielle Walters, "Zambia's Game Plan," *Topic Magazine* (U.S. Information Agency), no. 187 (1989); Roger Stone, "Zambia's Innovative Approach to Conservation," *World Wildlife Fund Letter*, no. 7 (1989); *WWF Project Folder #1652*.

40. Proceedings of the Workshop on Community Forest/Protected Area Management, Maumi Hotel, Yaounde, Cameroon, October 12–13, 1993, sponsored by the Cameroon Ministry of Environment and Forests; Roger Stone, "The View from Kilum Mountain," *World Wildlife Fund Letter*, no. 4 (1989); Michael Wright, "People-Centered Conservation: An Introduction," *Wildlands and Human Needs: A Program of World Wildlife Fund* (pamphlet) (Washington, D.C.: WWF, 1989); World Wildlife Fund, *1988–1989 Annual Report on the Matching Grant for a Program in Wildlands and Human Needs*, U.S. AID Grant #OTR–0158–A–00–8160–00 (Washington, D.C.: WWF, 1989).

41. Roger Stone, "Conservation and Development in St. Lucia," *World Wildlife Fund Letter*, no. 3 (1988).

42. See Vandana Shiva, "North-South Conflicts in Global Ecology," *Third World Network Features*, December 11, 1991; John Hough and Mingma Norbu Sherpa, "Bottom Up vs. Basic Needs: Integrating Conservation and Development in the Annapurna and Michiru Mountain Conservation Areas of Nepal and Malawi," *Ambio* 18, no. 8 (1989); Robin Broad, John Cavanaugh, and Walden Bellow, "Development: The Market Is Not Enough," *Foreign Policy*, no. 81 (Winter 1990); Hurst (fn. 65).

43. Outside contact may also splinter traditional associations, causing economic and social dislocation. See, for example, James Mittelman, *Out from Underdevelopment: Prospects for the Third World* (New York: St. Martin's Press, 1988), 43–44.

44. Bratton, "The Politics of Government-NGO Relations in Africa," *World Development* 17, no. 4 (1989), 574.

45. See "Whose Common Future," *Ecologist* (special issue) 22, no. 4 (July–August 1992); Robert McC. Adams, "Foreword: The Relativity of Time and Transformation," in B. L. Turner et al., eds., *The Earth as Transformed by Human Action* (New York: Columbia University Press with Clark University, 1990). For how these pressures work in one particular

area, see Susanna Hecht and Alexander Cockburn, *The Fate of the Forest: Developers, Destroyers and Defenders of the Amazon* (New York: Harper Perennial, 1990).

46. Hilary French, "Rebuilding the World Bank," in Lester Brown et al., *State of the World, 1994* (New York: W. W. Norton, 1994), 163.

47. See Bramble and Porter (fn. 2); "Withdraw from Sardar Sarovar, Now: An Open Letter to Mr. Lewis T. Preston, President of the World Bank," *Ecologist* 22 (September–October 1992); James Rush, *The Last Tree: Reclaiming the Environment in Tropical Asia* (New York: Asia Society, distributed by Boulder, Colo: Westview Press, 1991).

48. Robert Livernash, "The Growing Influence Of NGOs in the Developing World," *Environment* 34 (June 1992), 15.

49. Such funding was evident in the preparatory meetings organized for the United Nations Conference on Environment and Development (UNCED). Organizations such as WWF spent thousands of dollars to bring Third World NGOs to Geneva, New York, and eventually to Brazil to attend the proceedings.

50. Michael Cernea, "Nongovernmental Organizations and Local Development," *Regional Development Dialogue* 10 (Summer 1989), 117. One should note that although the overall trend is to fund local NGOs, the amount of money going to local NGOs decreased in 1987. It increased the following year, however.

51. Cernea (fn. 78), 118, table 1. One should note that the reason for this shift in funding is a combination of the perceived failure of governments to promote development, the proved effectiveness of NGO responses to recent famines throughout Africa, and donor's preference for private sector development. See Anne Drabek, "Editor's Preface," *World Development* 15, supplement (Autumn 1987).

52. Organization for Economic Cooperation and Development (OECD), *Development Cooperation in the 1990s: Efforts and Policies of Members of the Development Assistance Committee* (Paris: OECD, 1989), 82.

53. See Fisher (fn. 14).

54. For a discussion of the interface at the local level, see Philip Hirsch, "The State in the Village: The Case of Ban Mai," *Ecologist* 23 (November–December 1993).

PART THREE

THE PROSPECTS FOR INTERNATIONAL ENVIRONMENTAL COOPERATION

Effective responses to global environmental problems clearly require international cooperation. But the barriers to such cooperation are substantial and include uncertainty, mistrust, conflicting interests, different views of causality, complex linkages to other issues, and the myriad problems of coordinating the behavior of large numbers of actors.[1] Effective international cooperation will require both international agreements that respond to specific, pressing environmental problems and a more general commitment to reexamine and restructure existing international practices that are damaging the environment. In this section we take up the question of creating cooperative institutions and processes; Part Four then turns to the related question of reforming existing practices.

Barriers notwithstanding, there have been some hopeful signs. International agreements of varying scope and effectiveness now exist on a number of important issues, including the international trade in endangered species, international shipments of toxic waste, ocean dumping, the Antarctic environment, whaling, nuclear safety, and the protection of regional seas. Perhaps the most powerful example of international cooperation is provided by the international agreement on protecting the planet's ozone layer. The successful negotiation of the Montreal Protocol on Substances that Deplete the Ozone Layer in 1987, and its further strengthening in subsequent agreements, signaled what many hoped would be a new era of increased global environmental cooperation.

Certainly that enthusiasm carried over into the 1992 Earth Summit, where governments attempted to hammer out agreements that would slow global warming, protect biological diversity, and reduce rates of deforestation. But as the international community grappled with these more complex and contentious problems—involving more actors, greater scientific uncertainty, higher stakes, more deeply entrenched interests, and higher costs of adjustment—the momentum for forming ambitious new international environmental regimes stalled in the post-UNCED 1990s. It is too early to say that the ozone regime is an isolated exception to a chronic inability of governments to act collectively, but clearly it did not trigger a wave of effective new international agreements.

We begin with an overview compiled by the U.N. Environment Programme on the pattern of multilateral environmental agreements. The report's authors contrast the rapid growth in the number of agreements in recent decades, particularly since the 1972 Stockholm conference, with several chronic problems: implementation barriers, uneven compliance, incompatibilities across individual accords, inadequate funding, and difficulties assessing agreement effectiveness. One of the most important patterns in the data relates to the unevenness of existing agreements, with strong growth and development in some problem areas (regional seas, hazardous chemicals, air quality) and little or no institution building in others (freshwater ecosystems, forests, coastal zones).

The importance of international accords to global environmental governance notwithstanding, the uneven performance and development of accords across space and time has led many to look for alternative approaches to international institution building. Here we examine three such approaches: global bargaining, so-called "stakeholder" processes, and the development of formal organizations as governance instruments. As discussed in the introduction, we are now at the point of having essentially institutionalized the idea of global conferencing, with major events having taken place in Stockholm in 1972, Rio in 1992, and Johannesburg in 2002 (there was also a lower-key "Stockholm plus 10" event held in Nairobi in 1982). Whether this means the institutionalization of global *bargaining* is less clear. Rio sought to construct such a bargain, based on bridging the gap between environmental and developmental concerns through the idea of sustainability (see Part Five). As James Gustave Speth (a former head of the U.N. Development Programme and past president of the World Resources Institute) discusses, concrete steps to make this grand sustainability bargain a reality were relatively few in the decade between Rio and Johannesburg.

Richard Bissell summarizes a very different approach, exemplified by the World Commission on Dams (WCD). Rather than situate the question at hand in a sovereign interstate forum such as an international treaty or U.N. conference, the WCD brought a group of representative "stakeholders," ranging from environmental and human rights activists to dam-building industrialists and professionals. And rather than beginning with a least-common-denominator foundation of agreement, the WCD placed the core economic, social, and environmental controversies surrounding large dams at the heart of its work. Its relative success in hammering out a consensus statement on dams and development has led some to see the WCD as a potentially fruitful model for other thorny international controversies.[2] Questions remain, however: Who exactly is a stakeholder? How broadly participatory can and should such processes be? What constitutes legitimate knowledge? At the end of the day, doesn't the fate of the enterprise rest on the willingness of governments and other powerful actors to embrace the findings?

We continue our discussion of different institutional forms of global environmental governance with an excerpt from the *Jo'burg Memo.* Coordinated by Wolfgang Sachs and signed by a group of sixteen prominent environmental advocates and researchers from around the world, the *Jo'burg Memo* sought to frame the discussion at the Johannesburg summit in terms of core principles of environmental protection, the defense of people's livelihood rights, and socioeconomic equity. Here we present the section of the memo that calls for the development of "facilitating institutions"—formal organs including a World Environment Organization (WEO), an international renewable energy agency, and a formalized international mechanism for environmental dispute resolution. The WEO debate has been particularly contentious; proponents see the authority, monitoring capability, and enforcement muscle lacking in softer institutional arrangements, whereas opponents see a layer of global bureaucracy with an unclear mission and dubious prospects for effectiveness.[3]

One question that cuts across all institutional forms is the role of scientific knowledge in international cooperation. Is scientific consensus required for international cooperation to occur? Can the sheer power of scientific knowledge spur cooperative action? Sheila Jasanoff argues that although knowledge plays an important role, science alone is an inadequate compass to guide global action. People can examine the same scientific information and come up with dramatically different interpretations of the cause(s) of a particular natural phenomenon. They also might disagree strongly over the best course of action to remedy the situation even when they agree that a problem exists. Science is inevitably politicized, given the high stakes and great uncertainty surrounding environmental change. And Jasanoff makes the provocative claim that too much scientific information can paralyze efforts to achieve cooperation. Take the issue of climate change, for example. Every new finding regarding the role of some feedback mechanism involving cloud cover or the oceans or every new theory about the influence of solar flares or volcanoes can lead to calls for more research in lieu of moving toward more specific action. Under such circumstances, knowledge alone is no substitute for the political will to act, and science requires some value orientation and set of agreed-upon social goals in order to know which questions to ask.

Thinking Critically

1. Given UNEP's list of strengths and weaknesses of existing multilateral environmental regimes, do you think the glass is half empty or half full? Which are the most significant weaknesses, and what would it take to address them effectively?

2. Did the 2002 World Summit on Sustainable Development mark the death of the "global summit" approach to global environmental governance? Is it worth trying to revive broadly multilateral North-South bargaining on environment and development and, if so, what would it take for revival to occur?

3. Who is a "stakeholder" in global environmental controversies? If you were constituting, say, a World Commission on Climate along the lines of the World Commission on Dams, how would you decide who should have a voice?

4. Do we need a World Environment Organization along the lines envisioned in the *Jo'burg Memo*?

5. What role should science play in international environmental negotiations? Can it be a unifying force, or is it inevitably skewed toward the interests and values of a knowledge elite? Which is the greater barrier to cooperation—too much science or too little? If Jasanoff is correct in suggesting that science alone cannot guide us on questions that are fundamentally value-based, where is such guidance to be found?

6. In your opinion, how will history judge the world's progress in international environmental cooperation in the period from the Stockholm conference (1972) to the Johannesburg summit (2002)? Imagine that you are a journalist writing about the legacy of this period from the vantage point of someone living in the year 2032. What do you imagine the first paragraph of your story would say?

Notes

1. A classic work on barriers to cooperation is Mancur Olson, *The Logic of Collective Action: Public Goods and the Theory of Groups* (Cambridge, MA: Harvard University Press, 1965). For a more optimistic perspective on similar questions, see Elinor Ostrom, *Governing the Commons: The Evolution of Institutions for Collective Action* (London: Cambridge University Press, 1990).

2. See the symposium "The World Commission on Dams: A Model for Global Environmental Governance?" *Politics and the Life Sciences* 21, no. 1 (March 2002):37–71; Navroz K. Dubash, Mairi Dupar, Smitu Kothari, and Tundu Lissu, *A Watershed in Global Governance? An Independent Assessment of the World Commission on Dams* (Washington, DC: World Resources Institute, 2001).

3. On the pros and cons of a WEO, see the debate in *Global Environmental Politics* 1, no. 1 (February 2001).

I 2

MULTILATERAL ENVIRONMENTAL AGREEMENTS: A SUMMARY

UNITED NATIONS ENVIRONMENT PROGRAMME

Status of Multilateral Environmental Agreements

Development of Multilateral Environmental Agreements

The earliest multilateral treaty related to the environment dates back to 1868. Since then, the number has risen to at least 502 international treaties and other agreements related to the environment, of which 323 are regional. Nearly 60 percent, or 302, date from the period since 1972, the year of the Stockholm conference.

Many of the earlier agreements were restricted in scope to specific subject areas and were regional in focus. The largest cluster of pre-1972 agreements, albeit a very disjointed one, was made up of biodiversity-related or species-related agreements. Four global agreements which continue to be of major

Excerpted from "Multilateral Environmental Agreements: A Summary." Background paper presented by the UNEP secretariat to the Open-Ended Intergovernmental Group of Ministers or their Representatives on International Environmental Governance, New York, 18 April 2001. Reprinted with permission.

relevance to Governments are the International Convention for the Regulation of Whaling (1946), the International Plant Protection Convention (1951—revised in 1979 and 1997), the Convention on Fishing and Conservation of the Living Resources of the High Seas (1958) and the Convention on Wetlands (1971). Another large cluster dealt with the marine environment. Particularly significant in this cluster were the conventions on marine pollution adopted between 1954 and 1971 under the auspices of what is now the International Maritime Organization (IMO). A third but smaller cluster addresses nuclear energy, testing of nuclear weapons, and nuclear radiation. In addition, agreements were negotiated in a few international freshwater basins, mainly in Africa and Europe.

The period from 1972 to the present has witnessed an accelerated increase in the conclusion of agreements. Over 300 have been negotiated, nearly 70 percent of them regional in scope. The emergence of regional integration bodies concerned with the environment in regions such as Central America and Europe has contributed to this trend. Of greatest impact has been the emergence of 17 multisectoral regional seas conventions and action plans embracing 46 conventions, protocols, and related agreements. By far the largest cluster of such agreements is related to the marine environment, accounting for over 40 percent of the total, the most notable being the United Nations Convention on the Law of the Sea (1982), new IMO marine pollution conventions and protocols, the Global Programme of Action for the Protection of the Marine Environment from Land-based Activities (1995), and regional seas conventions and action plans and regional fisheries conventions and protocols. Biodiversity-related or species-related conventions form the second-largest cluster, including some key global conventions: the World Heritage Convention (1972), [the Convention on International Trade in Endangered Species of Wild Fauna and Flora (CITES)] (1973), [the Convention on the Conservation of Migratory Species of Wild Animals (CMS)] (1979), and [the Convention on Biological Diversity (CBD)] (1992). As in the earlier period, the cluster of nuclear-related agreements remains important, with the addition of nine global conventions and protocols and several regional agreements. Two important new clusters have emerged: the chemicals-related conventions, primarily of a global nature, including the International Labour Organization (ILO) conventions that address occupational hazards in the workplace, the Rotterdam Convention (1998), and the new convention on persistent organic pollutants expected to be adopted in Stockholm in May 2001; and the atmosphere/energy-related conventions, including the Vienna Convention for the Protection of the Ozone Layer (1985) and its Montreal Protocol (1987) and [the United Nations Framework Convention on Climate Change (UNFCCC)] (1992). Agreements on international freshwater basins have historically been the most difficult to negotiate. A number of conventions and protocols have been adopted, but they are concentrated in international freshwater basins in Africa and Europe.

From a combined global and regional perspective, the resultant proliferation of environmental agreements has placed an increasing burden on Parties to meet their collective obligations and responsibilities to implement environmental conventions and related international agreements.

For the purposes of the secretariat report, multilateral treaties are divided into three categories: core environmental conventions and related agreements of global significance; global conventions relevant to the environment, including regional conventions of global significance; and others, largely restricted in scope and geographical range. Agreements in the first category . . . constitute the focus of [this] report . . . .

Scope of the Core Environmental Conventions and Related International Agreements

The core environmental conventions and related international agreements are basically divided into five clusters: the biodiversity-related conventions, the atmosphere conventions, the land conventions, the chemicals and hazardous wastes conventions, and the regional seas conventions and related agreements. . . .

Cluster 1: Biodiversity-related conventions.   The scope of the biodiversity-related conventions ranges from the protection of individual species (e.g., CITES, CMS, the Agreement on the Conservation of African-Eurasian Migratory Waterbirds [AEWA], the Agreement on the Conservation of Bats in Europe [EUROBATS], the Agreement on the Conservation of Small Cetaceans of the Baltic and North Sea [ASCOBANS], and the Lusaka Agreement on Cooperative Enforcement Operations Directed at Illegal Trade in Wild Fauna and Flora) to the protection of ecosystems (e.g., CBD, the Convention on Wetlands, the World Heritage Convention and the International Coral Reef Initiative [ICRI]), or both (e.g., the Cartagena Protocol of CBD, the Agreement on the Conservation of Cetaceans of the Black Sea, Mediterranean Sea, and Contiguous Atlantic Area [ACCOBAMS] and protocols or annexes to five regional seas conventions on specially protected areas and wildlife). While all of these agreements aim at protecting species and/or ecosystems, several also promote their sustainable use (e.g., CBD, CITES, Wetlands, ICRI, and agreements on specially protected areas and wildlife).

Cluster 2: Atmosphere conventions.   The Vienna Convention on the Protection of the Ozone Layer and its Montreal Protocol and the United Nations Framework Convention on Climate Change and its Kyoto Protocol are closely associated with protection of the environment by eliminating or stabilizing anthropogenic emissions of substances that threaten to interfere with the atmosphere.

Cluster 3: Land conventions.   This cluster contains only one major global convention, [the United Nations Convention to Combat Desertification (UNCCD)], which aims to combat desertification and mitigate the effects of drought in countries experiencing serious drought and/or desertification, particularly in Africa. Given the sustainable development focus and the strong substantive linkages between climate change, desertification and drought and loss of biodiversity, UNCCD is very much associated with UNFCCC and CBD.

Cluster 4: Chemicals and hazardous wastes conventions.   The overarching objective of the chemicals and hazardous wastes conventions is the protection of human health and the environment from pollution by specific chemicals and hazardous substances by aiming to control trade in selected dangerous chemicals through informed consent (Rotterdam Convention), to phase out, restrict and reduce the production and use of certain chemicals (Stockholm Convention), and to reduce production of hazardous wastes and their transboundary movements (Basel Convention). Those global agreements are complemented by regional agreements.

Cluster 5: Regional seas conventions and related agreements.   Seventeen regional seas conventions and action plans form a global mosaic of agreements with one overarching objective: the protection and sustainable use of marine and coastal resources. These have evolved over the years into multisectoral agreements addressing integrated coastal area management, including in several cases links to the management of contiguous freshwater basins; land-based sources of pollution; the conservation and sustainable use of living marine resources; and the impacts of offshore exploration and exploitation of oil and gas. Also included in this cluster are the Global Programme of Action for the Protection of the Marine Environment from Land-based Activities and ICRI, for both of which the regional seas conventions and action plans are regional building blocks and vehicles for their implementation.

Legal Framework of the Core Agreements

Of the 40 agreements [that are the focus of this report], all but six are legally binding instruments. Sixteen are framework conventions such as UNFCCC, CBD, the Basel Convention, and the Barcelona Convention that can develop protocols for addressing specific subjects requiring more detailed and specialized negotiations. Eight are self-contained conventions that work through annexes or appendices, rather than protocols, which are revised periodically through the decisions of the conferences of the contracting parties. These include CITES, the World Heritage Convention, the Lusaka Agreement, UNCCD, the Rotterdam Convention, the Stockholm Convention, the Helsinki Convention on the Protection of the Marine Environment of the

Baltic Sea Area, and the Convention for the Protection of the Marine Environment of the North-East Atlantic. CMS is the only agreement that operates like an umbrella convention. It has fostered five independent regional treaties—the Agreement on the Conservation of Seals in the Wadden Sea, EUROBATS, ASCOBANS, ACCOBAMS, and AEWA—all of which continue to work closely with CMS.

The six that are not legally binding are all oceans-related agreements, of which two are global in nature—the Global Programme of Action and ICRI—and four are regional seas programmes—the South Asian Seas Programme, the North-West Pacific Action Plan, the East Asian Seas Action Plan, and the Arctic Council's programme for protection of the Arctic marine environment, which receives its mandate from a non-legally binding declaration, adopted in 1996 by the eight Arctic States. The three other regional seas programmes operate with action plans that were adopted in intergovernmental meetings.

The regional seas conventions and action plans have the distinction of being closely, and in some cases systematically, linked to global conventions and agreements and are proving to be useful regional instruments in supporting their implementation. For example, the protocols, amendments, and annexes on pollution from oil and harmful substances and on dumping from ships and aircraft are operationally linked to the IMO marine pollution conventions in these areas and the protocols on land-based sources of pollution are also operationally linked to the Global Programme of Action.

Institutional Structure and Governance

Multilateral environmental agreements adopted since 1972 generally have the following institutional elements: a Conference of the Parties, a secretariat, advisory bodies, a clearing-house mechanism, and a financial mechanism.

The Conference of the Parties to each convention or the Meeting of the Parties to a protocol to a convention are the ultimate decision-making bodies regarding the overall implementation and development of each agreement, including the programme of work, the budget, and the revision of annexes, where applicable. An important function is the adoption of protocols and annexes. The bureaus of the Conferences and Meetings of the Parties to several conventions (e.g., Vienna Convention and CBD) and protocols (e.g., Montreal Protocol) meet inter-sessionally. Most non-binding agreements (such as those on the South Asian Seas, the North-West Pacific, and the East Asian Seas) also have intergovernmental bodies for decision-making.

The main subsidiary bodies established under environmental agreements and assessment bodies established by or associated with them are . . . generally advisory in nature and present their recommendations to the Conference or Meeting of the Parties.

Several conventions and protocols and related international agreements have clearing houses, generally operated by the secretariats. Clearing houses promote and facilitate technical and scientific cooperation or facilitate the exchange of scientific, technical, environmental, and legal information and assist developing country Parties in the implementation of the agreement concerned.

A few conventions (e.g., Basel Convention) have established or are in the process of establishing regional centres. The purposes of these centres range from for training and technology transfer to provision of assistance in the implementation of the agreements

Corporate or business plans and strategic plans that form the basis for implementation and governance are periodically adopted under most agreements. Practically all of the newer agreements that have not entered into force or have only recently done so still lack corporate or business plans. . . .

Review of the Strengths and Weaknesses of Existing Arrangements

This review is based on the responses to the questionnaire provided by the secretariats.

Strengths

Clustering and opportunities for synergies.   The core environmental conventions within each cluster have much in common, and opportunities exist for closer cooperation. Opportunities for collaboration appear strongest for those agreements that fall within the cluster of biodiversity-related conventions. Those within the chemicals and hazardous wastes conventions cluster are also open to increasing cooperation, as are those in the regional seas cluster. Opportunities for collaboration along functional rather than substantive lines also exist. Because they are trade-related instruments, conventions such as CITES, the Montreal Protocol, the Basel Convention, and the Stockholm Convention have much in common. Opportunities exist for various agreements to work together in capacity-building programmes related to the development of national legislation that supports the implementation of conventions and protocols at the country level.

Opportunities for scientific cooperation.   The opportunity exists for closer cooperation among the scientific bodies set up under the agreements. Proposals mentioned in this regard include periodic meetings of the chairs of these bodies to maximize the benefits of the limited human and financial resources, and periodic production of a comprehensive report integrating the findings of the different scientific assessments, which would facilitate the work of Governments both locally and globally. Problematic issues where there exists scientific commonality among agreements would be better addressed through cooperation between them. Opportunities for collaboration at the scientific level among biodiversity-related conventions and among the chemicals conventions was viewed positively in several responses. It was felt the exchange of scientific data and information should be encouraged.

Increase in arrangements for cooperation among conventions. Cooperation has been increasing in recent years, demonstrating a growing political will and commitment by the agreements, particularly within the biodiversity-related conventions cluster and the cluster of regional seas conventions and related international agreements, to work together in a more integrated manner. In several cases, this is leading to the development of joint programmes of work in areas of common interest. The development of memoranda of understanding and other cooperative arrangements is being endorsed and supported by the Conferences of the Parties to some of these agreements. Cooperation among conventions within clusters may be hampered by differences in stages of implementation, but this might present opportunities for the more developed agreements to assist the less developed, as has been the case with the twinning arrangements between regional seas conventions.

Weaknesses

Reluctance of some agreements to cooperate with others. One convention secretariat felt that considerable lip service is paid to the synergies paradigm, but that when it comes to implementation, many conventions continue to be inward-looking and are reluctant to share or give away part of what they perceive as their "sovereignty."

Inadequate attention to the harmonization of national reporting. Little has been done in the area of harmonization of national reporting among environmental agreements. Some success in streamlining the reports of Parties to the Montreal Protocol and beneficiaries of the Multilateral Fund has been achieved. A new initiative supported by UNEP has been launched for the streamlining of national reporting to the five global biodiversity-related conventions (CBD, CITES, CMS, the Convention on Wetlands, and the World Heritage Convention) and the two regional seas conventions with biodiversity-related protocols (the Barcelona Convention and the Cartagena Convention). Attention needs to be given to harmonizing reporting under trade-related agreements in areas of common interest, such as work linked to customs and port authorities.

Inadequate implementation and coordination of efforts at the national level. Although coordination has focused on cooperation among Conferences and Meetings of the Parties, secretariats and their subsidiary bodies, insufficient attention is being given to the more critical issue of coordinating implementation of the agreements at the national level. Coordination problems are compounded by the fact that human and financial resources at the national level are inadequate for proper implementation.

Inadequate compliance and enforcement. It was felt that there was inconsistency at the national level as regards enforcement and compliance. A holistic approach is required that emphasizes such issues as adequate financial resources, access to technical expertise, and the development of core skills, supported by appropriate legislation and institutional frameworks at the national level, with a clear role for non-State actors. Weak and ineffective national focal points constitute a major impediment to the implementation of these agreements. Most of them lack verification mechanisms. Examples of successful compliance and enforcement need to be identified and shared with other agreements, including analysis of the key operational skills that led to success. Lack of funding for some conventions was perceived as a major obstacle to instituting effective compliance and enforcement mechanisms. Establishment of an inspectorate on enforcement and compliance within the UNEP framework was proposed.

Lack of environmental and performance indicators for measuring the effectiveness of an agreement. The overwhelming majority of the agreements have no scientifically or technically based indicators for appraising performance in improving the quality and sustainability of the environment.

Issues that are not being addressed effectively. According to the secretariats, there are significant gaps in terms of issues not being addressed effectively. Among these are:

- Control of new ozone-depleting substances
- Impact of climate change on migratory waterbirds
- Commercial fishing from an environmental perspective
- The impact of high seas fisheries on marine species such as mammals and birdlife
- Lack of sites on the World Heritage list nominated for their marine values
- Coastal zone management and information
- Information policies
- Impact of population, poverty, and urbanization on coastal resources
- Forests
- Tropical timber trade
- Freshwater resources

- River ecosystems
- Minimization of the production of wastes, including hazardous wastes
- The role of poverty and corruption in relation to environmental management practices
- The failure to identify and make available alternatives to bad environmental practices
- The failure to quantify and publicize the economic benefits of good environmental practices
- Economic instruments and incentives
- Practical indicators for measuring performance under the agreements
- Compliance and enforcement.

Inadequate funding for certain agreements.   Several secretariats strongly feel that inadequate funding hampers the effective implementation of their agreements, including the required support needed by many developing countries. Some are finding it difficult or impossible to access support from the Global Environment Facility (GEF). Areas particularly affected by inadequate funding are the development of synergies and cooperative activities among conventions.

I 3

PERSPECTIVE ON THE JOHANNESBURG SUMMIT

JAMES GUSTAV SPETH

"Obviously, this is not Rio," said United Nations Secretary-General Kofi A. Annan at the conclusion of the World Summit on Sustainable Development (WSSD) in Johannesburg in September 2002. And indeed, it was not. The Earth Summit ten years earlier in Rio de Janeiro was a landmark event. It produced an outstanding blueprint for sustainable development, Agenda 21; two major international conventions on climate and biodiversity protection and a commitment to a third on desertification; the Forest Principles for sustainable forest management; the beginnings of the Earth Charter; the important Rio Principles to guide international decisionmaking; and a commitment to doubling development assistance funding. By contrast, WSSD's Plan of Implementation was a faint echo, though it contains a few notable accomplishments.

Whether one judges the Johannesburg Summit a failure or a very modest success depends on the measuring stick one applies. If one asks whether the summit responded seriously to global-scale environmental threats or brought globalization and sustainable development together, the only honest answer is that it did not. In failing to rise to the moment, WSSD was a huge missed opportunity. Environmental leaders were almost unanimous in voicing dismay, although they did not lose their sense of humor. The World Wide Fund for Nature (WWF) called WSSD the "World Summit on Shameful Deals," and Greenpeace noted that the Plan of Action on energy "is not much of a plan and it contains almost no action."[1]

Environment vol. 45, no. 1, pp. 24–29, January/February 2003. Reprinted with permission of the Helen Dwight Reid Educational Foundation. Published by Heldref Publications, 1319 Eighteenth St. N.W., Washington, D.C. 20036-1802. © 2003.

When the heads of state took the podium in the final days, speaker after speaker attacked the Plan of Implementation as too weak. After formally agreeing to the text, the delegates from almost 200 nations applauded for just ten seconds. U.S. Secretary of State Colin Powell was heckled. The anger at the United States was palpable. Not only was President George W. Bush not among the 104 heads of state in attendance, but the United States fought with considerable success against tough targets and timetables, including the European proposal to set a goal of having 15 percent of countries' energy provided by renewable sources by 2015. Iran, Iraq, most members of the Organization of Petroleum Exporting Countries, and Japan joined the United States in this successful opposition.

In the preparation for Johannesburg, almost everyone accepted the proposition that the excellent agreements reached in Rio had not been implemented effectively and that this failure had been compounded by declining, rather than increasing, development assistance. WSSD, therefore, was to be about implementation. The Natural Resources Defense Council said WSSD should be the "Down to Earth Summit."[2]

A year before the summit, Maurice Strong, who ably led the previous environment and development conferences in Stockholm and Rio, wrote, "What is needed for Johannesburg is a clearly stated theme or goal, together with concrete measures and firm commitments to specific targets designed to measure progress along the way."[3] I was among those who vigorously agreed with Strong that Johannesburg would succeed if agreements were reached on specific plans of action to which governments were unambiguously committed, with targets and timetables and commitments to funding. Nothing else could close the huge credibility and accountability gaps that had opened since Rio. I had been scheduled to discuss these matters with UN Secretary-General Annan on 11 September 2001, and I arrived at New York's Grand Central Station just as the first of the World Trade Center towers collapsed. When I did finally meet with the secretary-general in October, we went over possible areas for which concrete plans of action with specific, funded, and time-bound objectives might be framed for WSSD. These areas included

- providing secure, committed funding and other support needed to meet the Millennium Development Goals, including the goal of halving world poverty by 2015;
- complementing the Kyoto Protocol with commitments to end energy subsidies and hasten the introduction of renewable energy;
- recognizing safe drinking water as a basic human right backed by the needed investments;
- breathing additional life into the biodiversity and desertification conventions and launching an effort to frame country-specific (North-South) compacts to stem deforestation and protect threatened ecosystems and biodiversity hotspots; and

- revamping global environmental governance and providing new institutional means to provide norms and rules for globalization.

In May 2002, Secretary-General Annan issued a major statement based on the "need for greater clarity on what Johannesburg is about and what it can achieve."[4] He called for a "strong program of action" and identified specific areas for which "concrete results are both essential and achievable": meeting the clean water and sanitation needs of the poor; providing access to modern energy services to the 2 billion people who currently lack them and increasing the use of renewables and energy efficiency; reversing the deterioration of agricultural lands and implementing the Desertification Convention; protecting biodiversity and marine fisheries; and protecting human health from toxic chemicals as well as unsanitary conditions.[5] These focal points became the five WEHAB areas (water, energy, health, agriculture, and biodiversity), and the UN secretariat produced useful reports in each area. Each of these reports was released shortly before the summit began.

The outcomes of WSSD bear no resemblance to the specific, monitorable plans of action many of us were advocating during the summit's preparatory process. What emerged instead was either nothing or next to nothing (as, for example, in the cases of renewable energy, desertification, development assistance funding, governance, and globalization) or very general and nonbinding targets with timetables for their accomplishment. The United States and many others typically opposed these targets and timetables, so it was considered a major accomplishment at WSSD when anything vaguely resembling a target and timetable was agreed upon. Among the more notable of these agreements were the following:

- "We agree to halve by the year 2015 . . . the proportion of people who do not have access to basic sanitation."
- We aim to achieve "by 2020 that chemicals are used and produced in ways that lead to the minimization of significant adverse effects on human health or the environment."
- "The following actions are required at all levels: (a) maintain or restore stocks [of fish] to levels that can produce the maximum sustainable yield with the aim of achieving these goals for depleted stocks on an urgent basis and where possible, not later than 2015."
- "The achievement by 2010 of a significant reduction in the current rate of loss of biological diversity will require the provision of new and additional financial and technical resources to developing countries."[6]

Clearly, transforming these and the few other time-bound "commitments" in the WSSD Plan of Implementation into major initiatives in the real world will require huge future efforts to move from generalities to specific plans of action and to garner the necessary political and financial commitments. If this happens, we can look back at the battles at Johannesburg and see provisions in these areas as the start of something important. It also is possible that these agreements will be ignored, as were most of the agreements at Rio. Unfortunately, the Plan of Implementation is silent on follow-up mechanisms for these agreements. As at Rio in 1992, the difficult issue of assuring accountability in the implementation process was largely ignored in Johannesburg.

There were many other signs of how difficult it was for governments to move the agenda forward at Johannesburg. It was viewed as a signal accomplishment to get the following sentence regarding climate change into the Plan of Implementation: "States that have ratified the Kyoto Protocol strongly urge States that have not already done so to ratify the Kyoto Protocol in a timely manner."[7] That was the summit's only fresh contribution to the most threatening of all environmental problems. Expanded reliance on fossil fuels was called for in numerous places without acknowledgment of climate risks.

In addition, negotiators struggled to achieve recognition of the Precautionary Principle previously adopted at Rio. Only a last-minute appeal by Ethiopia managed to delete words that would have made environmental treaties subservient to World Trade Organization (WTO) rules. The governments also could not agree on language that would guide WTO in implementing the Doha Agreement or in how to make economic globalization work for sustainable development rather than against it.[8] In the end, many were musing that the day of the UN mega-conference may have passed.

A more positive assessment of the Johannesburg outcomes is possible if one starts with low expectations and the premise that WSSD was sailing against stiff winds from the outset. In the year before the summit, the world economy had fared poorly. The U.S. administration was preoccupied with the war on terrorism and was generally hostile to both environmental causes and multilateral agreements. The developing world was both wary of and frustrated with the rich countries. The failure to implement the Rio agreements had cast a long shadow, raising questions about credibility and accountability in processes such as WSSD. Those who sought important outcomes at Johannesburg were aware of these and other negative factors but hoped that the fundamental importance of the issues involved would drive the agenda.

From this perspective, many were relieved that what they saw as a generally sensible, forward-looking document was created in the end. They were thankful for modest accomplishments. The targets and timetables that were agreed upon offered some hope. A number of parallel multilateral processes, including several environmental treaties and trade agreements, received a modest boost in the Plan of Implementation. So did the Millennium Development Goals, set at the UN Millennium Assembly, with their objective of halving the incidence of world poverty by 2015.[9] Poverty and environment linkages received much-needed visibility. The business community also was deeply and generally positively involved, much more so than at Rio. Indeed, the developing countries (and development assistance organizations) and

the business community left Johannesburg far happier than did the environmental community.

Importantly, there was tremendous vitality, commitment, and determina-
tion within nongovernmental organizations and, indeed, with many governments and agencies participating. As a lowest-common-denominator document, the WSSD Plan of Implementation was hardly reflective of the best of
our world.

WSSD pioneered the promotion of Type II outcomes—public-private and
other partnership initiatives for sustainable development. Hundreds of these
individual initiatives were showcased at Johannesburg. The United States
highlighted numerous U.S.-based partnership initiatives, said to be worth
$2.4 billion over several years. (Because the summit offered so little in the
Type I negotiations among governments, critics accused the United States of
seeking to derail the main purpose of the meeting with Type II agreements.)[10]
The UN Environment Programme presented awards for the ten best partnerships, including one involving Alcan, Inc., for school-based recycling in Asia,
and one between the Americas and Shell for a gas exploration project in the
Philippines. The United States committed $36 million over three years to help
protect Congo Basin forests.

Brazil, the Global Environment Facility, WWF, and the World Bank announced one especially promising partnership. The Amazon Regional Protected Area project ensures that 500,000 square miles of the Amazon will be
placed under federal protection. This is the largest-ever tropical forest protection plan, covering an area twice the size of the United Kingdom; it will triple
the amount that is already protected.

In another partnership of a very different sort, Greenpeace and the World
Business Council for Sustainable Development joined forces for the first time
to call upon governments "to tackle climate change on the basis of the Framework Convention on Climate Change and its Kyoto Protocol."[11] Independently, Russia used the occasion of the summit to announce that it would ratify the Kyoto Protocol.[12]

Several other important initiatives announced at Johannesburg planted
seeds for the future. The European Union announced that, having failed to
win green energy targets at WSSD, it would seek to organize a "coalition of the
willing," or like-minded, countries to push ahead with global goals for renewable energy development.[13] Germany's Chancellor Gerhard Schroeder announced that Germany was willing to host an international conference on renewables, saying that "climate change is no longer a skeptical prognosis but a
bitter reality."[14] Another group of like-minded countries, the fifteen biologically richest or megadiverse countries that are home to 70 percent of the
planet's biological diversity, came together to achieve reductions in the rate of
biodiversity loss, protect against biopiracy, and seek fairness and equity in
sharing the economic benefits derived from biodiversity.

In sum, one can hope that the sometimes perverse logic of these affairs might once again come into play. Rio was a great summit with extraordinary momentum during the preparatory process, but the wind went out of its sails shortly after the event. The Johannesburg preparations never developed any forward momentum, but perhaps the frustration and disappointment evident there will spur serious efforts after the event. The postsummit European initiative on renewable energy is an example of what is possible. The WEHAB documents generated late in the process in response to Secretary-General Annan's request provide another important entry point for postsummit action.

What Johannesburg Tells Us

Writing immediately after the Johannesburg Summit, it is difficult to forecast its long-term significance. But some conclusions are possible.

First, WSSD was a true sustainable development summit in the sense that advocates of all three dimensions of sustainable development—the "triple bottom line" of economy, environment, and society—were under one roof arguing their cases, raising real issues, and confronting those with different interests and perspectives. It was not a social summit dealing only with poverty, exclusion, and human rights. It was not an economic and globalization summit addressing only trade and investment, finance for development, and transfer of technology. And it was not an environmental summit focusing only on large-scale biotic impoverishment and pollution. Johannesburg was instead a summit about the intersections of these issues, and it was as sprawling and unwieldy as the sustainable development concept itself.

As a result, however, it accurately reflected the dynamics of these issues as they are in reality today. And every so often, the vision of sustainable development actually becoming the unifying concept for its three powerful components would appear like a quantum apparition, shimmer for a moment, but fade away. Perhaps with more leadership, better preparation, and a more focused agenda, sustainable development forums could provide the meeting ground to resolve real-world issues of inevitable difficulty and complexity. It is doubtful, however, if history is any judge, that the United Nations Commission on Sustainable Development is capable of providing such forums.

As it was, what Johannesburg did reveal in bringing all this together is that our world is badly divided on key issues: corporate accountability, globalization and WTO, trade and subsidies, climate and energy, development priorities and aid, and many others. The summit debates covered the core issue: making economic globalization supportive of sustainable development and raising many of the right issues. But in the end, delegates could only agree on platitudes. It is a sad commentary on the state of international discourse, but it is true. Next to nothing was accomplished to bridge these gaps. In all these senses we are still worlds apart.

Johannesburg also underscored the poor condition we are in regarding the status of environmental issues and institutions. Shortly after the summit, *The Economist* editorialized: "If the world had needed saving, it would have been wrong to expect an event such as the UN summit to rise to that challenge in the first place. Happily, though, the world does not need saving. . . . [I]t is ludicrous to suggest that the earth is in grave peril."[15]

A sense of mounting alarm regarding the state of the global environment was sometimes hard to find at Johannesburg outside circles of nongovernmental organizations and some governments. Although seriously wrongheaded, *The Economist*'s views did seem to capture a Panglossian perspective that often was present in Johannesburg.

The summit revealed that, in 2002, the world's governments were more prepared to discuss the economic and social pillars of sustainable development than the environmental pillar. In a similar vein, important questions about how to strengthen multilateral environmental institutions and global environmental governance were never on the table for discussion. The weakness of the summit's Plan of Implementation on environmental issues mirrors the current state of environmental institutions at the international level. The environmental community in and out of government has got its work cut out for it if it is to provide a powerful pillar of sustainable development.

Notes

1. S. Sawyer, Greenpeace, as quoted in World Wide Fund for Nature, "WSSD on Energy—Nothing for the Poor, Nothing for the Climate," press release (3 September 2002), accessible via http://panda.org/news_facts/newsroom/press_releases/index.cfm.

2. See, for example, W. P. Strobel, "Earth Summit Ends with Boos for Colin Powell," Knight Ridder News Service, 5 September 2002, accessed via the *Philadelphia Inquirer* web site at http://www.philly.com/mld/inquirer/news/front/4003812.htm.

3. Maurice F. Strong, President, Council of the University for Peace, and Chairman, Earth Council Foundation, remarks given at the World Summit for Sustainable Development International Eminent Persons Meeting on Inter-Linkages—Bridging Problems and Solutions to Work towards Sustainable Development, United Nations University Centre, Tokyo, 3 September 2001 (see http://www.unu.edu/interlink).

4. K. A. Annan, "Toward a Sustainable Future," *Environment*, September 2002, 10–15 (from a lecture given by Mrs. Nane Annan at the American Museum of Natural History's annual environmental lecture, New York, 14 May 2002).

5. Ibid.

6. World Summit on Sustainable Development, *Plan of Implementation* (advance unedited text), 4 September 2002. Documents prepared for the summit and the final agreed-upon texts can be found at http://www.johannesburgsummit.org/.

7. Ibid., 17.

8. For more information, see the World Trade Organization web site at http://www.wto.org.

9. United Nations Millennium Declaration, adopted at the Millennium Summit, New York, 6–8 September 2000.

10. "The Bubble-and-Squeak Summit," *The Economist,* 7 September 2002, 69–70.

11. R. Pomeroy, "Industry Joins Greenpeace to Demand Climate Action," *World Environment News,* 30 August 2002, accessible via http://www.planetark.org.

12. R. L. Swarns, "Broad Accord Reached at Global Environment Meeting," *New York Times,* 4 September 2002, A6.

13. "EU Seeks Green Energy Goals After Summit Defeat," *World Environment News,* 9 June 2002, accessible via http://www.planetark.org.

14. T. Czuczka, "Germany Pushes for Renewable Energy Conference," *Environmental News Network,* 6 September 2002, accessible via http://www.enn.com.

15. "Small Is All Right," *The Economist,* 7 September 2002, 13–14.

14

A PARTICIPATORY APPROACH TO STRATEGIC PLANNING

RICHARD E. BISSELL

There is a dismal history of international commissions—generally long-winded, obscenely expensive, producing reports with the conclusions decided from the beginning and destined to consume too many trees in publishing a list of platitudes. On occasion, history gets a rude shock. One report that belies such jaundiced prejudices of global observers is the report of the World Commission on Dams (WCD), *Dams and Development: A New Framework for Decision-Making*, released in November 2000.[1] WCD, comprising twelve commissioners, was created in 1998 to review the performance of large dams and make recommendations regarding future water and energy projects.

Consider the words of the commission's chair, Kader Asmal, in the first paragraph of the report: "If politics is the art of the possible, this document is a work of art." Rarely has a commission taken an intransigent international controversy further into politics rather than fulfilling the hopes of the initiators that the commission would find a nonpolitical answer. The commission rejected a purely nonpolitical role, instead opting for the conclusion that politics is inherent in macroscale decisions such as billion-dollar dam projects. The commission determined that it is essential to first establish a fair process, whereby a "rights and risk" approach will put the social and environmental dimensions of dams on a plane with traditional economic and engineering considerations. (A rights and risk approach is a new tool for participatory decisionmaking that recognizes all legitimate rights of stakeholders and requires a complete assessment of risks to provide a full and fair set of development

Environment vol. 43, no. 7, pp. 37–40, September 2001. Reprinted with permission of the Helen Dwight Reid Educational Foundation. Published by Heldref Publications, 1319 Eighteenth St. N.W., Washington, D.C. 20036-1802. © 2001.

choices.) In effect, the commission turned upside down the expectations of those who launched this effort—the World Bank and the World Conservation Union (IUCN)—by placing healthy politics at the center of a solution that gives due place to technical criteria that also are essential.

Given the terrible controversies over large dams in the past decade, people can be forgiven for having forgotten the history of water management, power issues, and dams in the twentieth century. In the last 100 years, 45,000 large dams (dams that are more than 15 meters in height) have been built, a record examined with great care by the commission's report. The "boom" in this technology—peaking from the 1930s to the 1950s—was followed by growing caution in the United States and northern Europe in the last two decades. It took many years of experience with dams before people realized that there was no "free lunch" to be had.

The report builds on the progress of recent decades by emphasizing the need for multidisciplinary analysis. In the not-too-distant past, dam construction and management was a preserve for civil engineers. In time, economists began to poach on the engineering preserve, demanding rates of return and other microeconomic standards. In some countries, there has been successful incorporation of people from other disciplines as well—including sociologists, environmentalists, anthropologists, and climatologists—who tended to take a role in dam debates as an assertion of veto rights. Too often the issue on the table was, "Should we build this dam and how high should it be?" rather than "Among the various alternatives, including this dam, how should we achieve the water, energy, development, and environmental goals set by responsible authorities?" There was no uniform standard among countries as these disciplines and questions were adopted.

In the widening gap between national standards, international financial institutions drew crossfire from all sides. The debate took on a particular virulence in the development banks—the one place where all countries met, whether rich or poor—to decide on major infrastructure investments. Developing, maintaining, and removing infrastructure involves enormous resources, and with the payoff occurring over many years, it was natural that developing countries with large hydroelectric potential would look to foreign financiers for the imported component costs—turbines, transmission systems, and engineering skills. Therefore, at one level, the World Bank and the regional development banks were inevitably drawn into the decisionmaking. There were other institutions, however, also stirring the pot. Export credit agencies where turbine manufacturers were located played a part, and bilateral-aid donor agencies often got involved except in rare cases (for example, when the U.S. Agency for International Development removed itself from the capital projects business in the early 1970s by transferring such projects to the World Bank). Finally, the nongovernmental environmental organizations could not resist the opportunity to push their agendas beyond national boundaries and join the debate as well.

The stage was set, therefore, for conflicts such as the Sardar Sarovar controversy in the Narmada Valley of India, a massive project likely to displace several hundred thousand people that ripped apart any semblance of international consensus on dams in the 1990s. The principal external financier of that project, the World Bank, was forced to withdraw in 1993 with the emergence of a profound split among the borrower, the government of India, and the Bank over what kind of conditions could be attached to a loan for construction of the dam. That controversy has been analyzed elsewhere on many occasions, but most importantly, it set the Bank on a course of attempting to clear up its rights and responsibilities with regard to borrowers.[2] The Bank first tried to find agreement on guidelines among its creditors and borrowers, even creating the Inspection Panel in 1994—a three-member, semi-independent body—to monitor and ensure compliance, inter alia, with dam-related policies.[3] Over the first five years of the Inspection Panel's existence, about half of all its project inspections related to the construction of dams in countries ranging from Nepal and India to Brazil, Paraguay, and Argentina.[4]

When it turned out that the effect of the Inspection Panel's presence was unlikely to dampen controversies, senior management of the Bank argued that they needed to either get out of the dam-building business altogether or find a new avenue for reconciliation with all of the stakeholders. Thus it was, in 1997, that the World Bank's Operations Evaluation Division (under the sage leadership of Robert Picciotto) proposed that IUCN host a "dialog" in Gland, Switzerland, bringing together the most outspoken opponents and supporters of dams. The dialog, as it turned out, was sufficiently cordial for the World Bank and IUCN to agree that they should explore the creation of an international commission to review the "development effectiveness" of dams (to be defined by the commission) and to make recommendations for future standards that could be applied globally.

There were skeptics on all sides of this proposal. Bank management had never before gone outside the Bank for policy guidance. Dam opponents had established a public position that *no* large dams were acceptable, limiting the scope for any kind of dialog that might lead to compromise. Dam builders and equipment suppliers had always left discussions with dam opponents to governments and the World Bank, finding the terms of the arguments rather distasteful. Utilities and government ministries of energy doubted the usefulness of dialog in stabilizing the long-term supply of power on which they depended. Despite all these doubts, there was one common element: Because of the ongoing war over each dam project, there was diminishing common ground and therefore less likelihood of persuading the parties of another view. Based on the slim thread of hope of each party that they could achieve more through dialog than confrontation, the planning for a World Commission on Dams went forward. Nevertheless, throughout the next three years, each stakeholder would, on more than one occasion, decide that the potential outcome was not worth the investment of time and political capital and threaten to withdraw. However, in the end, almost none withdrew.

The chair was chosen first: Kader Asmal, minister of water in South Africa, a veteran of the anti-apartheid movement and senior member of the African National Congress Executive Committee, known for bringing consensus out of the most intractable situations. The diverse commission was chosen, including the CEO of a major manufacturer of dam turbines, a leader of a militant protest group against dams in India's Narmada Valley, and a leading academic expert on the social and resettlement issues associated with dams.[5] The commissioners came from all regions of the world and covered most major fields of knowledge relevant to decisions on dams. Parallel to the choice of commissioners was an informal dialog among representatives of some forty to fifty organizations to ensure agreement on the mandate for the commission, the choice of staff and commissioners, the time frame, and the financing of the effort. Each decision had to reflect joint ownership of the commission and a strong sense of shared participation. By the spring of 1998, the commission held its first meeting in Washington, D.C., and began to establish the relationships that would enable them to produce a report by late 2000.[6]

The thirty months of labor that followed included a time-bound mandate and an expectation articulated by the chair that the commission probably would not fulfill 100 percent of its goals. Asmal argued that the commission had a choice: It could labor until it completely met its mandate, which might take decades, or it could use a specific amount of time to solve as much as it could and leave the remainder of the tasks to other bodies. He clearly chose the latter option, saying informally that if the commission could complete 80 percent of the job, it would be an enormous success. Indeed, it was argued that if the commission could establish 80 percent of a consensus, the momentum should be sufficient to carry the multi-stakeholder community towards eventual agreement. By leaving unclear just which issues might remain unsettled at the end of the day, Asmal's formulation served to create more negotiating room during the commission process itself, and he deliberately left all issues on the table throughout the several years of commission deliberations.

The commission went out of its way to create an inclusive process. Meetings were held on all continents, studies were commissioned from experts in any countries with large dams, and contributions were solicited from people and organizations of any orientation. The establishment of a Web site with voluminous information, including drafts of case studies, allowed participation by anyone with Internet access. On several occasions, the process was so open that organizations with established roles in the controversies felt bypassed and had to be persuaded that the openness was not an attempt to sideline them. The WCD experience on transparency and disclosure should be reviewed by anyone establishing a future commission on what can be achieved with current information technologies.

In pursuit of its first mandate—to review the development effectiveness of dams—the commission reviewed more than 1,000 dams to some degree and 125 dams in great detail. It undertook country studies in the two most controversial cases (India and China), and most importantly, conducted river basin studies in several parts of the world. It also commissioned seventeen thematic reviews that examined the global inventory of 45,000 large dams in the context of specific attributes and policy issues. The thematic reviews involved evaluations of the social, environmental, and economic implications of dam projects, alternatives to dams, and governance and institutional processes. For instance, past plans for building dams included only the dam site and thus, did not evaluate the effects of the dam on the rest of the river basin. The WCD staff developed an extensive review of river basins as a planning framework, drawing on the work of a generation of geographers, including the work of Gilbert F. White.[7] WCD proceeded to build a database from which the public could reach conclusions as readily as the commission and staff. The commission drew two lessons from its review of the development effectiveness of the world's large dams. The first lesson was predictable, that dams have brought significant benefits to publics throughout the world, and that a large cost, often unrecognized owing to its diffuse social and environmental impact, was also incurred. The second lesson was that the most successful dams historically shared three characteristics: They reflected a comprehensive approach to integrating social, environmental, and economic dimensions of development; they created greater levels of transparency and certainty for all involved; and they have resulted in increased levels of confidence in the ability of nations and communities to meet their future water and energy needs.

As previously mentioned, WCD accumulated a massive database on large dams in the process of meeting that first mandate. With the termination of the commission, the fate of that database is unclear. The research community needs to ensure its survival and maintenance.*

The second mandate of WCD—to develop internationally acceptable criteria, guidelines, and standards, where appropriate, for the planning, design, appraisal, construction, operation, monitoring, and decommissioning of dams, was the main challenge for the commission members. The solution reached by WCD comprised three international norms: international recognition of human rights, the right to development, and the right to a healthy environment. In that context, WCD established seven policy principles for decisionmakers to follow: gain public agreement, conduct a comprehensive options assessment, address existing dams, sustain rivers and livelihoods, recognize entitlements and share benefits, ensure compliance, and share rivers for peace, development, and security.[8] At a minimum, the seven principles would serve as a valuable agenda from which any negotiation over a dam project might begin.

The impact of these seven principles issued unanimously by WCD has already been felt in the months since the report's release in November 2000. Many of the environmental nongovernmental organizations applauded the

---

*Editors' note: The United Nations Environment Programme subsequently launched a follow-up "Dams and Development Project" initiative.

conclusions; WCD was cited as a legitimizing source by the Narmada Bachao Andolan (NBA)—a grassroots organization in the Narmada Valley of central India—in its press release about the Maheshwar hydroelectric project in India when a foreign financier pulled out.

On the other hand, the World Bank has experienced a major internal debate over the implications of the WCD report. The Bank's board of executive directors is visibly concerned about the "costs of compliance" with the WCD approach and is quite doubtful the Bank can afford the possible increase in design and compliance charges for dam projects. The private sector is reconfiguring its involvement; Asea Brown Boveri, Ltd. (ABB) has sold off its hydro turbine business to focus on other forms of energy-producing capital equipment. In the United States, the reviews of the Snake River dams in Idaho, as well as the Glen Canyon Dam in Arizona, should be conceptually reinforced by the WCD approach because the U.S. Bureau of Reclamation, which is involved in conducting the reviews, closely tracked the commission's process.

At the conceptual level, the WCD report should lead to more integrative, place-based analysis of projects, including alternatives. World Bank staff have already noted the practice in the Asian Development Bank of undertaking analyses of alternatives and impacts of proposed dams further "upstream" in the project design process. The need is not for mere assessment of a dam after deciding on the project but rather the consideration of alternative sources of power, water, and flood control. Indeed, a major contribution of WCD is to expand the contextual understanding for deciding whether to undertake a dam project; in effect, they have said that decisions must involve people from other disciplines besides just engineers and microeconomists. And if those involved in making decisions about whether to begin dam projects are going to include people from other fields, the central questions about rights and risks must be asked earlier in the process. For instance, by arguing that "displacement" is more than just physical loss of land, WCD implicitly endorses the World Bank's proposal to strengthen its policy on involuntary resettlement, an inevitable result of dam or other large infrastructure projects. Such projects also cause "livelihood displacement," because far more people lose their jobs than lose their land as a result of large dams.[9]

The report should also lead to greater focus on accountability for development decisions, a matter of concern to far more than the dam community. The decisionmaking that goes into building a dam is ultimately a political process as much as a technical issue, and therefore, a political body has to make the decisions about dams. Most environmental issues involve trade-offs between various public interests. The weighing of those trade-offs is not an exact science, and thus, WCD appropriately suggests that a body with political accountability has to make the decisions. Democracies know that to be true, but countries in transition are not sure whether to involve the public in decisions that may have major environmental impacts. WCD is clear: When in doubt, go public.

The commission model is a powerful one: Establish a clear mandate, work for two years, and go out of business. Its exemplar is international strategic planning rather than more international government. It keeps accountability in the appropriate places, locally, nationally, and internationally. It also establishes a means of periodically comparing experience among countries and regions on troubling issues. Finally, this particular commission did an especially outstanding job of keeping the various stakeholders on board. That may be a function of the personalities rather than the structure, but for whatever reason, it showed that it can and should be done. Other highly contentious global issues could benefit from similar treatment.

Notes

1. World Commission on Dams (WCD), *Dams and Development: A New Framework for Decision-Making* (London and Sterling, VA: Earthscan, November 2000). This report is available in its entirety at http://www.dams.org.

2. B. Morse and T. R. Berger, *Sardar Sarovar: The Report of the Independent Review* (Ottawa: Resource Futures International, 1992).

3. I. F. I. Shihata, *The World Bank Inspection Panel* (Oxford University Press, published for the World Bank, 1994).

4. A. Umana, ed., *The World Bank Inspection Panel: The First Four Years* (1994–1998) (Washington, DC: World Bank for the Inspection Panel, 1998); and R. E. Bissell, "Recent Practice of the Inspection Panel of the World Bank," *American Journal of International Law* 91, no. 4 (1997):741–744.

5. The commissioners who signed the report included Kader Asmal (South Africa), Lakshmi Chand Jain (India), Judy Henderson (Australia), Goran Lindahl (Sweden), Thayer Scudder (United States), Joji Carino (Philippines), Donald Blackmore (Australia), Medha Patkar (India), José Goldemberg (Brazil), Deborah Moore (United States), Jan Veltrop (United States), and Achim Steiner (Germany).

6. The author was asked by the World Conservation Union (IUCN) and the World Bank, the two initiators of the commission process, to coordinate the appointment of the chair and commission, to initiate the fundraising, to build consultative mechanisms involving all stakeholders, and after WCD's first meeting, to hand off the management of WCD to the secretariat in Cape Town.

7. G. F. White, "The River as a System: A Geographer's View of Promising Approaches," *Water International* 22, no. 2 (1997):79–81; G. F. White, "Water Science and Technology: Some Lessons from the 20th Century," *Environment* (January/February 2000):30–88; and I. Burton, R. W. Kates, and G. F. White, eds., *Selected Writings of Gilbert F. White* (Chicago: University of Chicago Press, 1986).

8. WCD, *Dams and Development,* xxxiv–v.

9. Ibid., 102.

EXCERPT FROM *THE JO'BURG MEMO: FAIRNESS IN A FRAGILE WORLD*

A Memorandum for the World Summit on Sustainable Development

HENRI ACSELRAD (BRAZIL)
FARIDA AKHTER (BANGLADESH)
ADA AMON (HUNGARY)
TEWOLDE BERHAN GEBRE EGZIABHER
(ETHIOPIA)
HILARY FRENCH (USA)
PEKKA HAAVISTO (FINLAND)
PAUL HAWKEN (USA)
HAZEL HENDERSON (USA)
ASHOK KHOSLA (INDIA)
SARA LARRAIN (CHILE)
REINHARD LOSKE (GERMANY)
ANITA RODDICK (GREAT BRITAIN)
WOLFGANG SACHS (GERMANY)
VIVIENE TAYLOR (SOUTH AFRICA)
CHRISTINE VON WEIZSÄCKER (GERMANY)
AND SVIATOSLAV ZABELIN (RUSSIA)

Facilitating Institutions

As awareness of the bio-physical constraints to growth has finally emerged, institutions responding to this shift in the historical condition are called for. Today, besides peace, the environmental challenge is the most essential issue around which the entire UN system should revolve.

Move Toward a
World Environment Organization

Mistakes, once committed, tend to endure. Already the 1972 UN Conference on the Human Environment in Stockholm had failed to build a solid institutional base for addressing environmental issues within the UN family of organizations. UNEP, the first major international environmental institution, was a child of the 1972 conference and was supposed to stay small forever. As a simple program of ECOSOC and not an independent organization of the United Nations, UNEP was expected to act as an initiator and coordinator for other organizations, without an autonomous budget nor programs of its own. Institutionally, therefore, Stockholm left only a rather small legacy.

The set-up did not change in Rio. Instead, confusion was added to weakness. Here as well, the institutional outcome of the 1992 conference, the Commission on Sustainable Development, was not designed to lend authority to environment and development issues. The CSD developed into a forum of opinion-building for governments and stakeholders, wide-ranging and participative, but without decisionmaking or implementation power. Apart from the CSD, a string of conventions and treaties emerged as well, but without mutual coordination, which in turn fragmented rather than consolidated institutional coherence. Institutionally, therefore, Rio left a rather confused legacy.

As a result, environmental concerns are surprisingly under-institutionalized at the multilateral level. They are insufficiently embedded into institutional power and operative competence. It is therefore not astonishing that the issue of bio-physical limits has never become a defining issue for the UN, although, admittedly, a number of specialized agencies have taken environmental questions on board. Further, the weaker presence of environmental issues among UN organizations contributed to the focal shift from the UN institutions to the Bretton Woods institutions in the 1990s. While UN institutions stand for public values such as peace, human rights, and coopera-

Excerpted from Wolfgang Sachs, coordinator and editor, *The Jo'Burg Memo: Fairness in a Fragile World* (Berlin: Heinrich Böll Foundation, 2002). Reprinted with permission. Full text of *The Jo'Burg Memo* is available for download at www.joburgmemo.org.

tion, the trinity of World Bank, IMF, and WTO embodies economic values of competitiveness, currency stability, and open markets. This shift in favor of economic values came in the wake of corporate-led globalization, while the human rights-centered globalization of the UN receded into the background. Any institutional attempt to rebalance social, environmental, and economic values is bound to improve the overall profile of the environment.

At present, environmental governance is weak, fragmented, and generally ineffective. Admittedly, the rather chaotic, bottom-up process that has so far characterized environmental governance tends to be flexible and less controllable by a superior authority, but time might now be ripe to develop clearer structures that would deepen commitment, focus efforts, and enjoy parity with both UN and Bretton Woods institutions. Only a balance between a plurality of institutions will guarantee a balance between a plurality of objectives, be they social, environmental, or economic ones. No system of checks and balances can be installed unless organizations like the ILO, the WHO, and the WTO are joined by an environmental organization of equal standing.

Furthermore, too much fragmentation undermines effectiveness. There are now over 500 international treaties and agreements related to the environment, more than 300 of which have been adopted since Stockholm 1972, and 41 of which are considered core conventions.[1] As the number of treaties has increased, problems of duplication and lack of coordination have arisen. Besides, each treaty creates its own mini-institutional machinery, including annual meetings and secretariats, which are scattered around the world, causing international environmental diplomacy to resemble at times a moving circus. Finally, the outreach in particular to Southern countries appears to be sketchy. The activities of UNDP notwithstanding, capacity building in environmental affairs cannot be taken for granted, although agreements increasingly presuppose the necessary competence. There is also no organizational setting, except perhaps the Global Environmental Facility, for the multiple financial transfers linked to environmental agreements. In both respects, an environmental organization could provide stability and transparency for North-South transfers.

To strengthen environmental concerns within the architecture of global governance we suggest upgrading UNEP into a World Environment Organization. Such a body should have its own budget, its own sources of reliable funding, its own legal personality, increased financial and staff resources, expanded competence, and an adequate governance structure. Funds could come from member governments and from new sources such as user fees on global commons. The elevation of UNEP to a World Environment Organization could be modeled either on the WHO and the ILO or on the UN Conference on Trade and Development (UNCTAD), a body established by the UN General Assembly for debate and cooperation on international trade policy. Apart from UNEP, the organization could integrate the relevant convention secretariats. Its main areas of activity would be to coordinate global environmental governance, oversee capacity building and transfers, and support the definition of multilateral standards and agreements. However, it should be emphasized that the organization should be horizontal in character rather than hierarchical. It will be an institution of cooperative governance and not an institution of global government. Its decisionmaking structure should be governed by a North-South parity system requiring a simple majority from either side.

Establish an International
Renewable Energy Agency

Moving toward solar economies worldwide implies a fundamental shift in the resource base of society. Eventually, the demand for energy and raw materials will be met from solar sources of energy and solar raw materials. Already now, a host of renewable energy technologies is available, including thermal and photovoltaic solar energy, wind power, regenerative biomass, wave as well as tidal power, and small hydroelectric power systems. As is well known, a transition to renewable energies is the regal road toward sustainability; they are climate-friendly, pollution-free, and inexhaustible.

Sunlight is most abundant where the majority of the world's poorest people live. Numerous studies have shown that, if efficiently used, insolation and biomass are sufficiently available to support a decent level of well-being continuously, indefinitely, and economically, everywhere on the globe. Indeed, in the future, renewables will have the potential to satisfy the actual world energy demand many times over. It is therefore only on the basis of renewables that Southern and transitional countries will be able to meet their growing energy needs. Besides, these technologies reduce the dependence on primary energy imports and save money usually spent on the infrastructure needed to distribute conventional forms of energy. In fact, renewable energy can be collected and converted for use at the very location where energy is needed. It is the only way to make power available without forbidding costs, since expensive energy grids will not have to be built and no long-distance transport is required. This is crucial, given that two billion people currently live in areas with no access to power grids.

Industrial countries—and the urban-industrial poles in many developing countries—face an analogous challenge, only from a different point of departure. Locked as they are in systems of conventional energy supply, they will have to back out of this dead end and embark upon a full-scale transformation of their resource base.

Recently, several such countries have demonstrated that high growth rates for renewable energies are possible when a favorable political framework exists. Incentives have been offered to stimulate manufacturing of renewable supply technologies at a large scale. If the use of renewables can be rendered economically viable, the market for them will expand. This has been achieved in several European countries by feed-in laws, which set the price at which grid operators have to purchase electricity produced by independent, decentralized producers. As a result, new production outlets have been built, and major cost reductions have been achieved. Experiences in Germany, Spain, Finland, and Austria suggest that a shift to renewables could be achieved in the course of a few decades. Moreover, the same experiences indicate that such a shift will not imply higher economic cost at the macro scale, but rather additional benefits, such as less damage caused by fossil and nuclear energy, less unemployment, independence from fuel imports, and greater supply security.

Since the transition to renewable fuels and materials must occur quickly and on a broad scale, there should be a specialized international agency created for this purpose. The proposal is for the establishment of an "International Renewable Energy Agency (IRENA)." Such a proposal was first launched in 1980 by the North-South Commission, presided over by Willy Brandt, and more recently promoted by EUROSOLAR. The organization describes the tasks of IRENA as follows:

- drawing up national programs for the introduction of renewable energies;
- supporting education, training, and the dissemination of information about renewables;
- implementing training activities for administrators, technicians, craftsmen, and for small and medium enterprises;
- the cooperative foundation of regional centers of research, development, and transfer of technologies of renewable energy;
- evaluating and processing information on applied technology and best practice experience;
- advising on and arranging financing options for renewables;
- collecting data and drawing up statistics.

It is advisable to set up such an agency in a decentralized fashion, following the model of the CGIAR, the institutes of agricultural research working under the auspices of the UN in different locations around the world. Interestingly, the International Atomic Energy Agency (IAEA), which was established in 1958, had among its tasks the noncommercial transfer of nuclear technology. What was deemed necessary at the time is now imperative for renewable energies. Indeed, as nuclear is obsolete, IRENA may well replace the IAEA one day. Furthermore, IRENA will have to be independent of economic interests and be financed by member countries. As with the founding of the IAEA, a movement on the part of just a handful of governments suffices for the creation of such an agency, which would offer membership to all interested nations. By putting its basic commitments into practice, the agency can establish a positive reputation and thus attract new member countries.

Transpose Dispute Resolution—
International Court of Arbitration

Global society, not unlike national societies, is pervaded by conflicts. As nations and corporations, communities and individuals bring extraordinarily diverse experiences, interests, and worldviews to bear on the global stage, conflict cannot be dreamed away; on the contrary, conflicts generate the upheavals, alliances, and ideologies of that amalgam called global society. There is no universal way of seeing; there are only context-bound viewpoints that offer particular perspectives. Any architecture of global governance is therefore well advised to start with the assumption that conflicts bubbling up from society are neither avoidable nor finally resolvable. In the best case, they can be identified before turning violent, peacefully settled, and redirected into a productive tension.

Liberal democracies have known that all along. For this reason, their political framework is based on institutions of conflict management. Parliaments, courts, and a debating public are the cornerstones of an order that aims at regulating conflicts rather than eliminating them. It is striking that there is a dearth of such institutions at the global level. Moreover, liberal states have adopted the principle of separation of powers, which, by dividing legislative, executive, and judicial powers, constrains authority with a system of checks and balances. This separation of powers too is still rudimentary, and in most cases nonexistent at the global level.

The World Trade Organization has staked out its claim in this gap. It has for all practical purposes become the supreme governance authority, one that implicitly distills legislative, executive, and judicial functions into one single institution. On a very straightforward level, trade affects everybody, but WTO committees are mainly populated by state representatives, economists, and males. By merely shaking up this composition and opening decisionmaking on trade to politicians, non-economists, and women, the picture would be markedly different; the world would cease to be dominated by the single worldview of neoclassical economics.

However, above all on an institutional level, the authority of the WTO derives from its dispute settlement system. Not only are the judges on the dispute panels appointed by the WTO and chosen for their trade background rather than for their social or environmental expertise (often required by the subject matter of the case), but it is a settlement system with teeth. The ruling of the Dispute Settlement Body is automatically adopted by the whole membership, and noncompliant countries face fines or punitive trade measures. Only consensus can overturn such a final decision, a situation that calls into question whether standards of due process are lacking. With this powerful instrument at hand, the WTO Dispute Settlement system makes pronouncements which affect areas beyond its mandate, namely environmental, social, and human rights matters, by redefining them as trade-relevant issues.

Thereby, the WTO usurps the competence to judge not only on trade but on broad aspects of public life. While the WTO competence needs to be scaled down, the competence of the UN system and organizations like the International Labor Organization, the World Health Organization, and eventually the World Environment Organization will have to be expanded. It is high time to restore a true balance of power between the two conflicting sets of global institutions, the WTO (along with World Bank and IMF) on the one side and the UN system on the other.

Conflicts are inevitable; therefore a supranational judicial body is needed for the impartial resolution of competing concerns. We argue for moving certain disputes out of the WTO Dispute Settlement system into an international court of arbitration.

Such a court already exists: the century-old Permanent Court of Arbitration in the Hague. In fact, taking into account the *lacunae* in existing dispute settlement mechanisms such as the WTO, the 94 Member States of the PCA adopted "Optional Rules for Arbitration of Disputes Relating to Natural Resources and/or the Environment" in June 2001. The PCA and its Environmental Rules have the following features:

- Not only states can bring cases to the PCA, but also any combination and number of nonstate actors, such as intergovernmental and nongovernmental organizations, corporations, and private parties.
- Parties voluntarily agree to enter arbitration and to accept outcomes as binding. They agree to settle a dispute on any issue, and may refer to provisions in existing contracts, agreements, conventions, etc., in relation to which or out of which a dispute arises. Consent to arbitrate may be given prior to the dispute in a contract or treaty, but may also be given *ad hoc* pursuant to a submission agreement.
- Arbitrators are chosen case by case. A list of experts in environmental law to draw from in selecting an arbitrator is available, as is a list of environmental science experts to assist the tribunal.
- The arbitral tribunal hears cases on the basis of statements by the claimant and the defense, possible witnesses, documents, and other kinds of evidence.
- The tribunal may order interim measures of protection falling within the subject matter of the dispute to preserve the rights of any party or to prevent serious harm to the environment falling within the subject matter of the dispute.
- The arbitral award is enforceable through national courts.

Because the PCA Environmental Rules can deal with questions of interpretation of the universe of environmental agreements, ensure access to justice for the global society, and offer access to environmental legal and scientific expertise, they represent the most advanced mechanism currently available for settling international environmental and/or natural resources disputes.

Notes

1. United Nations Environmental Programme, *International Environmental Governance: Multilateral Environmental Agreements (MEAs)*. Paper prepared for the Open-Ended Inter-governmental Group of Ministers on International Environmental Governance, Bonn, Germany, 2001.

16

SKINNING
SCIENTIFIC CATS

Sheila Jasanoff

Let me begin with the picture that unquestionably accounts for the birth of the modern environmental movement. The World Commission on Environment and Development has this to say in its influential work, *Our Common Future:*

> In the middle of the 20th century, we saw our planet from space for the first time. Historians may eventually find that this vision had a greater impact on thought than did the Copernican revolution of the 16th century. . . . From space we see a small and fragile ball, dominated not by human activity and edifice, but a pattern of clouds, greenery, oceans and soil. Humanity's inability to fit its activities into that pattern is changing boundary systems fundamentally.

The idea of the scientific revolution is never far from the minds of those who comment on the Apollo picture. Many environmentalists have argued that what the picture of the biosphere truly accomplished was a paradigm shift in our ways of thinking about how the world works: the "fourth discontinuity." It was a moment that displaced the human ego by making it conscious of the physical finiteness of the place it inhabits. The effect was on a par with the three great discontinuities of the past: the Copernican revolution, which displaced the earth from the centre of the human universe, the Darwinian revolution, which displaced human beings from the pinnacle of the tree of creation, and the Freudian revolution, which exposed the unconscious, and told humankind that we are not the masters in our own house.

Originally published in *New Statesman and Society,* 26 February 1993, pp. 29–30. Reprinted with permission.

But the scientific paradigm of ecological interconnectedness does not, in fact, provide answers to questions about what we human beings are entitled to do with our environment. What science is, and how we apply it to our needs, is thus far from straightforward.

The first point I want to make is that scientific inquiry, contrary to expectation, does not always lead to the same explanation for the same observed phenomenon. Consider the seasonal flooding in the plains of northern India, where two competing theories obstinately occupy the field. On the one hand, there is a "mountain theory," preferred by environmental bureaucrats and developers, that holds that population pressure in the foothills of the Himalayas is causing deforestation and soil erosion, and that these effects in turn are responsible for the flooding below.

The contrasting "plains theory," upheld by environmental activists and indigenous people living in the hilly regions, ascribes the flooding to poor resource-management practices lower down. For them, it is the indiscriminate clearing of forests, the damming of rivers, and the resulting siltation of river beds that lead to uncontrollable floods. Uphill tree cutting adds little or nothing in the way of separate environmental stress. So who is to blame? The non-modernised primitive practices of ecologically unconscious indigenous peoples somewhere up in the mountains? Or a model of development dominated by centralised money-lenders, international financial and other institutions?

Controversies of this kind are familiar to many people, and science seems unable to provide satisfying answers. For in the complex systems under study, enough suggestive and even persuasive evidence can be found to sustain very different overall stories about what is *really* going on. Lacking ways of testing or falsification, neither theoretical position is able to deal a body blow to the other. Ideology and politics thus become the primary determinants of choosing among competing scientific accounts of felt reality.

A second point of almost equal importance is that when people reach scientific conclusions about the reasons for a particular natural phenomenon, their explanations are not always the same. To take one case, US public health experts have been convinced for many years that an important reason to reduce lead levels in the environment is the damage the metal causes even at lowest-dose levels to children's learning behavior. When Britain decided to phase out lead additives from petrol, almost ten years after the US, the reasons the British experts provided did not prominently include children's health, an issue regarded as hopelessly uncertain and divisive. Rather their decision was based on findings that lead was toxic, even at very low doses, that it was highly persistent in the environment, and that alternatives to many current uses of lead could be found without damaging the economy. So, in the end, both these countries chose to phase lead additives out of petrol, but the scientific pathways they took to get to these results were very different.

A third point that complicates our initially simplistic connection between science and action is that what compels people to act upon a perceived problem is not necessarily knowledge that is endorsed by science. An example of such an unscientific consensus are the factors that produced agreement on the Mediterranean Action Plan. Many countries signed on to the treaty because of a mistaken but compelling notion that pollution anywhere in the Mediterranean basin would be equally harmful to all of the coastal states.

By some accounts, UN Environment Programme experts, who participated in the treaty negotiations, apparently knew that the ecological paradigm as applied to the Mediterranean did not in fact drive everybody's pollution up on everybody else's shores. But they withheld this knowledge from the participants, on the theory that it was desirable for the right decision to be taken, in environmental terms, even on the basis of the wrong scientific reason.

In fourth place, just as too little science can sometimes aid decision-making, so too much science sometimes overwhelms the capacity to act. There are many reasons why this can be the case. More information may, to begin with, simply create more grounds for argument, especially when strong enough refereeing agencies cannot be found. Information, too, can outstrip the capacity of our societies to analyse, synthesise and apply to programmes of action. In our own recent past, environmental problems that have reached such a stalemate of knowledge include, prominently, the acid rain controversy, where no new study, however compelling, was likely to change how people believed on that issue. Unless great care is taken, there are signs that at least aspects of the climate-change problem are in danger today of being studied to death in this fashion.

Fifth, and finally, I'd like to mention those instances when states or interest groups agree that a problem exists, but cannot agree about how the problem should be conceptualised for purposes of scientific investigation. To decide what needs to be studied, one needs, in effect, to impose a kind of moral map on the issue in question. And this map may differ from country to country, or even from one scientific organisation to another.

Let's take the so-called problem of human cancer. Now there appears to be good scientific agreement that some fraction of human cancers are caused by environmental factors, such as diet, smoking, certain lifestyle choices *and* by exposure to chemicals. Yet if you look across the spectrum of research-rich nations, the emphasis has not, in fact, been equal on all of these possible areas of explanation. No other country, to my knowledge, can match the US in the richness, intensity, scope and variety of programmes for researching the health effects of industrial chemicals, including their carcinogenicity.

As a result, many have found it difficult to avoid the conclusion that chemicals occupy a different niche in the collective American consciousness of environmental hazards from the niche they occupy in any other country. When it comes to studying the causes of complex environmental problems, there is almost always more than one way to skin the scientific cat. And these choices are not themselves scientific. They're deeply social, cultural, and ethical.

A historical example of this was the mid-century study, funded by the Rockefeller Foundation, to study and solve the problem of world hunger. We all know the miraculous results of that voyage of discovery, the creation of those high-yielding grain varieties that ushered in the green revolution. But students of the green revolution have come in time to ask not merely what was achieved and scientifically celebrated, but also what was not studied, what went unexplored or under-explored, like the environmental consequences of the heavy use of pesticides and fertilisers, which were needed to make the green revolution take root and flourish. The individual life experiences, or even the collective local knowledge of the groups that science was going to help, whose problem of hunger science was going to solve, never figured in the scientific agenda setting.

You will recognise that the implicit hierarchy that the green revolution scientists established is the hierarchy that dominates our western scientific sensibility that some approaches to understanding nature are superior to others. In this hierarchy, not surprisingly, it is the basic physical and biological sciences that occupy the top of the ladder. The social sciences are relegated to some indeterminate middle position. Much lower down, usually disappearing from the frame of inquiry completely, are the unsystematised or nonprofessionalised ways of knowing nature that are characteristic of the people often living closest to environmental problems.

If more international cooperation in science is necessary to do a better job of understanding and coping with environmental change, then we are not going to get much international cooperation unless we sit down together and address some very important prior questions: What is the problem we are trying to define? From whose point of view is it a problem? Why is it seen as scientific? What do we mean by science? And which areas of science are we going to privilege while we go about seeking solutions?

PART FOUR

INSTITUTIONS AS THOUGH THE EARTH MATTERED

Much of the effort to promote international environmental cooperation has focused on issue-specific agreements for pressing environmental problems such as climate change, depletion of the ozone layer, or the use of toxic chemicals. But as such agreements have come into force, it has become clear that their effectiveness can be limited by the environmentally destructive effects of more fundamental economic and political processes in the world system. Practices such as international trade, foreign investment, technology transfer, and development assistance can have effects that cut across issue-specific environmental concerns such as soils, forests, or water quality.

Oran Young has defined institutions as "social practices consisting of easily recognized roles coupled with clusters of rules or conventions governing relations among the occupants of these roles."[1] This definition of institutions, stressing roles and rules, is not synonymous with organizations, which are "material entities possessing physical locations (or seats), offices, personnel, equipment, and budgets."[2] Many institutions have a formal organizational base; others, such as language systems or the family, endure informally, being reproduced over time by the beliefs and practices of individuals and groups.

International trade, as codified in the General Agreement on Tariffs and Trade (GATT), the World Trade Organization (WTO), and regional arrangements such as the European Union and the North American Free Trade Agreement (NAFTA), is an example of an institution—in Young's sense of roles and rules—with important consequences for the global environment. Development assistance, as practiced by the World Bank, the other multilateral development banks, and the various bilateral programs linking Northern aid donors and Southern recipients, is another. As the environmental impact of these and other international economic practices has become more apparent, pressures have mounted for international institutional reform. In this chapter we examine trade and aid as two central components of this broader debate.

Environmentalists began to focus serious attention on links between trade and the environment in the 1990s. They did so for several reasons, including the increasingly apparent environmental consequences of trade, the growing importance of trade in the world economy, and an emerging flurry of efforts to rewrite the rules of the international trading game through agreements such as NAFTA and GATT. The ensuing trade-environment debate has reflected what are often fundamentally different perspectives about environmental externalities, about fairness in international trade competition, and about the appropriate way to view economic growth.[3] Although most participants in this debate agree on the importance of protecting the environment and promoting prosperity, they disagree strongly on which institutional path to take in order to achieve those goals.

Tony Juniper of Friends of the Earth International summarizes many of the standard criticisms of current international trade practices offered by environmentalists.[4] For Juniper, trade should be understood and judged not as an end in itself but as a means to the larger aim of sustainability, with decisions on trade liberalization taken accordingly. For Juniper, aggressive trade liberalization promotes materials-intensive, unsustainable economic growth; destabilizes local communities; worsens the income gap between rich and poor that lies at the heart of many environmental ills; and undermines multilateral environmental agreements (MEAs) that often seek to employ trade restrictions as compliance incentives.

Daniel Esty presents a more reform-minded perspective on the trade-environment linkage. In his view, much of the problem lies not with trade itself, which he sees as providing important economic benefits useful for sustainable development. Rather, for Esty much of the problem stems from the specific practices embraced by the WTO, which focus inadequate attention on legitimate environmental concerns and operate in a context of excessive exclusion and secrecy. In marked contrast to Juniper's structural critique, Esty offers a reformist agenda centered primarily on procedural changes to facilitate openness and dialogue between trade and environmental advocates. His more limited agenda for substantive reform centers on topics where environmentalists and trade advocates are said to have common ground, such as the elimination of subsidies that are both environmentally harmful as well as trade distorting.

Clearly, proponents and opponents of trade liberalization have different visions not simply of the environmental consequences of trade but of the costs and benefits of trade-based economic interdependence more generally. Advocates of trade liberalization often warn that we must pay careful attention to the stability of the international trading system.[5] In this view, we should not risk trade wars by implementing protectionist measures to promote what are often subjective, culturally specific environmental goals. Instead, environmental goals should be accomplished with diplomacy and domestic legislation that minimize the impact on the trading system. Those opposing trade liberalization on environmental grounds often argue that the assumptions behind the neoclassical vision of free trade, comparative advantage, and gains from specialization are no longer valid. Now that capital is so mobile internationally, it can easily move to those countries with less rigorous environmental, wage, or safety standards. The result is not enhanced global economic efficiency but the propagation of market distortions and externalities.

The case of development assistance provides an interesting contrast to international trade in that a process of institutional reform for the purposes of environmental protection is already well under way. The World Bank, in particular, as the financially and intellectually dominant international organization on the development scene, has felt substantial pressure to change its lending practices. Beginning in the mid-1980s, the World Bank's role in distributing tens of billions of dollars annually for development projects, including many with devastating environmental impacts, made it a target of criticism from non-governmental organizations in both the North and the South.[6] As a result, the Bank began to institute a series of internal reforms aimed at improving its environmental performance.

Frances Seymour and Navroz Dubash describe the campaign to change the World Bank's environmental practices and the Bank's response to those pressures. They highlight some achievements, particularly in the realm of new guidelines and procedures and a shift toward what the authors refer to as a "do no harm" philosophy. They also warn of a growing sense of complacency with the reform effort, if not outright retrenchment, which they find troubling in light of the Bank's still spotty record of performance in implementing these reforms at the project level.

Others offer a more optimistic view. According to Mohamed T. El-Ashry, writing in 1993 as the World Bank's Director of Environment:

All Bank-financed projects are now categorized according to their potential environmental impact. Only projects that are unlikely to have adverse environmental effects—projects such as family planning, education, health and nutrition projects—are not subject to environmental scrutiny. All others must undergo either an environmental analysis or a full-blown environmental assessment depending on the potential significance of their environmental consequences.[7]

El-Ashry described the World Bank's response to its critics as a four-part strategy: comprehensive environmental assessment procedures for Bank–funded projects; exploitation of the "synergies between poverty reduction and environmental improvement"; assistance to member countries in the development of national environmental institutions and the building of domestic bureaucratic and administrative capacity; and grants and technical assistance made through the Global Environment Facility.

As an indicator of the direction of new thinking within at least some parts of the World Bank, we present here a short essay on the "four capitals" of sustainability, coauthored by Ismail Serageldin, who served for several years as the Bank's Vice President for Socially and Environmentally Sustainable Development. Although preserving the emphasis on "capital" typical of what is at heart a financial institution, Serageldin's framework broadens the notion of capital substantially to take into account environmental goods and services (natural capital), networks of social ties (social capital), and the possibilities of knowledge and learning (human capital). In doing so, the authors recognize an overly narrow emphasis within the Bank traditionally on financial capital as the sole pillar of "development."

Despite organizational and procedural changes within the World Bank, even the optimists acknowledge that change in practice has been uneven. As with any large organization, reform in the Bank has collided with bureaucratic inertia and resistance. To underscore both the possibilities of and barriers to change, we include an extended excerpt from a report by the World Bank Inspection Panel, a body that was itself created as a result of criticism directed at the Bank. The Inspection Panel decides whether to investigate grievances brought by citizens in countries with Bank-funded projects; it can issue independent reports on whether the Bank has complied with its own rules and standards on issues such as environmental assessment, forced resettlement of local communities, and the treatment of indigenous people. Bank observers have had differing opinions on whether the panel constitutes evidence of a changing organizational culture.[8] The report excerpted here, on an agricultural colonization project in western China, is one of the panel's strongest criticisms to date of Bank practices. It documents numerous instances in which changed thinking and operational guidelines have not translated fully into good practices on the ground.

Reformers within and around the World Bank argue that despite such enduring problems, the process of change is now irreversible. This optimism is in stark contrast with the skepticism of some of the Bank's more vocal critics, who argue that the Bank is embedded in a set of institutional and political contradictions that limit the possibilities of its reform.[9] From this perspective the key to change is not better guidelines but rather for concerned groups from both the North and the South to continue to press the Bank to become more open and democratic in its operations.

One clear lesson from both the trade and aid domains is that implementing effective reforms will require careful attention to the internal workings of entities such as the WTO and the World Bank. Failure to take into account the incentive structures of the actors involved can be devastating to reform efforts. At the same time, we must ask whether internal change of the sort advocated by reformers can be effective if the skeptics are correct in concluding that prevailing institutions reflect a larger, structural logic in which environmental concerns are marginalized.

Thinking Critically

1. Compare Juniper's and Esty's ideas on the appropriate response to trade-environment controversies. To the extent that they differ, does the difference lie in the realm of theory, values, goals, evidence, or all of the above?

2. Do Esty's process-oriented reforms address Juniper's substantive concerns? If these were the opening statements in an actual face-to-face debate, what would you expect each to say in round 2? What sort of evidence would be required to settle their central points of disagreement?

3. How optimistic or pessimistic should we be about the possibilities for change in a large, centralized institution such as the World Bank? How might the problems identified in the World Bank Inspection Panel report be addressed? Are they problems of organizational culture, inadequate rule compliance, institutional design, monitoring, or . . . ?

4. Would the reforms advocated by Seymour and Dubash turn the World Bank into an agent of environmentally sustainable development? Would you expect support for or opposition to the proposed reforms from donor countries? From borrower countries? From within the Bank itself?

Notes

1. See Oran Young, *International Cooperation: Building Regimes for Natural Resources and the Environment* (Ithaca, NY: Cornell University Press, 1989), p. 32.

2. Ibid.

3. See for example the exchange between Herman Daly and Jagdish Bhagwati in the November 1993 issue of *Scientific American.*

4. See also Ken Conca, "The WTO and the Undermining of Global Environmental Governance," *Review of International Political Economy* 7, no. 3 (Autumn 2000):484–494.

5. On protectionism and the stability of the international trading system, see Jagdish Bhagwati, *Protectionism* (Cambridge, MA: MIT Press, 1989).

6. The origins of the campaign to change the World Bank are described in Pat Aufderheide and Bruce Rich, "Environmental Reform and the Multilateral Banks," *World Policy Journal* 5, no. 2 (Spring 1988):301–321.

7. Mohamed T. El-Ashry, "The Road from Rio: Implications of the UN Conference on Environment and Development for the World Bank," *Journal of Environment and Development* 2, no. 2 (Summer 1993):69.

8. See for example the exchange between Paul Nelson and Rodger Payne in *Journal of Peace Research* 34, no. 4 (1997).

9. Bruce Rich, *Mortgaging the Earth: The World Bank, Environmental Impoverishment, and the Crisis of Development* (Boston: Beacon Press, 1994).

17

PRESENTATION
TO THE WORLD TRADE
ORGANIZATION SYMPOSIUM

Geneva, 29 April 2002

TONY JUNIPER, FRIENDS
OF THE EARTH INTERNATIONAL

Friends of the Earth International—What Is It?

Friends of the Earth International is a federation of 68 grassroots and independent national member Friends of the Earth organizations working from
the local to the international level in pursuit of sustainable development. We
have members north, south, east, and west. Contrary to some perceptions, we
are not a Northern organization, but a global federation bringing local and
grassroots views not only to national and local policymakers, but to international forums too. . . .

The WTO Is Not Advancing the
Cause of Sustainable Development

The [World Trade Organization (WTO)] agreement preamble places the objective of "sustainable development" at the heart of the WTO's work. How-

Tony Juniper, Friends of the Earth International. Excerpted from presentation to the World Trade
Organization Symposium Geneva, 29 April 2002. Reprinted with permission.

ever, the rules that the WTO creates and maintains have not turned this rhetoric into reality.

Certainly we believe it is possible to achieve sustainable development. So do apparently the majority of the world's governments who promised ten years ago in Rio de Janeiro to deliver policies to do just that. Our contention, however, is that one of the most potent tools governments have, namely the creation and operation of multilateral rules governing trade, is presently being misused.

Far from promoting sustainability through the integration of economic, environmental, and social policy, international discussions on the liberalization of commerce are trading one agenda (the economy) against another (local communities and environment) in such a way as to not only present false choices (namely social justice and environment protection or development) but is also becoming dangerously confused about the extent to which sustainable development is primarily, or even only, about wealth creation.

The Impacts of Corporate-Led Trade Liberalization—Why It Is Not Conducive to Sustainable Development

The reality is that the impacts of trade liberalization have worsened some crucial sustainability trends rather than improved them.

- Perhaps the most fundamental flaw arises from the pursuit of growth at any cost and the increasing tendency toward the promotion of liberalization and trade as ends in themselves. This leads to, among other things, increased consumption, waste of natural resources, and transport pollution. And in many cases where trade rules have come into conflict with environmental regulations both internationally and nationally, almost always the trade rules take precedence. Look at the example of the USA and its choice to defend the competitiveness of its companies rather than reduce greenhouse gas emissions in line with its Kyoto obligations.
- Economic instability arising from financial deregulation has also caused economic chaos in some countries leading to, for example, capital flight and serious impacts on poor people. Also, in the least developed nations, largely as a consequence of trade and economic policies conceived in Northern-dominated institutions, investment has been concentrated on the production of primary commodities that has had the effect of overproduction leading to declining terms of trade for many exporter nations. This situation has not been helped by trade barriers to processed goods designed to protect industries in the richer importing countries. The effect of these circumstances has in turn been the promotion of policies to increase production, often associated with

very grave environmental impacts—the clearance of natural forests to make way for large-scale farms and mines, for example.

- Also, free trade policies, by establishing market conditions that require economic actors of different strengths to compete with each other on a legally equal footing, have pitted weak actors against strong ones and institutionalized the market dominance of transnational corporations (TNCs) in international (and increasingly in domestic) markets at the expense of small and medium enterprises—especially of those from developing and least developed countries. Small companies seeking to compete with the likes of Microsoft, Monsanto, McDonald's, and Mitsubishi stand little chance of commercial survival. The transnational corporations have thus thrived, often at the expense of smaller companies and local economies, and in the process virtually foreclosing the ability of local communities and governments—especially from developing and least developed countries—to foster and support domestic industries in ways that support sustainable development and progressively prepare them to compete globally.

- This trend has helped to ensure that the benefits of free trade have been unevenly distributed. It is the already wealthy who have gained most—the gap between the richest and poorest in global society grows ever wider: in 1960, the richest 20 percent of people were 30 times better off than the poorest 20 percent; by 1997, they were 70 times richer; today the disparity is even worse. This trend moved the [United Nations Development Programme] to remark in 1996 that "the imbalances in economic growth, if allowed to continue, will produce a world gargantuan in its excesses and grotesque in its human and economic inequalities." Far from solving the problem of poverty, it seems that in some parts of the world—especially among the developing and least-developed countries—that the international trading system is making matters worse.

- A consequence of all of this has been the accumulation of a vast ecological debt owed by the rich Northern consumer countries to the resource-providing nations of the South. Heavy financial debt burdens on impoverished countries encourage governments to facilitate increased exploitation of natural resources for export in order to generate foreign exchange. Export-led development programs have reinforced this short-term and damaging approach, creating a vicious circle in which world markets are oversupplied, commodity prices tumble, and poverty-stricken countries are forced to increase exports. In addition, heavily indebted countries are often forced to slash environmental and social spending, making it difficult for governments to pursue sustainability objectives. Thus rich, importing countries have ready access to cheap supplies of natural resources and have, in fact, incurred an ecological debt to the countries of the South—which, it should be noted, far, far outweighs the official financial debt owed to them by the South.

"Free" Trade Theory Is a Fundamentally Flawed Idea and Is Anyway Not a Sincerely Held Political Idea

These observations lead us to believe that free trade theory is out of date; capital is increasingly mobile and therefore the theory of comparative advantage is no longer tenable. The idea that each country should exploit its own unique advantages is being replaced with the reality of absolute advantage. This means that the win-win scenario promoted by advocates of free trade worldwide is increasingly one of win-lose. As the global economy is progressively opened, some will win, others will not.

Also there is, as far as we can see, no proof that economic liberalization even leads to economic growth—let alone sustainable development. Thus is the fragility of an idea that now shapes virtually all policymaking the world over.

And not only is the present system highly questionable from the evidence to show it works, it is also a questionable idea in terms of the practice. The behavior of the USA with respect to steel imports is a recent case in point: The free trade rhetoric was gladly abandoned there in order to cater for domestic political pressures. I wonder what would have been the reaction of the USA if one of the economically weak countries it trades with behaved in a similar way? Perhaps the approach of the U.S. toward Caribbean banana farmers gives a clue.

And what about the European Union with its vast farm subsidies? Developing nations are urged by European leaders to open their markets while the EU protects its own. Even now, while the demise of the CAP is virtually assured by political and economic changes inside the EU itself, Europeans refuse to hand over the CAP as a sign of goodwill in trade talks. They'd rather keep it for use as a bargaining chip to extract concessions elsewhere—perhaps in exchange for access to the services sector in dozens of developing countries.

Not only have developed countries, in the past six and a half years that the WTO has been in existence, not implemented in full the promises that they made in the Uruguay Round, but in the current Doha agenda, they are asking developing and least-developed countries to give them even more binding commitments in exchange for more promises. Not only has the Uruguay Round check bounced against developing and least-developed countries, but the North seems to be once again prepared to issue another bouncing check in exchange for more binding commitments from developing and least-developed countries under the Doha agenda.

These kinds of behaviors lead many of us in civil society to conclude that what governments call "free" trade is not about global collective interest or sustainable development—it is about national self-interest and national gain, not least on behalf of transnational corporations, especially in the North. If you are rich and powerful, in the win-lose world you stand to gain most; perhaps that is why the most assured free trade proponents are from the governments of the developed North and the transnational corporations based there.

The Specific Concerns We
Have about the Doha Mandate

The Doha agenda represents in itself a deepening of the applicability of
WTO rules into areas already covered under the Uruguay Round (i.e., agriculture, industrial goods, and services) and a possible expansion of such
rules into other areas (such as investment, competition policy, and government procurement, and trade facilitation) whose impacts on people and the
environment, especially in developing and least-developed countries, have
been and might be more negative than positive. Such possible expansion is
not necessary and may only serve to skew the global trading system even
more in favor of the "haves" and even more against the "have nots"—not
only in terms of economic equity and social justice but also in terms of environmental sustainability.

With these fundamental concerns in mind, Friends of the Earth International was present in Doha to make the case for deep reforms in how the trading system operates. Our basic point was to argue that governments should
review the impact of existing free trade policies on local communities and the
environment before embarking on new negotiations. In the light of what was
agreed in Doha, this remains our basic position: There should not be any expansion in the power or scope of trade agreements or the WTO, and that a
fuller understanding of what has been the effect of existing rules must be
achieved. Having said that, we should make a few more specific remarks
about the negotiating mandate on the environment.

Firstly, we are not convinced that a review of the relationship between the
WTO and the multilateral environmental agreements (MEAs) is sufficient a
step in seeking to identify and manage the environmental and sustainable development consequences of free trade. This is certainly a current and important question (for example, in relation to the operation of the Biosafety Protocol in relation to trade rules for farm produce and the Montreal Protocol on
the trade in ozone-depleting substances), but is not sufficient. We are also
concerned that in clarifying the relationship between MEAs and trade rules in
a trade forum might actually lead to a de facto weakening of the MEAs and a
more institutionalized notion of what now happens in practice—which is to
give precedence to trade rules over environmental ones. We will do all that we
can to ensure that this does not happen—but such an outcome is nonetheless
a serious risk.

Wider Issues Than MEAs

In respect of some of the wider questions that need to be tackled (and that
won't be in the Doha mandate), consider the following. What are the environ-

mental and sustainable development implications arising from the progressive liberalization of agriculture, and who is reviewing those?

As far as we can see, the industrialization of farming that is now happening worldwide continues to lead to really very serious social and environmental impacts. One is the continued erosion of biological diversity: not only from encroachment into natural habitats cleared to accommodate ever larger industrial-scale farms, but also within the farmed landscape as ever more intensive methods are used to enable producers to better compete in international markets. Linked to these trends, and to the TRIPs [trade-related intellectual property] agreement as well, is the progressive loss of the biodiversity that has been at the heart of food production for centuries—namely, the crop varieties honed by farmers to grow and thrive in local conditions. These are now being lost and replaced by patented varieties reliant on branded chemicals available only from the giant transnational seed and agrochemical firms.

Policies to promote export-led development in the agricultural sector are also leading to an increasing concentration of land and power in the hands of fewer people with one result being the marginalization and impoverishment of many others. By all means let us review the relationship of trade rules in respect of environmental ones, but let's also look at these more deep-seated trends too, including the ones related to the impacts of liberalization on people. If we had an independent review of these issues, we might get somewhere.

Similarly with respect to the impacts of pollution and transport infrastructure needed to shift goods and services around the globe. Although there is a weak international treaty in place that is established to manage the climate change question, it seems that "free" trade policies are pushing practice against the aims of the stated policy to reduce greenhouse gas as goods circulate ever further between producer and consumer—virtually all under power from fossil fuels.

And what will be the environmental implications arising from the negotiations on services and investment liberalization? Many colleagues around the world, not just in Friends of the Earth International but in a huge and growing coalition of civil society groups from north, south, east, and west are gravely worried. Many foresee powerful TNCs competing with domestic industries and undertaking profit-maximization activities in a variety of environmentally and socially sensitive sectors with governments handing over their future ability to manage and intervene in these sectors to promote sustainability.

For example, my colleagues from Uruguay last week identified a whole raft of environmentally sensitive "service" sectors named in a recent EU liberalization "hit list" for that country. These included construction and related engineering services, so called environmental services (such as water collection, purification, and distribution; wastewater management; solid/hazardous waste management; and protection of biodiversity and landscape; plus all other environmental protection services not classified elsewhere), transport services (including maritime, internal waterways, rail, road, and air freight), energy services (including services related to exploration and production; to the construction of energy facilities such as oil and gas pipelines and power lines; services related to energy distribution and transportation of natural gas and petroleum; and the wholesale, retail sale, trading, and brokering of electricity and energy products), and tourism and travel-related services.

Similarly with potential investment liberalization, both under the GATS* negotiations or in any potential WTO investments agreement, there are comparable concerns. For example, what will be the impact on government's ability to direct and regulate investment in key sectors such as natural resource management—including forestry and mining. The potential introduction of a multilateral framework for competition policy in the WTO might also foster increased TNC penetration of and activities in domestic economies, with possible add-on impacts relating to the loss of regulatory flexibility to ensure that both TNC and domestic economic actors support the objective of sustainable development. These implications of the possible introduction of the investment and competition issues as negotiating areas in the WTO must be studied and fully understood. No negotiations on these issues must therefore be launched until that is the case.

The Corporations Have Designed the System to Suit Themselves

We are in no doubt where the momentum for such a comprehensive liberalization agenda comes from. We know that international business works tirelessly behind the scenes to keep governments on track for the next round of trade reforms that will deliver still more growth and profits. The International Chamber of Commerce, the TransAtlantic Business Dialogue, the Biotechnology Industry Organization, the Intellectual Property Committee, various U.S. business advisory committees, the Investment Network, the European Services Network, the LOTIS committee, the European Roundtable of Industrialists—that has a committee on foreign economic relations chaired by a former [director general of the General Agreement on Tariffs and Trade]—and others all speak as one on what needs to be done next.

Such is the pressure from companies for more liberalization that it seems the traditional relationship between business and governments is being reversed.

---

*Editors' note: GATS stands for General Agreement on Trade in Services, an agreement negotiated during the Uruguay Round of trade talks. Liberalizing trade in services has been a continuing topic of WTO negotiations.

No longer is it the case that governments regulate industry; it seems more and more that it is industry writing the rules that will regulate governments.

Where Next?

With these reflections in mind, you will no doubt be wanting to hear what we want instead. We have published a detailed analysis and proposals on what we believe would be a more sustainable approach to policymaking in this area, and these can be found at the FoEI Web site (www.foei.org). To give you a flavor in the short time available now, however, here are a few of our more important points.

New Economic Objectives

Simply attempting to maximize GDP is no longer sufficient. Trade liberalization and economic deregulation, combined with increased production and consumption, is leading to increased socioeconomic inequity (especially between rich and poor countries and communities), increased environmental degradation (locally and globally), and increased resource use and pollution. In addition, the wealth generated tends to be very unequally distributed.

A credible and productive system should have as its goal the satisfaction of people's needs through the equitable and sustainable use of the planet's limited environmental capacities. Poverty eradication, social and cultural sustainability, intergenerational equity and human dignity, along with environmental protection, must be key objectives.

Economic Diversity

Another of our key points arises from our skepticism toward the one-size-fits-all approach applied to economic liberalization. To that extent, one of our main messages is that economic diversity should be enhanced and protected as an alternative to the imposition of global rules.

The prevailing neoliberal economic model reduces self-reliance and encourages a high degree of dependence on the global economy. There is little or no room for diversity. This inflexible approach has proved particularly difficult for many poorer countries wishing to build up infant industries, promote local employment, protect cultural diversity, and/or restrict resource exports.

The right of countries, especially developing and least-developed ones, to develop and steer their economies, within parameters agreed internationally (concerning equity, human rights, and global resource use limits, for example) and on the basis of democratic and participative decisionmaking (which effectively rules out old-style state-planned economies) toward the objective of sustainable development and the upliftment of the economic conditions of their peoples, should be clearly recognized, supported, and strengthened by the world trading system.

Economic Subsidiarity

Another key principle for Friends of the Earth International is the notion of economic subsidiarity. We simply don't see how sustainable development can emerge in a world where global rules are applied to local situations. More decisionmaking power must be returned to local communities and democratic institutions. This is not to say that all decisions should be taken locally. The nature of the issue in hand should determine whether it is dealt with locally, nationally, regionally, or internationally. Implementing the principles of economic subsidiarity and economic democracy, with decisionmaking taking place at a number of different levels in a democratic manner, should enhance input from the local level, encourage diverse economies, and provide checks and balances that discourage the abuse of power at any one level.

Rebalancing Trade

Linked to this is the wider question of relocalizing economic strength. We don't hold what might be regarded as protectionist views in Friends of the Earth International; we rather see our approach as integrated, internationalist, and based on the promotion of international cooperation. We do believe that for sustainable development to evolve from aspiration to reality that it will be necessary to rebalance trade such that local economic activity is promoted and enhanced. This should lead to changes in consumption patterns in rich countries and a corresponding improvement in the economic conditions of poor countries in ways that support sustainable development. People must have the right to strengthen protection of their local and national environments; to promote small-scale, sustainable economic activity; and to exert control over their local and shared natural resources. Local economies should be able to choose the extent to which they wish to be self-reliant, generating their own wealth and jobs while retaining the option to trade internationally if they wish. Deprioritizing international trade, giving a higher priority to local and regional trade (and small and medium-sized enterprises), and promoting more local self-reliance, we believe, is a prerequisite for sustainability.

Regulating International Companies

. . . We believe it is time to examine the relationship among international companies, the environment, and the societies they affect. With this in mind, Friends of the Earth International is calling on world leaders to commit to talks that will result in a new Corporate Accountability Convention. This will bind companies, especially TNCs, to best practices wherever they operate. This will also recognize the rights of access over natural resources of local communities, and establish legal remedies through which local communities negatively affected by TNC operations may seek compensation and redress against the company on an international level.

Large international companies have become hugely powerful politically and economically, not least arising from their successful advocacy for a level playing field for business on the global stage. Our call is for this level playing field to be extended to the realms of environmental protection and social engagement. If there really is no race to the bottom taking place as a result of trade and financial liberalization, then there should be no argument against this proposal.

Recognize the Ecological Debt

Finally, if there is to be a just foundation to international economic relations, a vital early step must be the cancellation of financial debt and the recognition of the growing ecological debt owed by the North to the South. Impoverished countries must be allowed the space to invest in more sustainable development policies and to permit changes in production and consumption patterns. Debt eradication should not be linked to export-led development, as debt relief is at the moment.

In conclusion, free trade is not the same as sustainable development. Trade is a potent tool that can advance the cause of sustainability, but that is by and large not happening in a focused or deliberate manner: either with respect to policy or practice. A process of reform is absolutely necessary, and it must begin with the post-Doha negotiations.

I 8

ENVIRONMENT AND THE TRADING SYSTEM: PICKING UP THE POST-SEATTLE PIECES

Daniel C. Esty

Seattle represents a watershed for the international trading system. The high-profile protests against globalization in general and the work of the World Trade Organization (WTO) in particular mark the end of the days in which trade negotiations can be conducted by a close-knit group of trade cognoscenti out of sight of the rest of the world. Trade policymaking is now a very high-profile business.[1] This fact transforms how future trade negotiations can and will be conducted. It also means that the substantive interaction between trade rules and procedures and other policy realms will have to be refined. Nowhere is this more true than with regard to the linkage between trade and the environment.

The public increasingly understands the central role that the WTO plays as part of the emerging structure of global governance.[2] The misleading suggestion advanced by some trade experts that the WTO is nothing more than an intergovernmental body that provides a forum for trade negotiations can no longer be sustained.[3] The rules and procedures of the trading system are now understood to be critical elements of the world community's efforts to manage economic interdependence.

Traditional trade community logic has argued that more liberalization can be accomplished if the public does not know what is going on than would be achieved through open debate in the light of day. This argument recognizes the "public choice" difficulties inherent in trade liberalization: The benefits are diffused across a great number of people who cannot easily be mobilized

---

Originally published in Jeffery J. Schott, ed., *The WTO After Seattle* (Washington, D.C.: Institute for International Economics, 2000): 243–252. Reprinted with permission.

for political support of open markets while there are a few "losers" who will fight hard to prevent increased competition from imports. In an open political process, the received wisdom has it, special interests manipulate outcomes in a welfare-reducing manner. But this view fails to take seriously the corrosive effects of the perception that trade policymaking is undemocratic and systematically biased toward the needs of multinational corporations. Whether the proposition favoring a cover-of-darkness approach to trade liberalization was ever correct is now moot. The WTO will never again be able to operate beneath the public's radar. Moreover, the demands at Seattle for a new WTO culture of openness came not just from environmentalists and civil society more broadly but also from officials from many developing countries who felt marginalized by the complex and arcane negotiating process.

To overcome the Seattle-fueled hostility toward globalization and to restore market-opening momentum will require a sweeping and convincing WTO commitment to transparency. In the months ahead, the WTO will have to redouble its efforts to hear and take seriously views from the South and simultaneously to institutionalize its outreach to civil society and to the many nongovernmental organizations (NGOs) that have been excluded from past trade policymaking.

Shifting to a "sunshine" strategy will not be easy. Almost all of the WTO officials and the national representatives who participate in WTO activities in Geneva are steeped in the traditional "diplomatic" approach to trade policymaking, involving complex horse trading in which confidentiality is essential and indirection is prized.[4] Ironically, many of the delegations from the developing world that were most outraged about their perceived exclusion from the *real* negotiations in the restricted-access "green rooms" in Seattle remain skeptical about greater NGO participation in global-scale trade policymaking.

Both the United States and the European Union recognize the necessity and inevitability of a more transparent trading system, and each advanced ideas in Seattle to open up the WTO in general and the dispute settlement process in particular. As the trading system is transformed from a system based on tit-for-tat tariff reductions to one that is rules-based, greater transparency is increasingly important. Simply put, the style of operation that served the trade community in the past will not serve it well in the future. The prevailing ethos of the WTO must shift from closed-door negotiating mode to process-conscious administrative law.

Why Link Trade and Environment Policies?

Though some continue to question the need to address environmental concerns in the context of trade liberalization, sophisticated political leaders and trade officials increasingly recognize that, because of the centrality of the trade regime in a highly interdependent world, the WTO cannot avoid rubbing up against other policy realms, such as the environment.[5] Indeed, the trade-environment link is not really a choice but a matter of fact. Beyond descriptive reality, the trade-environment link should be recognized as having normative value as well.

Trade policy, and particularly trade liberalization, inescapably affect the natural environment. And where environmental resources are mispriced, trade may magnify the harms. The WTO itself acknowledges this reality.[6] Simultaneously, environmental policy affects trade. The presence of regulatory requirements—health standards, emissions limits, disposal requirements, labeling rules, and so on—channels (and may confine) trade flows, creating a potential for trade-environment clashes. As economic interdependence grows, the number of points of intersection expands and concomitantly so does the potential for conflict.[7] The range of recent tensions—including the Venezuelan challenge to the reformulated gasoline regulations promulgated under the 1990 U.S. Clean Air Act, the ongoing U.S.-E.U. beef hormone dispute, and the WTO case arising from Thai shrimping practices that killed endangered sea turtles—supports this proposition.

Fundamentally, trade and environmental policy interactions are inevitable in a world of economic integration.[8] International commerce needs to be governed by rules and procedures that bound behavior; some of these requirements will relate to environmental matters. Setting boundaries creates the potential for differences of opinion and therefore dispute. As we push for further trade liberalization, the number of realms where environmental questions may be raised will grow. The question of how biotechnology will be regulated and to what degree genetically modified organisms will be permitted in food represents one high-profile example of the difficulties that lie ahead. Serious attempts to control greenhouse gases, which may radically alter the prices of fossil fuels and therefore affect the value of hundreds of billions of dollars in industrial assets and existing energy investments, could have significant competitiveness effects and create further trade-environment tensions. Similarly, efforts to take more seriously the need to protect biodiversity or to expand the linkage between the trade regime and the Convention on International Trade and Endangered Species (CITES) might also lead to future conflict.

Beyond these economic interactions, trade and environmental policy become entangled as a function of ecological realities. A number of environmental challenges are global in scale. From the depleted fisheries in many of the world's oceans, to the need to protect the ozone layer, to the buildup of greenhouse gas emissions that may produce climate change, a number of problems cannot be dealt with on a national basis because of their scale. Indeed, any country that sets out unilaterally to address a transboundary prob-

lem will find that its own efforts cannot resolve the issue. International cooperation is essential. From the perspective of sound economics, there must be
some mechanism in place to discipline "free riders," those who decline to bear
a fair share of the burden of addressing global challenges. Whether countries
are "doing their share" has to be understood as a question that has important
economic consequences and implications—and therefore a tight link to trade
policy.

The failure to address environmental harms that spill across national
boundaries represents an uninternalized externality that, if left unaddressed,
leads to market failure.[9] Pollution spillovers and mismanagement of shared
natural resources make a degree of trade-environment linkage not just in-
escapable but advisable.[10] The efficiency and integrity of the international
economic system depends on the presence of procedures to address transboundary environmental externalities. While leadership in establishing the
policies and mechanisms to ensure that these challenges are taken seriously
must come from environmental authorities, the trading system must support,
and not undermine, these efforts.[11] Where environmental policies have been
agreed upon at the international level, the trading system should reinforce the
obligations that have been spelled out. Trade measures should not be the only
tool available for enforcement of multilateral environmental agreements.[12]
But lacking other effective mechanisms and recognizing the inexorable link
between global-scale environmental harms and the efficiency as well as integrity of the international economic system, the WTO should provide a degree of discipline on those who might "free ride" on the efforts of others or
otherwise shirk their responsibilities.

A third reason to take the trade-environment linkage seriously derives
from the political economy of trade policymaking. In the United States, in
particular, successful efforts at trade liberalization in recent years have always
been accompanied by express strategies to address related environmental
questions. Most observers do not believe the North American Free Trade
Agreement (NAFTA) would have cleared the U.S. Congress but for the environmental provisions written into the agreement and the substantial environmental side agreement that was negotiated in parallel. Many Congress
watchers attribute the failure of the Clinton administration's 1997–1998 fast-
track proposal to the lack of a comparable environmental commitment.

More broadly, one of the key lessons from the WTO fiasco in Seattle is that
deeper economic integration depends on a sense of political community—
and a belief that there are shared values that justify a commitment to open
markets.[13] If trade policymakers fail to appreciate the need to address this political dimension of liberalization, their efforts to promote a new round of
multilateral negotiations will falter.

Perhaps more important, the long-term legitimacy and durability of the international trading system will be enhanced to the extent that international

economic policy evolves in ways that intersect constructively with other policymaking realms such as the environment.[14] WTO decisions will not win the degree of popular acceptance that that they must have to keep the trade system functioning smoothly unless the organization develops procedures to enhance the authoritativeness, procedural and substantive fairness, and representativeness of its policy choices and directions. At a very basic level, the world community needs a deeper and richer WTO "politics." To facilitate more vigorous debate, the WTO must develop more open procedures and a broader outreach to civil society as well as *all* member governments.

To a significant degree, of course, the problems of international environmental policy cannot be laid at the doorstep of the trade community. The deeply flawed global environmental regime must bear most of the responsibility. In this regard, a number of opinion leaders have recently called for the creation of a global environmental organization, or GEO.[15] A more robust global environmental governance structure, constructed out of some of the pieces of the existing system, including the United Nations Environment Program (UNEP), might facilitate a more systematic international response to challenges of pollution control and natural resources management.[16] A GEO might also provide support for better international environmental policymaking as well as facilitate information exchanges on cutting-edge policy approaches and technologies. Most important, a functioning global environmental regime would take pressure off the WTO, sparing it the burden of action as an adjudicator of environmental disputes that go beyond the realm of its well-established trade expertise.[17]

Trade and environmental policies cannot be kept on separate tracks. The points of intersection are too frequent and too significant to prevent these policy realms from becoming intertwined. Thus the question is not, do we want trade and environmental policy linkage? It must be, how will we integrate trade and environmental policymaking in ways that both promote open markets and environmental protection?

The policy focus must be on how to fold environmental sensitivity into the trading system. Integration of environmental considerations in the trade domain could be accomplished through responses to "trade and environment" crises and through dispute resolution cases. But such a haphazard approach to policymaking is unlikely to yield good long-term results. A much better alternative would be to expressly, deliberately, and thoughtfully negotiate how trade and environmental policies will intersect. The trade-environment agenda cannot be an environmentalist's wish list but rather should be a carefully defined, theoretically grounded, and narrow set of procedural and substantive advances that promotes the peaceful coexistence of these two important policy realms. Building an environmental dimension into the international trading system will require both procedural WTO reforms and substantive changes in the WTO rules.

Procedural Advances

The WTO's day-to-day procedures could be opened up to ensure greater environmental sensitivity. With regard to the WTO's "executive" operations, it would make sense to invite NGO (and media) observers to watch the General Council meetings, during which the 130 member states work through basic policies and administrative matters. Secrets cannot be kept in a meeting of this size, so the presence of NGOs will not chill candor nor otherwise change the tenor of these sessions. Opening these meetings would go a good distance toward demystifying the WTO and providing a window on what issues are discussed, what points of view are raised, what assumptions drive decision-making, and what arguments are deemed persuasive. It should also be possible to provide NGOs with a limited period in which they would be allowed to ask questions or offer comments on the issues under debate.

A number of ideas have been advanced for building greater transparency into the WTO's quasi-judicial dispute settlement procedures to ensure that environmental issues are raised and addressed carefully and systematically. First, dispute panels should conduct their hearings in public. The taking of evidence in open court is a fundamental element of sound judicial process in almost every country in the world. The existence of "secret tribunals" links the WTO in the minds of many to dictatorships and other undemocratic governance systems. Likewise, as part of an effort to ensure that the public is aware of the arguments that are driving dispute settlement outcomes, it would be useful to have all briefs or position statements made public. In addition, NGOs should be permitted to share with dispute panels their views on any issue in question. Such a procedure, akin to the *amicus curiae* briefs permitted in U.S. courts, would provide WTO dispute settlement decisionmakers with access to the broadest range of relevant information. To complete the commitment to transparency, the WTO should release dispute panel decisions as soon as they are rendered.

It might also be advantageous to have a more clearly defined mechanism for incorporating by reference the judgments of other bodies, notably environmental entities, into the WTO dispute settlement process. For example, if a question were raised about a country's compliance with a multilateral environmental agreement, it would be very helpful to have the judgment of the parties to that agreement on whether a violation has occurred. Such procedures already exist with regard to WTO advice from the International Monetary Fund (IMF).

Future trade negotiations might also be conducted somewhat more openly, leading to significant credibility and legitimacy benefits for the WTO. Obviously, at a certain point, there are trade-offs that must be made in negotiations, and national negotiators will have to keep secret some issues, particularly those relating to their willingness to compromise on certain points.

Nevertheless, many opportunities exist to inform the public about the issues under discussion. In this spirit of openness, it would make sense for the WTO to invest in an easily accessed interactive Web site and conduct regular briefings for NGOs about the progress of all ongoing negotiations.

Demystifying the international trade regime stands out as a critical job for the WTO in the weeks and months ahead. The organization's credibility and future viability are threatened by public perceptions of it as undemocratic and biased toward multinational corporations and other special interests.

To ensure that critical environmental questions are not overlooked during negotiations, environmental reviews should be undertaken at the outset. The U.S. government and a number of other countries have already committed to such reviews. It would be useful if the WTO, perhaps with help from UNEP or other UN bodies with environmental expertise, were to provide support to developing countries that would be interested in pursuing this sort of analysis.

The WTO's Committee on Trade and Environment (CTE) might also be called upon to instill environmental sensitivity into negotiations. In particular, the CTE might be empowered to serve as an environmental advisory board to each negotiating group so that whenever the negotiations touched upon pollution or resources management, a degree of expertise would be available and a sense of coherence over how to address environmental questions might emerge across the whole effort.

Opportunities for Substantive Progress

In Seattle's wake, finding a way forward on the substance of the trade-environment conflict will be difficult. The environmental community feels empowered by the "success" of the street protests. But, in fact, the Seattle outcome represents a major tactical failure from the environmental point of view. Developing-country officials now seem more convinced than ever that the proposed "trade and environment" agenda constitutes nothing more than a new guise for protectionism. The sight of hundreds of environmental protesters walking arm in arm with unabashedly protectionist union members provided all the corroboration that most developing-country officials needed to lump the environmentalists in with others who are irretrievably hostile to freer trade.

The easiest place to begin in creating a viable trade-environment agenda is with "win-win" opportunities such as the elimination of subsidies. Ending agricultural price supports, as well as energy, water, timber, and fisheries subsidies, would help remove important trade distortion, stop environmental harms, reduce the fiscal pressure on budget-burdened governments, and create opportunities for developing countries to export their products. Subsidy reduction stands out therefore as a "win-win-win-win" possibility.

A second potential "win-win" item might be "super-liberalization" of environmental goods and services. A bold goal, such as zero worldwide tariffs on all environmental goods and a real commitment to reducing nontariff barriers for environmental services, might galvanize broad-based support. Liberalizing trade in environmental goods and services would represent an important initiative to promote environmental technology transfer to the developing world. The recipient nations obtain access to better environmental results at lower costs. The exporting countries get expanded markets for their eco-goods and services. Everyone wins. Only countries that are profoundly confused could oppose super-liberalization in pursuit of environmental progress.

Refining the WTO's approach to circumstances where trade and environmental rules clash represents a particularly difficult set of issues, but one critical to reduced trade-environment tension. In this regard, the WTO might seek ways to ensure that the trading system reinforces, rather than undermines, existing multilateral environmental agreements. It would also be useful if the WTO were to bless the use of eco-labels, perhaps in exchange for a negotiated set of disciplines that would constrain the use of such labels. Codifying the results of recent GATT trade-environment jurisprudence, in particular the logic of the Appellate Body's decision in the recent shrimp-turtle case—endorsing the GATT-consistency of legitimate environmental policies—would also represent a significant advance on prior trading system thinking.

If the rules of international trade are clear—and if they are perceived to be supportive of important environmental values—then their legitimacy will be much greater. Over the long term, public support for the WTO depends on a perception that it is balanced and fair.[18] Efforts to address the issues identified above could greatly enhance the WTO's reputation. Competing trade and environmental principles could best be balanced through creation of an interpretive statement that focuses on how the "exceptions" spelled out in Article XX would be implemented, rather than through full-blown renegotiation of the environmental elements of the trading system.

Conclusion

The world trading system is undergoing a major transformation. It is evolving from a forum for negotiation where the dominant mode is horse trading into a rules-based system where disputes are settled in a peaceful fashion that facilitates trade, reflects broad public values, and provides predictability about what is acceptable in the realm of international commerce. Such a system is essential to the successful management of economic interdependence. A rules-based regime is also very much in the interest of the smaller countries, whose hope for getting a fair deal rises if there are broadly accepted disciplines and procedures that every nation, even the most powerful, is obliged to accept and follow.

Finding ways to address the environmental issues that inescapably arise in the context of deeper economic integration must be seen as an important trade policy priority, as a matter of WTO commitment to undergirding the trade regime with sound economic theory, and as a matter of political necessity. Building a trading system that is more sensitive to pollution control and natural resources management issues is mandated by the growing degree to which these realms intersect with trade and economic policy. Systematic and thoughtful efforts to make trade and environmental policies mutually reinforcing are also advisable to the extent that the presence of trade rules that internalize externalities will prove to be more economically efficient over time. Institutionalizing the links from the trade regime to environmental actors and other elements of civil society will also pay dividends. A culture of openness within the WTO is likely to generate policies that the public accepts and that therefore become more useful and durable.

Notes

1. Daniel C. Esty, "An Environmental Perspective on Seattle," *Journal of International Economic Law* 3, no. 1 (2000):10.

2. Jeffery Schott, "Challenges Facing the World Trade Organization," in Jeffrey J. Schott, ed., *The World Trading System: Challenges Ahead* (Washington, DC: Institute for International Economics, 1996); John H. Jackson, "Reflections on Constitutional Changes to the Global Trading System," *Chicago-Kent Law Review* 72 (1996):511; John H. Jackson, *The World Trading System.* (Cambridge: MIT Press, 1997).

3. Jeffery L. Dunoff, "Trade and Recent Developments in Trade Policy and Scholarship—And Their Surprising Political Implications," *Northwestern Journal of International Law and Business* 17, no. 2/3 (1997):759.

4. John H. Jackson, "World Trade Rules and Environmental Policies: Congruence or Conflict?" *Washington and Lee Law Review* 49 (Fall 1992):1227; Daniel C. Esty, "The Case for a Global Environmental Organization," in Peter B. Kenen, ed., *Managing the World Economy: Fifty Years After Bretton Woods* (Washington, DC: Institute for International Economics, 1994).

5. E.g., Lawrence Summers, Speech to the Confederation of Indian Industry, Bombay, 18 January 2000; Bill Clinton, Speech at the World Economic Forum Annual Meeting, Davos, Switzerland, 29 January 2000; Tony Blair, Speech at the World Economic Forum Annual Meeting, Davos, Switzerland, 28 January 2000.

6. Hakan Nordstrom and Scott Vaughan, *WTO Special Report 4: Trade and the Environment* (Geneva: World Trade Organization, 1999).

7. André Dua and Daniel C. Esty, *Sustaining the Asia Pacific Miracle: Environmental Protection and Economic Integration* (Washington, DC: Institute for International Economics, 1997).

8. Daniel C. Esty "Economic Integration and the Environment," in Norman J. Vig and Regina Axelrod, eds., *The Global Environment: Institutions, Law, and Policy* (Washington,

DC: CQ Press, 1999); Steve Charnovitz, "The World Trade Organization and the Environment," *Yearbook of International Environmental Law* 8 (1998):98.

9. William J. Baumol and Wallace E. Oates, *The Theory of Environmental Policy,* 2nd ed. (Cambridge: Cambridge University Press, 1988).

10. Robert E. Hudec, "GATT Legal Restraints on the Use of Trade Measures against Foreign Environmental Practices," in Jagdish Bhagwati and Robert Hudec, eds., *Fair Trade and Harmonization: Prerequisites for Free Trade?* (Cambridge: MIT Press, 1996).

11. Daniel C. Esty, *Greening the GATT: Trade, Environment, and the Future* (Washington, DC: Institute for International Economics, 1994).

12. Harold K Jacobson and Edith Brown Weiss, *Engaging Countries: Strengthening Compliance with International Environmental Accords* (Cambridge: MIT Press, 1997).

13. Robert Lawrence et al., *A Vision for the World Economy* (Washington, DC: Brookings Institution, 1996); Dua and Esty, *Sustaining the Asia Pacific Miracle.*

14. Daniel C. Esty, "NGOs at the World Trade Organization: Cooperation, Competition, or Exclusion," *Journal of International Economic Law* 1, no. 1 (1998):123.

15. Renato Ruggiero, Speech to the World Trade Organization Symposium on Trade and the Environment, Geneva, 15 March 1999; Jacques Chirac, Speech before the IUCN (World Conservation Union), Fontainebleau, France, 3 November 1999; "Why Greens Should Love Trade: The Environment Does Need to Be Protected but Not from Trade," *Economist,* 9 October 1999, 18.

16. Esty, "The Case for a Global Environmental Organization."

17. Dunoff, "Trade and Recent Developments."

18. Esty, "NGOs at the World Trade Organization."

19

WORLD BANK'S ENVIRONMENTAL REFORM AGENDA

Frances Seymour and Navroz K. Dubash

Environmental concerns have been at the leading edge of a movement to reform the World Bank over the past fifteen years. The bank has come under fire for financing a series of environmentally damaging projects, including dams on the Narmada River in India, transmigration in Indonesia, and road building into the Brazilian Amazon. These projects have led to a variety of adverse impacts in borrower countries, including deforestation and displacement of indigenous peoples.

In response to criticism voiced by environmental advocates and amplified through the U.S. Congress, the World Bank adopted policies and procedures in the late 1980s and early 1990s to assess and mitigate the adverse environmental impacts of individual projects. These reforms included mandatory environmental assessment procedures and the public disclosure of these assessments in advance of project approval. In addition, the bank's board of executive directors has mandated a series of sector-specific policies to guide World Bank investment in such areas as forestry and energy. For example, the bank's forestry policy prohibits the institution from financing logging in primary tropical forests.

Frustration with the World Bank's lack of vigilance in applying the new policies and procedures led environmental advocates to pursue a second gen-

Originally published in *Foreign Policy in Focus,* vol. 4, no. 10 (March 1999), a project of the Institute for Policy Studies and the Interhemispheric Resource Center. Reprinted with permission.

eration of reforms in the early 1990s focusing on increasing the transparency and accountability of lending operations. Again, conditions set by the U.S. Congress were crucial in pressuring bank management to agree to these reforms. As a result, the World Bank must now comply with an information disclosure policy governing the timing and content of documents released to the public. Moreover, the bank's actions are subject to review by an independent inspection panel established to investigate claims of those alleging that they were harmed by the bank's failure to abide by its own policies.

Along with these policy reform efforts, the World Bank has pursued structural changes and investment strategies intended to demonstrate its commitment to environmentally sustainable development. A separate environmental unit created in the 1980s has evolved into a vice-presidency for Environmentally and Socially Sustainable Development (ESSD) in the 1990s. The bank has recruited staff with technical environmental credentials to supplement the institution's professional core, which is overwhelmingly dominated by economists. By the mid-1990s, these staff had begun to develop a portfolio of environment-sector projects, ranging from support for national environmental agencies to investments in national parks.

Currently, this sequence of reforms is being replicated in the context of the World Bank's sister organizations, the International Finance Corporation (IFC) and the Multilateral Investment Guarantee Agency (MIGA), which provide financing and underwriting services directly to private sector entities. In 1998 the IFC adopted environmental policies and procedures, and MIGA [followed] suit in 1999. Also in 1999, an IFC ombudsman [was] appointed, and discussions are under way regarding extension of the bank's independent inspection panel to cover the IFC. The IFC has recruited a small (but growing) group of environmental professionals, and environment-specific projects—including venture capital funds dedicated to biodiversity conservation and renewable energy development—have begun to appear in the institution's portfolio.

These achievements have engendered a sense of complacency in official circles—including bank management and member governments—regarding the urgency of the World Bank's environmental reform agenda. In fact, World Bank President Wolfensohn's much touted "Strategic Compact" with the bank's board in 1997 did not feature environmental performance as a priority objective for improvement.

At the same time, the World Bank has evidenced a growing confidence in its ability to provide global leadership on environmental issues. In 1998, President Wolfensohn convened logging industry leaders from around the world to promote a shift to sustainable forestry practice. In the climate change arena, World Bank staffers have proposed a Prototype Carbon Fund, through which the bank would broker investment flows between industrialized and developing countries tied to reducing greenhouse gas emissions. Critics question the bank's legitimacy as an environmental leader, given its own poor performance record, its failure to mainstream environmental objectives into its lending portfolios, and its failure to engage key constituencies in borrower countries. The moment is clearly ripe for a reassessment of the World Bank's environmental reform agenda.

Despite the achievements highlighted above, the World Bank's mitigation-oriented, "do no harm" approach to the environment has had mixed results on its own terms and has failed to transform the institution into an agent of environmentally sustainable development. In fact, many environmental advocates fear that the World Bank is currently in a period of retrenchment from its environmental commitments. As evidence, they cite the disempowerment of environmental staff through recent reorganizations, the watering down of environmental policies through a recent reformatting exercise, and a proposed reconsideration of the bank's forestry policy in 1999. Moreover, they note that the bank's lending portfolio continues to include environmentally destructive projects, particularly in the energy sector.

A decade after the adoption of much-needed environmental policies and procedures, there continue to be significant lapses in the application of policy reforms. A recently published history of the World Bank characterized its environmental reforms as efforts to deflect outside criticism, not as significant changes in the bank's internal incentives or performance. The bank's continuing consideration of a major oil pipeline project in West Africa, despite the opposition of most internal environmental specialists, indicates that lending imperatives tied to traditional models of economic growth continue to outweigh environmental considerations.

The World Bank's project-by-project approach to environmental issues has also failed to address the fundamental choices faced by borrowers in determining which development path to follow. An internal review of the bank's environmental assessment procedures concluded that it has insufficiently considered alternative ways of meeting development goals. As it is, the bank's focus is usually on mitigating the impacts of its original project designs rather than exploring more environmentally sustainable ways of achieving project objectives. For example, environmental assessments of coal-fired power plants focus on technical methods for reducing the emissions of such plants rather than alternative ways of meeting demand for electricity or active management of that demand.

Environmental assessment procedures have not yet been adequately developed or implemented at the ecosystem, sectoral, or economy-wide levels. For example, in 1996 the World Bank failed to consider the likely impacts of rural road improvement on biologically rich forests as part of its transport sector loan to Cameroon. The narrow focus of the bank is also evident in its structural adjustment loans, which, in addition to increasing poverty, often provide incentives that accelerate natural resource exploitation, while forcing governments to cut budgets for social services and environmental protection.

The World Bank's Country Assistance Strategies, which provide a framework for policy advice and lending portfolios, tend not to highlight environmental issues or identify possible strategies to address environmental degradation.

Another problem is the tendency of many environmental advocates, both inside and outside the World Bank, to focus disproportionate attention on the merits of specific projects and on addressing international environmental issues such as biodiversity conservation and climate change at the global level. Though these efforts are important, they too often overshadow the need for the bank to address environmental issues more strategically through development of progressive investment portfolios and promotion of policy reform in individual borrower countries. For example, although it is important that the U.S. executive director on the World Bank's board vote against environmentally damaging projects, this is not sufficient to change the "upstream" dynamic that generates such projects in the first place.

Similarly, the Global Environment Facility (GEF)—the multilateral mechanism created to finance the incremental costs incurred by developing nations in their effort to comply with global environmental agreements—has largely failed to leverage the World Bank's wider investment portfolio toward environmental objectives. Indeed, in some borrower countries, the funds available from the GEF for projects that directly address global environmental problems have diverted the attention of bank staff and government officials away from the pressing need to support national policy reforms—such as ending subsidies for fossil fuel and timber extraction—that would not only serve national economic interests but would also benefit the global environment.

There is a widening (if unfounded) perception, particularly among borrower nations, that U.S. support for environmental standards is driven by Northern interests and that these standards threaten the sovereignty of Southern governments. Such concerns have fueled recent efforts to restrict the investigative powers of the bank's independent inspection panel and threaten to undo many of the reforms gained through U.S. leadership in the past.

Despite promises to mainstream environmental awareness into its overall lending program, the World Bank suffers from a credibility deficit. Its legacy of support for environmentally destructive projects and devastating structural adjustment programs has undermined its legitimacy as a proponent of environmental objectives. This credibility problem is evident in Indonesia, where the bank is attempting to promote forestry sector reform in the context of adjustment lending. Previous loans and grants to the Ministry of Forestry under the Suharto regime, allegations that the bank ignored that regime's corruption, and the inclusion of a Suharto crony in Wolfensohn's meeting of timber industry leaders all make it difficult for the World Bank to be accepted as a sincere proponent of forestry sector reform. Internationally, the bank's credibility as an advocate of climate protection has been undermined by its failure to redirect its own energy and transport sector lending portfolios away from fossil fuels and toward alternative investments in renewables and energy efficiency.

To meet its commitment to mainstream the environment, the World Bank must realign its internal incentive structures to ensure that sustainability objectives shape all its lending (not just the specifically environmental projects) as well as the policy reforms it advocates in all recipient countries. National policy reforms leveraged by World Bank loans can do more to advance sustainable development than either its lending for environment-specific projects or its engagement in global environmental policy arenas, although these channels are also important.

To ensure that borrower countries make natural resource management a priority concern and that the bank's role is perceived as legitimate, the World Bank should make certain that discussions with governments include those constituencies most likely to support environmental reforms. The bank's new emphasis on promoting participation at the project level and assisting borrowers to combat corruption should help ensure that vested interests do not shape government natural resource policies and investments. In the handful of cases where the World Bank has put environmental policy reform near the top of its agenda with borrower governments and has reached out to domestic constituencies, the response of progressive forces within government and civil society has been promising. For example, several Kenyan NGOs were cautiously positive when World Bank staff floated the idea of an "environmental adjustment" loan to Kenya to be focused explicitly on policy and institutional reforms necessary to promote environmentally sustainable and equitable development. Similarly, many environmental activists in Papua New Guinea supported the bank when it held up a structural adjustment loan conditioned on forest policy reforms.

U.S. foreign policy can assist the World Bank in these efforts in several ways. U.S. environmental leadership in governing the World Bank, in particular through its seat on the bank's executive board, continues to be essential and should be reinvigorated. To be more effective, however, this leadership needs to address new challenges.

First, although scrutiny of the environmental impacts of individual projects brought to the board for approval will always be necessary, more attention must be given to ensuring that environmental considerations are integrated upstream into the World Bank's country assistance strategies, sector strategies, and adjustment lending. The ongoing financial crisis in Asia provides an important test of the bank's ability to integrate environmental considerations into its response. The United States should monitor potential threats to the environment (such as accelerated export crop development at the expense of natural forests) as well as opportunities (such as the removal of economically inefficient subsidies for resource use) posed by bailout packages.

In this context, monitoring the environmental performance of multilateral development banks (MDBs), including the World Bank, currently undertaken by staff of the U.S. Agency for International Development, should be extended upstream from individual projects. This monitoring effort, which currently applies a "do no harm" standard at the project level, should be supplemented with assessments of how effectively MDBs are mainstreaming environmental objectives into their country and sector strategies and adjustment lending.

Second, U.S. environmental leadership on the bank's board requires increased investment in consensus building with both wealthy and developing nations at the board level and beyond. However, U.S. leadership and efforts at consensus building on an environmental reform agenda cannot succeed if limited to the level of the World Bank's board. They must be reinforced by the U.S. Treasury Department, the State Department, and the White House in multilateral forums such as the Group of Seven industrialized nations and in bilateral dialogues with other member governments. The environmental dimension of governance of international financial institutions in general and of the World Bank in particular deserves a higher profile and priority in U.S. diplomacy.

Finally, environmental advocates and the U.S. Congress should ensure that the United States inserts consideration of environmental sustainability into ongoing discussions about the design of a new global financial architecture recently occasioned by the series of financial crises in emerging market economies.

Specifically, the United States should forge a consensus conditioning continuation of the World Bank's existing mandates—and any new mandates—on its credibility as a proponent of environmentally sustainable development primarily in borrower countries and then at the global level.

20

EXPANDING
THE CAPITAL STOCK

ISMAIL SERAGELDIN
AND ANDREW STEER

Sustainable development means ensuring that future generations have as many opportunities as we have. Ensuring that this will be possible for the increased populations of the future requires increasing the world's stock of "capital." Four types of capital—which are often strong complements but weak substitutes for one another—need to be recognized.

Sustainable development is about development progress; it certainly is not a doctrine of "no-growth" environmental protectionism. But it is about a particular form of progress. Specifically, sustainable development places the focus on two groups of disenfranchised people: the poor of today and the generations of tomorrow. Its goals are to increase opportunities, improve livelihoods, and reduce the risk of disease or impoverishment for the 1 billion people who live below the line of acute poverty and the 2 billion who live not much above it, for the 1.7 billion who lack even basic sanitation services, the 1.4 billion who breathe badly polluted air, the hundreds of millions of farmers who are threatened by soil depletion or natural disturbance, and the 2.5 billion who yet cannot enjoy the benefits of modern energy.

Meeting the need of productive jobs, education, health, and infrastructure requires gains in productivity, pro-poor targeting of programs, and an expansion of the capital stock. But sustainable development also requires that such progress be *sustained;* today's progress must not be achieved at the expense of tomorrow's citizens. This is a more difficult concept to grapple with. Here

Originally published in Ismail Serageldin and Andrew Steer, eds., *Making Development Sustainable: From Concepts to Action* (Washington, D.C.: World Bank, 1994). Reprinted with permission.

again, it is helpful to focus on the need to preserve—and given the expected future growth of population, to expand—the capital stock to ensure the option of enjoying at least the same flow of income and services in the future as exists today.

Four Types of Capital

We need to recognize at least four categories of capital: human-made or "fabricated" capital (machines, factories, buildings, and infrastructure), natural capital (as discussed in many works of environmental economics), human capital (investments in education, health, and nutrition of individuals), and social capital (the institutional and cultural bases for a society to function).

Human-made capital. Most economic analysis focuses on the first category, humanmade capital, which is also the most measurable. Consistent with our tendency to "treasure what we measure," more efforts have gone into ensuring a rising stock of this type of capital than any other. For this reason discussions of sustainable development rightly tend to focus on the other forms of capital since it is there that remedial analysis and action are needed.

Natural capital. This is the stock of environmentally provided assets (such as soil, sub-soil minerals, forests, atmosphere, water, wetlands) that provide a flow of useful renewable and nonrenewable goods and services, which may be marketed or unmarketed. As we have moved from an "empty world" to a "full world," these environmentally provided assets have become increasingly scarce; thus it is appropriate that attention should shift from concern about the adequacy of human-made capital to concern about the adequacy and effective use of natural capital. The services derived from natural capital can be greatly expanded when such capital is cultivated—that is, combined with human-made and human capital, as in agriculture. However, care must be taken that increased yields derived from increasing applications of other factors do not mask an underlying deterioration of the basic natural capital stock. There is growing evidence that this may be happening in many parts of the world, for example, in arable agriculture and forestry, where continued increments of complementary inputs are ensuring ever-increasing yields while vital ecological and physical services are being eroded. Substitution of nonnatural capital for natural capital is possible in the short to medium term but eventually is limited. Thresholds can be crossed, after which yields will decline, often sharply, regardless of how many other inputs are supplied. Deepening our understanding of sustainability in such situations of cultivated natural capital is a high priority.

Human capital.   In the past three decades very considerable progress has been made in recognizing the importance of human capital formation; investment in people is now seen to be a very high return investment, especially in developing societies. The entire mainstream paradigm of development has been expanded to include investment in human resources as an essential, possibly the most essential, ingredient of development strategy.[1]

Investments in health and education and nutrition are increasingly central parts of national investment strategies. Nevertheless, we still have difficulties, methodologically, to define the monetary value of such investments, even if ingenious proxies, such as the discounted differential income stream, are used. However, even the most conservative measures in such proxies lead to an overwhelming positive value to such investments.

Less clear is the link between such investments and the shifting economic realities of an aging population profile in the industrialized countries and the persistence of unemployment and underemployment in many societies, both industrialized and developing. The negative and corrosive impacts of such phenomena on the social fabric and well-being of society as a whole, not only the individuals concerned, deserve more research and policy attention.

Social capital.   The last observation leads directly to the fourth form of capital. Without a degree of common identification with the forms of governance and of cultural expression and social behavior that make a society more than the sum of a collection of individuals, it is impossible to imagine a functioning social or economic order. The myriad institutions that we take for granted as essential premises of a functioning society must be grounded in a common sense of belonging by its members, and the institutions must reflect a sense of legitimacy in their mediation of conflicts and competing claims. In short, if that social capital is inadequate, the resulting failures make it impossible to talk of either economic growth, environmental sustainability, or human well-being. Examples are all too painfully evident—from Somalia to Yugoslavia to Rwanda.

But what constitutes this social capital? It is a difficult question, and the definition is clearly different from and broader than that of individual human capital. It is based on inclusion, participation, and the promotion of an enabling environment. Yet it is more. The most ambitious work to date on this subject has been the effort to deal empirically with the link between good governance and development. This requires efforts at definition and measurement that face formidable methodological obstacles, but, happily, headway is being made.

In a landmark study presented in *Making Democracy Work: Civic Traditions in Modern Italy,* Professor Robert D. Putnam of Harvard University and colleagues have made a convincing case that the existence of civic community is not only the precursor and guarantor of good governance but also the key to sustained socioeconomic development.[2]

Strong civic community is defined as a preponderance of *voluntary horizontal associations,* in contrast to *hierarchical vertical associations,* and the *den-*

sity of these voluntary horizontal institutions throughout the society. The Putnam study found a matrix of voluntary horizontal associations in prosperous, rapidly developing northern Italy while the less developed, less effective south of Italy is characterized by autocratic vertical institutions.

But which is the cause and which is effect? Does northern Italy have a dense network of horizontal institutions (choral societies, soccer clubs, parent-teacher associations) because it is rich and can afford them? Or is it rich because it has good, responsive government nurtured by long-standing citizen involvement in many such voluntary institutions? The evidence suggests the latter. The twenty-year study documents a strong causal link between civic traditions and the effectiveness of governments to promote sustained socioeconomic development. The Italian case has potentially vital relevance for a deeper understanding of how to promote environmentally sustainable development. Questions remain as to how to measure social capital, and as to whether and how it is possible to "invest" in such capital. Similarly, the causal impacts—for good or bad—of economic development on civil society still are not known. These areas of research need to be addressed.

Sustainability and the Capital Stock

How does the above view of capital stock enlighten our understanding of sustainability? It clearly enables us to set aside the simplistic view that sustainability requires leaving to the next generation exactly the same amount of composition of natural capital as we found ourselves, and to substitute a more promising concept of giving future generations the same, if not more, opportunities than we found ourselves. In other words, the stock of capital that we leave them, defined to include all four forms of capital, should be the same if not larger than what we found ourselves. This new paradigm immediately opens the door for substituting one form of capital for another. Arguably, it is the most worthwhile to reduce some natural capital, for example, reducing the amount of oil in the ground, to invest in increasing human capital, for example, educating girls. The question then becomes, in the language of development economists, of the degree to which we can

- measure each kind of capital;
- define the production function, in terms of the degree of substitutability and complementarity between the different kinds of capital, and how these may change in a dynamic context;
- define (in the absence of a common numeric) an "exchange rate" for the different kinds of capital, accepting that it, too, may be dynamic;
- define sustainability in terms of a context of thresholds within which the more efficient (highest return) activities could be selected, in such

a way that individual investments and entire strategies could be meaningfully evaluated.

Such an approach ultimately may be comprehensive and rigorous, but it is a long way off. A good way to think about proceeding is in a series of short steps. We have already made great strides in incorporating human capital into conventional economic analysis, and we are starting to incorporate various aspects of natural capital. This is where we should invest our primary efforts now, significantly improving our understanding of the interlinkages between these three kinds of capital. Social capital will take longer to elaborate, and in the meantime can be left to the political processes in each country to arbitrate.

This brings us to the definition of sustainability in terms of the maintenance of these four types of capital while producing an increasing stream of benefits to individuals and society as a whole.

Sustainability has several levels—weak, sensible, strong, and absurdly strong—depending on how strictly one elects to hew to the concept of maintenance or nondeclining capital.[3]

Weak sustainability is maintaining total capital intact without regard to the composition of that capital among the four different kinds of capital. This would imply that the different kinds of capital are substitutes, at least within the boundaries of current levels of economic activity and resource endowment.

Sensible sustainability would require that in addition to maintaining the total level of capital intact, some concern should be given to the composition of that capital (among natural, human-made, human, and social). Thus, oil may be depleted so long as the receipts are invested in other capital, for example, human capital development, elsewhere, but, in addition, efforts should be made to define critical levels of each type of capital, beyond which concerns about substitutability could arise. These levels should be monitored to ensure that patterns of development do not promote a decimation of one kind of capital, regardless of what is being accumulated in other forms of capital. This degree of sustainability still assumes that human-made and natural capital are to a large extent substitutable but recognizes that they are also complementary. The full functioning of the system requires at least a mix of the different kinds of capital. Since we do not know exactly where the boundaries of these critical limits for each type of capital lie, it behooves the sensible person to err on the side of caution in depleting resources (especially natural capital) at too fast a rate.

Strong sustainability requires maintaining different subcomponents of capital intact separately. Thus, for natural capital, loss of forest in one area should be replaced by new forest of a similar type elsewhere, and receipts from depleting oil should be invested in sustainable energy production. This assumes that natural and man-made capital are not really substitutes but complements in most production functions and that even within capital types, there is limited substitutability. Thus, a sawmill (human-made capital) is worthless without the complementary natural capital of a forest.

Absurdly strong sustainability would never deplete anything. Nonrenewable resources—absurdly—could not be used at all; for renewables, only net annual growth rates could be harvested, in the form of the overmature portion of the stock.

Pragmatism has to be our abiding concern in both the development of new measurements and methodologies and in the pursuit of policies and investments. Operationally, this translates into encouraging the growth of natural capital by reducing our level of current exploitation; by investing in projects to relieve pressure on natural capital stocks by expanding cultivated natural capital, such as tree plantations to relieve pressure on natural forests; and by increasing investment in human resources, particularly of the poor who are both the victims and the unwitting agents of economic degradation in many of the poorest societies on earth.

Methodologically, it is better to follow the wise advice of Nobel laureate Robert Solow, who advocated a series of imperfect steps to improve our current work rather than an interminable debate about the "perfect" formulation.[4] With this approach must come a major effort at improving our databases for the different kinds of capital, especially the physical stocks and flows of natural capital, and the interaction of these into coherent views of ecosystem integrity and resilience at the regional as well as the global level.

It is a tall order, and it will be a long journey before the concept of sustainability sketched here is operational in a meaningful sense. But the longest journey starts with a single step, and on this journey many steps have already been taken.

Notes

1. See World Bank, *World Development Report 1991: The Challenge of Development* (New York: Oxford University Press, 1991).

2. Robert D. Putnam (with Robert Leonardi and Raffaella Y. Nanetti), *Making Democracy Work: Civic Traditions in Modern Italy* (Princeton: Princeton University Press, 1993).

3. Ismail Serageldin, Herman Daly, and Robert Goodland, "The Concept of Environmental Sustainability," in *Principles of Sustainable Development*, ed. Wouter van Dieren (Amsterdam: Institute for Environment and Systems Analysis, 1994).

4. Robert M. Solow, "An Almost Practical Step Toward Sustainability." 40th Anniversary Lecture (Resources for the Future, Washington, DC, October 1992).

2 1

REPORT AND FINDINGS ON THE QINGHAI PROJECT: EXECUTIVE SUMMARY

WORLD BANK INSPECTION PANEL

Interpretation of the Bank's Policies and Procedures

... During the course of examining some twenty projects over the past five years, the Panel has encountered certain differences in views among staff on just how the Bank's operational policies and procedures should be applied. In this case, however, the Panel's interviews revealed an unusually and disturbingly wide range of divergent and, often, opposing views. These large differences pervade all ranks of the staff, from senior management to frontline professionals. And they apply to virtually all of the major decisions required by the policies. The implications of this for a reasonable application of the Bank's policies and procedures became a matter of serious concern to the Panel and ought to be of concern to the Bank generally since there is no way that the policies can be applied with reasonable consistency in the face of such wide divergences of opinion.

For example, a number of staff members felt that the Bank's Operational Directives and other policies were simply idealized policy statements and should be seen largely as a set of goals to be striven after. Others of equal or more senior rank disagreed with this view. They felt that this interpretation

Excerpted from World Bank Inspection Panel, *Inspection Panel's Report and Findings on the Qinghai Project: Executive Summary,* Washington, D.C., April 2000. Reprinted with permission.

could render the policies virtually meaningless and certainly incapable of being employed as benchmarks against which to measure compliance.

In discussions about compliance, staff often pointed out that the policies allow for flexibility of interpretation. The decisions made on the specific matters were thus covered and in compliance. It was simply a matter of "judgment at Management's sole discretion." The Management Response itself makes several claims in this respect. Other staff argued, however, that the policies are clear enough to distinguish areas that are binding from areas where some reasonable flexibility in interpretation is called for. Read in their entirety, the Panel feels that the directives cannot possibly be taken to authorize a level of "interpretation" and "flexibility" that would permit those who must follow these directives to simply override the portions of the directives that are clearly binding. . . .

Interviews with some staff were punctuated by the refrain that *"in China things are done differently."* This is echoed in the Management Response which states that: *"The level and quality of preparation and analysis for this Project were very much in line with Bank practice in applying social and environmental policies to projects in China in the context of its political and social systems."* The Panel has carefully examined the policies and has failed to find any grounds for the view that precedents in a country, or a country's "social and political systems," can in any way determine what is required by the policies. . . .

The Qinghai Project in Space and Time

The Environmental Assessment does not distinguish between short-term impacts and those that will only occur at some time in the future. This raises serious questions about the time horizons over which the Project was evaluated.

Moreover, in examining the Project documentation, the Panel found a high level of ambiguity, uncertainty and inconsistency in the use of the term "project area." This confusion is compounded by the fact that the documentation is poorly supported by maps. (The Panel had eventually to prepare its own set of maps . . . .) As a result, it appears that significant numbers of people, including members of minority nationalities, have been left out of the environmental and social assessments required by Bank policy. . . .

In the Panel's view, given the letter and intent of [Operational Directives] 4.01 [on environmental assessment], 4.20 [on indigenous peoples] and 4.30 [on involuntary resettlement], the actual scale of the area to be impacted by the Qinghai Project, the ethnic composition of the Project's impacted populations, the boundaries of the "project area" were far too narrowly defined by Management. As a result, the assessments fail to address many of the most significant social and environmental impacts of the Project on the potentially affected populations, including those who are members of minority nationalities. The Panel finds that this is not in compliance with these ODs.

The Consultation and Survey Method

. . . Four points can be made concerning the survey in the Move-out area. First, the questionnaires are not confidential. (All four surveys required the respondent to put his or her name on the survey.) Second, from the internal evidence of the questionnaires themselves, they must have been filled out by someone other than the individual respondents. Third, the very limited source of information about the subject matter of the survey is striking; 93 percent of respondents indicated that they learned of the resettlement from "government propaganda." Fourth, an examination of the questions asked, and the context in which they were asked, indicates that opinions and information gathered are probably not reliable because respondents will probably think that this questionnaire could directly influence whether they get selected for the resettlement project.

. . . [I]n the Panel's view, the expressions of opinion it heard and the incidents it witnessed indicate the need for far greater efforts to obtain public consultation under adequate conditions before Management can be said to have met the requirements for public consultation in the Operational Directives. The mere fact that opinions expressed were so strikingly different, and especially the fact that there was a strong perception of risk from those expressing opposition to the Project during the Inspection Team's visit, indicates that methods of public consultation used for this Project have so far been inadequate.

The Consideration of Project Alternatives

If there is no alternative there can be no choice. The Bank's policies and procedures leave no room for doubt as to the need for a careful and systematic consideration of a number of different types of alternatives, including investment alternatives, alternative sites, alternative project designs, alternative implementation plans. The purpose of considering these alternatives is to ensure that the option supported by the Bank will achieve the project's objectives most cost effectively, while meeting the Bank's safeguard policies.

One of the most noticeable and significant weaknesses of the assessments is that investment and project alternatives are neither identified nor systematically compared. For all practical purposes, the Environmental Assessment avoids consideration of alternatives. . . . From the documentation, it is not possible to deduce whether the Qinghai Project as proposed is the best way for the Bank to meet the Project's objectives or to ensure that the Bank's safeguard policies are being respected.

Management failed to ensure that those responsible for the [environmental assessment] understood their brief to include an examination of alternatives to resettlement in both the Move-out and Move-in areas. Instead, the Panel found that they understood the main purpose of their studies to be to assist in the optimal resettlement of around 60,000 people from the Move-out area into the Balong-Xiangride irrigation area. . . . There is no systematic study of *in situ* alternatives to resettlement, or of alternative resettlement sites, or of alternative development plans for the national minorities affected within the Move-in area.

Why the Bank accepted Assessments conducted in such a circumscribed and limiting manner is unclear. Whatever the reasons, the Panel finds that the Assessments do not make any meaningful analysis of realistic project alternatives as required by Bank policy.

Environmental Assessment of the Qinghai Project

Management adopted a very limited definition of "environment" in the Project with the result that the Assessment fails to analyze the full range of Project effects. The Assessment also fails completely to place the Project in proper time frames. As noted above, the spatial boundaries of the Move-out and Move-in areas are defined narrowly, or not at all, with the result that whole communities and populations, whose lives will be impacted by the Project, have been left out of the Environmental and Social Assessments. . . .

In May/June 1999, following the outbreak of public concern, Management tried to compensate for this by requiring a study to evaluate the environmental and social impacts of the Voluntary Settlement Implementation Plan. This study (which is to recommend measures to enhance the environmental sustainability and the living conditions of the people in the Move-out counties) is to be undertaken not later than three years after the implementation of the Plan has commenced. Undertaking an environmental and social assessment three years after the commencement of resettlement is a bit late, not only in terms of the policies, but also in terms of any elemental understanding of the purposes of such assessments. Within the social arena, this is comparable to requiring that the safety of a proposed dam should be studied within three years after it has been built! . . .

The EA and other Project documents fail to consider the appropriateness of implanting large-scale irrigated agriculture in this Region. It does not examine its suitability or viability in comparison with the traditional forms of land use. . . . There appears simply to be an assumption that irrigated agriculture is "a good thing" without consideration of alternatives and relative costs. . . .

The Panel finds that the Environmental Assessment of the Qinghai Project is not in compliance with Bank policies as set out in [Operational Directive] 4.01.

Involuntary Resettlement

. . . [Operational Directive] 4.30 [on involuntary resettlement] applies to those people who are displaced or adversely affected by the Project. As noted repeatedly, Management's narrow definition of the boundaries of the Project area resulted in many people and communities affected by the Project being left out of the assessments. This appears to be true of the population of persons who will be displaced by the Project, which is likely to be larger than that accounted for in Project documents. In the Panel's view, the Project is not in compliance with OD 4.30.

Paragraph 4 of OD 4.30 requires the development of a plan that will assist involuntarily resettled persons with their move and will provide fair compensation for their loss. . . . Adequate baseline data on pastoralism, including the data on land use and inheritance that would allow a proper assessment of the compensation offered, are unfortunately lacking for this Project. Although envisaged by the OD, it appears that this work was not done. Without the results of such work, it is difficult to assess the adequacy of the compensation offered, not only for the Panel but also, in the first instance, for Management. Indeed, it is difficult to understand how the OD's policy objectives can be achieved without this information.

PART FIVE

THE SUSTAINABILITY DEBATE

Effective responses to global environmental problems demand both international cooperation and institutional reform. As previous sections have indicated, these are substantial challenges. The prevailing structures and practices of the international system make attainment of these goals difficult, and they cannot be divorced from the larger political, economic, and cultural struggles that infuse world politics.

It would be a mistake, however, to study global environmental politics solely in terms of international treaties and institutional change. Perspectives on the essence of the global environmental problematique are another key variable, and one that has changed in important ways over time. Few would argue that ideas alone have the power to change history. But there is no doubt that paradigms—bundles of fundamental ideas and beliefs—shape the strategies and goals of actors in important ways. They influence how actors understand their interests, how policies are formulated, how resources are allocated, and which actors and institutions are empowered to make the critical decisions that affect global environmental quality.[1]

One powerful but controversial new paradigm that emerged in the build-up to the 1992 Rio de Janeiro Earth Summit is the idea of sustainability. As previously discussed, one of the central controversies at the Stockholm conference was the debate over whether economic growth and development are inherently destructive to the environment. This question revealed sharp cleavages between governments of the industrialized North and the developing South, as well as sharp divisions between growth-oriented governments in general and nongovernmental actors concerned about the negative consequences of continually expanding economic activity.

Concepts of sustainability and sustainable development appeal to many people because they hold out the promise of reconciling these divergent views. Sustainable development approaches are predicated on the premises that poverty and economic stagnation are themselves environmentally destructive and that all forms of economic organization and activity are not equal in their environmental impact. If these premises are true, then it might be possible to design environment-friendly forms of production and exchange that simultaneously facilitate economic development, alleviate the pressures of poverty, and minimize environmental damage. Such forms of production and exchange might be aimed at "development without growth"—that is, improvement in the quality of people's lives without an increase in the aggregate level of economic activity.[2] Or they might be tailored to forms of economic growth that are more acceptable ecologically. Whatever the path advocated, reconciling the tension between ecology and economy is the central goal of sustainable development.

The most frequently cited definition of sustainable development is found in *Our Common Future,* an influential report published by the World Commission on Environment and Development. In 1983 the United Nations General Assembly charged the commission—also known as the Brundtland Commission, after its chairperson, Norwegian Prime Minister Gro Harlem Brundtland—with devising a conceptual and practical "global agenda for change."[3] The commission, which included representatives from twenty-two nations on five continents, conducted a series of hearings around the world before preparing its final report and presenting it to the General Assembly in 1987. The report had an enormous influence on the global environmental debate and played a key role in shaping the content and format of the 1992 Earth Summit.

According to the Brundtland Commission, sustainable development is "development that meets the needs of the present without compromising the ability of future generations to meet their own needs."[4] To meet the goal of achieving sustainable development, the commission set forth a policy blueprint based on enhanced international cooperation, substantial changes in national policies, and a reoriented global economy. The report argues that the problem is not economic growth per se but the environmentally destructive character of many current activities and incentives. Economic growth remains vital, in the commission's view, given the substantial impact of poverty on the environment. Thus the commission combined its recommendations for ecologically sound forms of production and exchange with a call for renewed global economic growth to solve the problems of Third World poverty.

Some observers saw the commission's advocacy of these positions as inherently contradictory. The continued commitment to a basically unreformed global economic system is, in this view, the biggest impediment to true sustainability, rather than a prerequisite for managing environmental problems more effectively. In an editorial originally published in the British environmental journal *The Ecologist,* Larry Lohmann questions whether the Brundtland Commission has provided an agenda for change or simply a justification of business as usual. In Lohmann's view, the Brundtland proposals merely put a green face on current practices while perpetuating unequal relationships of power and wealth—both within individual countries and between the overdeveloped North and underdeveloped South. Sustainable development, Lohmann asserts, is less threatening to powerful interests than other approaches to environmental policy.[5]

Sharachchandra Lélé provides a different but in some ways equally critical assessment of the concept of sustainable development. A comprehensive review of the burgeoning literature on sustainability leads Lélé to conclude that the concept lacks a clear, widely accepted definition. There are many different conceptions of sustainable development, not all of which endorse the Brundtland Commission's formulation. Lélé argues that because of the many frequently contradictory uses of the term, sustainable development "is in real danger of becoming a cliché . . . —a fashionable phrase that everyone pays homage to but nobody cares to define."

Like Lohmann, Lélé writes from the perspective of one who accepts the goal of meeting current needs without compromising the ability of future generations to meet their requirements. His quarrel is with several of the assumptions embedded in mainstream sustainable development thinking. These include a narrowly technical focus on the problem of poverty while ignoring its fundamentally sociopolitical roots; a neoclassical emphasis on economic growth as an end in itself, rather than a more precise specification of how to meet people's basic needs; and a lack of clarity about exactly what is to be sustained, for whom, and for how long. Definitions that begin instead with the ecological goal of sustaining the conditions for human life and well-being avoid some of these problems, in Lélé's view. But they suffer from an equally debilitating flaw: Too often, they stress the *ecological* conditions required for ecological sustainability but overlook the complex array of *social* conditions that are also required.

Lélé also worries that mainstream notions of sustainable development place an undue burden of structural and value adjustment on the South in order to facilitate the continuation of current consumption practices in the North. In his view, the problem of excessive Northern consumption poses fundamental challenges that are not being adequately addressed with the "managed-growth" model of sustainable development. The idea that the challenge lies primarily in the South is more a reflection of the power of some actors and institutions to set the global agenda than an accurate reflection of the true scope of the problem.

Lélé's concern for a *global* perspective on sustainability forces us to ask what sustainable societies might look like in the North as well as the South. One vision is presented by the World Business Council for Sustainable Development, a coalition of more than 160 major international firms "united by a shared commitment to sustainable development" (and represented in this volume by a speech from the WBCSD president, Björn Stigson). The business leaders of the WBCSD have embraced the Brundtland Commission's notion of growth-oriented sustainability, emphasizing efficiency in the context of open markets to improve existing systemic structures such as free trade and a modern industrial economy. This perspective takes an optimistic view on the possibilities for "ecological modernization," in which advanced industrial societies are seen as able to make significant environmental progress through reform in production systems, management practices, and market-based incentives, while remaining within the parameters of a globalizing capitalist economy.[6]

Alan Durning, in contrast, sees a far deeper crisis of Northern unsustainability rooted in "the consumer society" and less amenable to technical and managerial solutions. High rates of population growth in the developing world are often identified as a major impediment to sustainability: Increasing numbers of poor people cannot afford the luxury of environmental stewardship as they struggle for survival. Yet for Durning, this depiction misses the larger part of the story—the consumption habits of the smaller but wealthier populations in the North. In a book published by the Worldwatch Institute, a Washington-based environmental think tank, Durning turns a critical eye to the acquisitive definition of the good life that undergirds high levels of material consumption. He addresses several questions that challenge mainstream consumer practices in industrial society: How much is enough? Can the Earth survive a world where more is always assumed to be better? Are technical fixes enough, when the dominant trend is for Madison Avenue and the World Bank to market this acquisitive logic to developing countries as the proper model for their own development?

In conclusion, we might well ask whether the idea of sustainability can break the North-South stalemate on environment and development that emerged at the Stockholm conference. To some extent, it already has; there is no question that the power of the concept—and in particular, its vision of harmonizing environmental quality and economic well-being—has fundamentally altered the global debate. The next and more difficult step is to clarify whether and how that vision can be attained. Whether the debate on sustainability moves to this higher level hinges on our ability to meet several challenges. We must redirect our gaze to encompass the system as a whole and not just the South; we must clarify and reconcile the goals that underlie radically different visions of a sustainable society; and we must broaden our vision to engage the contested issues of power, wealth, and authority that underlie current environmental problems.

Thinking Critically

1. In your judgment, does "sustainable development" represent a powerful synthesis of the twin needs for environmental protection and economic de-

velopment? Or is it a contradiction in terms? Is sustainability compatible with a wide array of definitions of "development" or does it narrowly limit what development can mean?

2. How do you think the members of the Brundtland Commission would respond to the criticisms voiced by Lohmann and Lélé?

3. Can there be a common framework for sustainability across the diverse societies of the global South? For North as well as South? Is a concept such as sustainability universal, or is it inherently contingent on culture?

4. Is the North's pathway to sustainability more likely to follow the course envisioned by Durning or by the World Business Council on Sustainable Development?

5. Are you an overconsumer, according to Durning's indicators of consumption? How much control do you have over your consumption? What aspects of your life would have to change in order for you to change from overconsumer to sustainer? What are the structural barriers to the sort of change Durning advocates?

Notes

1. For a view stressing the importance of paradigms in shaping global environmental futures, see Dennis C. Pirages, ed., *Building Sustainable Societies: A Blueprint for a Post-Industrial World* (Armonk, NY: M. E. Sharpe, 1996).

2. On the concept of development without growth, see Herman E. Daly and John B. Cobb Jr., *For the Common Good: Redirecting the Economy Toward Community, the Environment, and a Sustainable Future* (Boston: Beacon Press, 1989).

3. World Commission on Environment and Development (WCED), *Our Common Future* (New York: Oxford University Press, 1987), p. ix.

4. WCED, *Our Common Future*, p. 43.

5. A similar criticism has been made of the "global change" discourse that became increasingly influential in environmental circles beginning in the 1980s. See Frederick H. Buttel, Ann P. Hawkins, and Alison G. Power, "From Limits to Growth to Global Change," *Global Environmental Change* 1 (December 1990):57–66.

6. On ecological modernization, see Arthur P. J. Mol, "Ecological Modernization and the Global Economy," *Global Environmental Politics* 2, no. 2 (May 2002):92–115.

2 2

TOWARDS SUSTAINABLE DEVELOPMENT

WORLD COMMISSION ON ENVIRONMENT AND DEVELOPMENT

Sustainable development is development that meets the needs of the present without compromising the ability of future generations to meet their own needs. It contains within it two key concepts:

- the concept of 'needs,' in particular the essential needs of the world's poor, to which overriding priority should be given; and
- the idea of limitations imposed by the state of technology and social organization on the environment's ability to meet present and future needs.

Thus the goals of economic and social development must be defined in terms of sustainability in all countries—developed or developing, market-oriented or centrally planned. . . .

Development involves a progressive transformation of economy and society. A development path that is sustainable in a physical sense could theoretically be pursued even in a rigid social and political setting. But physical sustainability cannot be secured unless development policies pay attention to such considerations as changes in access to resources and in the distribution of costs and benefits. . . .

Excerpted from Chapter Two of World Commission on Environment and Development, *Our Common Future* (1987). Reprinted by permission of Oxford University Press.

The Concept of
Sustainable Development

The satisfaction of human needs and aspirations is the major objective of development. The essential needs of vast numbers of people in developing countries—for food, clothing, shelter, jobs—are not being met, and beyond their basic needs these people have legitimate aspirations for an improved quality of life. A world in which poverty and inequity are endemic will always be prone to ecological and other crises. Sustainable development requires meeting the basic needs of all and extending to all the opportunity to satisfy their aspirations for a better life.

Living standards that go beyond the basic minimum are sustainable only if consumption standards everywhere have regard for long-term sustainability. Yet many of us live beyond the world's ecological means, for instance in our patterns of energy use. Perceived needs are socially and culturally determined, and sustainable development requires the promotion of values that encourage consumption standards that are within the bounds of the ecological possible and to which all can reasonably aspire.

Meeting essential needs depends in part on achieving full growth potential, and sustainable development clearly requires economic growth in places where such needs are not being met. Elsewhere, it can be consistent with economic growth, provided the content of growth reflects the broad principles of sustainability and non-exploitation of others. But growth by itself is not enough. High levels of productive activity and widespread poverty can coexist, and can endanger the environment. Hence sustainable development requires that societies meet human needs both by increasing productive potential and by ensuring equitable opportunities for all.

An expansion in numbers can increase the pressure on resources and slow the rise in living standards in areas where deprivation is widespread. Though the issue is not merely one of population size but of the distribution of resources, sustainable development can only be pursued if demographic developments are in harmony with the changing productive potential of the ecosystem.

A society may in many ways compromise its ability to meet the essential needs of its people in the future—by overexploiting resources, for example. The direction of technological developments may solve some immediate problems but lead to even greater ones. . . . At a minimum, sustainable development must not endanger the natural systems that support life on Earth: the atmosphere, the waters, the soils, and the living beings.

Growth has no set limits in terms of population or resource use beyond which lies ecological disaster. Different limits hold for the use of energy, materials, water, and land. Many of these will manifest themselves in the form of rising costs and diminishing returns, rather than in the form of any sudden loss of a resource base. The accumulation of knowledge and the development of technology can enhance the carrying capacity of the resource base. But ultimate limits there are, and sustainability requires that long before these are reached, the world must ensure equitable access to the constrained resource and reorient technological efforts to relieve the pressure.

Economic growth and development obviously involve changes in the physical ecosystem. Every ecosystem everywhere cannot be preserved intact. . . . In general, renewable resources like forests and fish stocks need not be depleted provided the rate of use is within the limits of regeneration and natural growth. But most renewable resources are part of a complex and interlinked ecosystem, and maximum sustainable yield must be defined after taking into account system-wide effects of exploitation.

As for non-renewable resources, like fossil fuels and minerals, their use reduces the stock available for future generations. But this does not mean that such resources should not be used. In general the rate of depletion should take into account the criticality of that resource, the availability of technologies for minimizing depletion, and the likelihood of substitutes being available. . . . Sustainable development requires that the rate of depletion of non-renewable resources should foreclose as few future options as possible.

Development tends to simplify ecosystems and to reduce their diversity of species. . . . The loss of plant and animal species can greatly limit the options of future generations; so sustainable development requires the conservation of plant and animal species.

So-called free goods like air and water are also resources. . . . Sustainable development requires that the adverse impacts on the quality of air, water, and other natural elements are minimized so as to sustain the ecosystem's overall integrity.

In essence, sustainable development is a process of change in which the exploitation of resources, the direction of investments, the orientation of technological development, and institutional change are all in harmony and enhance both current and future potential to meet human needs and aspirations.

Equity and the Common Interest

. . . How are individuals in the real world to be persuaded or made to act in the common interest? The answer lies partly in education, institutional development, and law enforcement. But many problems of resource depletion and environmental stress arise from disparities in economic and political power. An industry may get away with unacceptable levels of air and water pollution because the people who bear the brunt of it are poor and unable to complain effectively. . . .

Ecological interactions do not respect the boundaries of individual ownership and political jurisdiction. . . . Traditional social systems recognized some aspects of this interdependence and enforced community control over agricultural practices and traditional rights relating to water, forests, and land. This enforcement of the 'common interest' did not necessarily impede growth and expansion though it may have limited the acceptance and diffusion of technical innovations.

Local interdependence has, if anything, increased because of the technology used in modern agriculture and manufacturing. Yet with this surge of technical progress, the growing 'enclosure' of common lands, the erosion of common rights in forests and other resources, and the spread of commerce and production for the market, the responsibilities for decision making are being taken away from both groups and individuals. This shift is still under way in many developing countries.

It is not that there is one set of villains and another of victims. All would be better off if each person took into account the effect of his or her acts upon others. But each is unwilling to assume that others will behave in this socially desirable fashion, and hence all continue to pursue narrow self-interest. Communities or governments can compensate for this isolation through laws, education, taxes, subsidies, and other methods. . . . Most important, effective participation in decisionmaking processes by local communities can help them articulate and effectively enforce their common interest. . . .

The enforcement of common interest often suffers because areas of political jurisdictions and areas of impact do not coincide. . . . No supranational authority exists to resolve such issues, and the common interest can only be articulated through international cooperation.

In the same way, the ability of a government to control its national economy is reduced by growing international economic interactions. . . . If economic power and the benefits of trade were more equally distributed, common interests would be generally recognized. But the gains from trade are unequally distributed, and patterns of trade in, say, sugar affect not merely a local sugar-producing sector, but the economies and ecologies of the many developing countries that depend heavily on this product.

The search for common interest would be less difficult if all development and environment problems had solutions that would leave everyone better off. This is seldom the case, and there are usually winners and losers. Many problems arise from inequalities in access to resources. . . . 'Losers' in environment/development conflicts include those who suffer more than their fair share of the health, property, and ecosystem damage costs of pollution.

As a system approaches ecological limits, inequalities sharpen. Thus when a watershed deteriorates, poor farmers suffer more because they cannot afford the same anti-erosion measures as richer farmers. . . . Globally, wealthier nations are better placed financially and technologically to cope with the effects of possible climatic change.

Hence, our inability to promote the common interest in sustainable development is often a product of the relative neglect of economic and social justice within and amongst nations.

Strategic Imperatives

The world must quickly design strategies that will allow nations to move from their present, often destructive, processes of growth and development onto sustainable development paths. . . .

Critical objectives for environment and development policies that follow from the concept of sustainable development include:

- reviving growth;
- changing the quality of growth;
- meeting essential needs for jobs, food, energy, water, and sanitation;
- ensuring a sustainable level of population;
- conserving and enhancing the resource base;
- reorienting technology and managing risk; and
- merging environment and economics in decision making.

Reviving Growth

. . . Development that is sustainable has to address the problem of the large number of people who . . . are unable to satisfy even the most basic of their needs. Poverty reduces people's capacity to use resources in a sustainable manner; it intensifies pressure on the environment. . . . A necessary but not a sufficient condition for the elimination of absolute poverty is a relatively rapid rise in per capita incomes in the Third World. It is therefore essential that the stagnant or declining growth trends of . . . [the 1980s] be reversed.

While attainable growth rates will vary, a certain minimum is needed to have any impact on absolute poverty. It seems unlikely that, taking developing countries as a whole, these objectives can be accomplished with per capita income growth of under 3 per cent. . . .

Growth must be revived in developing countries because that is where the links between economic growth, the alleviation of poverty, and environmental conditions operate most directly. Yet developing countries are part of an interdependent world economy; their prospects also depend on the levels and patterns of growth in industrialized nations. The medium-term prospects for industrial countries are for growth of 3–4 per cent. . . . Such growth rates could be environmentally sustainable if industrialized nations can continue the recent shifts in the content of their growth towards less material- and energy-intensive activities and the improvement of their efficiency in using materials and energy.

As industrialized nations use less materials and energy, however, they will provide smaller markets for commodities and minerals from the developing nations. Yet if developing nations focus their efforts upon eliminating poverty and satisfying essential human needs, then domestic demand will increase for both agricultural products and manufactured goods and some services. Hence the very logic of sustainable development implies an internal stimulus to Third World growth. . . .

Changing the Quality of Growth

Sustainable development involves more than growth. It requires a change in the content of growth, to make it less material- and energy-intensive and more equitable in its impact. These changes are required in all countries as part of a package of measures to maintain the stock of ecological capital, to improve the distribution of income, and to reduce the degree of vulnerability to economic crises.

The process of economic development must be more soundly based upon the realities of the stock of capital that sustains it. . . . For example, income from forestry operations is conventionally measured in terms of the value of timber and other products extracted, minus the costs of extraction. The costs of regenerating the forest are not taken into account, unless money is actually spent on such work. Thus figuring profits from logging rarely takes full account of the losses in future revenue incurred through degradation of the forest. . . . In all countries, rich or poor, economic development must take full account in its measurements of growth of the improvement or deterioration in the stock of natural resources. . . .

Yet it is not enough to broaden the range of economic variables taken into account. Sustainability requires views of human needs and well-being that incorporate such non-economic variables as education and health enjoyed for their own sake, clean air and water, and the protection of natural beauty. . . .

Economic and social development can and should be mutually reinforcing. Money spent on education and health can raise human productivity. Economic development can accelerate social development by providing opportunities for underprivileged groups or by spreading education more rapidly.

Meeting Essential Human Needs

The satisfaction of human needs and aspirations is so obviously an objective of productive activity that it may appear redundant to assert its central role in the concept of sustainable development. All too often poverty is such that people cannot satisfy their needs for survival and well-being even if goods and services are available. At the same time, the demands of those not in poverty may have major environmental consequences.

The principal development challenge is to meet the needs and aspirations of an expanding developing world population. The most basic of all needs is for a livelihood: that is, employment. Between 1985 and 2000 the labour force

in developing countries will increase by nearly 900 million, and new livelihood opportunities will have to be generated for 60 million persons every
year.[1] . . .

More food is required not merely to feed more people but to attack under-
nourishment. . . . Though the focus at present is necessarily on staple foods,
the projections given above also highlight the need for a high rate of growth
of protein availability. In Africa, the task is particularly challenging given the
recent declining per capita food production and the current constraints on
growth. In Asia and Latin America, the required growth rates in calorie and
protein consumption seem to be more readily attainable. But increased food
production should not be based on ecologically unsound production policies
and compromise long-term prospects for food security.

Energy is another essential human need, one that cannot be universally met
unless energy consumption patterns change. The most urgent problem is the
requirements of poor Third World households, which depend mainly on fuelwood. By the turn of the century, 3 billion people may live in areas where
wood is cut faster than it grows or where fuelwood is extremely scarce.[2] Corrective action would both reduce the drudgery of collecting wood over long
distances and preserve the ecological base. . . .

The linked basic needs of housing, water supply, sanitation, and health care
are also environmentally important. Deficiencies in these areas are often visible manifestations of environmental stress. In the Third World, the failure to
meet these key needs is one of the major causes of many communicable diseases such as malaria, gastro-intestinal infestations, cholera, and typhoid. . . .

Ensuring a Sustainable Level of Population

The sustainability of development is intimately linked to the dynamics of
population growth. The issue, however, is not simply one of global population
size. A child born in a country where levels of material and energy use are
high places a greater burden on the Earth's resources than a child born in a
poorer country. . . .

In industrial countries, the overall rate of population growth is under 1 per
cent, and several countries have reached or are approaching zero population
growth. The total population of the industrialized world could increase from
its current 1.2 billion to about 1.4 billion in the year 2025.[3]

The greater part of global population increase will take place in developing
countries, where the 1985 population of 3.7 billion may increase to 6.8 billion
by 2025.[4] The Third World does not have the option of migration to 'new'
lands, and the time available for adjustment is much less than industrial
countries had. Hence the challenge now is to quickly lower population growth
rates, especially in regions such as Africa, where these rates are increasing.

Birth rates declined in industrial countries largely because of economic and social development. Rising levels of income and urbanization and the changing role of women all played important roles. Similar processes are now at work in developing countries. These should be recognized and encouraged. Population policies should be integrated with other economic and social development programmes—female education, health care, and the expansion of the livelihood base of the poor. . . .

Developing-country cities are growing much faster than the capacity of authorities to cope. Shortages of housing, water, sanitation, and mass transit are widespread. A growing proportion of city-dwellers live in slums and shanty towns, many of them exposed to air and water pollution and to industrial and natural hazards. Further deterioration is likely, given that most urban growth will take place in the largest cities. Thus more manageable cities may be the principal gain from slower rates of population growth. . . .

Conserving and Enhancing the Resource Base

. . . Pressure on resources increases when people lack alternatives. Development policies must widen people's options for earning a sustainable livelihood, particularly for resource-poor households and in areas under ecological stress. . . .

The conservation of agricultural resources is an urgent task because in many parts of the world cultivation has already been extended to marginal lands, and fishery and forestry resources have been overexploited. These resources must be conserved and enhanced to meet the needs of growing populations. Land use in agriculture and forestry should be based on a scientific assessment of land capacity, and the annual depletion of topsoil, fish stock, or forest resources must not exceed the rate of regeneration.

The pressures on agricultural land from crop and livestock production can be partly relieved by increasing productivity. But shortsighted, short-term improvements in productivity can create different forms of ecological stress, such as the loss of genetic diversity in standing crops, salinization and alkalization of irrigated lands, nitrate pollution of ground-water, and pesticide residues in food. Ecologically more benign alternatives are available. Future increases in productivity, in both developed and developing countries, should be based on the better controlled application of water and agrochemicals, as well as on more extensive use of organic manures and non-chemical means of pest control. These alternatives can be promoted only by an agricultural policy based on ecological realities. . . .

The ultimate limits to global development are perhaps determined by the availability of energy resources and by the biosphere's capacity to absorb the by-products of energy use.[5] These energy limits may be approached far sooner than the limits imposed by other material resources. First, there are the supply problems: the depletion of oil reserves, the high cost and environmental impact of coal mining, and the hazards of nuclear technology. Second, there are emission problems, most notably acid pollution and carbon dioxide build-up leading to global warming.

Some of these problems can be met by increased use of renewable energy sources. But the exploitation of renewable sources such as fuelwood and hydropower also entails ecological problems. Hence sustainability requires a clear focus on conserving and efficiently using energy.

Industrialized countries must recognize that their energy consumption is polluting the biosphere and eating into scarce fossil fuel supplies. Recent improvements in energy efficiency and a shift towards less energy-intensive sectors have helped limit consumption. But the process must be accelerated to reduce per capita consumption and encourage a shift to non-polluting sources and technologies. The simple duplication in the developing world of industrial countries' energy use patterns is neither feasible nor desirable. . . .

The prevention and reduction of air and water pollution will remain a critical task of resource conservation. Air and water quality come under pressure from such activities as fertilizer and pesticide use, urban sewage, fossil fuel burning, the use of certain chemicals, and various other industrial activities. Each of these is expected to increase the pollution load on the biosphere substantially, particularly in developing countries, Cleaning up after the event is an expensive solution. Hence all countries need to anticipate and prevent these pollution problems. . . .

Reorienting Technology and Managing Risk

The fulfillment of all these tasks will require the reorientation of technology—the key link between humans and nature. First, the capacity for technological innovation needs to be greatly enhanced in developing countries. . . . Second, the orientation of technology development must be changed to pay greater attention to environmental factors.

The technologies of industrial countries are not always suited or easily adaptable to the socio-economic and environmental conditions of developing countries. To compound the problem, the bulk of world research and development addresses few of the pressing issues facing these countries. . . . Not enough is being done to adapt recent innovations in materials technology, energy conservation, information technology, and biotechnology to the needs of developing countries. . . .

In all countries, the processes of generating alternative technologies, upgrading traditional ones, and selecting and adapting imported technologies should be informed by environmental resource concerns. Most technological research by commercial organizations is devoted to product and process innovations that have market value. Technologies are needed that produce 'social goods,' such as improved air quality or increased product life, or that resolve problems normally outside the cost calculus of individual enterprises, such as the external costs of pollution or waste disposal.

The role of public policy is to ensure, through incentives and disincentives, that commercial organizations find it worthwhile to take fuller account of environmental factors in the technologies they develop. . . .

Merging Environment and Economics in Decision Making

The common theme throughout this strategy for sustainable development is the need to integrate economic and ecological considerations in decision making. They are, after all, integrated in the workings of the real world. This will require a change in attitudes and objectives and in institutional arrangements at every level.

Economic and ecological concerns are not necessarily in opposition. For example, policies that conserve the quality of agricultural land and protect forests improve the long-term prospects for agricultural development. . . . But the compatibility of environmental and economic objectives is often lost in the pursuit of individual or group gains, with little regard for the impacts on others, with a blind faith in science's ability to find solutions, and in ignorance of the distant consequences of today's decisions. Institutional rigidities add to this myopia. . . .

Intersectoral connections create patterns of economic and ecological interdependence rarely reflected in the ways in which policy is made. Sectoral organizations tend to pursue sectoral objectives and to treat their impacts on other sectors as side effects, taken into account only if compelled to do so. . . . Many of the environment and development problems that confront us have their roots in this sectoral fragmentation of responsibility. Sustainable development requires that such fragmentation be overcome.

Sustainability requires the enforcement of wider responsibilities for the impacts of decisions. This requires changes in the legal and institutional frameworks that will enforce the common interest. Some necessary changes in the legal framework start from the proposition that an environment adequate for health and well-being is essential for all human beings—including future generations. . . .

The law alone cannot enforce the common interest. It principally needs community knowledge and support, which entails greater public participation in the decisions that affect the environment. This is best secured by decentralizing the management of resources upon which local communities depend, and giving these communities an effective say over the use of these resources. . . .

Changes are also required in the attitudes and procedures of both public and private-sector enterprises. Moreover, environmental regulation must move beyond the usual menu of safety regulations, zoning laws, and pollution control enactments; environmental objectives must be built into taxation, prior approval procedures for investment and technology choice, foreign trade incentives, and all components of development policy.

The integration of economic and ecological factors into the law and into decision-making systems within countries has to be matched at the international level. The growth in fuel and material use dictates that direct physical linkages between ecosystems of different countries will increase. Economic interactions through trade, finance, investment, and travel will also grow and heighten economic and ecological interdependence. Hence in the future, even more so than now, sustainable development requires the unification of economics and ecology in international relations. . . .

Conclusion

In its broadest sense, the strategy for sustainable development aims to promote harmony among human beings and between humanity and nature. In the specific context of the development and environment crises of the 1980s, which current national and international political and economic institutions have not and perhaps cannot overcome, the pursuit of sustainable development requires:

- a political system that secures effective citizen participation in decision-making,
- an economic system that is able to generate surpluses and technical knowledge on a self-reliant and sustained basis,
- a social system that provides for solutions for the tensions arising from disharmonious development,
- a production system that respects the obligation to preserve the ecological base for development,
- a technological system that can search continuously for new solutions,
- an international system that fosters sustainable patterns of trade and finance, and
- an administrative system that is flexible and has the capacity for self-correction.

These requirements are more in the nature of goals that should underlie national and international action on development. What matters is the sincerity with which these goals are pursued and the effectiveness with which departures from them are corrected.

Notes

1. Based on data from World Bank, *World Development Report 1984* (New York: Oxford University Press, 1984).

2. FAO, *Fuelwood Supplies in the Developing Countries,* Forestry Paper No. 42 (Rome: 1983).

3. Department of International Economic and Social Affairs, *World Population Prospects and Projections as Assessed in 1984* (New York: United Nations, 1986).

4. Ibid.

5. W. Häfele and W. Sassin, "Resources and Endowments, An Outline of Future Energy Systems," in P. W. Hemily and M. N. Ozdas (eds.), *Science and Future Choice* (Oxford: Clarendon Press, 1979).

2 3

WHOSE
COMMON FUTURE?

LARRY LOHMANN

Never underestimate the ability of modern elites to work out ways of coming through a crisis with their power intact.

From the days of the American populists through the Depression, postwar reconstruction, the end of colonialism and the age of 'development,' our contemporary leaders and their institutions have sought to turn pressures for change to their advantage. The New Deal, the Marshall Plan, Bretton Woods, multilateral lending—all in their turn have taken challenges to the system and transformed them into ways of defusing popular initiatives and developing the economic and political domains of the powerful.

Now comes the global environmental crisis. Once again those in high places are making solemn noises about "grave threats to our common security and the very survival of our planet." Once again their proposed solutions leave the main causes of the trouble untouched. As ordinary people try to reclaim local lands, forests and waters from the depredations of business and the state, and work to build democratic movements to preserve the planet's health, those in power continue to occupy themselves with damage control and the containment of threats to the way power is currently distributed and held. The difference is important to keep in mind when listening to the calls to arms from the new statesmen and women of 'environmentalism.'

This article first appeared in the May/June 1990 issue of *The Ecologist*, Volume 20, No. 3, www.theecologist.org. Reprinted with permission.

Political Management of the Crisis

Two of the most prominent of these, former Norwegian Prime Minister Gro Harlem Brundtland and Canadian businessman Maurice Strong, . . . Secretary General of the 1992 United Nations Conference on Environment and Development (UNCED), were in Vancouver in March [1990] to reiterate the message that we all share a 'common future' in environmental preservation and 'sustainable development.' Their speeches at the 'Globe 90' conference and 'green' trade fair gave valuable clues about how the more progressive global elites are organizing themselves for the political management of the environment crisis.

The first instinct of those in high places when faced with a problem is to avoid analyzing its causes if doing so would put the current power structure in an unfavourable light. In Vancouver, Brundtland averted her gaze from the destruction brought about through economic growth, technology transfer and capital flows from North to South and vice versa, and instead rounded up the usual suspects of 'poverty,' 'population growth' and 'underdevelopment,' without exploring the origins of any of them. She spoke of global warming, a declining resource base, pollution, overexploitation of resources and a 'crushing debt burden' for the South, but omitted mentioning who or what might be responsible. Environmental problems, she implied, were mainly to be found in the South. Admittedly the North had made some mistakes, she said, but luckily it knows the answers now and can prevent the South from making the same errors as it toddles along behind the North on the path to sustainable development.

Whose Security?

The stress of a crisis also tends to drive those in power to the use of vague code words that can rally other members of the elite. In Vancouver the word was 'security.' Brundtland and Strong warned of the "new (environmental) threats to our security" and dwelt on the ideas of a 'global concept of security,' a 'safe future' and a new 'security alliance' with an obsessiveness worthy of Richard Nixon.

What was all this talk of 'security' about? In the rural societies where most of the world's people live, security generally means land, family, village and freedom from outside interference. Had the ex-Prime Minister of Norway and the Chairman of Strovest Holdings, Inc. suddenly become land reform activists and virulent opponents of the development projects and market economy expansion which uproot villagers from their farms, communities and livelihoods? Or were they perhaps hinting at another kind of security, the security that First World privilege wants against the economic and political chaos that would follow environmental collapse? In the atmosphere of Globe 90, where everyone was constantly assured that all humanity had 'common security' interests, it was not always easy to keep in mind the distinction between the first, which entails devolution of power, and the second, which requires the reverse.

A third instinct of crisis managers in high places is to seek the 'solution' that requires the least change to the existing power structure. Here Brundtland and Strong, as befits two contenders for the UN Secretary-Generalship, repeated a formula to be found partly in UN General Assembly documents relating to UNCED. This is:

1. reverse the financial flows currently coursing from South to North, using debt relief, new lending, and new infusions of aid possibly augmented by taxes on fossil fuels and transfers from military budgets;
2. transfer technology, particularly 'green' technology, from North to South; and
3. boost economic growth, particularly in the South.

This scheme has obvious attractions for the world's powerful. For one thing, a resumption of net North-South capital flows would provide a bonanza for Northern export industries. Funds from the West and Japan would be sent on a quick round trip through a few institutions in other parts of the world before being returned, somewhat depleted by payoffs to elites along the way, to the coffers of Northern firms. Third World income freed up by debt relief would add immensely to corporate profits. Buoyed up by a fresh flow of funds, Southern leaders would become more receptive to the advice of Northern-dominated institutions and more dependent on Northern technology and aid. Injections of remedial technology, in addition, might well provide an incentive for the South to follow the strategy of dealing with the effects rather than the causes of environmental degradation. That would mean more money for both polluting and pollution-correcting industries.

The scheme also shores up the present industrial and financial system by suggesting that the solution to the environmental crisis lies within that system. . . . It implies that environmental issues are technological and financial and not matters of social equity and distribution of power—discussion of which would call much of the system into question. The scheme invokes and reinforces the superstitions that it is lack of capital that leads to environmental crisis; that capital flows are going to 'expand the resource base,' replace soil fertility and restore water tables and tropical forests lost to commercial exploitation; that poverty will be somehow relieved rather than exacerbated by economic growth; and that capital flows 'naturally' in large quantities from North to South.[1]

Weighing Up the Costs

Admittedly, the UNCED plan has costs for those in power. Bankers may not be overjoyed at the prospect of debt relief, but since the alternatives seem to be either continued insupportable and destabilizing South-North net financial transfers or the perpetuation of the process of servicing Third World debts with new loans, they may agree in the end. Northern countries will also have to spend massively on 'green' technology now in order to be in a position to put pressure on the South to do the same later.[2] But this is not necessarily a bad thing for industry, which can 'clean up' the mess it itself makes around the world, perhaps in the process creating new problems which will require further business solutions. As one of Globe 90's organizers put it, "a solution to most environmental issues is a business opportunity."[3] Another obstacle to the UNCED scheme is that it may stir resistance among its Southern 'beneficiaries.'...

Perhaps a bigger problem for the UNCED scheme is that it does not actually address the environmental crisis in either North or South. By tailoring solutions not to the problems but to the interests of those who created them, the plan is in fact likely to make things worse.... The UNCED plan will reinforce Southern dependence on environmentally destructive models of development imposed by the North and increase the power of Southern elites over their societies. It will promote technology most of which, like the tree-planting machine on display at Globe 90, has only a spurious claim to being 'green' and which will have to be paid for eventually by cashing in resources. It does not examine the effects of importing large amounts of capital into the South and endorses the continuing devastating economization of the natural and social heritage of both North and South. It is, however, probably as far as elites can go at present without challenging their own position. As for the future, there is always the hope that, as the brochure of one Japanese organization present at Globe 90 put it, the problems of global warming, ozone depletion, acid rain, desertification and tropical forest destruction can someday be solved "through technological innovations."[4]

The 'New' Alliance

A fourth tendency among elite crisis managers is to identify the executors of the solution with the existing power structure....

The technical fixes of the UNCED agenda are to be promoted and implemented by a 'new global partnership' or environmental quadruple alliance consisting of industry, government, scientists and non-governmental organizations—"the most important security alliance we have ever entered into on this planet" according to Strong....

Seasoned observers . . . may wonder what is supposed to distinguish the new environmental alliance from the familiar sort of elite ententes that helped land the world in its current environmental mess—the old-boy networks and clubs typified by the military-industrial complex, the World Bank's web of clients, consultants and contractors, the Trilateral Commission, and so on.

Co-opting the NGOs

The answer is non-governmental organizations (NGOs). . . . Why the interest in NGOs? One reason is that they might be used to push business and government in a slightly less destructive direction. Another is that official or corporate environmental initiatives need credibility. Establishment political strategists have not failed to note the growing role of NGOs in recent popular movements from Latin America to South and Southeast Asia and Eastern and Central Europe. . . . 'New alliance' leaders are thus courting and manipulating NGOs, particularly tame NGO umbrella groups, groups with establishment links, and groups with jet-set ambitions, in the hope of being able to use their names to say that UNCED initiatives have the backing of environmentalists, youth, trade unions, women's groups, the socially concerned and "all the nations and peoples of the world."

These manoeuvres, however, cannot conceal the fact that grassroots NGO 'participation' in UNCED and other 'new alliance' activities, to say nothing of the participation of ordinary people, is a fraud. . . . It is governments who decide who is allowed to say what, just as it is governments who will be signing agreements. . . . NGOs are expected to carry governments' message to the people and help them stay in power.[5]

A Common Interest?

Outside official meetings, of course, it is business whose voice will inevitably carry above that of all others in the 'new alliance.' If Globe 90 is any indication, it is not likely to be a voice urging environmental and political sanity. Nor are grassroots-oriented environmental activists likely to be excited about joining a coalition carrying the industry agenda. . . .

Many environmentalists, nevertheless, will feel that joining the 'new global alliance' can do no harm if it presents an opportunity for nudging business and government in a more 'green' direction. Such a conclusion is questionable. It is one thing to pressure business and government into changing their ways with all the means at one's disposal. It is quite another to pledge allegiance in advance to a new elite coalition with a predetermined or unknown agenda which one will have little power to change.

Any alliance which tells us that we *must* seek consensus, that no opposition is to be brooked to Brundtland as Our Common Leader, or that there is a perfect potential community of interest between, say, a UN bureaucrat and a Sri Lankan subsistence fisherman, is one that deserves suspicion at the outset. Consensus-seeking is neither good nor necessary in itself—it may, after all, function merely to conceal exploitation—but only when it is agreed by all parties after full discussion to be possible and fruitful.

This is not to denigrate the ambitious professionals associated with the UNCED, but merely to state a fact. To seek genuine solutions it is necessary to accept, respect and explore differences, to face causes, and to understand the workings of power. It may well be that parties with wildly divergent interests can come to agreements on the crisis confronting the planet. Come the millennium, we may all even be able to form one grand coalition. But until then, it is best to remember the lesson of history: that no matter how warmly it seems to have embraced the slogans of the rebels, the Empire always strikes back.

Notes

1. Payer, C., 'Causes of the Debt Crisis' in B. Onimode (ed.), *The IMF, the World Bank and African Debt: the Social and Political Impact,* Zed, London, 1989, pp. 7–16.

2. 'Action for Whose Common Future?' *Solidarity for Equality, Ecology and Development Newsletter* 1, 1989, Torggt. 34, N–1083 Oslo 1, Norway, pp. 6–7.

3. Wiebe, J. D., Vice-President, Globe 90, Executive Vice-President, Asia Pacific Foundation, in *Globe 90 Official Buyers' Guide and Trade Fair Directory,* p. 13.

4. Global Industrial and Social Progress Research Institute brochure, p. 3.

5. United Nations General Assembly, A/CONF 151/PC/2, 23 February 1990, p. 8.

24

SUSTAINABLE DEVELOPMENT: A CRITICAL REVIEW

Sharachchandra M. Lélé

Introduction

The last few years have seen a dramatic transformation in the environment-development debate. The question being asked is no longer "Do development and environmental concerns contradict each other?" but "How can sustainable development be achieved?" All of a sudden the phrase Sustainable Development (SD) has become pervasive. . . . It appears to have gained the broad-based support that earlier development concepts such as "ecodevelopment" lacked, and is poised to become the developmental paradigm of the 1990s.

But murmurs of disenchantment are also being heard. "What *is* SD?" is being asked increasingly frequently without, however, clear answers forthcoming. SD is in real danger of becoming a cliché like appropriate technology—a fashionable phrase that everyone pays homage to but nobody cares to define. . . . Agencies such as the World Bank, the Asian Development Bank and the Organization for Economic Cooperation and Development have been quick to adopt the new rhetoric. The absence of a clear theoretical and analytical framework, however, makes it difficult to determine whether the new policies will indeed foster an environmentally sound and socially meaningful form of development. . . .

Originally published in *World Development* 19, 6 (June 1991):607–621. Reprinted with permission from Elsevier Science Ltd., Pergamon Imprint, Oxford, England.

The persuasive power of SD (and hence the political strength of the SD movement) stems from the underlying claim that new insights into physical and social phenomena force one to concur with the operational conclusions of the SD platform almost regardless of one's fundamental ethical persuasions and priorities. I argue that while these new insights are important, the argument is not inexorable, and that the issues are more complex than is made out to be. Hence . . . many of the policy prescriptions being suggested in the name of SD stem from subjective (rather than consensual) ideas about goals and means, and worse, are often inadequate and even counterproductive. . . .

Interpreting Sustainable Development

The manner in which the phrase "sustainable development" is used and interpreted varies so much that while O'Riordan (1985) called SD a "contradiction in terms," Redclift suggests that it may be just "another development truism" (Redclift, 1987, p. 1). These interpretational problems, though ultimately conceptual, have some semantic roots. Most people use the phrase "sustainable development" interchangeably with "ecologically sustainable or environmentally sound development" (Tolba, 1984a). This interpretation is characterized by: (a) "sustainability" being understood as "ecological sustainability"; and (b) a conceptualization of SD as a process of change that has (ecological) sustainability added to its list of objectives.

In contrast, sustainable development is sometimes interpreted as "sustained growth," "sustained change," or simply "successful" development. Let us examine how these latter interpretations originate and why they are less useful than the former one. . . .

Contradictions and Trivialities

Taken literally, sustainable development would simply mean "development that can be continued—either indefinitely or for the implicit time period of concern." But what is development? Theorists and practitioners have both been grappling with the word and the concept for at least the past four decades. . . . Some equate development with GNP growth, others include any number of socially desirable phenomena in their conceptualization. The point to be noted is that development is *a process of directed change*. Definitions of development thus embody both (a) the objectives of this process, and (b) the means of achieving these objectives.

Unfortunately, a distinction between objectives and means is often not made in the development rhetoric. This has led to "sustainable development" frequently being interpreted as simply a process of change that can be continued forever. . . . This interpretation is either impossible or trivial. When development is taken to be synonymous with growth in material consumption—which it often is even today—SD would be "sustaining the growth in material consumption" (presumably indefinitely). But such an idea contradicts the general recognition that *"ultimate* limits [to usable resources] exist"[1] (WCED, p. 45, emphasis added). At best, it could be argued that growth in the per capita consumption of certain basic goods is necessary in certain regions of the world in the short term. To use "sustainable development" synonymously with "sustain[ing] growth performance" (Idachaba, 1987) or to cite the high rates of growth in agricultural production in South Asia as an example of SD is therefore a misleading usage, or at best a short-term and localized notion that goes against the long-term global perspective of SD.

One could finesse this contradiction by conceptualizing development as simply a process of socio-economic change. But one cannot carry on a meaningful discussion unless one states what the objectives of such change are and why one should worry about continuing the process of change indefinitely. . . .

Sustainability

. . . The concept of sustainability originated in the context of renewable resources such as forests or fisheries, and has subsequently been adopted as a broad slogan by the environmental movement. Most proponents of sustainability therefore take it to mean "the existence of the ecological conditions necessary to support human life at a specified level of well-being through future generations," what I call *ecological sustainability*. . . .

Since ecological sustainability emphasizes the constraints and opportunities that nature presents to human activities, ecologists and physical scientists frequently dominate its discussion. But what they actually focus on are the ecological conditions for ecological sustainability—the biophysical "laws" or patterns that determine environmental responses to human activities and humans' ability to use the environment. The major contribution of the environment-development debate is, I believe, the realization that in addition to or in conjunction with these ecological conditions, there are social conditions that influence the ecological sustainability or unsustainability of the people-nature interaction. To give a stylized example, one could say that soil erosion undermining the agricultural basis for human society is a case of ecological (un)sustainability. It could be caused by farming on marginal lands without adequate soil conservation measures—the ecological cause. But the phenomenon of marginalization of peasants may have social roots, which would then be the social causes of ecological unsustainability. . . .

The Concept of Sustainable Development

Evolution of Objectives

The term sustainable development came into prominence in 1980, when the International Union for the Conservation of Nature and Natural Resources (IUCN) presented the World Conservation Strategy (WCS) with "the overall aim of achieving sustainable development through the conservation of living resources" (IUCN, 1980). Critics acknowledged that "By identifying Sustainable Development as the basic goal of society, the WCS was able to make a profound contribution toward reconciling the interests of the development community with those of the environmental movement" (Khosla, 1987). They pointed out, however, that the strategy restricted itself to living resources [and] focussed primarily on the necessity of maintaining genetic diversity, habits and ecological processes. . . . It was . . . unable to deal adequately with sensitive or controversial issues—those relating to the international economic and political order, war and armament, population and urbanization (Khosla, 1987). . . .

The United Nations Environment Program (UNEP) was at the forefront of the effort to articulate and popularize the concept. UNEP's concept of SD was said to encompass

1. help for the very poor, because they are left with no options but to destroy their environment;
2. the idea of self-reliant development, within natural resource constraints;
3. the idea of cost-effective development using nontraditional economic criteria;
4. the great issues of health control [*sic*], appropriate technology, food self-reliance, clean water and shelter for all; and
5. the notion that people-centered initiatives are needed (Tolba, 1984a).

This statement epitomizes the mixing of goals and means, or more precisely, of fundamental objectives and operational ones, that has burdened much of the SD literature. While providing food, water, good health and shelter have traditionally been the fundamental objectives of most development models (including UNEP's), it is not clear whether self-reliance, cost-effectiveness, appropriateness of technology and people-centeredness are additional objectives or the operational requirements for achieving the traditional ones. . . .

In contrast to the aforementioned, the currently popular definition of SD—the one adopted by the World Commission on Environment and Development (WCED)—is quite brief:

Sustainable development is development that meets the needs of the present without compromising the ability of future generations to meet their own needs (WCED, 1987; p. 43).

The constraint of "not compromising the ability of future generations to meet their needs" is (presumably) considered by the Commission to be equivalent to the requirement of some level of ecological and social sustainability.[2]

While the WCED's statement of the fundamental objectives of SD is brief, the Commission is much more elaborate about (what are essentially) the operational objectives of SD. It states that "the critical objectives which follow from the concept of SD" are:

1. reviving growth;
2. changing the quality of growth;
3. meeting essential needs for jobs, food, energy, water, and sanitation;
4. ensuring a sustainable level of population;
5. conserving and enhancing the resource base;
6. reorienting technology and managing risk;
7. merging environment and economics in decision making; and
8. reorienting international economic relations (WCED, 1987, p. 49).

Most organizations and agencies actively promoting the concept of SD subscribe to some or all of these objectives with, however, the notable addition of a ninth operational goal, viz.,

9. making development more participatory.[3]

This formulation can therefore be said to represent the mainstream of SD thinking. This "mainstream" includes international environmental agencies such as UNEP, IUCN and the World Wildlife Fund (WWF), developmental agencies including the World Bank, the US Agency for International Development, the Canadian and Swedish international development agencies, research and dissemination organizations such as the World Resources Institute, the International Institute for Environment and Development, the Worldwatch Institute (1984–88), and activist organizations and groups such as the Global Tomorrow Coalition. . . .

The Premises of SD

The perception in mainstream SD thinking of the environment-society link is based upon the following premises:

1. *Environmental degradation:*

- Environmental degradation is already affecting millions in the Third World, and is likely to severely reduce human well-being all across the globe within the next few generations.

- Environmental degradation is very often caused by poverty, because the poor have no option but to exploit resources for short-term survival.
- The interlinked nature of most environmental problems is such that environmental degradation ultimately affects everybody, although poorer individuals/nations may suffer more and sooner than richer ones.

2. *Traditional development objectives:*

- These are: providing basic needs and increasing the productivity of all resources (human, natural and economic) in developing countries, and maintaining the standard of living in the developed countries.
- These objectives do not necessarily conflict with the objective of ecological sustainability. In fact, achieving sustainable patterns of resource use is necessary for achieving these objectives permanently.
- It can be shown that, even for individual actors, environmentally sound methods are "profitable" in the long run, and often in the short run too.

3. *Process:*

- The process of development must be participatory to succeed even in the short run).

Given these premises, the need for a process of development that achieves the traditional objectives, results in ecologically sustainable patterns of resource use, and is implemented in a participatory manner is obvious.

Most of the SD literature is devoted to showing that this process is also feasible and can be made attractive to the actors involved. SD has become a bundle of neat fixes: technological changes that make industrial production processes less polluting and less resource intensive and yet more productive and profitable, economic policy changes that incorporate environmental considerations and yet achieve greater economic growth, procedural changes that use local non-governmental organizations (NGOs) so as to ensure grassroots participation, agriculture that is less harmful, less resource intensive and yet more productive, and so on. In short, SD is a "metafix" that will unite everybody from the profit-minded industrialist and risk-minimizing subsistence farmer to the equity-seeking social worker, the pollution-concerned or wildlife-loving First Worlder, the growth-maximizing policy maker, the goal-oriented bureaucrat, and therefore, the vote-counting politician.

Weaknesses

The major impact of the SD movement is the rejection of the notion that environmental conservation necessarily constrains development or that development necessarily means environmental pollution—certainly not an insignificant gain. Where the SD movement has faltered is in its inability to develop a set of concepts, criteria and policies that are coherent or consistent—both externally (with physical and social reality) and internally (with each other). The mainstream formulation of SD suffers from significant weaknesses in:

- its characterization of the problems of poverty and environmental degradation;
- its conceptualization of the objectives of development, sustainability and participation; and
- the strategy it has adopted in the face of incomplete knowledge and uncertainty.

Poverty and Environmental Degradation: An Incomplete Characterization

The fundamental premise of mainstream SD thinking is the two-way link between poverty and environmental degradation. . . .

In fact, however, even a cursory examination of the vast amount of research that has been done on the links between social and environmental phenomena suggests that both poverty and environmental degradation have deep and complex causes. . . .

To say that mainstream SD thinking has completely ignored [this complexity] would be unfair. But . . . inadequate technical know-how and managerial capabilities, common property resource management, and pricing and subsidy policies have been the major themes addressed, and the solutions suggested have been essentially techno-economic ones. . . . Deeper socio-political changes (such as land reform) or changes in cultural values (such as overconsumption in the North) are either ignored or paid lip-service. . . .

Conceptual Weaknesses

Removal of poverty (the traditional developmental objective), sustainability and participation are really the three fundamental objectives of the SD paradigm. Unfortunately, the manner in which these objectives are conceptualized and operationalized leaves much to be desired. On the one hand, economic growth is being adopted as a major operational objective that is consistent with both removal of poverty and sustainability. On the other hand, the concepts of sustainability and participation are poorly articulated, making it difficult to determine whether a particular development project actually promotes a particular form of sustainability, or what kind of participation will lead to what kind of social (and consequently, environmental) outcome.

The Role of Economic Growth. By the mid-1970s, it had seemed that the economic growth and trickle-down theory of development had been firmly rejected, and the "basic needs approach" (Streeten, 1979) had taken root in development circles. Yet economic growth continues to feature in today's debate on SD. In fact, "reviving [economic] growth" heads WCED's list of operational objectives quoted earlier. Two arguments are implicit in this adoption of economic growth as an operational objective. The first, a somewhat defensive one, is that there is no fundamental contradiction between economic growth and sustainability, because growth in economic activity may occur simultaneously with either an improvement or a deterioration in environmental quality. Thus, "governments concerned with long-term sustainability need not seek to limit growth in economic output so long as they stabilize aggregate natural resource consumption" (Goodland and Ledec, 1987). But one could turn this argument around and suggest that, if economic growth is not correlated with environmental sustainability, there is no reason to have economic growth as an operational objective of SD.[4]

The second argument in favor of economic growth is more positive. The basic premise of SD is that poverty is largely responsible for environmental degradation. Therefore, removal of poverty (i.e., development) is necessary for environmental sustainability. This, it is argued, implies that economic growth is absolutely necessary for SD. The only thing that needs to be done is to "change the quality of [this] growth" (WCED, 1987, pp. 52–54) to ensure that it does not lead to environmental destruction. In drawing such an inference, however, there is the implicit belief that economic growth is necessary (if not sufficient) for the removal of poverty. But was it not the fact that economic growth per se could not ensure the removal of poverty that led to the adoption of the basic needs approach in the 1970s?

Thus, if economic growth by itself leads to neither environmental sustainability nor removal of poverty, it is clearly a "non-objective" for SD. The converse is a possibility worth exploring, viz., whether successful implementation of policies for poverty removal, long-term employment generation, environmental restoration and rural development will lead to growth in GNP, and, more important, to increases in investment, employment and income generation. This seems more than likely in developing countries, but not so certain in developed ones. In any case, economic growth may be the fallout of SD, but not its prime mover.

Sustainability. The World Conservation Strategy was probably the first attempt to carry the concept of sustainability beyond simple renewable resource systems. It suggested three ecological principles for ecological sustainability (see the nomenclature developed above), viz., "maintenance of essential eco-logical pro-cesses and life-support systems, the preservation of genetic diver-sity, and the sustainable utilization of species and resources" (IUCN, 1980). This definition, though a useful starting point, is clearly recursive as it invokes "sustainability" in resource use without defining it. Many subsequent attempts to discuss the notion are disturbingly muddled. There is a very real danger of the term becoming a meaningless cliché, unless a concerted effort is made to add precision and content to the discussion. . . .

Any discussion of sustainability must first answer the questions "What is to be sustained? For whom? How long?" The value of the concept (like that of SD), however, lies in its ability to generate an operational consensus between groups with fundamentally different answers to these questions, i.e., those concerned either about the survival of future human generations, or about the survival of wildlife, or human health, or the satisfaction of immediate subsistence needs (food, fuel, fodder) with a low degree of risk. It is therefore vital to identify those aspects of sustainability that do actually cater to such diverse interests, and those that involve tradeoffs.

Differentiating between ecological and social sustainability could be a first step toward clarifying some of the discussion. Further, in the case of ecologi-cal sustainability, a distinction needs to be made between renewable re-sources, nonrenewable resources, and environmental processes that are cru-cial to human life, as well as to life at large. The few researchers who have begun to explore the idea of ecological sustainability emphasize its multidi-mensional and complex nature. . . .

In the rush to derive ecological principles of (ecological) sustainability, we cannot afford to lose sight of the social conditions that determine which of these principles are socially acceptable, and to what extent. Sociologists, eco-Marxists and political ecologists are pointing out the crucial role of socioeco-nomic structures and institutions in the pattern and extent of environmental degradation globally. Neoclassical economists, whose theories have perhaps had the greatest influence in development policy making in the past and who there-fore bear the responsibility for its social and environmental failures, however, have been very slow in modifying their theories and prescriptions. The SD movement will have to formulate a clear agenda for research in what is being called "ecological economics" and press for its adoption by the mainstream of economics in order to ensure the possibility of real changes in policy making.

Social sustainability is a more nebulous concept than ecological sustain-ability. Brown et al. (1987), in a somewhat techno-economic vein, state that sustainability implies "the existence and operation of an infrastructure (trans-portation and communication), services (health, education, and culture), and government (agreements, laws, and enforcement)." Tisdell (1988) talks about "the sustainability of political and social structures" and Norgaard (1988) ar-gues for cultural sustainability, which includes value and belief systems. De-tailed analyses of the concept, however, seem to be nonexistent.[5] Perhaps achieving desired social situations is itself so difficult that discussing their maintainability is not very useful; perhaps goals are even more dynamic in a social context than in an ecological one, so that maintainability is not such an important attribute of social institutions/structures. There is, however, no contradiction between the social and ecological sustainability; rather, they can complement and inform each other.

Participation. A notable feature of . . . some of the earlier SD literature was the emphasis placed on equity and social justice. . . . Subsequently, however, the mainstream appears to have quietly dropped these terms (suggesting at least a deemphasizing of these objectives), and has instead focused on "local participation."

There are, however, three problems with this shift. First, by using the terms equity, participation and decentralization interchangeably, it is being suggested that participation and decentralization are equivalent, and that they can somehow substitute for equity and social justice. . . .

Second, the manner in which participation is being operationalized shows up the narrow-minded, quick-fix and deceptive approach adopted by the mainstream promoters of SD. . . . Mainstream SD literature blithely assumes and insists that "involvement of local NGOs" in project implementation will ensure project success (Maniates, 1990; he dubs this the "NGOization" of SD).

Third, there is an assumption that participation or at least equity and social justice will necessarily reinforce ecological sustainability. Attempts to test such assumptions rigorously have been rare. But preliminary results seem to suggest that equity in resource access may not lead to sustainable resource use unless new institutions for resource management are carefully built and nurtured. . . . This should not be misconstrued as an argument against the need for equity, but rather as a word of caution against the tendency to believe that social equity automatically ensures environmental sustainability (or vice-versa).. . .

Concluding Remarks:
Dilemmas and Agendas

The proponents of SD are faced with a dilemma that affects any program of political action and social change: the dilemma between the urge to take strong stands on fundamental concerns and the need to gain wide political acceptance and support. . . . SD is being packaged as the inevitable outcome of objective scientific analysis, virtually an historical necessity, that does not contradict the deep-rooted normative notion of development as economic growth. In other words, SD is an attempt to have one's cake and eat it too.

It may be argued that this is indeed possible, that the things that are wrong and need to be changed are quite obvious, and there are many ways of fixing them without significantly conflicting with either age-old power structures or the modern drive for a higher material standard of living. . . . If, by using the politically correct jargon of economic growth and development and by packaging SD in the manner mentioned above, it were possible to achieve even 50% success in implementing this bundle of "conceptually imprecise" policies, the net reduction achieved in environmental degradation and poverty would be unprecedented.

I believe, however, that (analogous to the arguments in SD) in the long run there is no contradiction between better articulation of the terms, concepts, analytical methods and policy-making principles, and gaining political strength and broad social acceptance—especially at the grassroots. In fact, such clarification and articulation is necessary if SD is to avoid either being dismissed as another development fad or being coopted by forces opposed to changes in status quo. More specifically, proponents and analysts of SD need to:

A. clearly reject the attempts (and temptation) to focus on economic growth as [a] means to poverty removal and/or environmental sustainability;
B. recognize the internal inconsistencies and inadequacies in the theory and practice of neoclassical economics, particularly as it relates to environmental and distributional issues; in economic analyses, move away from arcane mathematical models toward exploring empirical questions such as limits to the substitution of capital for resources, impacts of different sustainability policies on different economic systems, etc.;
C. accept the existence of structural, technological and cultural causes of poverty and environmental degradation; develop methodologies for estimating relative importance of and interaction between these causes in specific situations; and explore political, institutional and educational solutions to them;
D. understand the multiple dimensions of sustainability, and attempt to develop measures, criteria and principles for them; and
E. explore what patterns and levels of source demand and use would be compatible with different forms or levels of ecological and social sustainability, and with different notions of equity and social justice.

There are, fortunately, some signs that a debate on these lines has now begun.

In a sense, if SD is to be really "sustained" as a development paradigm, two apparently divergent efforts are called for: making SD more precise in its conceptual underpinnings, while allowing more flexibility and diversity of approaches in developing strategies that might lead to a society living in harmony with the environment and with itself.

References

Brown, B. J., M. Hanson, D. Liverman, and R. Merideth, Jr. "Global Sustainability: Toward Definition," Environmental Management, Vol. 11, No. 6 (1987), pp. 713–719.

Brown, L. R., *Building a Sustainable Society* (New York: W. W. Norton, 1981).

Chambers, R., *Sustainable Livelihoods: An Opportunity for the World Commission on Environment and Development* (Brighton, UK: Institute of Development Studies, University of Sussex, 1986).

Daly, H., *Economics, Ecology, Ethics: Essays Toward a Steady-State Economy* (San Francisco: W. H. Freeman, 1980).

Goodland, R., and G. Ledec, "Neoclassical Economics and Principles of Sustainable Development," *Ecological Modelling*, Vol. 38 (1987), pp. 19–46.

Idachaba, F. S., "Sustainability Issues in Agriculture Development," in T. J. Davis and I. A. Schirmer (Eds.), *Sustainability Issues in Agricultural Development* (Washington, DC: World Bank, 1987), pp. 18–53.

IUCN, *World Conservation Strategy: Living Resource Conservation for Sustainable Development* (Gland, Switzerland: International Union for Conservation of Nature and Natural Resources, United Nations Environment Program and World Wildlife Fund, 1980).

Khosla, A., "Alternative Strategies in Achieving Sustainable Development," in P. Jacobs and D. A. Munro (Eds.), *Conservation with Equity: Strategies for Sustainable Development* (Cambridge, England: International Union for Conservation of Nature and Natural Resources, 1987), pp. 191–208.

Maniates, M., "Organizing for Rural Energy Development: Local Organizations, Improved Cookstoves, and the State in Gujarat, India," Ph.D. thesis (Berkeley: Energy & Resources Group, University of California, 1990).

Norgaard, R. B., "Sustainable Development: A Coevolutionary View," *Futures*, Vol. 20, No. 6 (1988), pp. 606–620.

———, "Three Dilemmas of Environmental Accounting," *Ecological Economics*, Vol. 1, No. 4 (1989), pp. 303–314.

O'Riordan, T., "Future Directions in Environmental Policy," *Journal of Environment and Planning*, Vol. 17 (1985), pp. 1431–1446.

Peskin, H. M., "National Income Accounts and the Environment," *Natural Resources Journal*, Vol. 21 (1981), pp. 511–537.

Redclift, M., *Sustainable Development: Exploring the Contradictions* (New York: Methuen, 1987).

Repetto, R., *World Enough and Time* (New Haven, CT: Yale University Press, 1986a).

Riddell, R., *Ecodevelopment* (New York: St. Martin's Press, 1981).

Sachs, I., *Environment and Development—A New Rationale for Domestic Policy Formulation and International Cooperation Strategies* (Ottawa: Environment Canada and Canadian International Development Agency, 1977).

Streeten, P., "Basic Needs: Premises and Promises," *Journal of Policy Modelling*, Vol. 1 (1979), pp. 136–146.

Tisdell, C., "Sustainable Development: Differing Perspectives of Ecologists and Economists, and Relevance to LDCs," *World Development*, Vol. 16, No. 3 (1988), pp. 373–384.

Tolba, M. K., "The Premises for Building a Sustainable Society. Address to the World Commission on Environment and Development," October 1984 (Nairobi: United Nations Environment Programme, 1984).

World Commission on Environment and Development, *Our Common Future* (New York: Oxford University Press, 1987).

Worldwatch Institute, *State of the World* (New York: Norton, various years).

Notes

1. More precisely, there are ultimate limits to the stocks of material resources, the flows of energy resources, and (in the event of these being circumvented by a major breakthrough in fission/fusion technologies) to the environment's ability to absorb waste energy and other stresses. The limits-to-growth debate, while not conclusive as to specifics, appears to have effectively shifted the burden of proof about the absence of such fundamental limits onto the diehard "technological optimists" who deny the existence of such limits.

2. Of course, "meeting the needs" is a rather ambiguous phrase that may mean anything in practice. Substituting this phrase with "optimizing economic and other societal benefits" (Goodland and Ledec, 1987) or "managing all assets, natural resources and human resources, as well as financial and physical assets for increasing long-term wealth and well-being" (Repetto, 1986a, p. 15) does not define the objectives of development more precisely, although the importance attached to economic benefits or wealth is rather obvious.

3. It is tempting to conclude that this nine-point formulation of SD is identical with the concept of "ecodevelopment"—the original term coined by Maurice Strong of UNEP for environmentally sound development (see Sachs, 1977 and Riddell, 1981). Certainly the differences are less obvious than the similarities. Nevertheless, some changes are significant—such as the dropping of the emphasis on "local self-reliance" and the renewed emphasis on economic growth.

4. Economists have responded by suggesting that currently used indicators of economic growth (GNP in particular) could be modified so as to somehow "build in" this correlation (e.g., Peskin, 1981). To what extent this is possible and whether it will serve more than a marginal purpose are, however, open questions (Norgaard, 1989).

5. Three other "social" usages of sustainability need to be clarified. Sustainable economy (Daly, 1980) and sustainable society (Brown, 1981) are two of these. The focus there, however, is on the patterns and levels of resource use that might be ecologically sustainable while providing the goods and services necessary to maintain human well-being, and the social reorganization that might be required to make this possible. The third usage is Chambers' definition of "sustainable livelihoods" as "a level of wealth and of stocks and flows of food and cash which provide for physical and social well-being and security against becoming poorer" (Chambers, 1986). This can be thought of as a sophisticated version of "basic needs," in that security or risk-minimization is added to the list of needs. It is therefore relevant to any paradigm of development, rather than to SD in particular.

WALKING THE TALK: THE BUSINESS CASE FOR SUSTAINABLE DEVELOPMENT

Björn Stigson

Good morning. It is a great pleasure to have been invited to your [Annual General Meeting]. I spent twenty-five years of my working life in four different multinational corporations—eight of those years as CEO. In this capacity I organized many investor meetings like yours here today and I know the challenges in selecting the right topics and speakers.

Therefore, I am honored and pleased to have been asked to address you this morning on a topic that is not new to you as investors of the Sustainable Performance Group: The Business Case for Sustainable Development.

Let me first acknowledge the context in which we are meeting here today. What happens to sustainable development in times of war? War, terror, and economic downturn can easily give the longer-term goals of sustainable development a lower priority. But judging from different events lately, such as the inclusion of sustainable development issues on the agenda of the G-8 meeting in Evian this June, sustainable development could very well also be the proper expression for the policies needed for a prosperous and politically stable future world: combining economic growth with greater social inclusion and respect for the physical limits of the planet.

Speech to the Annual General Meeting of the Sustainable Performance Group, May 7, 2003. Reprinted with permission.

Sustainable Development
on Three Levels

As investors of the [Sustainable Performance Group], you are all interested in advancing the ideas and practices of sustainable development. What does it take to do that? I would say that we need actions on three levels.

In companies.   The normal operations of companies are crucial for sustainable development. Companies provide economic growth and jobs; they pay taxes and contribute to resource efficiency via management practices and innovation. Investments in developing countries help to transfer skills and resources needed for economic growth to alleviate poverty.

By governments.   Businesses can do much to encourage eco-efficient practices, but they need an enabling framework from society if they are to move forward with any greater speed. It is the role of governments, in consultation with business, to create the conditions that allow business to contribute fully to sustainable development.

By the financial markets.   Financial markets are key in the pursuit of sustainable development because they hold the scorecard, allocate and price capital and provide risk coverage and price risks. If financial markets do not understand and reward sustainable behavior, progress will be slow. They are, however, as you well know, starting to recognize that companies focusing on sustainable development represent a lower financial risk and can also produce a better financial performance.

Against this background let me spend the next twenty minutes or so talking about the Business Case for Sustainable Development. In doing so, I will make reference to our book *Walking the Talk* that we published last year at the World Summit for Sustainable Development and that was made possible with much help and expertise by Sustainable Asset Management.

World Business Council
for Sustainable Development

At the outset, let me just say a few words about the World Business Council for Sustainable Development. The WBCSD is a coalition of 165 international companies united by a shared commitment to sustainable development. Our members are drawn from 35 countries and more than 20 major industrial sectors and are represented in the council by their CEOs or equivalent.

We also benefit from a Global Network of 40 national and regional business councils and partner organizations involving some 1,000 business leaders globally.

To give you a further idea of the scope of the WBCSD, member company turnover aggregates approximately $4,000 billion. The market capitalization of the WBCSD members is close to $2,700 billion and member companies employ approximately 11 million people. Even more interesting is that all of our member companies combined touch about 2 billion people daily, a third of the world's population, either through the sale of a product or the provision of a service.

The Evolution of Sustainable Development

I would first like to spend a couple of minutes outlining the framework of the global sustainable development agenda. This has been a thirty-year journey that started in 1972 with the UN conference in Stockholm on environmental issues. Twenty years later, in 1992, at the Rio Earth Summit, the focus had broadened to include both environment and development. And last year in Johannesburg, for the first time, a global summit looked at all three pillars of sustainable development in an integrated way.

The decade from Rio to Johannesburg had been focused on establishing *norms and principles* for sustainable development. Johannesburg marks the start of a new phase with an emphasis on *implementation.*

Legacies of Johannesburg

The main output from Johannesburg was the reconfirmation of the Millennium Development Goals, a Plan of Implementation for the Rio Agenda 21 program that specifies what actions governments agree are necessary, the call for partnerships, on which I will comment later on, and a serious doubt about whether a multilateral system is able to effectively address our sustainable development challenges.

Two Sustainable Development Agendas

Looking ahead, there are two sustainable development agendas that business needs to address.

- The first is a Public Policy Agenda driven by forces outside of business. This agenda deals with the framework conditions and policies that are set by society for business. Let me underline that this agenda is not something companies can choose to deal with. It is coming our way whether we like it or not.
- The second agenda, the Business Agenda, focuses on the Business Case for Sustainable Development. It has to do with why addressing sustainable development makes good business sense, and how you manage change toward sustainable development.

The Public Policy Agenda

The key issues of the Public Policy Agenda post-Johannesburg are:

- Globalization and global governance
- Poverty eradication
- Sustainable production and consumption
- Health of the ecosystems
- Energy and climate change
- The role of innovation and technology
- Accountability and reporting
- Risk

Why Should Companies and Investors Worry About This?

Business Assets

How well a corporation addresses this agenda has a large impact on its valuation in the marketplace. As you all know, the market capitalization of a corporation builds on the capacity to generate earnings of two types of assets: physical assets and intangible assets.

Physical assets, like land and manufacturing facilities, make up one part of the market capitalization of a corporation. The other part, up to 75 percent, comes from intangibles, such as reputation, brand, trust, credibility, and the ability to interact and work in partnership with stakeholders. The value of these intangible assets is highly influenced by how a company relates to the Public Policy Agenda. There are many examples of corporations that have failed to respond to changing societal demands and have thus seen dramatic impacts on their market valuation when being accused of using child labor, human rights abuses, environmental pollution, health risks and so on.

The Business Agenda
for Sustainable Development

Corporations cannot be managed based on philanthropy/do-good arguments. To stimulate line managers to take action, it is necessary to demonstrate that sustainable development makes good business sense. There is a proven track record of the following sustainable business practices:

- Eco-efficiency—"zero pollution"
- Safety—"no accidents"
- Local community interactions

We know that in most cases these practices increase efficiency and profitability while improving the environmental and social performance of a company. I have also noted lately that "sustainability" is being referred to more visibly in company advertisement, as a way of strategic differentiation from competitors.

Walking the Talk

Our book, *Walking the Talk,* has the subtitle *The Business Case for Sustainable Development.* It is devoted to showing that business, over the past ten years, has spent more efforts on working toward sustainable development than other parts of society. It is highlighting examples and case studies of what companies are doing to address the challenges we face.

The book specifies what we have called the "Ten Building Blocks" for sustainable societies. Some of these building blocks can be implemented directly by the business community. Others are framework conditions that government must establish.

1. *The market.* Sustainable development is best achieved through open markets. Due to their competitive nature, such markets encourage an efficient use of resources, deliver the most cost-effective solutions, promote transparency of information, and foster creativity innovation—all necessities for sustainable development.

Last year, we presented a report, "Tomorrow's Markets," that outlines what we see as the nineteen mega-trends that will shape the future markets and their implications for business.

The necessity for open markets is underlined by the fact that there is a striking correlation between the national scores on the Index of Economic Freedom and on the Human Development Index: roughly speaking, the more economic freedom, the higher the level of human development.

We must remember that markets are human constructs based on human values, laws and norms. They must be built, and they can always be improved.

2. *The right framework.* The WBCSD has always stressed that markets need to be well framed in order to encourage sustainable progress. This requires the rule of law, effective property rights, no corruption, and predictability of government interaction. To foster sustainable development within the private sector, a policy mix of command-and-control, voluntary initiatives and economic instruments must be set in place which should be supported by horizontal mechanisms such as education and research.

3. *Eco-efficiency.* A crucial element of the business case, over which business has immediate control, comes from the eco-efficiency concept that I mentioned earlier as part of the Business Agenda. "Creating more value with less impact" as it has been defined. Eco-efficiency has a proven track record as we have shown through our portfolio of case studies, gathered over the past ten years. Many of these moves from rhetoric to reality can be found in *Walking the Talk.*

4. *Corporate Social Responsibility (CSR).* CSR is the term that many companies have started using to express an enlightened approach to corporate citizenship, or, indeed, to addressing the Public Policy Agenda. Yet, what does it really mean in practical terms?

We at the WBCSD have gathered views from across the globe, exploring what CSR means to stakeholders. This has been brought together in our report, "CSR—Making Good Business Sense."

From these very extensive stakeholder dialogues it became clear that CSR means different things to people due to their religion, culture and traditions. There is no "one-size-fits-all" solution to the CSR challenge. Therefore, we are opposed to global codes of conduct that become less relevant to guide the action of an individual company. Rather, each company needs to find for themselves their "magnetic north." This meaning the vision and values that they stand for and by which they are prepared to be judged.

5. *Learning to change.* Buy-in and leadership from top management is absolutely crucial for successful change within companies toward sustainable operations. In order to motivate middle management, adequate incentive systems need to be set in place. Many of our member companies have included social and environmental aspects to their balanced scorecard, for example.

Many companies have quality education and training programs on environment and on health and safety, but there is a lack of good training tools for the social aspects of sustainable development. In response to this, the WBCSD and Cambridge University's Programme for Industry have developed an e-learning tool, called Chronos, which is now available for subscription.

6. *From dialogues into partnerships.* "Partnerships" was one of the key themes coming out of the Johannesburg Summit. It has become clear that governments cannot resolve the sustainable development challenges on their own. We have moved from a bipolar to a tripartite world in which government, business and civil society are moving from dialogues to active engagement and partnerships.

The challenges are also too big for any one company to handle on its own. We see a strong interest from our members in projects that look at the sustainable development challenges for the whole value chain of a particular industry sector. This comes both from an interest in better understanding the future challenges they will be facing, the need to create more stable platforms for future long-term investments and efficiency, and the need to strengthen their business license to operate. We have presently six such sector projects: forestry, mining, cement, mobility, electricity utilities and urban water.

7. *Informing and providing consumer choice.* Sustainability through the market requires informed consumers. It is debated to what extent consumers are willing to pay a premium for green products that do not harm the environment. But they can certainly be quick to turn away if companies are seen to be ignoring such concerns.

Corporate image will increasingly inform consumer choice. Therefore, brands of the future will have to stand not only for product quality and a desirable image, but will also have to signal something wholesome about the company behind the brand. This can be seen by the actions of companies such as Nestlé and Unilever that are increasingly trying to position not only the individual brand but also the corporation itself.

8. *Innovation.* Innovation is another of the Ten Building Blocks for sustainable societies to which business can significantly contribute. Even though there is no guarantee that it is sufficient to solve the dilemma between a growing population, increasing living standards, and the physical limitations of the planet, innovation is an important tool to address sustainable development. But a particular challenge is to make new innovations and technologies acceptable to society. This is well illustrated by the debates around [genetically modified organisms] or nuclear power, as examples.

One problem is that we in business have had a tendency to argue our case too much in scientific and technical terms—and not explaining sufficiently the benefits to society. Who is trusted when deciding on the risks and benefits of new technologies? There has been a growing distrust in science. So you cannot take for granted that using your scientists to bring forward your messages will be successful. "Exit men in white coats," as I have called it.

9. *Reflecting the worth of the earth.* Sustainability through the market will not work if we have the wrong price signals for the use of resources. We do not protect what we do not value. Many of nature's ecosystem services, such as providing clean air and water, are currently not monetized. Those that have tried to put a price tag on the ecosystems have concluded that the ongoing erosion of the world's natural capital is costing many times more than the conservationist alternative. In this context, distorting governmental subsidies for agricultural products or water, for example, provide a special problem that needs to be addressed.

10. *Making markets work for all.* The growth in future consumer markets and labor will to a high degree come from the emerging markets. To stimulate these huge markets, dominated by young populations, it is in the interest of business to support a supply of products and services that are affordable and will increase the quality of life for the poor.

The WBCSD is actively engaged in a new project, Sustainable Livelihoods. If we want to maintain the open global markets, then the benefits of globalization must increasingly also come to the poor part of the world's population. We, from business, have so far developed products and services targeted at less than half of the world's population. This is not sustainable. Business must play a positive role in the creation of sustainable livelihoods for the poor, and this requires new business approaches.

The Business Case

A few years back, I gave a speech that I called "Clean, Green, and Rich." Today being "clean" is a must for companies. Is there a positive value in being "green"? It seems so, but the evidence remains mostly anecdotal. What about "rich"? Indices such as the Dow Jones Sustainability Index or FTSE 4 Good have been met with much positive recognition. They show that companies that focus on sustainable development outperform their peers over the longer run. Admittedly, this is not the case over the shorter term. Other research, such as a study recently conducted by the Institute of Business Ethics, shows that there is a reliable correlation between "business integrity" and above average financial performance.

Why could that be? We do not yet know exactly, but it seems that companies that focus on sustainable development are more in tune with the market trends and society, are faster to change, and are generally better managed.

WBCSD Work Program

. . . Let me introduce two of our programs that I believe are of particular interest to you: our Sustainability and the Financial Sector, and Accountability and Reporting projects.

Sustainability and the Financial Sector

For the WSSD in Johannesburg, our project Sustainability in the Financial Sector produced a call for action signed by eleven CEOs of WBCSD financial sector members. The headlines of this document illustrate the issues facing the Financial Sector:

> Integrating sustainable development into our business is a prerequisite for the continuous success of our companies as well as for creating long-term shareholder value.
> We will promote proactive sustainable development thinking.
> We recognize our role as drivers for change, although the limits of responsibility and influence of the financial services industry need to be further explored.
> We clearly see a need to improve transparency as a matter of urgency and will seek to increase mutual trust.

As a next step we saw the need to broaden the discussion to include perspectives of other industrial players and the strategic impact of the financial industry as a pivotal force in the global economy and international policy agenda. This means that we will move to a phase in which the project will no longer be named Sustainable Development *in* the Financial Sector but rather, Sustainability *and* the Financial Sector.

Accountability and Reporting

We live today in an information society where "everyone knows everything about you all the time." There is no place to hide. The growing demand for corporate accountability was clearly visible in Johannesburg. There is new national legislation in countries like France and the U.K., and many codes of conduct have emerged. New reporting guidelines are coming from the Global Reporting Initiative, for example. Further, we see a significant growth in Socially Responsible Investments and in their demands for information. In response to these issues, we have examined the questions of corporate accountability in a variety of ways over the past few years and have launched a report, "Sustainable Development Reporting: Striking the Right Balance." This initiative focused on the key questions, why should a company engage in sustainable development reporting, and more specifically, how should a company approach this task?

The working group on Accountability and Reporting will now grapple with a number of dilemmas, such as, how do we strike a balance between what stakeholders find interesting to know [and] what they have the right to know? All stakeholders are not equal. Some are more direct than others—like shareholders, employees, suppliers, local communities around business facilities—who all have a right to information and a strong voice in the company. Then there are a number of more or less indirect stakeholders whose influence on a company has less justification. Also, what kind of information can be put to meaningful use in companies? This also needs to be weighed against the cost of reporting, which can be quite significant.

Window of Opportunity

Society increasingly recognizes that business is a key solutions provider for a sustainable development future and that sustainable development is not possible without the active involvement of business. Thus, business is listened to in a way that was not the case some years ago. This is a window of opportunity for business to contribute to society's formulation of the political agenda for sustainable development that will not be there forever and from which business should benefit.

Conclusion

To conclude, the key challenge for business in contributing to a sustainable future will, I believe, not be how we manage our own corporations. It will instead be how we address the expectation that we should play a larger role in building well-functioning societies. Business cannot and should not replace governments. But it is also impossible to provide in a sustainable way goods and services in nonfunctioning societies. As we at the WBCSD have often expressed it, "Business cannot succeed in a society that fails."

2 6

HOW MUCH IS ENOUGH?

ALAN DURNING

The Conundrum of Consumption

For Sidney Quarrier of Essex, Connecticut, Earth Day 1990 was Judgment Day—the day of ecological reckoning. While tens of millions of people around the world were marching and celebrating in the streets, Sidney was sitting at his kitchen table with a yellow legal pad and a pocket calculator. The task he set himself was to tally up the burden he and his family had placed on the planet since Earth Day 1970.[1]

Early that spring morning he began tabulating everything that had gone into their house—oil for heating, nuclear-generated electricity, water for showers and watering the lawn, cans of paint, appliances, square footage of carpet, furniture, clothes, food, and thousands of other things—and everything that had come out—garbage pails of junk mail and packaging, newspapers and magazines by the cubic meter, polluted water, and smoke from the furnace. He listed the resources they had tapped to move them around by car and airplane, from fuel and lubricants to tires and replacement parts. "I worked on that list most of the day," Sid remembers. "I dug out wads of old receipts, weighed trash cans and the daily mail, excavated the basement and shed, and used triangulation techniques I hadn't practiced since graduate school to estimate the materials we used in the roofing job."[2]

Manufacturing and delivering each of the objects on his list, Sid knew, had required additional resources he was unable to count. National statistics suggested, for example, that he should double the energy he used in his house

SOURCE: Worldwatch Institute, *How Much Is Enough? The Consumer Society and the Future of the Earth*, copyright © 1992, www.worldwatch.org. Reprinted with permission.

and car to allow for what businesses and government used to provide him with goods and services. He visualized a global industrial network of factories making things for him, freighters and trucks transporting them, stores selling them, and office buildings supervising the process. He wondered how much steel and concrete his state needed for the roads, bridges, and parking garages he used. He wondered about resources used by the hospital that cared for him, the air force jets and police cars that protected him, the television stations that entertained him, and the veterinary office that cured his dog.

As his list grew, Sid was haunted by an imaginary mountain of discarded televisions, car parts, and barrels of oil—all piling up toward the sky on his lot. "It was a sober revisiting of that period. . . . It's only when you put together all the years of incremental consumption that you realize the totality." That totality hit him like the ton of paper packaging he had hauled out with the trash over the years: "The question is," Sid said, "Can the earth survive the impact of Sid, and can the Sids of the future change?"[3]

That *is* the question. Sidney Quarrier and his family are no gluttons. "During those years, we lived in a three-bedroom house on two-and-a-half acres in the country, about 35 miles from my job in Hartford," Sidney recounts. "But we have never been rich," he insists. "What frightened me was that our consumption was typical of the people here in Connecticut."[4]

Sid's class—the American middle class—is the group that, more than any other, defines and embodies the contemporary international vision of the good life. Yet the way the Quarriers lived for those 20 years is among the world's premier environmental problems, and may be the most difficult to solve.

Only population growth rivals high consumption as a cause of ecological decline, and at least population growth is now viewed as a problem by many governments and citizens of the world. Consumption, in contrast, is almost universally seen as good—indeed, increasing it is the primary goal of national economic policy. The consumption levels exemplified in the two decades Sid Quarrier reviewed are the highest achieved by any civilization in human history. They manifest the full flowering of a new form of human society: the consumer society.

This new manner of living was born in the United States, and the words of an American best capture its spirit. In the age of U.S. affluence that began after World War II, retailing analyst Victor Lebow declared: "Our enormously productive economy . . . demands that we make consumption our way of life, that we convert the buying and use of goods into rituals, that we seek our spiritual satisfaction, our ego satisfaction, in consumption. . . . We need things consumed, burned up, worn out, replaced, and discarded at an ever increasing rate." Most citizens of western nations have responded to Lebow's call, and the rest of the world appears intent on following.[5]

In industrial lands, consumption now permeates social values. Opinion surveys in the world's two largest economies—Japan and the United States—show that people increasingly measure success by the amount they consume.

The Japanese speak of the "new three sacred treasures": color television, air conditioning, and the automobile. One-fourth of Poles deem "Dynasty," which portrays the life-style of the richest Americans, their favorite television program, and villagers in the heart of Africa follow "Dallas," the television series that portrays American oil tycoons. In Taiwan, a billboard demands "Why Aren't You a Millionaire Yet?" A *Business Week* correspondent beams: "The American Dream is alive and well . . . in Mexico." Indeed, the words "consumer" and "person" have become virtual synonyms.[6]

The life-style made in the United States is emulated by those who can afford it around the world, but many cannot. The economic fault lines that fracture the globe defy comprehension. The world has 202 billionaires and more than 3 million millionaires. It also has 100 million homeless people who live on roadsides, in garbage dumps, and under bridges. The value of luxury goods sales worldwide—high-fashion clothing, top-of-the-line autos, and the other trappings of wealth—exceeds the gross national products of two-thirds of the world's countries. Indeed, the world's average income, about $5,000 a year, is below the U.S. poverty line.[7]

The gaping divide in material consumption between the fortunate and unfortunate stands out starkly in their impacts on the natural world. The soaring consumption lines that track the rise of the consumer society are, from another perspective, surging indicators of environmental harm. The consumer society's exploitation of resources threatens to exhaust, poison, or unalterably disfigure forests, soils, water, and air. We, its members, are responsible for a disproportionate share of all the global environmental challenges facing humanity. . . .

Ironically, high consumption is a mixed blessing in human terms too. People living in the nineties are on average four-and-a-half times richer than their great-grandparents were at the turn of the century, but they are not four-and-a-half times happier. Psychological evidence shows that the relationship between consumption and personal happiness is weak. Worse, two primary sources of human fulfillment—social relations and leisure—appear to have withered or stagnated in the rush to riches. Thus many of us in the consumer society have a sense that our world of plenty is somehow hollow— that, hoodwinked by a consumerist culture, we have been fruitlessly attempting to satisfy with material things what are essentially social, psychological, and spiritual needs.[8]

Of course, the opposite of overconsumption—destitution—is no solution to either environmental or human problems. It is infinitely worse for people and bad for the natural world too. Dispossessed peasants slash-and-burn their way into the rain forests of Latin America, hungry nomads turn their herds out onto fragile African rangeland, reducing it to desert, and small farmers in India and the Philippines cultivate steep slopes, exposing them to the erosive powers of rain. Perhaps half the world's billion-plus absolute poor are caught in a downward spiral of ecological and economic impoverishment. In desperation, they knowingly abuse the land, salvaging the present by savaging the future.[9]

If environmental destruction results when people have either too little or too much, we are left to wonder, How much is enough? What level of consumption can the earth support? When does having more cease to add appreciably to human satisfaction? Is it possible for all the world's people to live comfortably without bringing on the decline of the planet's natural health? Is there a level of living above poverty and subsistence but below the consumer life-style—a level of sufficiency? Could all the world's people have central heating? Refrigerators? Clothes dryers? Automobiles? Air conditioning? Heated swimming pools? Airplanes? Second homes?

Many of these questions cannot be answered definitively, but for each of us in the consumer society, asking is essential nonetheless. Unless we see that more is not always better, our efforts to forestall ecological decline will be overwhelmed by our appetites. Unless we ask, we will likely fail to see the forces around us that stimulate those appetites, such as relentless advertising, proliferating shopping centers, and social pressures to "keep up with the Joneses." We may overlook forces that make consumption more destructive than it need be, such as subsidies to mines, paper mills, and other industries with high environmental impacts. And we may not act on opportunities to improve our lives while consuming less, such as working fewer hours to spend more time with family and friends.

Still, the difficulty of transforming the consumer society into a sustainable one can scarcely be overestimated. We consumers enjoy a life-style that almost everybody else aspires to, and why shouldn't they? Who would just as soon not have an automobile, a big house on a big lot, and complete control over indoor temperature throughout the year? The momentum of centuries of economic history and the material cravings of 5.5 billion people lie on the side of increasing consumption.

We may be, therefore, in a conundrum—a problem admitting of no satisfactory solution. Limiting the consumer life-style to those who have already attained it is not politically possible, morally defensible, or ecologically sufficient. And extending that life-style to all would simply hasten the ruin of the biosphere. The global environment cannot support 1.1 billion of us living like American consumers, much less 5.5 billion people, or a future population of at least 8 billion. On the other hand, reducing the consumption levels of the consumer society, and tempering material aspirations elsewhere, though morally acceptable, is a quixotic proposal. It bucks the trend of centuries. Yet it may be the only option.

If the life-supporting ecosystems of the planet are to survive for future generations, the consumer society will have to dramatically curtail its use of resources—partly by shifting to high-quality, low-input durable goods and partly by seeking fulfillment through leisure, human relationships, and other nonmaterial avenues. We in the consumer society will have to live a technologically sophisticated version of the life-style currently practiced lower on the economic ladder. Scientific advances, better laws, restructured industries, new treaties, environmental taxes, grassroots campaigns—all can help us get there. But ultimately, sustaining the environment that sustains humanity will require that we change our values.

The Consumer Society

The world has three broad ecological classes: the consumers, the middle income, and the poor. These groups, ideally defined by their per capita consumption of natural resources, emissions of pollution, and disruption of habitats, can be distinguished in practice through two proxy measures: their average annual incomes and their life-styles (see Table 28.1).

The world's poor—some 1.1 billion people—includes all households that earn less than $700 a year per family member. They are mostly rural Africans, Indians, and other South Asians. They eat almost exclusively grains, root crops, beans, and other legumes, and they drink mostly unclean water. They live in huts and shanties, they travel by foot, and most of their possessions are constructed of stone, wood, and other substances available from the local environment. This poorest fifth of the world's people earns just 2 percent of world income.[10]

The 3.3 billion people in the world's middle-income class earn between $700 and $7,500 per family member and live mostly in Latin America, the Middle East, China, and East Asia. This class also includes the low-income families of the former Soviet bloc and of western industrial nations. With notable exceptions, they eat a diet based on grains and water, and lodge in moderate buildings with electricity for lights, radios, and, increasingly, refrigerators and clothes washers. (In Chinese cities, for example, two-thirds of households now have washing machines and one-fifth have refrigerators.) They travel by bus, railway, and bicycle, and maintain a modest stock of durable goods. Collectively, they claim 33 percent of world income.[11]

The consumer class—the 1.1 billion members of the global consumer society—includes all households whose income per family member is above $7,500. Though that threshold puts the lowest ranks of the consumer class scarcely above the U.S. poverty line, they—rather, we—still enjoy a life-style unknown in earlier ages. We dine on meat and processed, packaged foods, and imbibe soft drinks and other beverages from disposable containers. We spend most of our time in climate-controlled buildings equipped with refrigerators, clothes washers and dryers, abundant hot water, dishwashers, microwave ovens, and a plethora of other electric-powered gadgets. We travel in private automobiles and airplanes, and surround ourselves with a profusion of short-lived, throwaway goods. The consumer class takes home 64 percent of world income—32 times as much as the poor.[12]

The consumer class counts among its members most North Americans, West Europeans, Japanese, Australians, and the citizens of Hong Kong, Singapore,

Table 26.1   World Consumption Classes, 1992

Category of Consumption	Consumers (1.1 billion)	Middle (3.3 billion)	Poor (1.1 billion)
Diet	meat, packaged food, soft drinks	grain, clean water	insufficient grain, unsafe water
Transport	private cars	bicycles, buses	walking
Materials	throwaways	durables	local biomass

SOURCE: Worldwatch Institute

and the oil sheikdoms of the Middle East. Perhaps half the people of Eastern Europe and the Commonwealth of Independent States are in the consumer class, as are about one-fifth of the people in Latin America, South Africa, and the newly industrializing countries of Asia, such as South Korea.[13] . . .

A Culture of Permanence

. . . The future of life on earth depends on whether we among the richest fifth of the world's people, having fully met our material needs, can turn to non-material sources of fulfillment. Whether we—who have defined the tangible goals of world development—can now craft a new way of life at once simpler and more satisfying. Having invented the automobile and the airplane, can we return to bicycles, buses, and trains? Having pioneered sprawl and malls, can we recreate human-scale settlements where commerce is an adjunct to civic life rather than its purpose? Having introduced the high-fat, junk-food diet, can we instead nourish ourselves on wholesome fare that is locally produced? Having devised disposable plastics, packaging without end, and instantaneous obsolescence, can we design objects that endure and a materials economy that takes care of things?

If our grandchildren are to inherit a planet as bounteous and beautiful as we have enjoyed, we in the consumer class must—without surrendering the quest for advanced, clean technology—eat, travel, and use energy and materials more like those on the middle rung of the world's economic ladder. If we can learn to do so, we might find ourselves happier as well, for in the consumer society, affluence has brought us to a strange pass. Who would have predicted a century ago that the richest civilizations in history would be made up of polluted tracts of suburban development dominated by the private automobile, shopping malls, and a throwaway economy? Surely, this is not the ultimate fulfillment of our destiny.

In the final analysis, accepting and living by sufficiency rather than excess offers a return to what is, culturally speaking, the human home: to the ancient order of family, community, good work, and good life; to a reverence for skill, creativity, and creation; to a daily cadence slow enough to let us watch a sunset and stroll by the water's edge; to communities worth spending a lifetime in; and to local places pregnant with the memories of generations. Perhaps Henry David Thoreau had it right when he scribbled in his notebook beside Walden Pond, "A man is rich in proportion to the things he can afford to let alone."[14]

Notes

1. Sidney Quarrier, geologist, Connecticut Geological & Natural History Survey, Hartford, Conn., private communication, February 25, 1992.

2. Ibid.

3. Ibid.

4. Ibid.

5. Lebow in *Journal of Retailing*, quoted in Vance Packard, *The Waste Makers* (New York: David McKay, 1960).

6. Sepp Linhart, "From Industrial to Postindustrial Society: Changes in Japanese Leisure-Related Values and Behavior," *Journal of Japanese Studies*, Summer 1988; Richard A. Easterlin and Eileen M. Crimmins, "Recent Social Trends: Changes in Personal Aspirations of American Youth," *Sociology and Social Research*, July 1988; "Dynasty" from "Harper's Index," *Harper's*, December 1990; "Dallas" from Jerry Mander, *In the Absence of the Sacred* (San Francisco: Sierra Club Books, 1991); Taiwan from "Asian Century," *Newsweek*, February 22, 1988; Stephen Baker and S. Lynne Walker, "The American Dream Is Alive and Well—in Mexico," *Business Week*, September 30, 1991.

7. Billionaires from Jennifer Reese, "The Billionaires: More Than Ever in 1991," *Fortune*, September 9, 1991; millionaires estimated from Kevin R. Phillips, "Reagan's America: A Capital Offense," *New York Times Magazine*, June 18, 1990; homelessness from U.N. Center for Human Settlements, New York, private communication, November 1, 1989; luxury goods from "The Lapse of Luxury," *Economist*, January 5, 1991; gross national product from United Nations Development Programme, *Human Development Report 1991* (New York: Oxford University Press, 1991); member countries in United Nations from U.N. Information Center, Washington, D.C., private communication, January 14, 1992; world average income from 1987, in 1987 U.S. dollars adjusted for international variations in purchasing power, from Ronald V. A. Sprout and James H. Weaver, "International Distribution of Income: 1960–1987," Working Paper No. 159, Department of Economics, American University, Washington, D.C., May 1991; U.S. 1987 poverty line for an individual from U.S. Bureau of the Census, *Statistical Abstract of the United States: 1990* (Washington, D.C.: U.S. Government Printing Office, 1990).

8. Four-and-a-half times richer from Angus Maddison, *The World Economy in the 20th Century* (Paris: Organisation for Economic Co-Operation and Development, 1989).

9. Alan Durning, *Poverty and the Environment: Reversing the Downward Spiral*, Worldwatch Paper 92 (Washington, D.C.: Worldwatch Institute, November, 1989).

10. Estimated annual earnings per family member, in 1988 U.S. dollars of gross domestic product (GDP) per capita adjusted for international variations in purchasing power,

and share of world income from Ronald V.A. Sprout and James H. Weaver, "1988 International Distribution of Income" (unpublished data) provided by Ronald V.A. Sprout, U.N. Economic Commission for Latin America and the Caribbean, Washington Office, Washington, D.C., private communication, January 2, 1992. Sprout and Weaver combined income distribution data and purchasing-power adjusted GDP per capita data to disaggregate 127 countries into five classes each and reaggregate these segments into five global classes; see Ronald V.A. Sprout and James H. Weaver, "International Dimensions of Income: 1960–1987," Working Paper No. 159, Department of Economics, American University, Washington, D.C., May 1991. Number in each class adjusted to mid-year 1992 population from Machiko Yanagishita, demographer, Population Reference Bureau, Washington, D.C., private communication, February 26, 1992.

11. Income range and share of world income estimated from Sprout and Weaver, "1988 International Distribution of Income"; Chinese appliances from "TV Now in 50% of Homes," *China Daily,* February 15, 1988.

12. Income range and share of world income from Sprout and Weaver, "1988 International Distribution of Income"; comparison to U.S. poverty line from U.S. Bureau of the Census, *Statistical Abstract of the United States: 1990* (Washington, D.C.: U.S. Government Printing Office, 1990). As used in this book, "consumers," "consumer class," and "global consumer society" are synonymous and refer to the richest fifth of humanity as measured by per capita income or lifestyle. The global consumer society, of course, does not share the institutions that a national society does, but it does share a way of life and many values.

13. Sprout and Weaver, "1988 International Distribution of Income." See also Nathan Keyfitz, "Consumerism and the New Poor," *Society,* January/February 1992.

14. Henry David Thoreau, *Walden* (1854; reprint, Boston: Houghton-Mifflin, 1957).

PART SIX

FROM ECOLOGICAL CONFLICT TO ENVIRONMENTAL SECURITY?

As seen in the previous section, the concept of sustainability has emerged as a powerful paradigm shaping the interpretations, goals, and behavior of a broad range of actors on the global environmental stage. But the global environmental debate of the past three decades has engaged not only economic issues of welfare, production, and livelihood but also political questions of international conflict, violence, and geopolitics. It is not surprising that paradigms focused on the conflictual dimensions of environmental problems also have begun to emerge.

One attempt to grapple with these intensely political themes is the paradigm of "environmental security." Like sustainability, environmental security offers a potentially powerful but also controversial way to think about the social dimensions of environmental problems. The environmental security paradigm rests on a series of claims: that environmental change is an important source of social conflict; that many societies face graver dangers from environmental change than from traditional military threats; and that security policies must be redefined to take account of these new realities.

The essay by Thomas Homer-Dixon addresses the connection between environmental change and violent conflict. Homer-Dixon argues that environmental change is becoming an increasingly important source of social instability, civil strife, and violence within societies. The growing scarcity of renewable resources—principally water, fish stocks, forests, and fertile land—already promotes such conflict, and it is likely to cause a surge in violence in the future. Homer-Dixon stresses that political and economic institutions remain central to determining specific patterns of conflict. But he also argues that "environmental scarcity"—driven by environmental change, population growth, and the unequal social distribution of natural resources—is an increasingly important factor. Given such conflict potential, proponents of environmental security have argued that there is an urgent, compelling need to "redefine" the concept of security.[1]

The United Nations Development Programme (UNDP) proposes that security issues be viewed within the broader category of "human security," the definition of which encompasses environmental as well as other specific concerns. The UNDP's seven components of human security, enumerated in the 1994 edition of its influential annual *Human Development Report,* hold up human well-being as what should be "secured" or provided to individuals and societies. Just as economic considerations have become increasingly important in security policy deliberations, so too must environmental concerns be raised to the level of "high politics." The UNDP's call for redefining security, and others like it, also stress that cooperation, and not defensive preparation for conflict, is the most effective way to address nonmilitary threats. Current military means are deemed inadequate to counter the new threats of environmental degradation, violent crime, economic inequities, food shortages, and infectious diseases.

The arguments for redefining security make clear that environmental security is more than an effort to reconceptualize the nature of the present and future threats that societies face. It is also a political agenda aimed at mobilizing the state and society toward a new set of goals and at redirecting resources and energies away from exclusively military concerns. Some proponents argue that only by framing the environmental problematique in security terms can the necessary level of governmental attention and social mobilization be ensured.[2] Others argue that security institutions could contribute directly to environmental protection, given their financial resources, monitoring and intelligence-gathering capabilities, and scientific and technological expertise.[3]

Thus, although the origins of the environmental security paradigm can be traced at least to the early post–World War II period,[4] it is surely no accident that the idea of rethinking security policy in ecological terms flourished in the post–Cold War era. Policymakers, military institutions, and entire societies have begun to reconsider the character of the threats they face. Many proponents of environmental security are driven by the belief that the end of the Cold War opened a window of opportunity for fundamental changes in security policies and a reordering of social priorities.

Among the many controversies surrounding the paradigm of environmental security, two are central. First, is there enough evidence to support the claim that ecological change is, or will be, a major new source of conflict? Although a growing body of research points to specific cases in which environmental change seems to have played a role in promoting or exacerbating social conflict, many questions remain. Why does environmental stress produce such conflict in some cases but not in others? Is it possible that environmental problems are a *symptom* of conflict-prone social systems rather than a root cause of conflict? Observers who pose these questions are indicating their doubt that environmental change is an important, independent source of conflict. A second set of questions involves the more nebulous concept of "security." Are the advantages of linking environmental problems to security concerns worth the risk of militarizing a society's responses to environmental problems?

The essay by Daniel Deudney raises both sets of questions. Deudney is skeptical that environmental change precipitates acute conflict, at least in the form of war; he argues that environmental problems have little in common with the traditional security problem of interstate violence.[5] Deudney is also wary of evoking the powerful concept of security in order to mobilize society: "For environmentalists to dress their programs in the blood-soaked garments of the war system betrays their core values and creates confusion about the real tasks at hand." Others have voiced stronger criticisms, suggesting that the powerful association between the concept of security and the use of military force creates the danger of turning environmental problems into sources of military tension and conflict.[6] Matthias Finger argues that "the military must be addressed as a cause and not a cure of global environmental problems." In Finger's view, worldwide militarization wastes scarce resources that could be deployed in the struggle against environmental degradation and is itself a source of massive amounts of pollution.[7] These critics share Deudney's view that the conflictual mind-set and the military tools of security institutions are poorly suited to the global environmental problematique.

Grounded in the experiences of South Asia, Adil Najam is confident that the complex relationship between insecurity and environmental resources can be effectively redressed within the broader human security frame, while still accounting for the concerns of skeptics such as Deudney and Finger. Najam stresses the need to place resource scarcity in the larger context of poverty and weak governance institutions when considering environment and security linkages. Social disruption at the societal level, even when explicit violence is not present, constitutes more salient environment and security links for populations throughout South Asia struggling daily to survive. The human security frame encompasses these wider concerns, tying this human-centered version of the ecological security paradigm firmly to the sustainability frame of Part Five.

Balakrishnan Rajagopal provides a dramatic portrayal of the violence often associated with development of natural resources when the human rights dimension of this human security frame is neglected. Rajagopal contends that the forced displacement of tens of millions to make way for large dams, so-called "development cleansing," disproportionately affects poor and minority populations (see also Part Seven). This displacement contributes to the poverty and societal violence that Najam identifies as widespread and central to the livelihood struggles of the global South (more so than in Homer-Dixon's scarcity-driven model of environmentally induced violence).

The environmental security debate is further complicated by the way in which it intersects the North-South axis in world politics. The focus of ecological conflict research tends to be on the economically less-developed regions of the planet; most analysts emphasize these

regions when identifying likely sites of future environmentally induced conflicts. There are many reasons for this focus on the South:
its limited financial and technological resources, high population
growth rates, preexisting political instability, and the day-to-day
struggles for survival that engulf large segments of its population.

However, even if it is plausible to claim that the South will be the
site of environmental conflicts, this concern cannot be divorced from
the broader pattern of North-South relations. The essay by Egyptian
diplomat Somaya Saad reflects the deep suspicion with which many
Southern governments have viewed the North's concern for "security" in the South, environmental or otherwise. She sees the rhetoric
of environmental security as an excuse to continue the North's long-
standing practice of military and economic intervention. She also suggests that the extensive focus on the South is a way for the North to
deny its own overwhelming responsibility for the deteriorating state
of the planet. Saad's concerns emphasize the importance of history
and context. In a world where many people feel their security threatened by other people, calls for changes in security policies may seem
like a way to break the cycle of violence, suspicion, and zero-sum
thinking; but given the purposes that security policies have served in
the past, such calls also raise deep suspicions about ulterior motives.

Social science may lack the tools to tell us exactly when and where
environmental problems will produce violence. Nevertheless, the capacity of environmental change to disrupt people's lives, erode standards of living, and threaten established interests tells us that the possibility of widespread violent conflict must be taken seriously. Research
that helps us understand when and where such conflict is likely to occur could be an important tool for conflict avoidance, international
confidence building, and nonviolent conflict resolution. But the paradigm of environmental security remains controversial because it links
plausible claims about conflict to the symbolically powerful and highly
charged concept of security. At best, linking environment and security
could be a way to build trust among nations and make security a cooperative, global endeavor, while at the same time steering resources
and public energy toward the resolution of environmental problems.[8]
At worst, tying environmental concerns to militarized approaches to
social conflict could itself be a recipe for greater violence in the future.

Thinking Critically

1. Can you think of examples that run counter to the Homer-Dixon argument—that is, cases where the conditions for environmentally induced violent conflict seem to exist but violence does not occur? What social institutions or other conditions are likely to influence whether violence occurs? Is

the connection between environment and conflict solely a problem for the developing world?

2. Which seems more likely: the "greening" of security policy or the militarization of environmental policy? Are Deudney's concerns about the mismatched tools of traditional security institutions well founded? Can we generalize across countries in answering this question?

3. Najam and Rajagopal argue that social disruptions associated with poverty, weak institutions, and large development projects should be central to a human security paradigm. Are these economic and political dynamics crowding out environmental considerations in efforts to redefine security?

4. Is environmental security an idea with more appeal in the North than the South? Are Saad's fears of Northern intent legitimate? Does the broader definition of security enunciated by Najam speak convincingly to the problems of the South?

Notes

1. See for example Lester Brown, "Redefining National Security," Worldwatch Paper no. 14 (Washington, DC: Worldwatch Institute, 1977); Jessica Tuchman Mathews, "Redefining Security," *Foreign Affairs* 67 (1989):162–177; Norman Myers, "Environment and Security," *Foreign Policy* 74 (Spring 1989):23–41.

2. Former Vice President Albert Gore discusses this theme in his book on the global environment, *Earth in the Balance: Ecology and the Human Spirit* (New York: Houghton Mifflin, 1992).

3. Kent Hughes Butts, "Why the Military Is Good for the Environment," in Jyrki Käkönen, ed., *Green Security or Militarized Environment* (Aldershot, UK: Dartmouth, 1994). For a discussion of how the U.S. government has operationalized environmental security ideas in a variety of ways, see Geoffrey D. Dabelko and P. J. Simmons, "Environment and Security: Core Ideas and U.S. Government Initiatives," *SAIS Review* 17 (Winter–Spring 1997):127–146. See also all issues of the *Environmental Change and Security Project Report* published by the Washington-based Woodrow Wilson International Center for Scholars.

4. Early examples include Fairfield Osborn, *Our Plundered Planet* (Boston: Little, Brown, 1953), and Harrison Brown, *The Challenge of Man's Future* (New York: Viking, 1954).

5. For a similar critique regarding the role of the environment in causing conflict, see Marc A. Levy "Is the Environment a National Security Issue?" *International Security* 20, no. 2 (Fall 1995):35–62; Thomas F. Homer-Dixon and Marc A. Levy, "Correspondence: Environment and Security," *International Security* 20, no. 3 (Winter 1995–1996):189–194.

6. See, for example, Ken Conca, "In the Name of Sustainability: Peace Studies and Environmental Discourse," *Peace and Change* 19, no. 2 (April 1994):91–113.

7. Matthias Finger, "The Military, the Nation State, and the Environment," *Ecologist* 21, no. 5 (September–October 1991):220–225.

8. See, for example, Ken Conca and Geoffrey D. Dabelko, eds., *Environmental Peacemaking* (Washington, DC, and Baltimore: Woodrow Wilson Center Press and Johns Hopkins University Press, 2002).

2 7

ENVIRONMENTAL
SCARCITIES AND VIOLENT
CONFLICT: EVIDENCE
FROM CASES

Thomas F. Homer-Dixon

Within the next fifty years, the planet's human population will probably pass nine billion, and global economic output may quintuple. Largely as a result, scarcities of renewable resources will increase sharply. The total area of high-quality agricultural land will drop, as will the extent of forests and the number of species they sustain. Coming generations will also see the widespread depletion and degradation of aquifers, rivers, and other water resources; the decline of many fisheries; and perhaps significant climate change.

If such "environmental scarcities" become severe, could they precipitate violent civil or international conflict? I have previously surveyed the issues and evidence surrounding this question and proposed an agenda for further research.[1] Here I report the results of an international research project guided by this agenda.[2] . . .

In brief, our research showed that environmental scarcities are already contributing to violent conflicts in many parts of the developing world. These conflicts are probably the early signs of an upsurge of violence in the coming decades that will be induced or aggravated by scarcity. The violence will usually be sub-national, persistent, and diffuse. Poor societies will be

Abridged article reprinted from *International Security* 19, no. 1 (1994):5–40. © 1994 The President and Fellows of Harvard College and the Massachusetts Institute of Technology. Reprinted with permission from MIT Press.

particularly affected since they are less able to buffer themselves from environmental scarcities and the social crises they cause. These societies are, in fact, already suffering acute hardship from shortages of water, forests, and especially fertile land.

Social conflict is not always a bad thing: mass mobilization and civil strife can produce opportunities for beneficial change in the distribution of land and wealth and in processes of governance. But fast-moving, unpredictable, and complex environmental problems can overwhelm efforts at constructive social reform. Moreover, scarcity can sharply increase demands on key institutions, such as the state, while it simultaneously reduces their capacity to meet those demands. These pressures increase the chance that the state will either fragment or become more authoritarian. The negative effects of severe environmental scarcity are therefore likely to outweigh the positive.

General Findings

Our research was intended to provide a foundation for further work. We therefore focused on two key preliminary questions: does environmental scarcity cause violent conflict? And, if it does, how does it operate?

The research was structured as I proposed in my previous article. Six types of environmental change were identified as plausible causes of violent intergroup conflict:

- greenhouse-induced climate change;
- stratospheric ozone depletion;
- degradation and loss of good agricultural land;
- degradation and removal of forests;
- depletion and pollution of fresh water supplies; and
- depletion of fisheries.

We used three hypotheses to link these changes with violent conflict. First, we suggested that decreasing supplies of physically controllable environmental resources, such as clean water and good agricultural land, would provoke interstate "simple-scarcity" conflicts or resource wars. Second, we hypothesized that large population movements caused by environmental stress would induce "group-identity" conflicts, especially ethnic clashes. And third, we suggested that severe environmental scarcity would simultaneously increase economic deprivation and disrupt key social institutions, which in turn would cause "deprivation" conflicts such as civil strife and insurgency. . . .

Resource Depletion and Degradation

Of the major environmental changes facing humankind, degradation and depletion of agricultural land, forests, water, and fish will contribute more to social turmoil in coming decades than will climate change or ozone depletion.

When analysts and policymakers in developed countries consider the social impacts of large-scale environmental change, they focus undue attention on climate change and stratospheric ozone depletion.[3] But vast populations in the developing world are already suffering from shortages of good land, water, forests, and fish; in contrast, the social effects of climate change and ozone depletion will probably not be seen till well into the next century. If these atmospheric problems do eventually have an impact, they will most likely operate not as individual environmental stresses, but in interaction with other, long-present resource, demographic, and economic pressures that have gradually eroded the buffering capacity of some societies.

Mexico, for example, is vulnerable to such interactions. People are already leaving the state of Oaxaca because of drought and soil erosion. Researchers estimate that future global warming could decrease Mexican rain-fed maize production up to 40 percent. This change could in turn interact with ongoing land degradation, free trade (because Mexico's comparative advantage is in water-intensive fruits and vegetables), and the privatization of communal peasant lands to cause grave internal conflict.[4]

Environmental Scarcity

Environmental change is only one of three main sources of scarcity of renewable resources; the others are population growth and unequal social distribution of resources. The concept "environmental scarcity" encompasses all three sources.

Analysts often usefully characterize environmental problems as resource scarcities. Resources can be roughly divided into two groups: non-renewables, like oil and iron ore, and renewables, like fresh water, forests, fertile soils, and the earth's ozone layer. The latter category includes renewable "goods" such as fisheries and timber, and renewable "services" such as regional hydrological cycles and a benign climate.

The commonly used term "environmental change" refers to a human-induced decline in the quantity or quality of a renewable resource that occurs faster than it is renewed by natural processes. But this concept limits the scope of environment-conflict research. Environmental change is only one of three main sources of renewable-resource scarcity. The second, population growth, reduces a resource's per-capita availability by dividing it among more and more people.[5] The third, unequal resource distribution, concentrates a resource in the hands of a few people and subjects the rest to greater scarcity.[6] The property rights that govern resource distribution often change as a result of large-scale development projects or new technologies that alter the relative values of resources.

In other words, reduction in the quantity or quality of a resource shrinks the resource pie, while population growth divides the pie into smaller slices for each individual, and unequal resource distribution means that some groups get disproportionately large slices.[7] Unfortunately, analysts often study resource depletion and population growth in isolation from the political economy of resource distribution.[8] The term "environmental scarcity," however, allows these three distinct sources of scarcity to be incorporated into one analysis. Empirical evidence suggests, in fact, that the first two sources are most pernicious when they interact with unequal resource distribution.

We must also recognize that resource scarcity is, in part, subjective; it is determined not just by absolute physical limits, but also by preferences, beliefs, and norms. This is illustrated by a debate about the role of population growth and resource scarcity as causes of the conflict between the Sandinista government and the Miskito Indians in Nicaragua.[9] Bernard Nietschmann argues that the Nicaraguan state's need for resources to sustain the country's economic and agricultural development caused environmental degradation to spread from the Pacific to the Atlantic coast of the country. As this happened, indigenous Miskitos in the east came into conflict with the central government. Sergio Diaz-Briquets responds that the Sandinistas expropriated Miskito lands because of ideology, not scarcity. The Atlantic coastal region was largely ignored by the Nicaraguan state under Somoza. Following the revolution, the Sandinistas had ample newly expropriated land to distribute to their followers; but the new government—guided by Marxism—saw the Miskitos as a backward people with a competing worldview and a precapitalist mode of production, whose land rightfully belonged to a state that was removing impediments to the historical progress of the working class.

The gap between the two views can be bridged by noting that scarcity is partly subjective. Marxist ideology encouraged the Sandinistas to adopt a strategy of state-directed industrialization and resource-use; this led them to perceive resources as more scarce than had the Somoza regime.

Interaction of Sources of Environmental Scarcity

The three sources of environmental scarcity often interact, and two patterns of interaction are particularly common: "resource capture" and "ecological marginalization.". . .

A fall in the quality and quantity of renewable resources can combine with population growth to encourage powerful groups within a society to shift resource distribution in their favor. This can produce dire environmental scarcity for poorer and weaker groups whose claims to resources are opposed by these powerful elites. I call this type of interaction "resource capture." Unequal resource access can combine with population growth to cause migrations to regions that are ecologically fragile, such as steep upland slopes, areas at risk of desertification, and tropical rain forests. High population densities in these areas, combined with a lack of knowledge and capital to protect local resources, cause severe environmental damage and chronic poverty.[10] This process is often called "ecological marginalization."[11] . . .

Hypothesis 1:
Simple-Scarcity Conflicts Between States

There is little empirical support for the first hypothesis that environmental scarcity causes simple-scarcity conflicts between states. Scarcities of renewable resources such as forests and croplands do not often cause resource wars between states. This finding is intriguing because resource wars have been common since the beginning of the state system. For instance, during World War II, Japan sought to secure oil, minerals, and other resources in China and Southeast Asia, and the 1991 Gulf War was at least partly motivated by the desire for oil.

However, we must distinguish between non-renewable resources, such as oil, and renewable resources. Arthur Westing has compiled a list of twelve conflicts in the twentieth century involving resources, beginning with World War I and concluding with the Falklands/Malvinas War.[12] Access to oil or minerals was at issue in ten of these conflicts. Just five conflicts involved renewable resources, and only two of these—the 1969 Soccer War between El Salvador and Honduras, and the Anglo-Icelandic Cod War of 1972–73—concerned neither oil nor minerals (cropland was a factor in the former case, and fish in the latter). However, the Soccer War was not a simple-scarcity conflict between states; rather it arose from the ecological marginalization of Salvadorean peasants and their consequent migration into Honduras.[13] It is evidence in support, therefore, of our second and third hypotheses (below), but not for the first. And, since the Cod War, despite its name, involved very little violence, it hardly qualifies as a resource war.

States have fought more over non-renewable than renewable resources for two reasons, I believe. First, petroleum and mineral resources can be more directly converted into state power than can agricultural land, fish, and forests. Oil and coal fuel factories and armies, and ores are vital for tanks and naval ships. In contrast, although captured forests and cropland may eventually generate wealth that can be harnessed by the state for its own ends, this outcome is more remote in time and less certain. Second, the very countries that are most dependent on renewable resources, and which are therefore most motivated to seize resources from their neighbors, also tend to be poor, which lessens their capability for aggression.

Our research suggests that the renewable resource most likely to stimulate interstate resource war is river water.[14] Water is a critical resource for personal and national survival; furthermore, since river water flows from one area to another, one country's access can be affected by another's actions. Conflict is most probable when a downstream riparian is highly dependent on river water and is strong in comparison to upstream riparians. Downstream riparians often fear that their upstream neighbors will use water as a means of coercion. This situation is particularly dangerous if the downstream country also believes it has the military power to rectify the situation. The relationships between South Africa and Lesotho and between Egypt and Ethiopia have this character.[15] . . .

However, our review of the historical and contemporary evidence shows that conflict and turmoil related to river water are more often internal than international. The huge dams that are often built to deal with general water scarcity are especially disruptive. Relocating large numbers of upstream people generates turmoil among the relocatees and clashes with local groups in areas where the relocatees are resettled. The people affected are often members of ethnic or minority groups outside the power hierarchy of their society, and the result is frequently rebellion by these groups and repression by the state. Water developments can also induce conflict over water and irrigable land among a country's downstream users, as we saw in the Senegal River basin.[16]

Hypothesis 2:
Population Movement and Group-Identity Conflicts

There is substantial evidence to support the hypothesis that environmental scarcity causes large population movement, which in turn causes group-identity conflicts. But we must be sensitive to contextual factors unique to each socio-ecological system. These are the system's particular physical, political, economic, and cultural features that affect the strength of the linkages between scarcity, population movement, and conflict.

For example, experts emphasize the importance of both "push" and "pull" factors in decisions of potential migrants.[17] These factors help distinguish migrants from refugees: while migrants are motivated by a combination of push and pull, refugees are motivated mainly by push. Environmental scarcity is more likely to produce migrants than refugees, because it usually develops gradually, which means that the push effect is not sharp and sudden and that pull factors can therefore clearly enter into potential migrants' calculations.

Migrants are often people who have been weak and marginal in their home society and, depending on context, they may remain weak in the receiving society. This limits their ability to organize and to make demands. States play a critical role here: migrants often need the backing of a state (either of the receiving society or an external one) before they have sufficient power to cause conflict, and this backing depends on the region's politics. Without it, migration is less likely to produce violence than silent misery and death, which rarely destabilizes states.[18] We must remember too that migration does not always produce bad results. It can act as a safety valve by reducing conflict in the sending area. Depending on the economic context, it can ease labor shortages in the receiving society, as it sometimes has, for instance, in Malaysia. Countries as different as Canada, Thailand, and Malawi show the astonishing capacity of some societies to absorb migrants without conflict. . . .

Hypothesis 3:
Economic Deprivation, Institutional
Disruption, and Civil Strife

Empirical evidence partially supports the third hypothesis that environmental scarcity simultaneously increases economic deprivation and disrupts key social institutions, which in turn causes "deprivation" conflicts such as civil strife and insurgency. Environmental scarcity does produce economic deprivation, and this deprivation does cause civil strife. But more research is needed on the effects of scarcity on social institutions.

Resource degradation and depletion often affect economic productivity in poor countries and thereby contribute to deprivation. For example, erosion in upland Indonesia annually costs the country's agricultural economy nearly half a billion dollars in discounted future income.[19] The Magat watershed on the northern Filipino island of Luzon—a watershed representative of many in the Philippines—suffers gross erosion rates averaging 219 tons per hectare per year; if the lost nutrients were replaced by fertilizer, the annual cost would be over $100 per hectare.[20] Dryland degradation in Burkina Faso reduces the country's annual gross domestic product by nearly 9 percent annually because of fuelwood loss and lower yields of millet, sorghum, and livestock.[21] . . .

I originally hypothesized that scarcity would undermine a variety of social institutions. Our research suggests, however, that one institution in particular—the state—is most important. Although more study is needed, the multiple effects of environmental scarcity, including large population movements and economic decline, appear likely to weaken sharply the capacity and legitimacy of the state in some poor countries.

First, environmental scarcity increases financial and political demands on governments. For example, to mitigate the social effects of loss of water, soil, and forest, governments must spend huge sums on industry and infrastructure such as new dams, irrigation systems, fertilizer plants, and reforestation programs. Furthermore, this resource loss can reduce the incomes of elites directly dependent on resource extraction; these elites usually turn to the state for compensation. Scarcity also expands marginal groups that need help from government by producing rural poverty and by displacing people into cities where they demand food, shelter, transport, energy, and employment. In response to swelling urban populations, governments introduce subsidies that drain revenues, distort prices, and cause misallocations of capital, which in turn hinders economic productivity. Such large-scale state intervention in the marketplace can concentrate political and economic power in the hands of a small number of cronies and monopolistic interests, at the expense of other elite segments and rural agricultural populations.

Simultaneously, if resource scarcity affects the economy's general productivity, revenues to local and national governments will decline. This hurts elites that benefit from state largesse and reduces the state's capacity to meet the increased demands arising from environmental scarcity. A widening gap between state capacity and demands on the state, along with the misguided economic interventions such a gap often provokes, aggravates popular and elite grievances, increases rivalry between elite factions, and erodes the state's legitimacy.

Key contextual factors affect whether lower economic productivity and state weakening lead to deprivation conflicts. Civil strife is a function of both the level of grievance motivating challenger groups and the opportunities available to these groups to act on their grievances. The likelihood of civil strife is greatest when multiple pressures at different levels in society interact to increase grievance and opportunity simultaneously. Our third hypothesis says that environmental scarcity will change both variables, by contributing to economic crisis and by weakening institutions such as the state. But numerous other factors also influence grievance and opportunity. . . .

A Combined Model

There are important links between the processes identified in the second and third hypotheses. For example, although population movement is sometimes caused directly by scarcity, more often it arises from the greater poverty caused by this scarcity. Similarly, the weakening of the state increases the likelihood not only of deprivation conflicts, but of group-identity conflicts.

It is useful, therefore, to bring the hypotheses together into one model of environment-conflict linkages. . . . Decreases in the quality and quantity of renewable resources, population growth, and unequal resource access act singly or in various combinations to increase the scarcity, for certain population groups, of cropland, water, forests, and fish. This can reduce economic productivity, both for the local groups experiencing the scarcity and for the larger regional and national economies. The affected people may migrate or be expelled to new lands. Migrating groups often trigger ethnic conflicts when they move to new areas, while decreases in wealth can cause deprivation conflicts such as insurgency and rural rebellion. In developing countries, the migrations and productivity losses may eventually weaken the state which in turn decreases central control over ethnic rivalries and increases opportunities for insurgents and elites challenging state authority. . . .

South Africa and Haiti illustrate this combined model. In South Africa, apartheid concentrated millions of blacks in some of the country's least productive and most ecologically sensitive territories, where population densities were worsened by high natural birth rates. In 1980, rural areas of the Ciskei homeland had 82 people per square kilometer, whereas the surrounding Cape province had a rural density of 2. Homeland residents had little capital and few resource-management skills and were subject to corrupt and abusive local governments. Sustainable development in such a situation was impossible, and wide areas were completely stripped of trees for fuelwood, grazed down to bare dirt, and eroded of top soil. A 1980 report concluded that nearly 50 percent of Ciskei's land was moderately or severely eroded, and nearly 40 percent of its pasturage was overgrazed.[22]

This loss of resources, combined with a lack of alternative employment and the social trauma caused by apartheid, created a subsistence crisis in the homelands. Thousands of people have migrated to South African cities, which are as yet incapable of adequately integrating and employing these migrants. The result is the rapid growth of squatter settlements and illegal townships that are rife with discord and that threaten the country's move to democratic stability.[23]

In Haiti, the irreversible loss of forests and soil in rural areas deepens an economic crisis that spawns social strife, internal migration, and an exodus of "boat people." When first colonized by the Spanish in the late fifteenth century and the French in the seventeenth century, Haiti was treasured for abundant forests. Since then, Haiti has become one of the world's most dramatic examples of environmental despoliation. Less than two percent of the country remains forested, and the last timber is being felled at four percent per year.[24] As trees disappear, erosion follows, worsened by the steepness of the land and by harsh storms. The United Nations estimates that at least 50 percent of the country is affected by topsoil loss that leaves land "unreclaimable at the farm level."[25] So much soil washes off the slopes that the streets of Port-au-Prince have to be cleared with bulldozers in the rainy season.

Unequal land distribution was not a main cause of this catastrophe. Haiti gained independence in 1804 following a revolt of slaves and ex-slaves against the French colonial regime. Over a period of decades, the old plantation system associated with slavery was dismantled, and land was widely distributed in small parcels.[26] As a result, Haiti's agricultural structure, unique to Latin America, has 73 percent of cropland in private farms of less than 4 hectares.[27]

But inheritance customs and population growth have combined to produce scarcity, as in Bangladesh. Land has been subdivided into smaller portions with each generation. Eventually the plots cannot properly support their cultivators, fallow periods are neglected, and greater poverty prevents investment in soil conservation. The poorest people leave for steeper hillsides, where they clear the forest and begin farming anew, only to exhaust the land in a few years.[28] Many peasants try to supplement their falling incomes by scavenging wood for charcoal production, which contributes to further deforestation.

These processes might have been prevented had a stable central government invested in agriculture, industrial development, and reforestation. Instead, since independence Haiti has endured a ceaseless struggle for power between black and mulatto classes, and the ruling regimes have been solely interested in expropriating any surplus wealth the economy generated. Today, over 60 percent of the population is still engaged in agriculture, yet capital is unavailable for agricultural improvement, and the terms of exchange for crop production favor urban regions.[29] The population growth rate has actually increased, from 1.7 percent in the mid-1970s to over 2 percent today: the UN estimates that the current population of 6.75 million will grow to over 13 million by 2025.[30] As the land erodes and the population grows, incomes shrink: agricultural output per capita has decreased 10 percent in the last decade.

Analysts agree that rising rural poverty has caused ever-increasing rural-rural and rural-urban migration. In search of work, agricultural workers move from subsistence hillside farms to rice farms in the valleys. From there, they go to cities, especially to Port-au-Prince, which now has a population of over a million. Wealthier farmers and traders, and even those with slimmer resources, try to flee by boat. . . .

Implications for International Security

Environmental scarcity has insidious and cumulative social impacts, such as population movement, economic decline, and the weakening of states. These can contribute to diffuse and persistent sub-national violence. The rate and extent of such conflicts will increase as scarcities worsen.

This sub-national violence will not be as conspicuous or dramatic as inter-state resource wars, but it will have serious repercussions for the security interests of both the developed and the developing worlds. Countries under such stress may fragment as their states become enfeebled and peripheral regions are seized by renegade authorities and warlords. Governments of countries as different as the Philippines and Peru have lost control over outer territories; although both these cases are complicated, it is nonetheless clear that environmental stress has contributed to their fragmentation. Fragmentation of any sizeable country will produce large outflows of refugees; it will also hinder the country from effectively negotiating and implementing international agreements on collective security, global environmental protection, and other matters.

Alternatively, a state might keep scarcity-induced civil strife from causing its progressive enfeeblement and fragmentation by becoming a "hard" regime that is authoritarian, intolerant of opposition, and militarized. Such regimes are more prone to launch military attacks against neighboring countries to divert attention from internal grievances. If a number of developing countries evolve in this direction, they could eventually threaten the military and economic interests of rich countries.

A state's ability to become a hard regime in response to environmentally induced turmoil depends, I believe, on two factors. First, the state must have sufficient remaining capacity—despite the debilitating effects of scarcity—to mobilize or seize resources for its own ends; this is a function of the internal organizational coherence of the state and its autonomy from outside pressures. Second, there must remain enough surplus wealth in the country's ecological-economic system to allow the state, once it seizes this wealth, to pursue its authoritarian course. Consequently, the countries with the highest probability of becoming "hard" regimes, and potential threats to their neighbors, are large, relatively wealthy developing countries that are dependent on a declining environmental base and that have a history of state strength. Candidates include Indonesia and, perhaps, Nigeria. . . .

Conclusions

Our research shows that environmental scarcity causes violent conflict. This conflict tends to be persistent, diffuse, and sub-national. Its frequency will probably jump sharply in the next decades as scarcities rapidly worsen in many parts of the world. Of immediate concern are scarcities of cropland, water, forests, and fish, whereas atmospheric changes such as global warming will probably not have a major effect for several decades, and then mainly by interacting with already existing scarcities.

The degradation and depletion of environmental resources is only one source of environmental scarcity; two other important sources are population growth and unequal resource distribution. Scarcity often has its harshest social impact when these factors interact. As environmental scarcity becomes more severe, some societies will have a progressively lower capacity to adapt. Of particular concern is the decreasing capacity of the state to create markets and other institutions that promote adaptation. The impact of environmental scarcity on state capacity deserves further research.

Countries experiencing chronic internal conflict because of environmental stress will probably either fragment or become more authoritarian. Fragmenting countries will be the source of large out-migrations, and they will be unable to effectively negotiate or implement international agreements on security, trade, and environmental protection. Authoritarian regimes may be inclined to launch attacks against other countries to divert popular attention from internal stresses. Any of these outcomes could seriously disrupt international security. The social impacts of environmental scarcity therefore deserve concerted attention from security scholars.

Notes

1. Thomas Homer-Dixon, "On the Threshold: Environmental Changes as Causes of Acute Conflict," *International Security*, Vol. 16, No. 2 (Fall 1991), pp. 76–116.

2. The three-year Project on Environmental Change and Acute Conflict brought together a team of thirty researchers from ten countries. It was sponsored by the American Academy of Arts and Sciences and the Peace and Conflict Studies Program at the University of Toronto.

3. For example, see David Wirth, "Climate Chaos," *Foreign Policy*, No. 74 (Spring 1989), pp. 3–22; and Neville Brown, "Climate, Ecology and International Security," *Survival*, Vol. 31, No. 6 (November/December 1989), pp. 519–532.

4. Diana Liverman, "The Impacts of Global Warming in Mexico: Uncertainty, Vulnerability and Response," in Jurgen Schmandt and Judith Clarkson, eds., *The Regions and Global Warming: Impacts and Response Strategies* (New York: Oxford University Press, 1992), pp. 44–68; and Diana Liverman and Karen O'Brien, "Global Warming and Climate Change in Mexico," *Global Environmental Change*, Vol. 1, No. 4 (December 1991), pp. 351–364.

5. Peter Gleick provides a potent illustration of the effect of population growth on water scarcity in Table 3 of "Water and Conflict: Fresh Water Resources and International Security," *International Security*, Vol. 18, No. 1 (Summer 1993), p. 101.

6. The second and third types of scarcity arise only with resources that can be physically controlled and possessed, like fish, fertile land, trees, and water, rather than resources like the climate or the ozone layer.

7. Since population growth is often a main cause of a decline in the quality and quantity of renewable resources, it actually has a dual impact on resource scarcity, a fact rarely noted by analysts.

8. James Boyce, "The Bomb Is a Dud," *The Progressive*, September 1990, pp. 24–25.

9. Bernard Nietschmann, "Environmental Conflicts and Indigenous Nations in Central America," paper prepared for the Project on Environmental Change and Acute Conflict (May 1991); and Sergio Diaz-Briquets, "Comments on Nietschmann's Paper," ibid.

10. Jeffrey Leonard, "Overview," *Environment and the Poor: Development Strategies for a Common Agenda* (New Brunswick, N.J.: Transaction, 1989), p. 7. For a careful analysis of the interaction of population and land distribution in El Salvador, see chap. 2 in William Durham, *Scarcity and Survival in Central America: The Ecological Origins of the Soccer War* (Stanford, Calif.: Stanford University Press, 1979), pp. 21–62.

11. Arthur Westing, "Appendix 2. Wars and Skirmishes Involving Natural Resources: A Selection from the Twentieth Century," in Arthur Westing, ed., *Global Resources and International Conflict: Environmental Factors in Strategic Policy and Action* (Oxford: New York, 1986), pp. 204–210.

12. See Durham, *Scarcity and Survival*.

13. Peter Gleick, "Water and Conflict," Occasional Paper No. 1, Project on Environmental Change and Acute Conflict (September 1992); and Gleick, "Water and Conflict: Fresh Water Resources and International Security," *International Security*, Vol. 18, No. 1 (Summer 1993), pp. 79–112.

14. In 1980, Egyptian President Anwar el-Sadat said, "If Ethiopia takes any action to block our right to the Nile waters, there will be no alternative for us but to use force";

quoted in Norman Myers, "Environment and Security," *Foreign Policy*, No. 74 (Spring 1989), p. 32. See also chap. 6, "The Nile River," in Thomas Naff and Ruth Matson, eds., *Water in the Middle East: Conflict or Cooperation?* (Boulder, Colo.: Westview, 1984), pp. 125–155.

15. See Thayer Scudder, "River Basin Projects in Africa," *Environment*, Vol. 31, No. 2 (March 1989), pp. 4–32; and Scudder, "Victims of Development Revisited: The Political Costs of River Basin Development," *Development Anthropology Network*, Vol. 8, No. 1 (Spring 1990), pp. 1–5.

16. Astri Suhrke, "Pressure Points: Environmental Degradation, Migration, and Conflict," Occasional Paper No. 3, Project on Environmental Change and Acute Conflict (March 1993).

17. Ibid.

18. Robert Repetto, "Balance-Sheet Erosion—How to Account for the Loss of Natural Resources," *International Environmental Affairs*, Vol. 1, No. 2 (Spring 1989), pp. 103–137.

19. This estimate does not include the economic costs of lost rooting depth and increased vulnerability to drought, which may be even larger. See Wilfrido Cruz, Herminia Francisco, and Zenaida Conway, "The On-Site and Downstream Costs of Soft Erosion in the Magat and Pantabangan Watersheds," *Journal of Philippine Development*, Vol. 15, No. 1 (1988), p. 88.

20. Ed Barbier, "Environmental Degradation in the Third World," in David Pearce, ed., *Blueprint 2: Greening the World Economy* (London: Earthscan, 1991), Box 6.8, p. 90.

21. Francis Wilson and Mamphela Ramphele, *Uprooting Poverty: The South African Challenge* (New York: Norton, 1989); George Quail et al., *Report of the Ciskei Commission* (Pretoria: Conference Associates, 1980), p. 73.

22. See Mamphela Ramphele and Chris McDowell, eds., *Restoring the Land: Environment and Change in Post-Apartheid South Africa* (London: Panos, 1991); and Chris Eaton, "Rural Environmental Degradation and Urban Conflict in South Africa," Occasional Paper of the Peace and Conflict Studies Program, University of Toronto, June 1992.

23. World Resources Institute, *World Resources, 1992–93* (New York: Oxford University Press, 1992), p. 286.

24. Global Assessment of Soil Degradation, *World Map on Status of Human-Induced Soil Degradation*, Sheet 1, North and South America.

25. Thomas Weil et al., *Haiti: A Country Study* (Washington, D.C.: Department of the Army, 1982), pp. 28–33.

26. Anthony Catanese, "Haiti's Refugees: Political, Economic, Environmental," *Field Staff Reports*, No. 17 (Sausalito, Calif.: Universities Field Staff International, Natural Heritage Institute, 1990–91), p. 5.

27. Elizabeth Abbott, "Where Waters Run Brown," *Equinox*, Vol. 10, No. 59 (September/October 1991), p. 43.

28. Marko Ehrlich et al., *Haiti: Country Environmental Profile, A Field Study* (Washington, D.C.: U.S. Agency for International Development, 1986), pp. 89–92.

29. WRI, *World Resources, 1992–93*, p. 246.

30. Ibid., p. 272.

THE CASE AGAINST LINKING ENVIRONMENTAL DEGRADATION AND NATIONAL SECURITY

Daniel Deudney

Introduction

. . . Environmental issues are likely to become an increasingly important dimension of political life at all levels—locally, inside states, as well as internationally. How institutions respond to these emerging constraints is likely to shape politics in a profound manner. Because state and interstate conflict are such central features of both world politics and geopolitical theory, there is a strong tendency for people to think about environmental problems in terms of national security and to assume that environmental conflicts will fit into the established patterns of interstate conflict.

The aim of this essay is to cast doubt upon this tendency to link environmental degradation and national security. Specifically, I make three claims. First, it is analytically misleading to think of environmental degradation as a national security threat, because the traditional focus of national security—interstate violence—has little in common with either environmental problems or solutions. Second, the effort to harness the emotive power of nationalism to help mobilise environmental awareness and action may prove

Millennium: Journal of International Studies. This article first appeared in *Millennium* 19, no. 3, 1990, and is reproduced with the permission of the publisher.

counterproductive by undermining globalist political sensibility. And third, environmental degradation is not very likely to cause interstate wars.

The Weak Analytical Links between Environmental Degradation and National Security

One striking feature of the growing discussion of environmental issues in the United States is the attempt by many liberals, progressives and environmentalists to employ language traditionally associated with violence and war to understand environmental problems and to motivate action. Lester Brown, Jessica Tuchman Matthews, Michael Renner and others have proposed 'redefining national security' to encompass resource and environmental threats.[1] More broadly, Richard Ullman and others have proposed 'redefining security' to encompass a wide array of threats, ranging from earthquakes to environmental degradation.[2] Hal Harvey has proposed the concept of 'natural security,'[3] and US Senator Albert Gore has spoken extensively in favour of thinking of the environment as a national security issue.[4] During the renewed Cold War tensions of the late 1970s and early 1980s, such concepts were advanced to prevent an excessive focus on military threats. As the Cold War winds down, such links are increasingly popular among national security experts and organisations looking for new missions. . . .

Historically, conceptual ferment of this sort has often accompanied important changes in politics.[5] New phrases are coined and old terms are appropriated for new purposes. Epochal developments like the emergence of capitalism, the growth of democracy and the end of slavery were accompanied by shifting, borrowing and expanding political language. The wide-ranging contemporary conceptual ferment in the language used to understand and act upon environmental problems is therefore both a natural and an encouraging development.

But not all neologisms and linkages are equally plausible or useful. Until this recent flurry of reconceptualising, the concept of 'national security' (as opposed to national interest or well-being) has been centred upon *organised violence*.[6] As is obvious to common sense and as Hobbes argued with such force, security from violence is a primal human need, because loss of life prevents the enjoyment of all other goods. Of course, various resource factors, such as access to fuels and ores, were understood as contributing to states' capacities to wage war and achieve security from violence.

Before either 'expanding' the concept of 'national security' to encompass both environmental and violence threats, or 're-defining' 'national security' or 'security' to refer mainly to environmental threats, it is worth examining just how much the national pursuit of security from violence has in common with environmental problems and their solutions.

Military violence and environmental degradation are linked directly in at least three major ways. First, the pursuit of national-security-from-violence through military means consumes resources (fiscal, organisational and leadership) that could be spent on environmental restoration. Since approximately one trillion US dollars is spent worldwide on military activities, substantial resources are involved. However, this relationship is not unique to environmental concerns, and unfortunately there is no guarantee that the world would spend money saved from military expenditures on environmental restoration. Nor is it clear that the world cannot afford environmental restoration without cutting military expenditures.

Second, war is directly destructive of the environment. In ancient times, the military destruction of olive groves in Mediterranean lands contributed to the long-lasting destruction of the lands' carrying capacities. More recently, the United States' bombardment and use of defoliants in Indochina caused significant environmental damage. Further, extensive use of nuclear weapons could have significant impacts on the global environment, including altered weather (i.e., 'nuclear winter') and further depletion of the ozone layer. Awareness of these environmental effects has played an important role in mobilising popular resistance to the arms race and in generally de-legitimising use of nuclear explosives as weapons.

Third, preparation for war causes pollution and consumes significant quantities of resources. In both the United States and the Soviet Union, significant quantities of radioactive waste have been produced as a by-product of the nuclear arms race, and several significant releases of radiation have occurred—perhaps most disastrously when a waste dump at a Soviet nuclear weapons facility exploded and burned, spreading radioactive materials over a large area near the Urals. Military activities have also produced significant quantities of toxic wastes.

In short, war and the preparation for war are clearly environmental threats and consume resources that could be used to ameliorate environmental degradation. In effect, these environmental impacts mean that the war system has costs beyond the intentional loss of life and destruction. Nevertheless, most of the world's environmental degradation is not caused by war and the preparation for war. Completely eliminating the direct environmental effects of the war system would leave most environmental degradation unaffected. Most of the causes and most of the cures of environmental degradation must be found outside the domain of the traditional national security system related to violence.

The war system is a definite but limited environmental threat, but in what ways is environmental degradation a threat to 'national security'? Making such an identification can be useful if the two phenomena—security from violence and security from environmental threats—are similar. Unfortunately, they have little in common, making such linkages largely useless for analytical and conceptual purposes. Four major dissimilarities . . . deserve mention.

First, environmental degradation and violence are very different types of threats. Both violence and environmental degradation may kill people and may reduce human well-being, but not all threats to life and property are threats to security. Disease, old age, crime and accidents routinely destroy life and property, but we do not think of them as 'national security' threats or even threats to 'security.' (Crime is a partial exception, but crime is a 'security' threat at the individual level, because crime involves violence.) And when an earthquake or hurricane strikes with great force, we speak about 'natural disasters' or designate 'national disaster areas,' but we do not speak about such events threatening 'national security.' If everything that causes a decline in human well-being is labelled a 'security' threat, the term loses any analytical usefulness and becomes a loose synonym of 'bad.'

Second, the scope and source of threats to environmental well-being and national-security-from-violence are very different. There is nothing about the problem of environmental degradation which is particularly 'national' in character. Since environmental threats are often oblivious of the borders of the nation-state, they rarely afflict just one nation-state. Nevertheless, this said, it would be misleading to call most environmental problems 'international.' Many perpetrators and victims are within the borders of one nation-state. Individuals, families, communities, other species and future generations are harmed. A complete collapse of the biosphere would surely destroy 'nations' as well as everything else, but there is nothing distinctively national about either the causes, the harms or the solutions that warrants us giving such privileged billing to the 'national' grouping.

A third misfit between environmental well-being and national-security-from-violence stems from the differing degrees of *intention* involved. Violent threats involve a high degree of intentional behaviour. Organisations are mobilised, weapons procured and wars waged with relatively definite aims in mind. Environmental degradation, on the other hand, is largely unintentional, the side-effects of many other activities. No one really sets out with the aim of harming the environment (with the so far limited exception of environmental modification for military purposes).

Fourth, organisations that provide protection from violence differ greatly from those in environmental protection. National-security-from-violence is conventionally pursued by organisations with three distinctive features. First, military organisations are secretive, extremely hierarchical and centralised, and normally deploy vastly expensive, highly specialised and advanced technologies. Second, citizens typically delegate the goal of achieving national security to remote and highly specialised organisations that are far removed from the experience of civil society. And third, the specialised professional group staffing these national security organisations are trained in the arts of killing and destroying.

In contrast, responding to the environmental problem requires almost exactly opposite approaches and organisations. Certain aspects of virtually all mundane activities—for example, house construction, farming techniques, sewage treatment, factory design and land use planning—must be reformed. The routine everyday behaviour of practically everyone must be altered. This requires behaviour modification in situ. The professional ethos of environmental restoration is husbandmanship—more respectful cultivation and protection of plants, animals and the land.

In short, national-security-from-violence and environmental habitability have little in common. Given these differences, the rising fashion of linking them risks creating a conceptual muddle rather than a paradigm or world view shift—a *de-definition* rather than a *re-definition* of security. If we begin to speak about all the forces and events that threaten life, property and well-being (on a large-scale) as threats to our national security, we shall soon drain the term of any meaning. All large-scale evils will become threats to national security. To speak meaningfully about actual problems, we shall have to invent new words to fill the job previously performed by the old spoiled ones.

The Risks in Harnessing the Rhetorical and Emotional Appeals of National Security for Environmental Restoration

Confronted with these arguments, the advocate of treating environmental degradation as a national security problem might retort:

> Yes, some semantic innovation without much analytical basis is occurring, but it has a sound goal—to get people to react as urgently and effectively to the environmental problem as they have to the national-security-from-violence problem. If people took the environmental problem as seriously as, say, an attack by a foreign power, think of all that could be done to solve the problems!

In other words, the aim of these new links is not primarily descriptive, but polemical. It is not a claim about fact, but a rhetorical device designed to stimulate action. Like William James, these environmentalists hope to find a 'moral equivalent to war' to channel the energies behind war into constructive directions. . . .

At first glance, the most attractive feature of linking fears about environmental threats with national security mentalities is the sense of urgency engendered, and the corresponding willingness to accept great personal sacrifice. If in fact the basic habitability of the planet is being undermined, then it stands to reason that some crisis mentality is needed. Unfortunately, it may be difficult to engender a sense of urgency and a willingness to sacrifice for extended periods of time. . . . A second apparently valuable similarity between the national security mentality and the environmental problem is the tendency to use worse case scenarios as the basis for planning. However, the extreme conservatism of military organisations in responding to potential threats is not unique to them. The insurance industry is built around preparations for the worst possibilities, and many fields of engineering, such as aeronautical design and nuclear power plant regulation, routinely employ extremely conservative planning assumptions. These can serve as useful models for improved environmental policies.

Third, the conventional national security mentality and its organisations are deeply committed to zero-sum thinking. 'Our' gain is 'their' loss. Trust between national security organisations is extremely low. The prevailing assumption is that everyone is a potential enemy, and that agreements mean little unless congruent with immediate interests. If the Pentagon had been put in charge of negotiating an ozone layer protocol, we might still be stockpiling chlorofluorocarbons as a bargaining chip.

Fourth, conventional national security organisations have short time horizons. The pervasive tendency for national security organisations to discount the future and pursue very near-term objectives is a poor model for environmental problem solving.

Finally, and perhaps most importantly, is the fact that the 'nation' is not an empty vessel or blank slate waiting to be filled or scripted, but is instead profoundly linked to war and 'us vs. them' thinking. The tendency for people to identify themselves with various tribal and kin groupings is as old as humanity. In the last century and a half, however, this sentiment of nationalism, amplified and manipulated by mass media propaganda techniques, has been an integral part of totalitarianism and militarism. Nationalism means a sense of 'us vs. them,' of the insider vs. the outsider, of the compatriot vs. the alien. The stronger the nationalism, the stronger this cleavage, and the weaker the transnational bonds. Nationalism reinforces militarism, fosters prejudice and discrimination, and feeds the quest for 'sovereign' autonomy. . . .

Thus, thinking of national security as an environmental problem risks undercutting both the globalist and common fate understanding of the situation and the sense of world community that may be necessary to solve the problem. In short, it seems doubtful that the environment can be wrapped in national flags without undercutting the 'whole earth' sensibility at the core of environmental awareness.

If pollution comes to be seen widely as a national security problem, there is also a danger that the citizens of one country will feel much more threatened by the pollution from other countries than by the pollution created by their fellow citizens. This could increase international tensions and make international accords more difficult to achieve, while diverting attention from internal cleanup. Citizens of the United States, for example, could become much more concerned about deforestation in Brazil than in reversing the centuries of North American deforestation. Taken to an absurd extreme—as national security threats sometimes are—seeing environmental degradation in a neighboring country as a national security threat could trigger various types of interventions, a new imperialism of the strong against the weak.

Instead of linking 'national security' to the environmental problem, environmentalists should emphasise that the environmental crisis calls into question the national grouping and its privileged status in world politics. The environmental crisis is not a threat to national security, but it does challenge the utility of thinking in 'national' terms. . . .

Environmental Degradation and Interstate War

Many people are drawn to calling environmental degradation a national security problem, in part because they expect this phenomenon to stimulate interstate conflict and even violence. States often fight over what they value, particularly if related to 'security'. If states begin to be much more concerned with resources and environmental degradation, particularly if they think environmental decay is a threat to their 'national security,' then states may well fight resource and pollution wars. . . . In general, I argue that interstate violence is not likely to result from environmental degradation, because of several deeply rooted features of the contemporary world order—both material and institutional—and because of the character of environmental and resource interests.

Few ideas seem more intuitively sound than the notion that states will begin fighting each other as the world runs out of usable natural resources. The popular metaphor of a lifeboat adrift at sea with declining supplies of clean water and rations suggests there will be fewer and fewer opportunities for positive-sum gains between actors. . . .

There are, however, three strong reasons for concluding that the familiar scenarios of resource war are of diminishing plausibility for the foreseeable future. First, the robust character of the world trade system means that states no longer experience resource dependency as a major threat to their military security and political autonomy. During the 1930s, the world trading system had collapsed, driving states to pursue autarkic economies. In contrast, the resource needs of contemporary states are routinely met without territorial control of the resource source, as Ronnie Lipschutz has recently shown.[7]

Second, the prospects for resource wars are diminished, since states find it increasingly difficult to exploit foreign resources through territorial conquest. Although the invention of nuclear explosives has made it easy and cheap to annihilate humans and infrastructure in extensive areas, the spread of small arms and national consciousness has made it very costly for an invader, even one equipped with advanced technology, to subdue a resisting population—as France discovered in Indochina and Algeria, the United States in Vietnam and the Soviet Union in Afghanistan. . . .

Third, the world is entering what H. E. Goeller and Alvin M. Weinberg have called the 'age of substitutability,' in which industrial civilisation is increasingly capable of taking earth materials such as iron, aluminum, silicon and hydrocarbons (which are ubiquitous and plentiful) and fashioning them into virtually everything needed.[8] The most striking manifestation of this trend is that prices for virtually every raw material have been stagnant or falling for the last several decades, despite the continued growth in world output. In contrast to the expectations voiced by many during the 1970s—that resource scarcity would drive up commodity prices to the benefit of Third World raw material suppliers—prices have fallen, with disastrous consequences for Third World development.

In a second scenario, increased interstate violence results from internal turmoil caused by declining living standards. . . . Faced with declining living standards, groups at all levels of affluence can be expected to resist this trend by pushing the deprivation upon other groups. Class relations would be increasingly 'zero-sum games,' producing class war and revolutionary upheavals. Faced with these pressures, liberal democracy and free-market systems would increasingly be replaced by authoritarian systems capable of maintaining minimum order.[9]

The international system consequences of these domestic changes may be increased conflict and war. If authoritarian regimes are more war-prone because of their lack of democratic control and if revolutionary regimes are more war-prone because of their ideological fervour and lack of socialisation into international norms and processes, then a world political system containing more such states is likely to be an increasingly violent one. The historical record from previous economic depressions supports the general proposition that widespread economic stagnation and unmet economic expectations contribute to international conflict.

Although initially compelling, this scenario has flaws as well. First, the pessimistic interpretation of the relationship between environmental sustainability and economic growth is arguably based on unsound economic theory. Wealth formation is not so much a product of cheap natural resource availability as of capital formation via savings and more efficient ways of producing. The fact that so many resource-poor countries, like Japan, are very wealthy, while many countries with more extensive resource endowments are poor, suggests that there is no clear and direct relationship between abundant resource availability and national wealth. Environmental constraints require an end to economic growth based on increasing raw material through-puts, rather than an end to growth in the output of goods and services.

Second, even if economic decline does occur, interstate conflict may be dampened, not stoked. . . . How societies respond to economic decline may in large measure depend upon the rate at which such declines occur. An offsetting factor here is the possibility that as people get poorer, they will be less willing to spend increasingly scarce resources for military capabilities. In this regard, the experience of economic depressions over the last two centuries may not be relevant, because such depressions were characterised by underutilised production capacity and falling resource prices. In the 1930s, increased military spending had a stimulative effect, but in a world in which economic growth had been retarded by environmental constraints, military spending would exacerbate the problem. . . .

Environmental degradation in a country or region could become so extreme that the basic social and economic fabric comes apart. Should some areas of the world suffer this fate, the impact of this outcome on international order may not, however, be very great. If a particular country, even a large one like Brazil, were tragically to disintegrate, among the first casualties would be the capacity of the industrial and governmental structure to wage and sustain interstate conventional war. As Bernard Brodie observed in the modern era, 'the predisposing factors to military aggression are full bellies, not empty ones.'[10] The poor and wretched of the earth may be able to deny an outside aggressor an easy conquest, but they are themselves a minimal threat to outside states. Offensive war today requires complex organisational skills, specialised industrial products and surplus wealth.

In today's world everything is connected, but not everything is tightly coupled. Regional disasters of great severity may occur, with scarcely a ripple in the rest of the world. After all, Idi Amin drew Uganda back into savage darkness, the Khmer Rouge murdered an estimated two million Cambodians and the Sahara has advanced across the Sahel without the economies and political systems of the rest of the world being much perturbed. Indeed, many of the world's citizens did not even notice.

A fourth possible route from environmental degradation to interstate conflict and violence involves pollution across state borders. It is easy to envision situations in which country A dumps an intolerable amount of pollution on a neighboring country B (which is upstream and upwind), causing country B to attempt to pressure and coerce country A into eliminating its offending pollution. We can envision such conflict of interest leading to armed conflict.

Fortunately for interstate peace, strongly asymmetrical and significant environmental degradation between neighboring countries is relatively rare. Probably more typical is the situation in which activities in country A harm parts of country A and country B, and in which activities in country B also harm parts of both countries. This creates complex sets of winners and losers, and thus establishes a complex array of potential intrastate and interstate coalitions. In general, the more such interactions are occurring, the less likely it is that a persistent, significant and highly asymmetrical pollution 'exchange' will result. The very multitude of interdependency in the contemporary world, particularly among the industrialised countries, makes it unlikely that intense cleavages of environmental harm will match interstate borders, and at the same time not be compensated and complicated by other military, economic or cultural interactions. Resolving such conflicts will be a complex and messy affair, but the conflicts are unlikely to lead to war.

Finally, there are conflict potentials related to the global commons. Many countries contribute to environmental degradation, and many countries are harmed, but since the impacts are widely distributed, no one country has an incentive to act alone to solve the problem. Solutions require collective action, and with collective action comes the possibility of the 'free rider.' . . .

It is difficult to judge this scenario, because we lack examples of this phenomenon on a large scale. 'Free-rider' problems may generate severe conflict, but it is doubtful that states would find military instruments useful for coercion and compliance. . . .

Conclusion

The degradation of the natural environment upon which human well-being depends is a challenge of far-reaching significance for human societies everywhere. But this challenge has little to do with the national-security-from-violence problem that continues to plague human political life. Not only is there little in common between the causes and solutions of these two problems, but the nationalist and militarist mindsets closely associated with 'national security' thinking directly conflict with the core of the environmentalist world view. Harnessing these sentiments for a 'war on pollution' is a dangerous and probably self-defeating enterprise. And fortunately, the prospects for resource and pollution wars are not as great as often conjured by environmentalists.

The pervasive recourse to national security paradigms to conceptualise the environmental problem represents a profound and disturbing failure of imagination and political awareness. If the nation-state enjoys a more prominent status in world politics than its competence and accomplishments warrant, then it makes little sense to emphasise the links between it and the emerging problem of global habitability.[11] Nationalist sentiment and the war system have a long-established logic and staying power that are likely to defy any rhetorically conjured 're-direction' toward benign ends. The movement to preserve the habitability of the planet for future generations must directly challenge the tribal power of nationalism and the chronic militarisation of public discourse. Environmental degradation is not a threat to national security. Rather, environmentalism is a threat to 'national security' mindsets and institutions. For environmentalists to dress their programmes in the blood-soaked garments of the war system betrays their core values and creates confusion about the real tasks at hand.

Notes

1. Lester Brown, *Redefining National Security* (Washington, DC: Worldwatch Paper, No. 14, October 1977); Jessica Tuchman Mathews, 'Redefining Security,' *Foreign Affairs* (Vol. 68, No. 2, 1989), pp. 162–77; Michael Renner, *National Security: The Economic and Environmental Dimensions* (Washington, DC: Worldwatch Paper, No. 89, May 1989); and Norman Myers, 'Environmental Security,' *Foreign Policy* (No. 74, 1989), pp. 23–41.

2. Richard Ullman, 'Redefining Security,' *International Security* (Vol. 8, No. 1, Summer 1983), pp. 129–53.

3. Hal Harvey, 'Natural Security,' *Nuclear Times* (March/April 1988), pp. 24–26.

4. Philip Shabecoff, 'Senator Urges Military Resources to Be Turned to Environmental Battle,' *The New York Times*, 29 June 1990, p. 1A.

5. Quentin Skinner, 'Language and Political Change,' and James Farr, 'Understanding Political Change Conceptually,' in Terence Ball et al., (eds.), *Political Innovation and Conceptual Change* (Cambridge: Cambridge University Press, 1989).

6. For a particularly lucid and well-rounded discussion of security, the state and violence, see Barry Buzan, *People, States, and Fear: The National Security Problem in International Relations* (Chapel Hill, NC: University of North Carolina Press, 1983), particularly pp. 1–93.

7. Ronnie D. Lipschutz, *When Nations Clash: Raw Materials, Ideology and Foreign Policy* (New York: Ballinger, 1989).

8. H. E. Goeller and Alvin Weinberg, 'The Age of Substitutability,' *Science* (Vol. 201, 20 February 1967). For some recent evidence supporting this hypothesis, see Eric D. Larson, Marc H. Ross and Robert H. Williams, 'Beyond the Era of Materials,' *Scientific American* (Vol. 254, 1986), pp. 34–41.

9. For a discussion of authoritarian and conflictual consequences of environmental constrained economies, see William Ophuls, *Ecology and the Politics of Scarcity* (San Francisco, CA: Freeman, 1976), p. 152. See also Susan M. Leeson, 'Philosophical Implications of the Ecological Crisis: The Authoritarian Challenge to Liberalism,' *Polity* (Vol. 11, No. 3, Spring 1979); Ted Gurr, 'On the Political Consequences of Scarcity and Economic Decline,' *International Studies Quarterly* (No. 29, 1985), pp. 51–75; and Robert Heilbroner, *An Inquiry Into the Human Prospect* (New York: W. W. Norton, 1974).

10. Bernard Brodie, 'The Impact of Technological Change on the International System,' in David Sullivan and Martin Sattler (eds.), *Change and the Future of the International System* (New York: Columbia University Press, 1972), p. 14.

11. For a particularly lucid argument that the nation-state system is over-developed relative to its actual problem-solving capacities, see George Modelski, *Principles of World Politics* (New York: The Free Press, 1972).

29

THE HUMAN DIMENSIONS OF ENVIRONMENTAL INSECURITY

Some Insights from South Asia

ADIL NAJAM

In the past half century the term "security" was primarily a matter of states and their military alliances, principally applied to the "security" of borders and institutions from outside threats. The bipolar nature of world dynamics that prevailed during the period intensified the emphasis on external threats. Such a definition, although considered minimalist by some, is accepted by many because military threats to security are easily identifiable and carry clear and often extreme consequences. In contrast, nonmilitary threats within nations, such as poverty, social vulnerability or ecological resiliency are generally not perceived as concrete and tangible. Yet, one could argue that the wrong end of a smoke stack can be as much of a security concern to humans as the barrel of a gun. A key conceptual difference between the two approaches is that the traditional definition of security presupposes that threats arising from outside the state are more dangerous to the state than threats that arise within it.

Recent debates on whether and how the concept of security might be expanded beyond issues of geo-polity, international power-balance, military strategy, and statecraft have been both intense and rich.[1] One strand of this debate on nontraditional security issues relates to the increase in attention

Adil Najam. "The Human Dimensions of Environmental Insecurity: Some Insights from South Asia." *Environmental Change and Security Project Report* No. 9 (2003):59–73. Reprinted with permission.

paid to the connection between environment and security. Scholarly discourse in this area has been prolific, though not always conclusive.[2]

This essay presents the key insights that emerge from a regional research project that explored environment and security links in the context of South Asia.[3] ... Our focus here is on what the South Asian experience can contribute to the larger literature on environment and security, or to be more precise, on sustainable development and human security. Of particular interest to us is the currently emerging interest in looking at the issue from the perspective of human security and embedding it within the concept of sustainable development.

Broadening the Base:
Focusing on Human Security

The literature on environment and security has evolved over the years from its early focus on trying to expand the definition of "security," to the incorporation of environmental and related concerns, to its more recent preoccupation with understanding how environmental change can be a cause or amplifier of violent conflict. An emerging trend within this evolution has been a move toward greater emphasis on the concept of *human* security.[4]

This broadening of the base is not in opposition to the earlier trends of redefining security or of mapping the environmental roots of violent conflict. In fact, it is an outgrowth of these trends. Indeed, many of the early attempts to broaden the definition of "security" used very similar language to those who debate on "human security" today. For example, consider the following definition from Norman Myers's *Ultimate Security*:

> Security applies most at the level of the individual citizen. It amounts to human well-being: not only protection from harm and injury but access to water, food, shelter, health, employment, and other basic requisites that are the due of every person on Earth. It is the collectivity of these citizen needs—overall safety and quality of life—that should figure prominently in the nation's view of security.[5]

By a similar token, those who have focused on explicating the environmental causes of violent conflict have also brought the debate closer to the notion of human security, most noticeably by focusing on intrastate, and often local, insecurities. In sum, they have each pushed the debate toward "the concept of 'human security' [which] offers a third perspective that allows us to move beyond conventional security thinking, appreciates both the local and global dimensions of the many insecurities experienced by real individuals and groups, and identifies useful ways of linking security and development policies."[6]

While the concept of human security has earlier roots, its recent prominence comes from the 1994 *Human Development Report* of the United Nations

Development Programme (UNDP).[7] Suhrke points out that "while offering an imprecise and controversial definition, the starting point for the UNDP was poverty rather than war—but 'security' suggested an escape from both."[8] The currency of the concept was further advanced by the importance given to it in the report of the Commission on Global Governance.[9] Both reports tried to shift the direction of the security discussion by focusing on issues of "human life and human dignity" rather than on weapons and territory.

Lorraine Elliott points out two dimensions of the human security paradigm that are of particular relevance:

> The first is that the concept of "human security" provides an antidote to the more conventional focus on states, borders and territorial integrity. The answer to the question, "security for whom" is not the state but the individual and communities, which suggests that even when a state is secure from external threats or internal instabilities, security for its people is not guaranteed. Protecting individuals and communities from the consequences of environmental decline (in this case) is therefore a security issue. The second dimension is that human insecurity (which includes equity, gender, human rights and identity concerns) is a central factor in social tensions and political instabilities and conflicts that can . . . become a feature of state insecurity. . . . If peoples and communities are insecure (economically, socially, politically, environmentally), state security can be fragile or uncertain. Environmental scarcity becomes a distributive equity problem rather than one simply of market failure, externalities or zero-sum calculations about access to resources and environmental services.[10]

. . . Indeed, as Elliott recognizes, the human security paradigm "turns the conventional security aphorism—secure states means secure people—on its head."[11] Dabelko, Lonergan, and Matthew add that the concept also "helps understand the complex interactions that determine the relative distribution of security and insecurity."[12] They point out that "under certain conditions, such as war, the distribution and composition of force may be the most important determinant of security and insecurity." However, "in many other situations, security and insecurity will be most closely related to poverty or resource scarcity or social discrimination." Importantly, this leads to the conclusion that "in these cases, traditional security institutions may have only a minor contribution to make, or none at all."

While Dabelko, Lonergan, and Matthew also point out the similarity between the goals of enhancing human security and sustainable development, they are likely to agree with Astri Suhrke that a key relationship exists between the concepts of "human security" and "human development." According to the UNDP *Human Development Report*, "human development is a broader concept, defined as a process of widening the range of people's choices. Human security means that people can exercise these choices safely and freely." Suhrke also argues that this relationship is more important to understanding the concept of human security:

There are two possible starting points for exploring the substantive core of "human security." One is in relation to the security of states, the other in relation to human development. . . . The major contribution of the 1994 UNDP report was its attempt to define human security and human development, and sort out their relationship. The result, however, was confusingly circular. "Human security" was presented both as an end-state of affairs—"safety from such chronic threats as hunger, disease and repression"—and a process in the sense of "protection from sudden and hurtful disruptions in the patterns of daily life." . . . Human security was seen as essential for human development; without minimal stability and security in daily life, there could be no development—human or otherwise. But the obverse was true as well. Long-term development that improves social and economic life would produce human security, the UNDP report concluded. In this reasoning, there is no difference between development and human security, or between process and end-state.[13]

In trying to place this emerging interest in human security within the context of the evolution of the environment and security debate, one might propose a simple heuristic. For the purpose of exposition, Figure 1 conceives of an environment and security "space" that is defined on one axis by the unit of analysis (ranging from state-centered to society-centered analysis) and on the other by sources of insecurity (ranging from violent conflict to social disruptions).

As previously discussed, the early literature on the subject was concerned predominantly with state-centered discussions. While it did flirt with expanding the discussion of insecurity beyond traditional confines to also include social disruptions, it was mostly focused on interstate conflict (since the audience of this literature was mostly restricted to the "traditional security community"). Hence, the emphasis of the environment and security analysis very often turned to discussions of whether or not *interstate war* was a likely outcome. The "second wave" of the literature honed in on the emphasis on violent conflict but made the focus of analysis more society-centered. The emphasis of the discussion, therefore, moved to whether and to what extent environmental change was a trigger for *civil strife*. The new focus on *human insecurity* is also society-centered, but is more concerned with social disruptions than with violent conflict as the principal source of insecurity. One of the key benefits of using such a heuristic is that it begins to point us towards other formalizations of the problematique that are not yet dominant in the available literature. In this case, Figure 1 points out the insecurity that emerges from social disruptions at the level of the state rather than the level of society. Based on the conclusions reached by researchers in South Asia,[14] one can posit that such insecurity is most likely to manifest itself as *institutional failure* and can be best understood through a focus on the mechanisms of societal governance.

There is no implication in this figure that any one kind of insecurity is any more or any less important than any other. However, there is the clear message that the environment-security problematique is composed of multiple

FIGURE 29.1   Organizing the Environment and Security

Sources of Insecurity

		Violent Conflict	Social Disruptions
Unit of Analysis	State-centered	Focus on Interstate War	Focus on Institutional Failure
	Society-centered	Focus on Civil Strife	Focus on Human Insecurity

forms of insecurity. Analysis centered on the state and on violent conflict is likely to define the environment-security discussion in terms of interstate war; those using a more society-centered lens but focusing on violent conflict are more likely to use examples of civil strife as their evidence; human insecurity is the likely focus of those whose analysis operates at the level of social disruptions and society-centered processes; and those who focus on social disruptions and state-centered analysis are likely to view institutional failure as the key evidence of environmental insecurity. These, of course, are very broad categories with hazy (although recognizable) boundaries between them. The purpose here is not to pigeonhole scholarship but to suggest that the space within which environmental insecurity manifests itself is rather wide and broad and needs to be recognized in its entirety.

Although this heuristic is tentative and in need of further empirical validation, it provides us with one way to organize and understand the discussion. Interestingly, but not surprisingly, the conclusions emerging from country-focused as well as issue-focused studies from South Asia lie very much in the right-hand half of Figure 1 and predominantly in the bottom-right quarter.[15] The emphasis is very much on environment-related insecurities as manifest in social disruption rather than in outright conflict. In order to begin understanding how, and why, issues of institutional failure and human insecurity are more immediate to the concerns of South Asians, let us quickly review what this region looks like.

South Asia in Context: Poverty as the Key Link Between Environment and Insecurity

. . . Table 1 presents a brief profile of the five largest countries of the region. It is clear from the table that on all the variables presented, South Asian countries are not only significantly behind the world as a whole but also well behind developing countries as a group (measured here as the average of all low- and medium-income countries). These are the roots of human insecurity in the region, which have significant implications for the environment. Table 1 also highlights the fact that although there are important differences

Table 29.1   South Asia's Many Roots of Insecurity

	Bangladesh	India	Nepal	Pakistan	Sri Lanka	Developing Countries	World
Area 1,000 sq. km. (1999)	144	3,288	147	796	66	101,487	133,572
Population millions (1999)	128	998	23	135	19	5,084	5,975
Population growthrate annual (1990–1999)	1.6	1.8	2.4	2.5	1.2	1.9	1.7
GNP per capita US dollars (1999)	370	450	220	470	820	1,240	4,890
GNP per capita PPP dollars (1999)	1,475	2,144	1,219	1,757	3,056	3,410	6,490
Under-5 mortality per 1,000 (1998)	96	83	107	120	18	79	75
Life expectancy M/F (1998)	58/59	62/64	58/58	61/63	71/76	63/67	65/69
Adult illiteracy % population 15 and above M/F (1998)	49/71	33/57	43/78	42/71	6/12	18/33	18/32
Urban sanitation % with access (1990–1996)	77	46	34	53	33	–	–
Children 10–14 in labor force % of age group (1999)	29	13	43	16	2	13	12
Gini index (1995–1997)	33.6	37.8	36.7	31.2	34.4	–	–
Public spending on education % of GNP (1997)	2.2	3.2	3.2	2.7	3.4	4.1	4.8
Public spending on health % of GDP (1990–1998)	1.6	0.6	1.3	0.9	1.4	1.9	2.5
External debt % of GNP (1998)	22	20	31	41	41	–	–

SOURCE: World Bank, *World Development Report 2000/2001: Attacking Poverty* (New York: Oxford University Press and World Bank, 2000)

within the region (for example, in terms of education), there is a certain uniformity in the development profiles of the region.

... The research from South Asia validates and advances new nuances to two key findings from the larger literature. First, it substantiates one of the conclusions that Geoffrey Dabelko, Steve Lonergan, and Richard Matthew reached in their major literature review of the subject: "research on environment and security often strengthens the conclusion that poverty is a key factor in causing tension, unrest and, eventually, conflict."[16] This is borne out quite strikingly. All across South Asia, poverty emerges as the key variable both in terms of defining environmental degradation and outlining human insecurity. Importantly, poverty is both the causal motivator of environmental stress as well as the most important manifestation of human insecurity. The key conceptual insight here is subtle, but critical: Not only is poverty one of the key elements that exacerbates the causal chain that can lead from environmental degradation to violence and insecurity, but research from South Asia also suggests that it can play a more central role in this chain of causality than much of the literature seems to acknowledge. The point that emerges here is that it is not scarcity but poverty that is driving environmental insecurity.

Contrary to the thrust of the mainstream literature, which struggles, often unconvincingly, to express the environmental problematique in the language of state-centric "national" security, the discussions from South Asia are presented in the language of society-centric "human" security.[17] More than that, poverty—rather than resource scarcity—emerges as the defining link between environment and security. . . . The local case studies from these countries highlight how it is poverty, as manifested in livelihood insecurity, that leads to pressures on resources such as fisheries (Bangladesh), forests (Pakistan), biodiversity (Sri Lanka), and land (India), rather than resource scarcity in and of itself that is the prime motor of insecurity. . . . [T]he key point that comes through (particularly from the experience of forests in Northern Pakistan) is that unless rooted in the larger goal of poverty alleviation, restrictive resource conservation policies (such as forest enclosures) can sometimes aggravate insecurity rather than relieve it. . . .

As already discussed, the findings of our study do emphasize that the causality often begins not as much with simple resource scarcity as with livelihood insecurity that translates into pressures on those resources. In other cases, however, the pressure can come not from poverty but from institutional failure in the form of resource capture. This seems to be the lesson from the water sector as well as parts of the forestry sector in Pakistan. The capture of precious forest resources by the so-called "forest mafia" in Pakistan has resulted not only in resource scarcity but also exclusion of communities that were traditionally dependent on this resource. The latter, in turn, has placed even greater pressures on the resource. The key, however, is the institutional and governance structure that originally enabled the resource capture and eventually failed to check the violence by not providing civil means of dispute resolution.

The critical role of weak institutions of governance as the precursor, and sometimes trigger, of conflict over environmental resources is borne out strikingly in the case of various irrigation projects in Nepal. While the importance of resource scarcity is not to be denied, it was the weakness of state institutions and their inability to accommodate community institutions that has led to a near permanent conflict between these institutions, which, in turn, spills into occasional conflicts between stakeholders. . . .

Linking the two insights described above, it can be argued that chronic and structural impoverishment forges the connection between environmental degradation and violent conflict. Such a conception leads to a focus on social disruptions at the level of the society (rather than the state).. . .

Importantly, shifting the focus of the discussion from resource scarcity to the motors that cause such scarcity—including poverty and the institutions of governance—has a very valuable benefit in that it provides us with defined areas of policy intervention. Both poverty and governance are areas of high policy salience (unlike resource conservation) in most developing countries and certainly in all South Asian countries. To highlight that environmental security flows best out of policies that target these areas is to build synergistically on existing priorities instead of positing resource conservation as a competitor to other policy demands. . . .

Five Key Lessons

Lesson 1: For South Asia in particular, and developing countries in general, environment and security are best conceptualized within the context of sustainable development.

. . . Placing the environment and human security problematique within the sustainable development complex has at least two important implications. First, such a conceptualization allows for articulating issues related to environment and security at the level of, and in the language of, policy and practice. Second, it contributes toward a better understanding of what sustainable development means in practice. Such a conceptual focus broadens the scope of the inquiry from whether and how environmental degradation might lead to societal and state insecurities to also include how human insecurities influence, or are influenced by, accelerated environmental degradation. Imperfect as it might be, sustainable development policy becomes a potential means of addressing the twin challenges of environmental degradation and human insecurity; it works best, however, when both challenges are taken seriously, and neither is deemed subservient to the other. . . .

Lesson 2: The challenge of environment and security in South Asia is principally a challenge at the domestic, even local, level; but it is a challenge common to the region.

One of the conclusions reached by Dabelko, Lonergan, and Matthew in their review of the literature on the subject is that "the most severe challenges for individual well-being in many parts of the world may not be external (to the country of residence), but internal, although internal problems are likely to be affected in some way by external forces."[18] This lesson is echoed and amplified by the experience in South Asia. Indeed, there is a distinct tendency to bring the problem "down" to the ground level rather than raise it "up" to national, let alone regional, levels. This is not to suggest that the regional dimensions are unimportant; however, it is to underscore the view that the local challenges are more numerous as well as more profound.

This, of course, is a surprise given the intensity of regional tensions in South Asia. Paradoxically, it is that very intensity that makes it unlikely that environmental issues will become significant international security concerns in the region. The argument is that the countries in the region have so many other and more pressing disputes to keep them busy that environmental issues slip down the list of potential flare-up points. At the same time, one must recognize the possibility that such issues can easily become embroiled in existing and unrelated disputes within the region. . . .

Lesson 3: The challenge of environment and security in South Asia is, at its core, not just a problem of resource endowments or geography but, quite distinctly, a problem of institutions and governance, if only because it is the latter rather than the former that we have the ability to change.

. . . In many cases, a lack of appropriate institutions and governance can help explain not only the levels of human insecurity but also the scarcity and degradation of environmental resources. Institutional and governance weaknesses can lead to significant human insecurity even in the absence of severe environmental scarcity or degradation. The later condition only worsens the former.

The implication of this point is that the solutions to issues of environment and security will not come from techno-fixes and mega-projects that might somehow "overrule" the forces of geography and nature; the solutions are more likely to come from institutional and governance reform. . . . The insight here is that resource scarcity does not simply turn into conflict; it turns into conflict when there is an institutional failure because democratic, transparent, culturally appropriate, localized, and participatory means of managing resources and dealing with disputes are not available or are systematically sidelined. . . .

Lesson 4: The prospects of interstate violence in South Asia over environmental issues are slim; however, given the region's history of distrust and dispute, environmental differences can add to existing tensions and apprehensions and perpetuate the general sense of insecurity that pervades interstate relations in the region.

. . . Indeed, there is unanimity amongst our authors on the belief that the prospects of outright war in South Asia over these issues are not high. . . .

Environmental deterioration, then, can be a source of *additional stress* that is likely to deepen existing lines of conflict (rather than create new ones). Although the main challenge is domestic, the regional context cannot be ignored. Regional environmental disputes, even when they may be relatively minor in and of themselves, can flare into larger conflicts because they are played out in a context of general distrust.

Lesson 5: There is the potential—albeit small—for a new generation of security relations in the region emerging around the nexus of environment and security that is based on the principles of mutual trust, harmony, and cooperation rather than on legacies of distrust and dispute.

... To end on a positive note, one might suggest that the environment has the potential to become an "entry point" for wider regional cooperation. On the one hand, the very nature of the environmental problematique points towards the urgency of adopting a cooperative mind-set. On the other hand, the language of human security at least allows for the potential of focusing on regional security without necessarily regurgitating stylized debates about traditional hurdles to cooperation. . . .

Notes

1. B. Buzan, *People, States, and Fear: An Agenda for International Security Studies in the Post–Cold War Era,* 2nd ed. (Boulder: Lynne Reinner, 1991); S. Dalby, "Security, Modernity, Ecology: The Dilemmas of Post–Cold War Security Discourse," *Alternatives* 17 (1992):95–134; J. Galtung, *Environment, Development, and Military Activity: Toward Alternative Security Doctrines* (New York: Columbia University Press, 1982); J. T. Mathews, "Redefining Security," *Foreign Affairs* 68, no. 2 (1989):162–177; R. H. Ullman, "Redefining Security," *International Security* 8, no. 1 (1983):129–153; S. M. Walt, "The Renaissance of Security Studies," *International Studies Quarterly* 35, no. 2 (1991):211–239.

2. G. Dabelko, S. Lonergan, and R. Matthew, *State-of-the-Art Review on Environment, Security, and Development Co-operation,* prepared for the Working Party on Development Cooperation and Environment, OECD Development Assistance Committee, Paris, 2000; P. F. Diehl and N. P. Gleditsch, eds., *Environmental Conflict* (Boulder: Westview Press, 2000); D. H. Deudney and R. A. Matthew, eds., *Contested Grounds: Security and Conflict in the New Environmental Politics* (Albany: State University of New York Press, 1999); P. Gleick, "Environment and Security: The Clear Connections," *Bulletin of the Atomic Scientists* (April 1991):17–21; T. F. Homer-Dixon, "On the Threshold: Environmental Changes as Causes of Acute Conflict," *International Security* 16, no. 2 (1991):76–116; M. Levy, "Is Environment a National Security Issue?" *International Security* 20, no. 2 (1995):35–62; S. Libiszewski, *What Is an Environmental Conflict?* Environment and Conflict Project (ENCOP) Occasional Paper No. 6. (Zurich: Center for Security Studies and Conflict Research, 1992); N. Myers, *Ultimate Security: The Environmental Basis of Political Stability* (New York: W. W. Norton, 1993); A. H. Westing, *Global Norms, War, and the Environment* (Oxford: Oxford University Press, 1988).

3. A. Najam, ed., *Environment, Development, and Human Security: Perspectives from South Asia* (Lanham, MD: University Press of America, 2003). This volume contains detailed analysis and discussion of the study, which was conducted with Ford Foundation funding for the Regional Centre for Security Studies (RCSS), Colombo, Sri Lanka. The ten chapters of the book— all written by authors from South Asia (three authors each from India, Pakistan, and Bangladesh, and two each from Nepal and Sri Lanka)—explore environment and security links in specific countries of the region (Bangladesh, India, Nepal, Pakistan, and Sri Lanka) as well as looking at cross-country trends on key policy areas (land and agriculture, energy, and water).

4. Dabelko, Lonergan, and Matthew, *State-of-the-Art Review*. See also L. Elliott, "Regional Environmental Security: Pursuing a Non-Traditional Approach," in *Non-Traditional Security Issues in Southeast Asia,* ed. A.T.H. Tan and J.D.K. Boutin (Singapore: Select Publishing, 2001).

5. Myers, *Ultimate Security,* 31.

6. Dabelko, Lonergan, and Matthew, *State-of-the-Art Review,* 48.

7. United Nations Development Programme, *Human Development Report, 1994* (Oxford: Oxford University Press, 1994).

8. A. Suhrke, "Human Security and the Interest of States," *Security Dialogue* 30, no. 3 (1999):269.

9. Commission on Global Governance, *Our Common Neighborhood: Report of the Commission on Global Governance* (Oxford: Oxford University Press, 1995).

10. Elliott, "Regional Environmental Security," 449.

11. Ibid., 449.

12. Dabelko, Lonergan, and Matthew, *State-of-the-Art Review,* 48–49.

13. Suhrke, "Human Security," 270–271.

14. Najam, ed., *Environment, Development and Human Security.*

15. Ibid.

16. Dabelko, Lonergan, and Matthew, *State-of-the-Art Review,* 56.

17. D. H. Deudney, "The Case Against Linking Environmental Degradation and National Security," *Millennium* 19, no. 3 (1990):461–476; N. P. Gleditsch, "Armed Conflict and the Environment," in *Environmental Conflict,* ed. P. F. Diehl and N. P. Gleditsch (Boulder: Westview Press, 2001); Homer-Dixon, "On the Threshold"; Mathews, "Redefining Security"; and Myers, *Ultimate Security.*

18. Dabelko, Lonergan, and Matthew, *State-of-the-Art Review,* 56.

30

FOR WHOSE BENEFIT?
REDEFINING SECURITY

Somaya Saad

The Quest for a Redefinition of Security

Today, the North is preoccupied by environmental threats. Indeed, since the Stockholm Conference of 1972, a very different approach to the environment has become evident.

Twenty years ago, the emphasis was on ending the pollution that the industrialized North had been inflicting on the nations of the South. The goals were clean air and water and arable land—the requisites of a decent life; and the modality was international cooperation.

Today, however, the North has seized hold of environmental issues by using them to cloak its own security concerns. The new ideology—or, to some, religion—of the environment allows its proponents to ignore nationalities and national boundaries.

Earth Rights or National Rights?

For some, a parallel meeting of non-government organizations at the . . . [1992] United Nations Conference on Environment and Development could be the forum for redefining security and sovereignty. The aim is to exert pressure on the participating national governments.

Excerpted from an article originally published in *Eco-Decisions*, September 1991, pp. 59–60.

The call for such a meeting is highly revealing. For those making it, the cause of the environment is to be used as a tool that can efface national boundaries and uproot national affiliations. They appeal instead to wider concepts: the sovereignty of the earth, the Global Commons, humanity or universal rights.

That approach could undermine national solidarity, stir up local conflicts, put individuals at odds with their governments, and cause governments to be judged without due consideration for the particular conditions that they face.

Such an approach might distort the issue. After all, it is the comparatively weaker states—who also happen to be developing nations—that have the bulk of the world's remaining natural resources. And it is these same countries that have relatively clean environments. Now these nations are being told to limit their military expenditures for the sake of development.

The Tilt toward the "Haves"

Even in the boundary-free global utopia that some imagine lies ahead, a form of administration would still be required. Very likely, that "administration" would cover not territory but rather particular aspects of human activity.

Of these, most important is the domain of development. Within this area falls the entire range of environmental concerns: population, migration, poverty, the use of resources, patterns of production and consumption, and finally pollution. All these are shaped by the asymmetry in the global distribution of power.

That imbalance has political and military aspects. As a result, certain nations, cultures and lifestyles exert dominance over others. If those not favoured by the current arrangement try to redress the balance, their efforts are met with resistance which can escalate into conflict.

In consequence, the present division of power is likely to be maintained. The balance—whether military, economic or technological—is tilted in favour of the nations of the North, who now are seeking international cooperation in their bid to put their own house in order. Outside the North, there are strict limits on the amount of permitted national or regional power.

Redefining the Environment

Some nations are redefining the environment as a territory-free, non-geographical issue in which supranational institutions may intervene. They seek to mediate when necessary between other nations, and to force them to follow particular policies. Apparently their aim is to impose the economic and political norms and lifestyles of the North on the rest of the world, instead of allowing other nations to develop their own norms. The outcome will be a still greater tilt in favour of those that already hold economic and political power.

This trend will produce a new division of labour between nations. The powerful will gain more power, while the weak will lose what little power they have.

What Kind of Future?

Such a development naturally arouses questions. For instance, what does the brave talk of global security mean? Security, after all, implies the protection of a particular territory by one group against another. We need to know who will define the new concept of security. And herein lies the danger.

There are indications that now that the Cold War is ended, the larger countries consider the environment as a major field of security concern. Defined in those terms, the environment will present an ugly face particularly to the developing world.

In the new order taking shape, who or what will be sacrificed? There are several possible scenarios.

One is that weak nations will be subjugated to powerful ones. Some analysts point to the inadequacy of a world order based on state sovereignty. According to these thinkers, the passing of the Cold War may mark the passing of the nation states created by the earlier great wars of this century, replacing them with an order having a new basis. The tool used will be the economic leverage which the North exerts over the rest of the world.

Another possibility is an increase in tensions within and between nations. Environmental concerns could provoke disagreements that would exacerbate internal problems. Further, if sovereignty, regional and international legal standards and instruments are all swept away, the new so-called environmental rights could serve as a pretext for more conflicts.

Still another outcome might be the imposition of the norms, cultures and lifestyles of powerful nations on the others. Evidence for such a development is provided by the move to attach conditions to international assistance, and the banding together of the powerful nations in such groupings as the Enterprise of the Americas (starting with the United States, Canada and Mexico) and Europe 1992. Nations that refuse to accept this domination might be subjected to restrictions that could endanger their growth and even their survival.

It would be highly ironic if the move to protect the environment ended up thus destroying some cultures and peoples. Are the interests of humanity to be sacrificed to the interests of the earth?

31

THE VIOLENCE
OF DEVELOPMENT

BALAKRISHNAN RAJAGOPAL

"Ethnic cleansing"—the forcible dislocation of a large number of people belonging to particular ethnic groups—is an outlawed practice. Individuals who
are accused of ethnic cleansing are subjected to indictment by international
criminal tribunals, and even domestic courts are increasingly used in the West
to prosecute those who commit mass violence abroad.

Yet most large forced dislocations of people do not occur in conditions of
armed conflict or genocide but in routine, everyday evictions to make way for
development projects. A recent report by the World Commission on Dams estimates that 40 million to 80 million people have been physically displaced by
dams worldwide, a disproportionate number of them being indigenous peoples. Indeed, this "development cleansing" may well constitute ethnic cleansing in disguise, as the people dislocated so often turn out to be from minority
ethnic and racial communities.

In the Philippines, almost all the large dam schemes are on the land of the
country's 6 million to 7 million indigenous people. In India, 40 percent to 50
percent of those displaced by development projects—a total estimated at
more than 33 million since 1947—are tribal people, who account for just 8
percent of the country's 1 billion population.

Still, international human rights monitors remain oblivious to the violence of
development. A biased focus on international criminal justice—the pursuit of a
Milosevic, for example—has blinded the world's conscience to mass crimes that
are often as serious as those that occurred in Rwanda and the former Yugoslavia.

The millions of people forcibly dislocated from their lands are usually from
among the poorest and most vulnerable sections of populations. Upon dislo-

Originally published in *The Washington Post*, August 8, 2001. Reprinted with permission of the author.

cation, these communities are pushed into further poverty and violence. These conditions are themselves grave human rights violations, but they also lead to further violations—for example, by exacerbating conflicts between large communities that lose land and are resettled and the communities into which they move.

Forcible dislocation destroys the livelihoods of entire communities as large dams and inappropriate agricultural projects alter the land-use patterns that traditionally support farming, grazing and fishing. And the number of people forcibly dislocated is probably far larger than reported, as the displaced are systematically undercounted—for example, by as much as 47 percent in the case of the projects funded by the World Bank. In China's Western Poverty Reduction Project in Qinghai, the World Bank Complaints Panel found that entire towns of thousands of Tibetan and Mongol minorities were not counted as affected.

The United Nations has declared mass eviction to be a violation of the human right to housing. And because of growing conflicts over water and natural resources, the World Commission on Dams was established in 1998 by the World Bank, the International Conservation Union and others. But despite these efforts, human rights violations continue in the name of development.

For instance, a judgment by the Indian Supreme Court in October 2000 will allow the construction of a mega-dam on the Narmada River to go forward. This is deeply disappointing given the Indian judiciary's history as the protector of the rights of the underprivileged. It is also tragic because the project will lead to the displacement of more than 200,000 people and the elimination of the rich ecological resources in the Narmada Valley, one of India's most fertile.

The Narmada Valley dam project is the second largest in the world, after the Three Gorges dam project in China, which is known for its excessive human and environmental costs. The World Bank, which originally was to have funded the Narmada project, withdrew funding in 1993 after being criticized for violating its own internal regulations on resettlement and rehabilitation and environmental clearance. Every funder since then—Japanese and Germans included—has withdrawn after running into criticism, and the project is now being funded by Indian state governments, redirecting scarce funds from much-needed health and education projects.

A broad coalition opposing the dam, consisting of the people of the Narmada Valley as well as domestic and foreign intellectuals, social activists, journalists, judges and lawyers, has repeatedly pointed out technological alternatives for producing power and providing water, but these have been dismissed by the Indian Supreme Court.

On the other side is the developmental nationalism displayed by Indian Home Minister L. K. Advani, who says opponents of such projects are working at the behest of "foreign nations"—a response commonly given by governments that commit gross human rights abuses.

It is clear that international indifference toward the violence of development projects needs to end.

PART SEVEN

ECOLOGICAL JUSTICE

Some of the main controversies surrounding the paradigms of sustainable development and ecological security involve questions of justice. Critics have raised concerns that these paradigms can blur questions of fairness, power, and distribution. Worse yet, environmental arguments might be used to justify measures that worsen social inequality, promote authoritarian measures, or otherwise concentrate power in the hands of elites. Thus, questions of justice are raised not only by the unequal effects of pollution and ecosystem destruction but also by the socially unequal effects of environmental policy responses.

Concerns about the relationship between environmental protection and social equity have been voiced since the Stockholm conference first placed the environment on the international agenda.[1] As the pace of environmental degradation has accelerated and policy responses to environmental problems have grown more complex and ambitious, the question of how various forms of environmental change affect different social groups has become increasingly central to environmental debates.

Today the link between ecology and justice is being articulated by a diverse array of voices: people of color in cities throughout the United States challenging the "environmental racism" of concentrating toxic facilities in minority communities; rural women in India protesting the impact of damming or deforestation on their lives and communities; green activists in Europe drawing links between militarism, patriarchy, and environmental destruction; Third World activists arguing that the North imposes both environmental problems and inappropriate solutions to those problems on the South; indigenous peoples of both the North and South organizing to reclaim their lands and their traditions as an alternative to the ecological onslaught of modernity.[2] In some cases, long-standing environmental and human rights groups have discovered one another and begun to work together, as in the "Defending Environmental Defenders" campaign launched jointly by Amnesty International and the Sierra Club.[3]

Given this diversity, is it possible to identify a single paradigm of ecological justice based on a common set of core arguments? While there are many different visions of an ecologically just world, a number of common themes lie at the heart of the ecological justice paradigm: first, the close linkage between violence against nature and violence against human beings; second, the linkage between the power to control nature and the power to control people; third, the observation that not all people or groups are affected equally by environmental problems or by the responses to those problems; fourth, the pursuit of solutions that are both ecologically sound *and* socially just, because neither can endure in the absence of the other; and fifth, the need for a fundamental transformation of politics, economics, and society.

The eco-justice paradigm can be used to analyze questions of ecology and justice at many different social levels. The question of justice among nations, with a particular focus on North-South inequality, was a central dispute at the Stockholm conference in 1972 (see the selection by Castro in Part One). Twenty years later at the Rio Earth Summit the question had not been resolved. According to Malaysian Prime Minister Mahathir Mohamad, addressing the Rio conference:

> We know that the 25 per cent of the world population who are rich consume 85 per cent of its wealth and produce 90 per cent of its waste. Mathematically speaking, if the rich reduce their wasteful consumption by 25 per cent, worldwide pollution will be reduced by 22.5 per cent. But if the poor 75 per cent reduce consumption totally and disappear from this earth altogether, the reduction in pollution will only be by 10 per cent.
>
> It is what the rich do that counts, not what the poor do, however much they do it. . . . The rich will not accept a progressive and meaningful cutback in their emissions of carbon dioxide and other greenhouse gases because it will be a cost to them and retard their progress. Yet they expect the poor people of the developing countries to stifle even their minute growth as if it will cost them nothing. . . . Malaysia will do what can reasonably be expected of it for the environment.[4]

Despite the optimism at Rio that "sustainable development" merged the conflicting concerns of North and South with regard to environment and development, distributional issues remain central to the North-South environmental debate. Mahathir Mohamad and others have stressed that the question of justice applies not only to who should pay the costs of environmental protection in poor societies but also to who holds decisionmaking power and who bears historical responsibility for the planet's predicament.

One of the most important themes of the eco-justice paradigm, however, is the idea that global environmental justice is not simply a question of equity among nation-states. Power and risk are distributed unequally not only among nations but also within them, in social divisions based on race, class, gender, ethnicity, and region. Inequality of voice is an issue not only in interstate negotiations but also within societies, in the workings of intergovernmental organizations, and even in dealings among environmentalists and other nonstate actors.

The experiences of indigenous peoples around the world illustrate these linkages among inequality, power, voice, and the environment at levels ranging from local to global. Here we present two letters published in 1989—during the height of the international furor over the destruction of tropical rainforests—by the Coordinating Body for the Indigenous Peoples' Organizations of the Amazon Basin (COICA). COICA argues that the future of the Amazon basin and the fate of its indigenous occupants are inherently linked. The rampant quest for modernization, colonization, territorial occupation, and economic development of the Amazon basin has damaged natural ecosystems and destroyed indigenous communities. The destruction has been driven by governments of the Amazon basin countries, which have largely excluded indigenous communities from decisionmaking about the region. Much of the destructive activity has been funded by external sources, including multinational corporations and multilateral development agencies such as the World Bank. Decisions about the fate of the Amazon forest and its people, whether made at the national or the international level, have excluded those who are most directly affected by such decisions.

COICA addressed the first letter to the multilateral development banks that fund so many projects and policies threatening indigenous peoples (see the material on the World Bank in Part Four). The second letter is addressed to the international environmental movement, which is also taken to task for its lack of attention to indigenous concerns. While acknowledging the efforts of environmentalists and the potential for common cause between the environmental and indigenous peoples' movements, the letter points out that governments, international organizations, and Northern environmental groups have struck bargains that leave out the people most directly and immediately affected. The members of COICA defend an alternative vision: Given the long history of sustainable interaction between indigenous peoples and the region's ecology, they argue, the best way to ensure an ecologically sound future is to restore and protect the land rights and lifestyles of indigenous peoples.

The struggles of indigenous peoples bear much in common with the movement against "environmental racism" that grew and spread rapidly in the United States during the 1990s.[5] This movement has both urban and rural components: the struggle of urban communities of color against the practice of locating toxic facilities in the inner city, and the struggle of rural communities to combat the health and safety risks of environmentally unsound agricultural practices (in particular the heavy use of toxic agricultural chemicals)—risks borne disproportionately by low-paid agricultural workers. In both the North American and the South American case the goal is not merely to change environmental outcomes but also to return greater decision-making power to the community. And in both cases the notion that current practices are inherently unjust has been an important weapon in the struggle.

Advocates of ecological justice have played a crucial role in pointing out that environmental problems often cause greater harm to the poor and powerless than to other groups. Another important theme is that the "solutions" to environmental problems also can be unjust, both locally and globally—and that such outcomes may not be solutions at all. This idea is evident in COICA's rejection of environment-development dialogues that exclude indigenous peoples. The next essay, by Nancy Peluso, raises the same concerns in an even more provocative fashion. Peluso argues that international environmental organizations, detached from the reality of local resource struggles, have sometimes participated in environmental preservation efforts that demonize local people and bolster oppressive, authoritarian regimes. Using wildlife conservation efforts in Kenya as an example, Peluso argues that the result—"coercing conservation"—pits the environment against social justice considerations, precluding an outcome that is both socially and ecologically sustainable.

These themes of unequal burdens, voice, powerlessness, and the potential for coercive "solutions" are central to contentious global debates over population and reproductive health and their links to environmental conditions. Gita Sen shows some of the complex ways in which the construction of gender roles in society empowers men and disempowers women. In this essay, Sen's particular focus is on the population debate. Failure to grasp the link between gender and power—a link that operates at the interpersonal level of the household as well as at the national or international level—produces a flawed understanding of the forces driving population growth. The common result is an unjust and ineffective response to the urgent problem of rapid population growth.

Sen's focus on the links among gender, ecology, and power are the concern of a body of thought known as *ecofeminism*.[6] Karen Warren summarizes the central tenets of ecofeminist perspectives:

> Ecological feminism is the position that there are important connections—historical, symbolic, theoretical—between the domination of women and the domination of nonhuman nature. . . . Any feminist theory with any environmental ethic which fails to take seriously the interconnected dominations of women and nature is simply inadequate.[7]

Some ecofeminists see an inherent difference in how men and women relate to and interact with nature, and explain environmentally destructive societies as a consequence of male dominance. Other ecofeminists have pointed out that gender is in many important ways a socially constructed set of roles and rules and not a biological fact. These "social" ecofeminists tend to see patriarchy and environmental destruction as stemming from a common source: the hierarchical concentration of power in society.[8]

Recognition of the connections among women, power, and the environment is at the heart of encouraging trends in attempts to address sustainability needs in both environment and population. In its annual *State of World Population 2001,* the United Nations Population Fund (UNFPA) acknowledged the damage done by polemical characterizations of population growth's negative effects on the environment. UNFPA counters these gross simplifications with a way forward captured in the "Cairo consensus," the internationally sanctioned approach to reproductive health negotiated at the 1994 International Conference on Population and Development held in Cairo, Egypt. Women's education, health, and economic empowerment are worthy development ends but are also recognized as highly effective means to alleviate poverty and foster sustainability.

Despite the optimism created by the Cairo consensus, challenges remain for widespread implementation of a human rights-based approach to reproductive health and linked environmental efforts. The unequal power relationships on the ground are often resistant to change. The donors' funding promises and specific development targets remain unfulfilled. And even the human rights–based approach of the Cairo consensus has been increasingly called into question at subsequent sustainability conferences, such as the 2002 World Summit on Sustainable Development in Johannesburg.

Together, the chapters in this part reject the Stockholm-era assertion that effective environmental protection requires increasingly authoritarian governance. In contrast, they argue that genuine sustainability and meaningful environmental security will require responses to environmental problems that are both ecologically effective and socially just.

Thinking Critically

1. After reading the essays in this section, are you persuaded that the environment is a social justice issue? Must there be social justice in order for there to be environmental protection? Are there difficult trade-offs to be made between these two values?

2. Do you accept the suggestion that some types of global environmental protection impose an unfair burden on the global South? Does this mean that the resistance of many governments of the South to particular forms of international environmental protection has the effect of promoting social

justice? What might COICA have to say to a Third World head of state such as Mahathir Mohamed? How might he respond?

3. Contrast the picture of international environmental NGOs drawn by Peluso with the essay by Wapner in Part Two. How can we account for the dramatically different interpretations of these two observers?

4. Can you identify other environmental issues that confront the sort of broad and deep differences of perspective that Sen describes on the population issue? How can such differences be overcome? Must they be overcome in order to promote global environmental protection? In order to promote global social justice?

5. The UNFPA recommendations for balancing population and development concerns with environmental concerns suggest that win-win solutions are possible. What are the impediments to these cross-sectoral or integrated efforts? Can they be overcome?

Notes

1. For a discussion of some of these issues prior to the Stockholm conference, see United Nations, *Development and Environment: Report and Working Papers of a Panel of Experts Convened by the Secretary General of the U.N. Conference on the Human Environment,* Founex, Switzerland, June 4–12, 1971.

2. For a discussion of the links between ecology and social justice, see Nicholas Low and Brendan Gleeson, *Justice, Society, and Nature* (New York: Routledge, 1998).

3. See Sierra Club and Amnesty International, *Environmentalists Under Fire: Ten Urgent Cases of Human Rights Abuses,* 2nd ed., January 2000.

4. Mahathir Mohamed, "Statement to the U.N. Conference on Environment and Development, *Environmental Policy and Law* 22, no. 4 (1992):232.

5. On environmental racism, see Robert D. Bullard, *Dumping in Dixie: Race, Class, and Environmental Quality,* 2nd ed. (Boulder: Westview Press, 1994); Luke W. Cole and Sheila R. Foster, *From the Ground Up: Environmental Racism and the Rise of the Environmental Justice Movement* (New York: New York University Press, 2000).

6. Irene Diamond and Gloria Feman Orenstein, *Reweaving the World: The Emergence of Ecofeminism* (San Francisco: Sierra Club Books, 1990); Wendy Harcourt, ed., *Feminist Perspectives on Sustainable Development* (London: Zed Books, 1994); Carolyn Merchant, *Earthcare: Women and the Environment* (New York: Routledge, 1995). For a criticism of some variants of ecofeminism, see Janet Biehl, *Rethinking Ecofeminist Politics* (Boston: South End Press, 1991).

7. Karen Warren, "The Power and the Promise of Ecological Feminism," *Environmental Ethics* 12 (Summer 1990):125–146, 125.

8. See Biehl, *Rethinking Ecofeminist Politics.*

32

TWO AGENDAS ON AMAZON DEVELOPMENT

COORDINATING BODY FOR THE INDIGENOUS PEOPLES' ORGANIZATIONS OF THE AMAZON BASIN (COICA)

For Bilateral and Multilateral Funders

(This document is addressed to the World Bank, the Inter-American Development Bank, the US Agency International Development, and the European Economic Community.)

We, the Indigenous Peoples, have been an integral part of the Amazon Biosphere for millennia. We have used and cared for the resources of that biosphere with a great deal of respect, because it is our home, and because we know that our survival and that of our future generations depends on it. Our accumulated knowledge about the ecology of our home, our models for living with the peculiarities of the Amazon Biosphere, our reverence and respect for the tropical forest and its other inhabitants, both plant and animal, are the keys to guaranteeing the future of the Amazon Basin, not only for our peoples, but also for all of humanity.

Originally published in *Cultural Survival Quarterly* 13, 4 (1989):75–78. Reprinted with permission.

What COICA Wants

1. The most effective defense of the Amazonian Biosphere is the recognition and defense of the territories of the region's Indigenous Peoples and the promotion of their models for living within that Biosphere and for managing its resources in a sustainable way. The international funders of Amazonian development should educate themselves about the Indigenous Peoples' relationship with their environment, and formulate new concepts of Amazonian development together with new criteria for supporting Amazonian development projects which would be compatible with the Indigenous Peoples' principles of respect and care for the world around them, as well as with their concern for the survival and well-being of their future generations.

2. The international funders must recognize the rights of Indigenous Peoples as those are being defined within the Working Group on Indigenous Peoples, established by the UN Human Rights Commission. These rights should form the basis of the institution's policy towards the Indigenous Peoples and their territories who live in those areas where the funder is supporting development work. The funders should consult directly with the organizations of the Indigenous Peoples throughout the process of establishing this policy and should distribute that policy widely among governments and the organizations of Indigenous Peoples.

3. There can be no development projects in indigenous areas without the informed consent of the Indigenous Peoples affected. The funders must make every effort, through field research conducted by personnel of the funding institution, to verify the existence of an indigenous population, or the possible negative impact on an indigenous population, in areas where they are considering the implementation of a project. If either is the case, the funder must openly recognize the existence of this population or the negative impact on them, and then should establish as a condition for further funding the project

   - that the government responsible for implementing the project also recognize the existence of the population and/or the negative impact;
   - that the affected population be informed of the plans and impact of the plans; and
   - that the affected population consent to the implementation of the plans.

These conditions should be monitored by both the funder and the organization which represents the affected population.

4. If the indigenous population has given its informed consent to the implementation of a development project within its territory, the project must

be designed in such a way that it respects the territories of the population as they define them, their economy and their social organization, according to the institutional policy as described in Point One. There should be special components of the project which lend support directly to the indigenous population for their own needs and for the development proposals which they may have. The organization which represents the affected population should participate in the design of the project.
5. The international funders should enter into a direct relation of collaboration and mutual respect with the organizations of Indigenous Peoples, through their representatives. This relation should establish the basis for:

- *consultations* on all aspects of projects implemented in areas with an indigenous population or which have an impact on an indigenous population;
- *participation* of representatives of Indigenous Peoples in the planning, implementation, and evaluation of projects;
- *exchange* of information of mutual interest on plans, projects, activities, and needs of both. . . .

Indigenous Peoples' Alternatives for Amazonian Development

An important task of the Coordinating Body is to present to the international community the alternatives which we indigenous peoples offer for living with the Amazonian Biosphere, caring for it and developing within it. This is one of our important contributions to a better life for humankind. The following represent, in general terms, our program for the defense of the Amazonian Biosphere.

1. The best defense of the Amazonian Biosphere is the defense of the territories recognized as homeland by Indigenous Peoples, and their promotion of our models for living within that biosphere and for managing its resources. This implies:

- education for the national and international communities regarding the Indigenous Peoples' concept of the unity between people and territory, and regarding our models for managing and caring for our environment.
- work with national governments, environmental organizations, and international institutions which fund Amazon development to develop new concepts and models for occupying and using the Amazon Basin in keeping with our long-term perspective (future generations),

our respect for the interdependence between humankind and our environments, and our need to improve the well-being of the entire community; further work with the same institutions to translate these new concepts into concrete programs for developing and caring for the Amazon Basin and its inhabitants.

- work with national governments, environmental organizations, and international funders to reorganize the occupation of supposedly empty Amazonian territories by combining indigenous territories, with forest, wildlife, and extractive reserves in favor of the indigenous and other current inhabitants; by discouraging the "conquest and colonization" of our homeland; and by recuperating those vast areas devastated by state policies of conquest and colonization.
- research on the natural resources and traditional crops used by Indigenous Peoples, on the traditional systems for utilizing and conserving resources, and on models for the extraction of renewable resources.
- evaluation and systematization of the development projects implemented by Indigenous Peoples which attempt to combine the demands of the market with a respect for indigenous principles of development.

2. The defense of the Amazon Biosphere/Indigenous territories must go hand-in-hand with the recognition of and respect for the territorial, political, cultural, economic, and human rights of the Indigenous Peoples. This implies:

- continued participation and support for the UN process for establishing an international instrument recognizing the rights of Indigenous Peoples.
- education for the national and international communities regarding the rights of Indigenous Peoples.
- establishment of mechanisms at both the national and international level for defending the rights of Indigenous Peoples in cases of violations of or conflicts over those rights.

3. The right of self-determination for Indigenous Peoples within their environment/territory is fundamental for guaranteeing the well-being of the indigenous population and of the Amazonian Biosphere. This implies:

- respect for our autonomous forms of community, ethnic, and regional government.
- indigenous control over the economic activities within the indigenous territories, including the extraction of mineral reserves.
- respect for indigenous customary law and the indigenous norms for social control.

4. Concrete Proposals for International Cooperation: For many decades now, most of our peoples have been experimenting with ways to participate in the encroaching market economies of our respective countries while trying to survive as peoples intimately linked to the Amazonian forest. We have done this despite the hostility shown us by the frontier society and despite the fact that, within the context of the market economy, we are desperately poor. For these reasons, we have organized ourselves in new ways and developed and managed a variety of small programs to improve our health, education, and economy. . . . It is these small scale, locally controlled initiatives which should be the cornerstone of future Amazonian development. . . .

To the Community of Concerned Environmentalists

We, the Indigenous Peoples, have been an integral part of the Amazonian Biosphere for millennia. We use and care for the resources of that biosphere with respect, because it is our home, and because we know that our survival and that of our future generations depend on it. Our accumulated knowledge about the ecology of our forest home, our models for living within the Amazonian Biosphere, our reverence and respect for the tropical forest and its other inhabitants, both plant and animal, are the keys to guaranteeing the future of the Amazon Basin. A guarantee not only for our peoples, but also for all of humanity. Our experience, especially during the past 100 years, has taught us that when politicians and developers take charge of our Amazon, they are capable of destroying it because of their shortsightedness, their ignorance and their greed.

We are pleased and encouraged to see the interest and concern expressed by the environmentalist community for the future of our homeland. We are gratified by the efforts you have made in your country to educate your peoples about our homeland and the threat it now faces as well as the efforts you have made in South America to defend the Amazonian rain forests and to encourage proper management of their resources. We greatly appreciate and fully support the efforts some of you are making to lobby the US Congress, the World Bank, USAID, and the InterAmerican Development Bank on behalf of the Amazonian Biosphere and its inhabitants. We recognize that through these efforts, the community of environmentalists has become an important political actor in determining the future of the Amazon Basin.

We are keenly aware that you share with us a common perception of the dangers which face our homeland. While we may differ about the methods to be used, we do share a fundamental concern for encouraging the long-term conservation and the intelligent use of the Amazonian rain forest. We have the same conservation goals.

Our Concerns

We are concerned that you have left us, the Indigenous Peoples, out of your vision of the Amazonian Biosphere. The focus of concern of the environmental community has typically been the preservation of the tropical forest and its plant and animal inhabitants. You have shown little interest in its human inhabitants who are also part of that biosphere.

We are concerned about the "debt for nature swaps" which put your organizations in a position of negotiating with our governments for the future of our homelands. We know of specific examples of such swaps which have shown the most brazen disregard for the rights of the indigenous inhabitants and which are resulting in the ultimate destruction of the very forests which they were meant to preserve.

We are concerned that you have left us Indigenous Peoples and our organizations out of the political process which is determining the future of our homeland. While we appreciate your efforts on our behalf, we want to make it clear that we never delegated any power of representation to the environmentalist community nor to any individual or organization within that community.

We are concerned about the violence and ecological destruction of our homeland caused by the increasing production and trafficking of cocaine, most of which is consumed here in the US.

What We Want

We want you, the environmental community, to recognize that the most effective defense of the Amazonian Biosphere is the recognition of our ownership rights over our territories and the promotion of our models for living within that biosphere.

We want you, the environmental community, to recognize that we Indigenous Peoples are an important and integral part of the Amazonian Biosphere.

We want you, the environmental community, to recognize and promote our rights as Indigenous Peoples as we have been defining those rights within the UN Working Group for Indigenous Peoples.

We want to represent ourselves and our interests directly in all negotiations concerning the future of our Amazonian homeland.

What We Propose

We propose that you work directly with our organizations on all your programs and campaigns which affect our homelands.

We propose that you swap "debt for indigenous stewardship" which would allow your organizations to help return areas of the Amazonian rain forest to our care and control.

We propose establishing a permanent dialogue with you to develop and implement new models for using the rain forest based on the list of alternatives presented with this document.

We propose joining hands with those members of the worldwide environmentalist community who:

- recognize our historical role as caretakers of the Amazon Basin.
- support our efforts to reclaim and defend our traditional territories.
- accept our organizations as legitimate and equal partners.

We propose reaching out to other Amazonian peoples such as the rubber tappers, the Brazil-nut gatherers, and others whose livelihood depends on the nondestructive extractive activities, many of whom are of indigenous origin.

We propose that you consider allying yourselves with us, the Indigenous Peoples of the Amazon, in defense of our Amazonian homeland.

3 3

COERCING
CONSERVATION

NANCY LEE PELUSO

The flurry of ecological awareness and action in the late 1980s has led to a proliferation of international environmental agreements among nation-states. . . . Such agreements assume that each nation-state, including those which have only recently emerged from colonialism, has the capacity, the internal legitimacy, and the will to manage all resources falling within its territorial boundaries. The implication is that the nation-state should be able to control the behavior of all users of all resources located within the state's (self) declared jurisdiction, whatever the origin of the state's claim, whatever the nature of competition for those resources, and whatever the nature or origins of resistance to the state's resource control.[1]

These strategies have elicited the formal commitment of many Third World officials and policymakers who, not surprisingly, stand to benefit from their involvement in such initiatives. Some states or state interests, however, appropriate the conservation concerns of international environmental groups as a means of eliciting support for their own control over productive natural resources. Indeed, some tropical developing states use conservation ideology to justify coercion in the name of conservation, often by using violence. The state's mandate to defend threatened resources and its monopolization of legitimate violence combine to facilitate state apparatus-building and social control. "Legitimate" violence in the name of resource control also helps states control people, especially recalcitrant regional groups, marginal groups, or minority groups who challenge the state's authority.

Excerpted from "Coercing Conservation: The Politics of State Resource Control," in Ronnie D. Lipschutz and Ken Conca, eds., *The State and Social Power in Global Environmental Politics* (New York: Columbia University Press, 1993). © 1993 Columbia University Press. Reprinted with permission.

The environmental community, perhaps inadvertently, justifies coercive-protective actions on the basis of moral high grounds which are difficult to dispute, such as the preservation of the world's biological heritage or our common security. Indeed, the recognition of the "urgent need" to defend at any cost endangered species, endangered habitats, or whole ecosystems, is becoming a more frequent part of the discourse of conservation.[2] Those who abhor state violence against its people are in some cases willing to turn a blind eye to the practice of violence or the threat of violence when conservation for (global) common security is being protected.[3] . . . Nevertheless, when a state must resort to violent means of protecting its own or the global community's claims to natural resources, it is an indicator of a failed, incomplete, or nonexistent legitimacy to govern society. Moreover, the states in question may (and often do) apply the tools and equipment they use to establish their resource sovereignty beyond the conservation endpoints envisioned by international facilitators of conservation, and appropriate the moral ideology of global conservation to justify state systems of resource extraction and production. . . .

Clashes between Central States and Local Resource Users

It is in developing countries, many of which are still struggling to redress the legacies of colonialism and the difficulties of maintaining multiethnic nation-states, that the most difficult circumstances for conservation are found. The origins of their territorial integration lie in colonialism, and were enforced by colonial armies and arms. Though international colonial pressures may have largely died down in the wake of worldwide independence movements, world market linkages continue to influence the decisions of former colonies by increasing the returns of market activities to the national elites who control the trading links.[4] Despite their contempt for the colonial regimes that preceded them, many contemporary developing states have adopted colonial policies for land and resource control, sometimes making them even more coercive.[5] Moreover, to enforce control where state hegemony is tenuous—because of deep-seated rifts between social groups, regional disparities in resource distribution, or competing concepts of appropriate or rightful use of resources—in many Third World countries, state leaders are increasingly members of, controlled by, or strongly allied with the military.[6]

Power struggles between the state and society are played out constantly in the process of allocation, control, and accessing of resources. Both internal and external pressures on states cause them to manage resources using particular tactics to achieve conservation or (sustainable) production management objectives. A state or a faction of the state may coerce conservation under one or all of three circumstances: when the resources are extremely valuable, when the state's legitimate control of the resource is questioned or challenged by other resource users, and when coercion is considered either the last resort or the easiest means of establishing control over people and territory. . . .

The conservation agenda, which is generally depicted as being in the common interest of the entire global community, is seen by some as a justification for external intervention in what were previously the sole affairs of states.[7] From a local perspective, however, both states and international conservation groups may be seen as illegitimate controllers of local resources. . . .

International intervention or support does not guarantee the realization of environmental goals or state legitimacy, however. Replacing or strengthening power holders in order to control resources may encourage increasing local resistance or rebellion against state or international controls on local resources. State concerns with the economic value of resources may influence conservation groups to use economic terms to justify their protection and preservation strategies. Whether for intensive production or for preservation, valuation strategies for resource territories frequently disenfranchise local people who had long histories of local resource use and may have played significant, though unrecognized, roles in creating "wild" habitats. Not only does this often have the effect of undermining conservation; it also changes the way resources are perceived, defined, valued, allocated, and used. When these management strategies change who has access to and control over local resources, the use of violence becomes an expedient means of exerting state control, in the name of "conservation" or "legitimate domain."

In sum, externally based resource claimants (including the state itself) frequently redefine resources, the means by which they will be conserved or harvested, and the distribution of benefits from their protection. Such redefinitions often override, ignore, or collide with local or customary forms of resource management. When competition between external and local legitimation mechanisms is played out in the environmental arena, the result is social and political conflict, which causes environmental degradation and ultimately fails to achieve the goals of international conservation interests.

Nevertheless, the state may not "lose." Even if conservation goals are not achieved, the state may succeed in strengthening its capacity to govern via the use of force.[8] No one monitors this type of aggression or this outcome of international conservation strategy. The means of violence and the ideologies of state stewardship of global resources, obtained directly or indirectly from the international conservation community, may facilitate the state's imposition and enforcement of its right to govern. . . .

Kenya

The resources discussed in this section are the lands set aside for national parks and wildlife reserves and resources within those lands (wildlife, pasture, and water). The traditional users of these lands, the Maasai, Somalis, and pastoralists of other ethnic groups, have been excluded from access to these lands to various degrees over the past century. State claims to nearly two-thirds of traditional Maasai lands were first made by the British colonial state at the turn of the twentieth century. In 1904 the Maasai, who used to occupy all the land from Mt. Kenya in the north to the border with (and into) what is today Tanzania, were resettled in two reserves. Several years later, those in the northern reserve were resettled again in an extension of the southern reserve. By 1912, they were confined to an area of approximately 38,000 square kilometers.[9] The British allocated some of the Maasai's traditional lands to European planters whose activities were believed by colonial officials to be "more productive."[10] Early on, however, the British did not subscribe to the theory that the Maasai could not coexist with wildlife. Thus, in 1906 they created the Southern Game Reserve—a wildlife reserve *within* the Maasai reserve because the Maasai were not believed to threaten wildlife, having coexisted with the region's wild game for thousands of years.[11]

It was not until the 1940s and 1950s that the colonial government gave in to pressures from game hunters and some conservation groups to set aside rangeland exclusively for wild game. At that same time, the state wanted to settle the Maasai in fixed places, which meant changing their traditional migratory cattle-raising practices. The Amboseli Basin, occupying some 3,200 km of both the Maasai Reserve and the Southern Game Reserve, was an important source of water during dry season for the region's wildlife as well as the Maasai and their cattle. Dams and boreholes to provide water outside the Amboseli basin were constructed to benefit the Maasai. As the number of Maasai cattle increased, as they continued to migrate to areas where wild game also sought drinking water, and as hunters threatened wildlife in a different manner, conservationist interests grew more concerned that the wildlife dependent on the Basin waters were being threatened. Along with big game hunters, they pressured the colonial government to create reserves where human use would be more restricted. The Southern Game Reserve was abolished in 1952 and four smaller reserves were created, including a new one outside the area of the old Southern Game Reserve, called Maasai Mara. In the 1950s, hunting was first outlawed within these reserves, although the government issued permits for hunting outside the reserves. In the early 1960s livestock grazing was also forbidden in an 80 km² area of the Amboseli reserve, which was a direct threat to Maasai lifestyles and livelihoods.[12]

The Maasai did not so easily give up their traditional patterns of migration to seasonal water supplies; nor were water development efforts sufficient to permit them to do so. When their principal means of livelihood was restricted by reserve authorities, the Maasai responded by killing rhinoceroses and elephants. A decade later, some allegedly began collaborating with ivory poachers. They also resisted further appropriation of their access rights by increasing their use of the area surrounding the livestock-free zone, and later demanded tenure rights to all these lands.[13]

Meanwhile, another development increased the state's direct interest in the protection of wild game and the reservation of parklands: the increase in wildlife-oriented tourism beginning in the 1960s. Some tourism revenues, including hunting fees, were given to various Maasai district councils as an incentive to win their acceptance of the reserves.[14] Fees and revenues grew through the 1960s and early 1970s, after Kenyan independence. Not all district councils, however, truly represented the interests of the people in the immediate vicinity of the reserves and parks. In Amboseli, for example, the Kajiado Council receiving park revenues was 150 km from the park boundaries. Thus some Maasai were benefitting from the Park's existence, but not necessarily those who had the most to lose from the Park's creation.

The value of wildlife tourism soon became clear to the central government. In 1974, the government designated 488 km^2 of the Amboseli basin as a national park, while still negotiating with the Maasai. In 1977 this area was reduced to 390 km^2, which was gazetted as a park and would remain free of livestock. A de facto buffer zone was to be established around the core area of the park, and group ranches—a brand-new form of social organization for these Maasai—were established to further the government's intentions of sedentarizing the Maasai. In addition, the Maasai were expected to allow wildlife to graze on these ranches in exchange for a "wildlife utilization fee," which was supposed to compensate them for losses of water and grazing area to their own livestock.[15]

By 1989, tourism in Kenya was contributing about 20 percent of the nation's total foreign exchange.[16] By 1991, tourists were spending some 50 million dollars a year to view elephants and other wildlife.[17] In this way, as Knowles and Collett have pointed out, the creation of national parks to protect wildlife has not only separated the Maasai from their livestock production base and created a mythical nature devoid of humans for tourist consumption but also provided the government with the financial means to "develop" and "modernize" them.[18] Moreover, "National Parks and Game Reserves are never justified solely in terms of the economics of tourism: both the conservationists and national governments support the creation and maintenance of these areas with *moral arguments* based on the need to conserve wildlife and the intangible benefits that conservation confers on humanity."[19]

The plans for development of the Maasai in Amboseli have not worked as well as they have in Mara. Some blame the failure on the basic conflict in the lifestyles of the Maasai and their unwillingness to allow outsiders to make decisions about their lives and their uses of resources. Collett, for example, claims that the main reason the provision of water supplies outside the park has not achieved the government's development goals is the preference of the Maasai for a migratory, pastoralist lifestyle.[20] However, a recent report by the World Bank indicates that there were also significant technical problems:

> [The conflicts] may be attributed . . . to failure to implement the agreements, to the lack of an official written agreement outlining the management responsibilities of the different parties and policy changes. The water pumping system, financed by the New York Zoological Society and the World Bank, worked well for a few years and then began to fail due to technical and administrative problems which were not corrected by the central Government which had built it. An inadequate water supply left the Maasai little option but to return to find water inside the Park. The problems were aggravated by a drought in 1984, in which the Maasai lost a substantial part of their livestock and received no assistance from the Park authorities. The wildlife utilization fees were paid regularly until about 1981, then the payments became sporadic without explanation to the Maasai. The agreement for group ranches to retain a portion of Park entry fees fell through, perhaps due to administrative changes. . . . Anticipated income from tourism did not increase as quickly as expected. . . . Construction of new lodges and viewpoint circuits on group ranch lands did not materialize as expected. Finally, the 1977 hunting ban eliminated anticipated income from safari hunting license fees.[21]

In the past few years, the basic conflicts over land and resource fights in Kenyan national parks and reserves have been reconstructed in terms of a government mandate to stop the poaching of wildlife, especially of elephants and rhinoceroses. Major international environmental organizations, including the Worldwide Fund for Nature, the African Wildlife Foundation, World Conservation International (WCI), the International Union for the Conservation of Nature (IUCN), Conservation International, and the National Geographic Society have publicized the poaching issue and its threat to global and African biodiversity. The efforts of these and other environmental groups led to the creation of the Convention on International Trade in Endangered Species (CITES). By 1991, 105 world nations had signed the CITES declaration to ban the raw ivory trade in their effort to protect elephants in Asia and Africa.[22]

A great deal, however, has been left out of the international discussion of the poaching issue, and neither the origins nor the implications of the proposed solutions to the poaching problem have received the critical analysis they merit. Two gaps in the conservation community's discussion are particularly glaring. The first is the lack of historical perspective on the political and ecological contexts within which parks were created to protect wildlife, and the resulting dismissal of local people in creating particular environments. The other is the failure to consider the political-economic implications of the provision of arms and other equipment intended (at least ostensibly) to protect wildlife.

In April 1989, Richard Leakey became the director of Kenya's Wildlife Service. Since then Leakey has made his mark by firing administrative and field staff believed to be involved in the illegal ivory or rhino horn trade, by giving raises to underpaid and overworked park rangers, and by arming these rangers with automatic rifles and helicopter gunships in order to wage war more effectively on the poachers invading Kenya's national parks. Wage war they have: within two years of his taking over, more than a hundred poachers had been killed, many of them with no chance for discussion or trial; the rangers are licensed, like military in a state of emergency, to shoot-to-kill.[23] The Wildlife Service has also reclaimed direct control over the Maasai Mara Reserve, where the combination of wildlife management with local participation and benefits had reportedly been more successful. The government claimed that the reserve had been inadequately maintained and was deteriorating, denying earlier reports that elephants and rhinoceros populations within this park had been increasing while antipoaching costs were virtually negligible.[24]

. . . In their campaigns to save animals, international conservation groups never specify who the poachers are, although some fingers are pointed and accusations made. A letter to members from the WWF, for example, says, "Some poachers, tribesmen displaced from traditional occupations by drought or civil war, use primitive methods to kill elephants and transport tusks. But most use high-powered weapons and even airplanes and various sorts of poisons."[25]

What tribe these "tribesmen" are from is not clarified, whether they are Maasai, or Kikuyu, or one of the smaller ethnic minorities within the country. Later in the letter, however, "Somali tribesmen" are directly implicated, as well as people from an apparently different social group, i.e., "Somali officials." In reference to ivory tusks sold or stockpiled within Somalia, the letter says, "These tusks were not legally confiscated. Instead, they probably were poached from Kenya's nearby Tsavo National Park by well-equipped Somali tribesmen, then smuggled out of Kenya with the complicity of Somali officials."[26] The Somali president himself also apparently wrote a letter guaranteeing his government's purchase of ivory tusks from neighboring countries.[27]

The WWF does not specifically accuse the Maasai of killing wildlife for ivory, but implies that their increasing populations are a major threat to the survival of the elephants and other wildlife. Nowhere in the letter to WWF members is it mentioned that the Maasai and other pastoral and hunter-gatherer groups coexisted with elephants and other savannah wildlife over thousands of years; or that people—as well as the elephants—play an important role in creating and maintaining the contemporary savannah habitat that supports them both. Rather, they imply that the presence of the Maasai is a new phenomenon to which elephants must adapt: "One broad cause of the decrease in elephant numbers is surely the advance of human populations into *their* habitat. . . . To some extent, elephants are able to adapt to the growing presence of pastoralists such as Kenya's Maasai."[28]

Chadwick, writing for *National Geographic,* reflects a more explicit "people versus wildlife" view, with only conservation researchers and supporters exempt:

Tusks became a sort of underground currency, like drugs, spreading webs of corruption from remote villages to urban centers throughout the world. . . . The seventies saw the price of ivory skyrocket. Suddenly, to a herder or subsistence farmer, this was no longer an animal, but a walking fortune, worth more than a dozen years of honest toil. . . . Ivory was running above a hundred dollars a pound, and officials from poorly paid park rangers to high ranking wildlife ministers had joined the poaching network. . . . Poaching gangs, including bush-wise bandits called *shifta* from Somalia, armed with AK-47 assault rifles, were increasingly turning their guns on tourists. This has all but shut down Meru National Park in the north.[29]

What is wrong with this description is its "snapshot" of a contemporary situation, with the camera angled in such a way as to keep the background out of focus. Everyone in the picture is considered equally guilty, regardless of the roots of their involvement, their power to prevent its happening, their public stance, or the historical basis of their claims to being where they are in relation to the wildlife and the lands. Both the average reader and the writer of the article are unfamiliar with the social history of these "wildlife habitats" and this gap in understanding is neither missed nor deemed necessary. The story, after all, is about people against nature. The people for nature, the heroes, are not the local people who lived alongside wildlife for thousands of years before their lands were appropriated by colonial and contemporary state agencies and carved into parks. The implicit heroes are Western wildlife scientists, environmental activists, and the conservation armies who rout the poachers. The indigenous people are implicated because of their proximity to the parks and the logistics of outside poachers gaining access, although it is unlikely that any "peasant farmer" sees one hundred dollars for any pound of ivory he has had a hand in obtaining. Peasants in this view are also guilty of "encroachment" on the elephants' habitat—the areas from which they were excluded not many decades ago: "Ultimately, though, people, not poachers, and growth, not guns, pose the most serious long-term threat to the elephant's survival."[30]

Ironically, Chadwick hints at another motive underlying the involvement of certain state and would-be state actors in this conservation drama: "To currency-strapped governments and revolutionaries alike [ivory poaching] was a way to pay for more firearms and supplies. In the eighties Africa had nearly ten times the weapons present a decade earlier, which encouraged more poaching than ever."[31]

Hence the "need" for increasing the power of the "good" government officials, particularly those working in the parks. As the WWF letter explained,
"Anti-poaching forces have been traditionally paid poorly, had insufficient
training and equipment, and were understaffed. Moreover, they rarely enlisted the aid of nearby villagers by offering them economic incentives."[32]

As a result, WWF and its partners (IUCN, TRAFFIC, and WCI) began providing "emergency assistance to key African wildlife departments," improving
ranger incentives and providing antipoaching equipment and training. They
claim that "the only long-term security for elephants in Africa lies in strengthening national capabilities in wildlife conservation and management." Moreover, to its credit, WWF and other groups are "working to ensure that protected areas benefit from the income generated through access fees."[33] Leakey
also asked the African Wildlife Federation for assistance, which AWF has provided, including airplanes and vehicles for antipoaching patrols in Tsavo National Park. Though it is a relatively small operation, AWF occasionally takes a
more direct role in coercive wildlife protection by "mounting extra patrols
when an emergency arises."[34]

That these aircraft, radios, vehicles, night-goggles, and other antipoaching
equipment might serve another purpose besides conservation has been a secondary consideration in view of the emergency status of the quest to protect
these wildlife. And yet, in an article appearing in January 1989, three months
before Leakey's takeover and the subsequent high-powered, highly publicized
crackdown on poaching, reports from Kenya showed how the government
was already using its mandate to protect and manage resources to assert its
authority where local people had resisted state controls on their activities
since the colonial period.[35]

Ostensibly to settle a dispute over grazing rights between Somali and Borana groups residing in the north, the government sent in police, army heli-
copters, military aircraft and the paramilitary General Service Unit. Over 600
people were detained and "large numbers" were killed in the course of the
current incident. The conflict is not a new one: a 1984 clash left 2,169 people
dead, and in 1987 some 200–300 Home Guards, none of them Somali, were
armed "to assist in policing grazing rights and local disputes."[36]

Many of these disputes date from the time that the Kora National Reserve
was created, when Somali pastoralists were excluded from access to parklands
for grazing. Whole communities of Somalis were resettled onto arid lands in
Borana districts. In the course of their resettlement, they were deprived of
pasture and water for their livestock. Seeking these resources in the vicinity of
the reserve, they are harassed by the Kenyan security forces in the same manner as illegal Somalis engaged in the smuggling trade. The present government's harassment of both the settled and nomadic Somali in the region is
couched in conservation rhetoric, but dates back to the region's efforts to se-
cede from independent Kenya in 1967. The colonial government also had difficulty establishing its authority previously. In the course of the recent clash

near the Kora reserve, it was reported that "under the state of emergency, se-curity forces have powers to act without warrant and detain without specific reason . . . clean-up operations are commonplace."[37] Moreover, the officials involved in the political security operations now form an integral part of the antipoaching operations.

The political implications of this trend in conserving Kenyan wildlife are clear. Though equipment and funds may be allocated to protect nature, they can directly or indirectly be used by the state to serve its own political ends. In this way, the commitment to preservation of wildlife for tourism and research serves both the economic and political interests of the Kenyan government, while its actual effectiveness in doing so is questionable. . . .

Conclusion

The environmental community's tacit or explicit support of coercive conser-vation tactics has far-reaching consequences. First, local resistance to what are perceived as illegitimate state claims and controls over local resources is likely to heighten, and may lead to violent response, sabotage of resources, and degradation.[38] Second, and most important, the outside environmental com-munity may be weakening local resource claimants who possess less firepower than the state. While some conservationists are also "arming" local non-government organizations with symbolic and financial support, their ulti-mate goal is as much or more to influence state policy as to empower local re-source users. The ethics underlying the spread of Western conservation ideologies, without considering their inevitable transformation when ac-cepted or appropriated by developing states, require close reexamination. . . .

[A] growing body of evidence show[s] that, wherever the state directly claims, controls, or manages land-based resources, state organizations and in-dividual state actors have strong vested interests in the commercial exploita-tion of resources. Their control over the territories within which the resources occur, and over the people living within them, is a major aspect of their strate-gic territorial control. Militaries, paramilitary organizations, and state agen-cies often create or exacerbate resource-based conflicts by their participation in protective activities, their involvement as actors, or their coercive tactics. . . . Just as some military leaders can be co-opted to work for the sake of conservation agendas, conservation groups' resources and ideologies can be co-opted for separate military agendas. Once coercive conservation tactics are accepted, such co-optation is nearly impossible to prevent.

Failing to venture beyond the *concept* of thinking globally and acting lo-cally, the writers of international conservation initiatives often brush aside or simply ignore the political implications of empowering states to coercively control access to natural resources. The militarization of resource control—

whether for protection or production—leads to damaging relations with the environment, not benign ones. Whatever their approach on the ground, these conservation groups seek ultimately to change state policy and practice. Unfortunately, coercive conservation also strengthens or extends the state's military capacity—not only with the weapons of enforcement but also with new "moral" justifications to legitimate coercion in enforcing a narrowly defined "global community's" environmental will.

Notes

1. Piers Blaikie, *The Political Economy of Soil Erosion in Developing Countries* (London: Longman, 1985); Nancy Lee Peluso, *Rich Forests, Poor People: Resource Control and Resistance in Java* (Berkeley, CA: University of California Press, 1992).

2. Daniel Deudney, "Case Against Linking Environmental Degradation and National Security," *Millennium: Journal of International Studies* 19, no. 3 (1990):461–476.; Jeffrey A. McNeeley, Kenton R. Miller, Walter V. Reid, Russell A. Mittermeier, and Timothy B. Wemer, *Conserving the World's Biodiversity* (Washington, DC: Worldwide Fund For Nature, 1988).

3. Deudney, "Case Against Linking."

4. Eric Wolf, *Europe and the People Without History* (Berkeley, CA: University of California Press, 1982).

5. Michael Watts, *Silent Violence: Food, Famine, and Peasantry in Northern Algeria* (Berkeley, CA: University of California Press, 1983); Ramachandra Guha, *The Unquiet Woods: Ecological History and Peasant Resistance in the Indian Himalaya* (Berkeley, CA: University of California Press, 1990); Peluso, *Rich Forests, Poor People.*

6. Charles Tilly, "War-Making and State-Making as Organized Crime," in Peter B. Evans, Dietrich Rueschemeyer, and Theda Skocpol, eds., *Bringing the State Back In* (Cambridge: Cambridge University Press, 1985).

7. World Commission on Environment and Development, *Our Common Future* (New York: Oxford University Press, 1987); Lester Brown et al., *State of the World 1990* (New York: W. W. Norton, 1990).

8. Tilly, "War-Making and State-Making"; Migdal, *Strong Societies.*

9. W. K. Lindsay, "Integrating Parks and Pastoralists: Some Lessons from Amboseli," in David Anderson and Richard Grove, eds., *Conservation in Africa: People, Policies, and Practice* (Cambridge: Cambridge University Press, 1987), pp. 152–155.

10. David Collett, "Pastoralists and Wildlife: Image and Reality in Kenya Maasailand," in Anderson and Grove, *Conservation in Africa,* p. 138.

11. Ibid.

12. Lindsay, "Integrating Parks," pp. 153–155.

13. David Western, "Amboseli National Park: Enlisting Landowners to Conserve," *Ambio* 11, no. 5:304; Lindsay, "Integrating Parks," p. 155.

14. Western, "Amboseli National Park," p. 305; Lindsay, "Integrating Parks," p. 154.

15. Lindsay, "Integrating Parks," pp. 156–157; Agnes Kiss, *Wildlife Conservation in Kenya* (Washington, DC: World Bank, 1990), p. 72.

16. Joan N. Knowles and D. P. Collett, "Nature as Myth, Symbol, and Action: Notes Towards an Historical Understanding of Development and Conservation in Kenyan Maasailand," *Africa* 59, no. 4 (1989):452.

17. Douglas H. Chadwick, "Elephants—Out of Time, Out of Space," *National Geographic* 179, no. 5 (1991):11, 17.

18. Knowles and Collett, "Nature as Myth," p. 452.

19. Collett, "Pastoralists and Wildlife," p. 129; emphasis added.

20. Ibid., p. 144.

21. Kiss, *Wildlife Conservation,* p. 72.

22. Chadwick, "Elephants," p. 14.

23. Ibid., pp. 26–31.

24. Kiss, *Wildlife Conservation,* pp. 71, 74.

25. World Wildlife Fund, "A Program to Save the African Elephant," World Wildlife Fund Letter, no. 2, 1989, p. 6.

26. Ibid., pp. 8–9.

27. Ibid., p. 9.

28. Ibid., pp. 4–5; emphasis added.

29. Chadwick, "Elephants," p. 24.

30. Ibid., p. 14.

31. Ibid., p. 24.

32. World Wildlife Fund, "A Program to Save the African Elephant," World Wildlife Fund Letter, no. 2, 1989, p. 7.

33. Ibid., p. 10.

34. African Wildlife Foundation, "1989 Was a Very Good Year: Annual Report," *Wildlife News* 25, no. 2:3–5.33.

35. "Kenya: Crackdown on Somalis," Africa Confidential 30, no. 1 (1989):6–7.

36. Ibid.

37. Ibid.

38. Blaikie, *The Political Economy of Soil Erosion;* Susanna Hecht and Alexander Cockburn, *The Fate of the Forest: Developers, Destroyers, and Defenders of the Rainforest* (New York: Verso, 1989); Guha, *Unquiet Woods;* Peluso, *Rich Forests, Poor People.*

34

WOMEN, POVERTY, AND POPULATION: ISSUES FOR THE CONCERNED ENVIRONMENTALIST

GITA SEN

Introduction

Differences in perceptions regarding the linkages between population and environment became particularly acute during the preparatory build-up to the UN Conference on Environment and Development, variously known as the Earth Summit and Rio 92.[1] Disagreement between Southern and Northern countries on the extent of attention to be given to population received considerable publicity. At the non-governmental level too, the issue of population has been, of late, a subject of considerable debate among environmentalists (especially those from the North), feminists and population lobbyists.

The basis of these differences often appears baffling; the apparent lack of willingness to compromise, or to acknowledge the obvious merits of opposing views seems to indicate a lack of analytical rigour. The debate appears, to some at least, to be based on passionately held but ultimately ephemeral differences. I wish to argue that, although the positions taken in the policy debate have been exaggerated at times, some of the oppositions have deeper roots. They arise from conceptual and possibly paradigmatic differences

Originally published in Wendy Harcourt, ed., *Feminist Perspectives on Sustainable Development* (London: Zed Books, 1994). Reprinted with permission of Zed Books Ltd.

rather than from disagreements regarding the 'truth-value' of particular scientific propositions. These shape the protagonists' perceptions of problems,
the analytical methods used, and weights assigned to different linkages and
relationships. In particular, varying views regarding development strategies,
the linkages between poverty and population growth, and the role of gender
relations in shaping those links colour the positions taken in the debate.

This chapter is an attempt to examine the different perspectives on these issues held by environmental scientists and environmental activists[2] on one
hand, and women's health researchers and feminist activists on the other. Its
motivation is twofold: first, to identify the positions taken by these two broad
groupings within the larger discourses on development and on population;
secondly to propose a possible basis for greater mutual understanding.[3]

Gender in the Population Field

In the history of population policy, women have been viewed typically in one
of three ways. The narrowest of these is the view of women as principal 'targets' of family planning programmes; of women's bodies as the site of reproduction, and therefore as the necessary locus of contraceptive technology, and
reproductive manipulation. The early history of population programmes is
replete with examples of such views; but even more recently, the 'objectification' of women's bodies as fit objects for reproductive re-engineering, independent of a recognition of women as social subjects, continues apace. (Hubbard, 1990)

A second view of women which gained currency after the Bucharest Population Conference in 1983 was women as potential decision-makers whose
capabilities in managing childcare, children's health in particular, could be
enhanced through greater education. Women began to be viewed as social
subjects in this case, but the attention given to women's education has not
spun off (in the population policy literature) into a fuller consideration of
the conditions under which the education of girls takes hold in a society,
and therefore the extent to which education is embedded within larger social processes and structures. While this view represented a step away from
objectification, women were still perceived as a means to a demographic
end, with their own health and reproductive needs becoming thereby inci-
dental to the process.

A third view which grew in the 1980s focused on maternal mortality as an
important health justification for family planning. This view, which was at the
core of the Safe Motherhood Initiative, attempted to claim a health justification for family planning on the basis of rates of maternal mortality. In practice, the initiative has received relatively little funding or support.

Conceptual Approaches

Economic theories of fertility are closely associated with the 'new' household economics. Premised on the belief that children are a source of both costs and benefits to their parents, such theories argue that parents determine their 'optimum' number of children based on a balancing of costs and benefits at the margin. As a description of differences between societies where children are viewed as a source of both present and future streams of income vs. those where children are essentially a cost to parents (balanced by a measure of psychological satisfaction but not by a significant flow of money income), the theory has an appealing simplicity. It purports to explain why the former societies may be more pro-natalist than the latter. It also suggests that shifting children away from child labour (a source of parental income) towards schooling (a parental cost) might work to reduce fertility.

Such theories have been criticized on a number of grounds. (Folbre, 1988) The main criticism centres on the assumption that actual fertility is the result of choices made by a homogenous household unit innocent of power and authority relations based on gender and age. Once such relations are acknowledged, and there is enough anthropological and historical evidence of their existence, the basis of decision-making within households has to be rethought in terms of differential short-term gains and losses for different members, as well as strategic choices by dominant members which will protect and ensure their continued dominance. For example, if the costs of child-raising increase, ceteris paribus, there may be little impact on fertility if the increased costs are largely borne by subordinate members of the household (such as younger women) who do not have much say in household decision-making.

Traditionally, in many societies the costs of high fertility in terms of women's health and work-burdens are rarely acknowledged as such, as long as the benefits in terms of access to a larger pool of subordinate children's labour or the social prestige inherent in being the father of many sons continue to accrue to men. Such authority relations are further cemented by ideologies which link woman's own personal status within the authoritarian household to her fertility. Newer game-theoretic models of household behaviour (Sen, 1987) provide more interesting and complex theories that take better account of the differential distribution of types of assets as well as gains and losses within the household. These have not thus far, however, generated adequate explanations of fertility outcomes.[4]

Against the Stream:
Gender Relations and Reproductive Rights

Many of the influential approaches to theory and policy within the population field have been less than able or equipped to deal with the complexity and pervasiveness of gender relations in households and the economies and societies within which they function. Both feminist researchers and activists within women's health movements have been attempting to change the terms of the debate and to expand its scope. An important part of this challenge is the critique of population policy and of family-planning programmes as being biased (in gender, class and race terms) in their basic objectives and in the methods that they predominantly use.

The definition of a social objective of population limitations[5] which does not recognize that there may be costs to limiting family size that are differential across social classes and income groups, has long been criticized.[6] In particular, such costs are likely to be less than transparent in non-democratic polities or even within democratic states where the costs are disproportionately visited on groups that are marginal on ethnic or racial bases and therefore do not have sufficient voice.[7]

Population policy has also been criticized by some as being a substitute for rather than complementary to economic development strategies that are broad-based in their allocation of both benefits and costs. For example, if impoverished peasants were persuaded or coerced to limit family size on the premise that their poverty is a result of high fertility, independent of the possible causal impact of skewed land-holding patterns, commercialization processes, or unequal access to development resources, then it is questionable whether smaller families would make them more or less poor.

The critique becomes more complicated once the gender dimension is introduced. Critics of population policy on class grounds have sometimes been as gender blind as the policy itself. Having many children may be an economic imperative for a poor family in certain circumstances, but the costs of bearing and rearing children are still borne disproportionately by the women of the household. Gender concerns cannot be subsumed under a notion of homogeneous national or global concerns. For feminist critics of population policy, development strategies that otherwise ignore or exploit poor women, while making them the main target of population programmes, are highly questionable. But they do not believe that the interests of poor women in the area of reproduction are identical to those of poor men.

In general terms, the feminist critique agrees with many other critics that population control cannot be made a surrogate for directly addressing the crisis of economic survival that many poor women face. Reducing population growth is not a sufficient condition for raising livelihoods or meeting basic needs.[8] In particular, the critique qualifies the argument that reducing fertility reduces the health risks of poor women and therefore meets an important basic need. This would be true provided the means used to reduce fertility did not themselves increase the health hazards that women face, or were considerably and knowably less than the risks of childbearing. If family-planning programmes are to do this, critics argue, they will have to function differently in the future than they have in the past.

The most trenchant criticism questions the objectives (population control rather than, and often at the expense of, women's health and dignity), the strategies (family planning gaining dominance over primary and preventive health care in the budgets and priorities of departments), the methods (use of individual incentives and disincentives for both 'target' populations and programme personnel, targets and quotas for field personnel, overt coercion, the prevalence of 'camps' and absence of medical care either beforehand or afterwards, inadequate monitoring of side-effects), and the birth-control methods (a narrow range of birth prevention methods, technology that has not been adequately tested for safety, or which has not passed regulatory controls in Northern countries) advocated and supplied through population programmes. A now extensive debate around the 'quality of care' has focused particularly on the implications of alternative programme methods and birth-control techniques for the quality of family programme services. (Bruce, 1989) More broad-ranging evaluations of population policy objectives and strategies have found them guilty of biases of class, race/ethnicity and gender. (Hartmann, 1987)

Viewed as a development strategy, the critics see population policies as usually falling within a class of strategies that are 'top-down' in orientation, and largely unconcerned with (and often violating) the basic human rights needs of target populations. Even the developmentalist concern with improving child health and women's education has received little real support from population programmes despite the extensive research and policy debate it has generated.

The critical perspective argues that ignoring co-requisites, such as economic and social justice and women's reproductive health and rights, also makes the overt target of population policies (a change in birth rates) difficult to achieve. Where birth rates do fall (or rise as the case may be) despite this, the achievement is often predicated on highly coercive methods, and is antithetical to women's health and human dignity. The women's health advocates argue for a different approach to population policy—one that makes women's health and other basic needs more central to policy and programme focus, and by doing so increases human welfare, transforms oppressive gender relations, and reduces population growth rates. (Germain and Ordway, 1989)

Around the world there is a growing emergence of positive statements about what human rights in the area of reproduction might encompass. (Petchesky and Weiner, 1990) Many of these statements are culturally and contextually specific, but they usually share a common critique of existing population programmes, and a common understanding of alternative principles. Many of them prioritize the perspective of poor women, although they recognize that the reproductive rights of all women in most societies are less than satisfactory. Their attempt to recast population policies and programmes is also, therefore, a struggle to redefine development itself to be more responsive to the needs of the majority.

Enter the Environmentalists

Environmentalist concern with population growth pre-dates the public debate sparked by the UN Conference on Environment and Development (UNCED). Probably some of the most influential early documents were the Club of Rome's *Limits to Growth* and Ehrlich and Ehrlich's *The Population Bomb.* (Ehrlich, 1969) The interest in global and local carrying capacity, vis-à-vis growing human population sizes and densities, stimulated the production of considerable literature, both scientific and popular. Unfortunately, the popular and activist literature has tended to ignore some of the important anthropological debates about carrying capacity, as well as to disregard the inconclusiveness of empirical evidence linking environmental change to population growth.[9] It tends, furthermore, to treat the population-environment linkages as simple mathematical ones, linking numbers of people to their environments through technology.

But the argument of both developmentalists in the population field and women's health and rights advocates has been precisely that population is not just an issue of numbers, but of complex social relationships which govern birth, death and migration. People's interactions with their environments can be only partially captured by simple mathematical relationships which fail to take the distribution of resources, incomes and consumption into account; such mathematical relationships by themselves may therefore be inadequate as predictors of outcomes or as guides to policy.[10]

Furthermore, from a policy point of view, more precise modelling of population-environment interactions has not, thus far, provided much better guidance about appropriate population policy programmes. Ignoring the wide disparities in the growth rates of consumption between rich and poor within developing countries and hence their relative environmental impacts, as well as the critiques of women's health advocates outlined in previous sections, leads to single-minded policy prescriptions directed once more simply to increasing family-planning funding and effort. The leap from over-aggregated population-environmental relations to policy prescriptions favouring increased family planning becomes an implicit choice of politics, of a particular approach to population policy, to environmental policy, and to development. Because it glosses over so many fundamental issues of power, gender and class relations, and of distribution, and because it ignores the historical experience of population programmes, it has come to be viewed by many as a retrograde step in the population-development discourse.

Population Actors

The preceding discussion suggests that important actors in the population field are as follows.

First come those population specialists who traditionally have focused on the size and growth of populations, on age structures, migration and population composition. In general, they enter the development discourse primarily through their concern with what impact population growth might have on rates of economic growth. In addition, population projections are mapped onto planning needs in areas such as food production, energy, and other infrastructures, as well as health, education, and so on. These mappings can be said to belong to a class of simple mathematical planning models which usually ignore problems of distribution (based as they tend to be on per capita needs and availabilities), as well as the social and institutional aspects of making a plan actually work.

The second group are the developmentalists who focus less on the impact of demographic change, and more on the prerequisites of sustained decline in mortality and fertility rates. In particular they stress the importance of improving health and women's education. They thus represent a major revision of traditional population approaches, but all too often stop short of addressing the problem of sustainability or of livelihoods.

A third group, the fundamentalists, has become increasingly important in the population field during the 1980s, gaining political legitimacy through their links to mainstream political organizations. Their primary interest is not the size or growth of populations, but rather control over reproduction and a conservative concern to preserve traditional family structures and gender rules. The moral overtones of the US abortion debate notwithstanding, their interest in procreation appears to derive largely from an opposition to changing gender relations in society.

The fourth group are the Northern environmentalists. At the risk of oversimplification, one might argue that many of these individuals and groups focus mainly on the links between economic growth and ecological sustainability on the one hand, and the size and growth of population on the other.

The fifth important group of actors are the women's health groups which have evolved either out of the feminist movement or out of other social movements or population organizations. Their understanding of the population problem is distinctive in that they define it as primarily a question of reproductive rights and reproductive health, in the context of livelihoods, basic needs and political participation. They often acknowledge that economic growth and ecological sustainability are concerns, but believe these ought to be viewed in the context of reproductive rights and health. In particular, many of them give priority to the needs and priorities of poor women in defining issues, problems and strategies.

Each of these sets of population actors has a view of the population question that is consistent with a particular view of development; as such they tend to overlap with particular sets of development actors, and find a niche within a particular set of development ideas. For example, population specialists are attracted to problems of economic growth, developmentalists to basic needs issues, and women's health activists to the problems of livelihoods, basic needs and political empowerment. Many Northern environmentalists, on the other hand, tend to view population solely through the lens of ecological sustainability, and this accounts for a considerable amount of the dissonance between their views and those of grassroots groups in the South.

Towards More Synergy between Environmentalists and Feminists

Despite the dissonance provoked by the population-environment debate, there is much in common between feminists and environmentalists in their visions of society and in the methods they use. Both groups (or at least their more progressive wings) have a healthy critical stance towards ecologically profligate and inequitable patterns of economic growth, and have been attempting to change mainstream perceptions in this regard. Both use methods that rely on grassroots mobilization and participation, and are therefore sensitive to the importance of political openness and involvement. As such, both believe in the power of widespread knowledge and in the rights of people to be informed and to participate in decisions affecting their lives and those of nations and the planet. Indeed, there are many feminists within environmental movements (North and South) and environmentalists within feminist movements.

Greater mutual understanding on the population question can result from a greater recognition that the core problem is that of development within which population is inextricably meshed. Privileging the perspective of poor women can help ground this recognition in the realities of the lives and livelihoods of many within the South.

Economic growth and ecological sustainability must be such as to secure livelihoods, basic needs, political participation and women's reproductive rights, not work against them. Thus, environmental sustainability must be conceptualized so as to support and sustain livelihoods and basic needs, and not in ways that automatically counterpose 'nature' against the survival needs of the most vulnerable. Where trade-offs among these different goals exist or are inevitable, the costs and burdens must not fall on the poorest and most vulnerable, and all people must have a voice in negotiating resolutions through open and genuinely participatory political processes. Furthermore, environmental strategies that enhance livelihoods and fulfill needs can probably help lay the basis for reduced rates of mortality and fertility.

Population and family-planning programmes should be framed in the context of health and livelihood agendas, should give serious consideration to women's health advocates, and be supportive of women's reproductive health and rights. This has to be more than lip service; it requires reorienting international assistance and national policy, reshaping programmes and rethinking research questions and methodologies. Using the language of welfare, gender equity or health, while continuing advocacy for family planning as it is at present practised, will not meet the need.

Reproductive health strategies are likely to succeed in improving women's health and making it possible for them to make socially viable fertility decisions if they are set in the context of an overall supportive health and development agenda. Where general health and social development are poorly funded or given low priority, as has happened in the development agendas of many major development agencies and countries during the last decade, reproductive rights and health are unlikely to get the funding or attention they need. Reproductive health programmes are also likely to be more efficacious when general health and development are served. A poor female agricultural wage-labourer, ill-nourished and anaemic, is likely to respond better to reproductive health care if her nutritional status and overall health improve at the same time.

The mainstream Northern environmental movement needs to focus more sharply on gender relations and women's needs in framing its own strategies, as well as on the issues raised by minority groups. These issues (such as those raised by native peoples and African Americans in the US) tend to link environmental issues with livelihoods and basic needs concerns in much the same way as do the people's organizations in the South.[11] Greater sensitivity to the one, therefore, might bring greater awareness of the other.

Wide discussion and acknowledgement of these principles could help to bridge some of the current gaps between feminists and environmentalists, and make it possible to build coalitions that can move both agendas forward.

References

Bruce, J. (1989) 'Fundamental Elements of the Quality of Care: A Simple Framework.' The Population Council, Programmes Division Working Papers No. 1, May, New York.

Caldwell, J., and P. Caldwell (1987) 'The Cultural Context of High Fertility in Sub-Saharan Africa,' in *Population and Development Review* 13:3, September, pp. 409–438.

Ehrlich, P. (1969) *The Population Bomb*. Ballantine Books, New York.

Folbre, N. (1988) 'The Black Four of Hearts: Towards a New Paradigm of Household Economics,' in J. Bruce and D. Dwyer (eds.), *A Home Divided: Women and Income in the Third World*. Stanford University Press, Stanford.

Germain, A., and J. Ordway (1989) *Population Control and Women's Health: Balancing the Scales*. International Women's Health Coalition, New York.

Hartmann, B. (1987) *Reproductive Rights and Wrongs: The Global Politics of Control and Contraceptive Choice*. Harper and Row, New York.

Hubbard, R. (1990) *The Politics of Women's Biology*. Rutgers University Press, New Brunswick.

Little, P. (1992) 'The Social Causes of Land Degradation in Dry Regions' (manuscript). Institute of Development Anthropology, Binghamton.

Mamdani, M. (1974) *The Myth of Population Control*. Monthly Review Press, New York.

Petchesky, R., and J. Weiner (1990) *Global Feminist Perspectives on Reproductive Rights and Reproductive Health*. Report on the Special Sessions at the Fourth International Interdisciplinary Congress on Women, Hunter College, New York, NY.

Scott, J. (n.d.) 'Norplant: Its Impact on Poor Women and Women of Color.' National Black Women's Health Project Public Policy/Education Office, Washington, DC.

Sen, A. K. (1987) 'Gender and Cooperative Conflicts.' Discussion Paper No. 1342. Harvard Institute of Economic Research, Cambridge.

Shaw, R. P. (1989) 'Population Growth: Is It Ruining the Environment?' in *Populi* 16:2, pp. 21–29.

Notes

1. This chapter is based on a longer article written for a collaborative project of the International Social Sciences Association, the Social Science Research Council, and Development Alternatives with Women for a New Era (DAWN) on 'Rethinking Population and the Environment.' I am grateful for comments on an earlier draft by Carmen Barroso, David Bell, Lincoln Chen, Adrienne Germain and Jael Silliman. The usual disclaimers apply.

2. The dissonance addressed in this chapter is between mainstream environmentalists from the North and women's health researchers and activists from both North and South.

3. My own position is that of someone who has come to these debates from a background of working on issues of gender and development, and this chapter will perforce tilt heavily towards spelling out the positions taken from within the women's movements. I do not claim to be able to explicate how the mainstream of the environmental movement (especially in the North) has come to the particular definitions it has of 'the population problem.'

4. A different theoretical approach that takes better account of the shifts in patterns of inter-generational transfers, and therefore of age-based hierarchies, is contained in the work of Caldwell and Caldwell (1987).

5. Or, in the case of many parts of Europe, of population expansion through increased fertility.

6. For an influential early critique, see Mamdani (1974).

7. See Scott (n.d.) for a look at Norplant use in the contemporary United States.

8. Even rapid fertility decline may sometimes be indicative of a strategy of desperation on the part of the poor who can no longer access the complementary resources needed to put children's labour to use.

9. Examples of the former are Little (1992), Blaikie (1985); of the latter, Shaw (1989) and UN (1992). The latter argues, for example, that 'The failure to take fully into account the possible effects of other factors that might contribute to environmental degradation characterizes many analyses of population-environmental interrelationships at the national and global levels and thus limits their value in assessing the impact of demographic variables.'

10. An example is the well known Ehrlich-Holden identity, I = PAT, linking environmental impact (I) with population growth (P), growth in affluence/consumption per capita (A), and technological efficiency (T).

11. Personal discussion with V. Miller, co-founder of West Harlem Environmental Action in New York City.

35

FOOTPRINTS AND MILESTONES: POPULATION AND ENVIRONMENTAL CHANGE

United Nations Population Fund

The Connections

Population and the environment are closely related, but the links between them are complex and varied, and depend on specific circumstances. Generalizations about the negative effects of population growth on the environment are often misleading. Population scientists long ago abandoned such an approach, yet policy in some cases still proceeds as if it were a reality.[1]

As human populations increase and globalization proceeds, key policy questions are: how to use available resources of land and water to produce food for all; how to promote economic development and end poverty so that all can afford to eat; and, in doing so, how to address the human and environmental consequences of industrialization and concerns like global warming, climate change and the loss of biological diversity.

Environmental devastation is not simply a waste of resources; it is a threat to the complex structures that support human development.

Understanding the ways in which population and environment are linked requires detailed consideration of the way in which factors interrelate, includ-

Excerpted from United Nations Population Fund, *State of the World Population 2001* (New York: UNFPA, 2001). Reprinted with permission.

ing affluence, consumption, technology and population growth, but also previously ignored or underrated social concerns such as gender roles and relations, political structures, and governance at all levels.

The relationships among environment, population and social development are increasingly better understood. There is broad agreement on means and ends. Women's empowerment, for example, is a development end in itself. Removing the obstacles to women's exercise of economic and political power is also one of the means to end poverty.

Reproductive health is part of an essential package of health care and education. It is a means to the goal of women's empowerment, but it is also a human right and includes the right to choose the size and spacing of the family. Achieving equal status between men and women, guaranteeing the right to reproductive health, and ensuring that individuals and couples can make their own choices about family size will also help to slow population growth rates and reduce the future size of world population.

Among other things, slower population growth in developing countries will contribute measurably towards relieving environmental stress.

Demographic Challenges and Opportunities

Changes in the size, rate of growth and distribution of human populations have a broad impact on the environment and on development prospects. A variety of demographic changes in different areas provide new challenges and opportunities.

Population and Fertility Trends

Fertility is highest in the poorest countries and among the poorest people in these countries. Failures in health, education and other services, especially for women, contribute to poverty in these countries. Reproductive health services cannot meet even the existing needs of women who want to prevent or delay pregnancy, and demand is expected to increase rapidly in the next twenty years.[2] Maternal mortality is high and rates of contraceptive use low (often less than 15 percent of all couples).

These countries are also among the most severely challenged by soil and water degradation and the most severely affected by food deficits. In some ecologically rich but fragile zones, known as "biodiversity hotspots," population growth is well above the global average of 1.3 percent a year.[3] Rising demand from more affluent areas adds to the pressures on natural resources in these ecosystems.

The good news is that fertility in developing countries as a whole has dropped to just under three children per woman, about half what it was in 1969, and the expectation is that it will fall further, to 2.17 children per woman by 2045–2050. At the same time, global life expectancy has increased to an average of 66 (up from 46 in 1950), and—outside the areas worst affected by HIV/AIDS—people are healthier throughout the life cycle than at any time in history.[4]

The AIDS pandemic will have severe demographic effects. By 2015, life expectancy in the worst affected countries will be 60, five years lower than it would be in the absence of AIDS. . . .

In industrial countries, fertility is now 1.6 children per woman, below replacement level.[5] Their populations are rapidly aging, and in some countries might actually shrink unless supplemented by migration. The downward trend in fertility is well established. However, recent studies in the United Kingdom show that family size in some low-income families is smaller than the parents desire.

The vast bulk of consumption is in the industrial countries, but it is rising fast elsewhere as incomes grow. Measures to conserve energy, curb pollution and promote sustainable use of natural resources are essential for sustainable development in the future.

Parallel measures are needed to stabilize global population growth. Whether world population in 2050 reaches the high projection of 10.9 billion, the low of 7.9 billion or the medium projection of 9.3 billion will depend on choices and commitments in the coming years. Two actions are central: first, ensuring that the right to education and health, including reproductive health, becomes a reality for all women; and second, bringing an end to the absolute poverty that affects the 1.2 billion people who live on less than $1 a day. These two aims are closely linked because most of the absolutely poor are female; action towards one will reinforce the other.

Governments, international donors, civil society and, in many cases, the private sector all have important roles to play in achieving these goals and creating a virtuous circle of smaller, healthier families, healthier and better-educated children with expanded opportunities, and increased progress towards population stabilization and environmental sustainability. . . .

As populations grow and demand increases, the search for water, food, and energy resources and the resulting impact on the environment are calling sustainability into question. The limits of technologies and the wisdom of our use of them are growing challenges, and questions of governance, social organization and human rights are increasingly important to a sustainable outcome.

Milestones

In the past decade we have learned more about the deepening ecological footprint resulting from the growth of human numbers, changing population distributions and unsustainable consumption and production patterns. The stark challenges to sustainable development have become clearer. At the same time, there are some important signs of positive change, including a growing international consensus on actions to promote development while protecting the environment.

Important milestones in this regard are the agreements of the United Nations conferences of the 1990s. The United Nations Conference on Environment and Development (UNCED), held in Rio de Janeiro in 1992, was one such milestone. The international community recognized that environmental protection and natural resource management had to be integrated with action to alleviate poverty and underdevelopment.

Progress recognizing the importance of population and women's rights and empowerment to the development agenda was marked at the Vienna Conference on Human Rights (1993), the International Conference on Population and Development (ICPD, 1994) and the Fourth World Conference on Women (1995). Participatory development strategies featured strongly in the World Summit on Social Development (1995).

The ICPD agreed on an explicit and detailed series of goals, using an approach based on human rights and individual decisionmaking. Among them are elimination of the gender gap in primary and secondary education by 2005, and universal primary education before 2015; sharp reductions in maternal mortality and in infant and under-5 mortality; and universal access to reproductive and sexual health services including a full range of safe and reliable family planning methods by 2015. Attaining these goals would also lead to early population stabilization.

Implementing the ICPD recommendations for development (including better reproductive health and moves towards gender equality) will help defeat poverty and protect the environment. By promoting slower population growth, it will buy time in which critical decisions can be made. . . .

Returns for Slower Growth

Policies and programmes addressing issues of population growth, reproductive health and women's empowerment meet pressing human needs and advance human rights. They also have important environmental benefits. It is hard to quantify these, because of the multiple interactions. But it is clear that providing full access to reproductive health services, which are relatively inexpensive, is far less costly in the long run than the environmental consequences of the faster population growth that will result if reproductive health needs are not met. There would also be substantial benefits in terms of health and economic and social opportunity.

Recommendations

Promoting human rights, eradicating poverty, improving reproductive health and achieving a balance between population and development needs and environmental protection will require a broad range of actions. Some priorities are to:

- Implement the global consensus agreement of the International Conference on Population and Development.
- Provide incentives for the dissemination, further development and use of more sustainable production processes.
- Improve the information base for more-sustainable population, development and environment practices.
- Implement internationally agreed actions to reduce poverty and promote social development.

Action on population, environment and development issues is both necessary and practical. The various international environmental agreements and the international consensus on population and development are being translated into working realities. These agreements only underline the need for broader and more extensive efforts.

Notes

1. Polemics against such simplistic positions are still being written. See, for example: Food and Agriculture Organization of the United Nations, *The State of the World's Forests* (Rome: Food and Agriculture Organization of the United Nations, 1999); and Scott R. Templeton and Sara J. Scherr, "Effects of Demographic and Related Microeconomic Change on Land Quality in Hills and Mountains of Developing Countries," *World Development* 27, no. 6 (1999):903–918.

2. UNFPA, *The State of World Population 1999: 6 Billion—A Time for Choices* (New York: UNFPA, 1999); and UNFPA, *The State of World Population 2001: Lives Together, Worlds Apart* (New York: UNFPA, 2000).

3. R. P. Cincotta and R. Engelman, *Nature's Place: Human Population and the Future of Biological Diversity* (Washington, DC: Population Action International, 2000).

4. United Nations, *World Population Prospects: The 2000 Revision—Highlights* (New York: U.N. Department of Economic and Social Affairs, Population Division, 2001).

5. Replacement-level fertility is the level necessary to ensure that the population replaces itself over the long run. For most populations, replacement is ensured with a fertility of 2.1 children per woman.